ONE YEAR TO AN
# ORGANIZED LIFE WITH BABY

ALSO BY REGINA LEEDS

*One Year to an Organized Financial Life*

*One Year to an Organized Work Life*

*One Year to an Organized Life*

*The Complete Idiot's Guide to Decluttering*

*Sharing a Place without Losing Your Space:*
*A Couples Guide to Blending Homes, Lives, and Clutter*

*The Zen of Organizing: Creating Order and Peace*
*in Your Home, Career, and Life*

## Praise for Regina Leeds' *One Year to an Organized Work Life*

"Use this guide to organize your office   and mind."
—*Shape*

"Streamline one domain a month to prune clutter and spur productivity."
—*Self*

"Readers should find plenty of smart, straightforward and rewarding ways
to eliminate chaos from their work lives."
—*Publishers Weekly*

## Praise for Regina Leeds' *One Year to an Organized Life*

"Making your New Year's resolutions? If your goal is to finally clear the clutter,
*One Year to an Organized Life* will break the task down week by week."
—*Parade*

"This 12-month guide offers the chronically messy a genuine sense of serenity."
—*USA Today*

"Not only shows us the importance of organization, [but] takes us week-by-week
through the chaos of our lives and tells us how to get it together, from schedules
to scrapbooks to celebrating holidays."
—*Minneapolis Star Tribune*

"If this week-by-week guide to getting yourself organized
won't do the trick, give up."
—*Newsday*

"This easy-to-use … domicile detox program will help you
tackle every inch of your life."
—*Women's Health*

"The perfect book for anyone wanting to find important papers instantly
or have a navigable closet. Full of useful information for everyone,
from the person who needs simply to clean a messy desk to the person
requiring a whole new approach to life; highly recommended."
—*Library Journal*

# ONE YEAR TO AN
# ORGANIZED LIFE
# WITH BABY

From Pregnancy to Parenthood,
the Week-by-Week Guide to
Getting Ready for Baby and
Keeping Your Family Organized

# REGINA LEEDS
## WITH MEAGAN FRANCIS

Da Capo

LIFE
LONG

A Member of the Perseus Books Group

Editorial production by *Marra*thon Production Services. www.marrathon.net

DESIGN BY JANE RAESE
Set in 12-point Bulmer

Library of Congress Control Number: 2010936293

ISBN 978-0-7382-1455-9

First Da Capo Press edition 2011

Published by Da Capo Press
A Member of the Perseus Books Group
www.dacapopress.com

Note: This book is intended only as an informative guide for those wishing to know more about health issues. In no way is this book intended to replace, countermand, or conflict with the advice given to you by your own physician. The ultimate decision concerning care should be made between you and your doctor. We strongly recommend you follow his or her advice. Information in this book is general and is offered with no guarantees on the part of the authors or Da Capo Press. The authors and publisher disclaim all liability in connection with the use of this book.

Da Capo Press books are available at special discounts for bulk purchases in the U.S. by corporations, institutions, and other organizations. For more information, please contact the Special Markets Department at the Perseus Books Group, 2300 Chestnut Street, Suite 200, Philadelphia, PA, 19103, or call (800) 810-4145, ext. 5000, or e-mail special.markets@perseusbooks.com.

10 9 8 7 6 5 4 3 2 1

This book is dedicated to the Divine Mother present in all beings. With special thanks to Lynn Decker Hernandez, Ann Lucien Walsh, and Christina Naify Zilber—three women who have taught me what motherhood looks like when it's done with grace, dedication, attention to detail, and love.

We are more than just physical beings,
we are Whispers of Love dancing in the breeze.

—MICHAEL TEAL

# CONTENTS

# Introduction

Love is the capacity to take care, to protect, to nourish . . .

. . . if you are not capable of taking care of yourself, of nourishing yourself,

of protecting yourself—it is very difficult to take care of another person.

– THICH NHAT HANH

YOU'RE GOING TO HAVE A BABY. Whether you're thrilled, terrified, or ambivalent about this news, one fact remains: You'll have a lot to think about over the next twelve months. From choosing a birth team to registering for your shower to actually finding a home for the veritable tidal wave of baby gear that is about to enter your life, you will be dealing with new information and details every day. And soon, you'll have a baby filling your arms and demanding lots of your time. The sooner you can create systems that work for you and make your transition to motherhood easier, the better! This book will show you how, one step at a time.

*"I have a daughter, Regina."* My friend Jeremy's voice seemed to float from a cloud. We were looking at little Melissa in her hospital bassinet. She was all of eleven hours old. "And she's beautiful," he added, as if I might be oblivious to her charms. As I turned to look at Jeremy, I could feel the mantle of fatherhood set-

tling on his shoulders. Jeremy and his wife Ellen had tried for years to have a child. Fertility treatments proved expensive and fruitless. But as so often happens, soon after they gave up, Melissa showed up.

When I next came to visit, I was amazed to see a literal explosion of baby paraphernalia in their home. Melissa was as tiny as a sack of flour and yet it seemed that a boatload of items had accompanied her arrival.

Many parents never really crawl out from under that initial avalanche of baby stuff. I once worked with a woman named Sheila who seemed to always be living in some previous stage of her child's life. Her oldest baby's drawers always held clothes that were too small, and dressing him became a fifteen-minute ordeal of picking through to find things that might actually fit. When her baby was two years old, Sheila told me, she still couldn't figure out where to store his tiny baby bathtub and teeny newborn socks. Just as Sheila thought she was getting things under control, another baby came along. By this time, she'd stored away the socks and bathtub . . . so thoroughly that she couldn't remember where they were and had to buy new ones. By the time she called me, Sheila's children were eight, six, and four years old, and yet her family room was still cluttered with their toddler toys. On the other hand, when we cleaned out her attic, we found thousands of dollars worth of things that had been so haphazardly packed away that Sheila couldn't find them when it was time to have another baby. She had three almost-identical bouncy seats! And who knows how many copies of each child's birth certificate . . . whenever one was needed, she would have to write the county for another copy. What a waste of time and money!

This doesn't have to happen to you. It *is* possible to get organized during your pregnancy and for initial new-baby chaos to give way to streamlined systems and routines. Ellen and Jeremy soon created a place for every new item. And everything was religiously returned to its designated spot. Their storage system allowed them to easily find packed-away items when it was time to reuse them or give them away. And systems allowed them to easily keep track of the myriad appointments, milestones, and records that come with having a new baby.

I've been getting into the organizing trenches with pregnant women and young moms for more than twenty years. My clients come from all walks of life: I've worked with movie stars, business executives, housewives, and everyone in be-

tween. No matter what your status in life, the physical, financial, and emotional challenges of having a baby are pretty much the same. My style of organizing—what I call "Zen Organizing"—encompasses the organizing tips and tricks you would expect, coupled with elements of psychology and spirituality to create a calm, peaceful, and functional home. My goal is for your environment to be converted from a space that sabotages you at every turn to one that nurtures and supports your best efforts in life. And what could be more important than bringing new life into the world?

I couldn't have written this guide, however, without the incomparable Meagan Francis by my side. Among other things, Meagan is the mother of five children, ranging in age from one to thirteen. She's a nurturing mom, a talented writer, and one organized woman! (Throughout this book we present a united front. To avoid confusion, you'll find the pronoun "I" used for organizing tips throughout, along with specific stories and tips from Meagan's experience as a mom.)

As I started writing this book, I came across an exchange between two of my Facebook friends. They were both in the final stages of being pregnant and were lamenting how little they had accomplished. They were facing the daunting task of preparing the new baby's room at the very moment they each felt "as big as a house." Even if you know all the things you have to accomplish (each of these women has three children), you can get sidetracked. And if this is your first baby, you might be amazed by how much more challenging it can be to stay on top of all the details and things involved in caring for such a small person. With this book as your companion, instead of flying blind, you will have a plan to follow.

## THE GIFT OF ORDER

We give children lessons in every sport and artistic endeavor imaginable. We review their homework to be sure they are getting the best grades possible. We are careful to save for their higher education. One gift that is often overlooked, however, is the gift of an organized environment. It isn't that some parents don't care or don't want their children to live with order, peace, and calm. They simply never learned the skill of organizing from *their* parents. No one can teach something they don't understand. For most people, the knee-jerk reaction to this reality is to feel shame. This is one of the reasons I developed the concept of Zen Organizing. I wanted a system that not only is practical and useful, but also fosters self-confidence and healthy self-love, and never entertains the concepts of guilt or shame. They are neither productive nor useful.

Pregnancy and birth are life-changing events. Raising a child is no doubt the most important undertaking of your life. My job is to help you feel in control during this time of transition and preparation. When you feel in control, you can accomplish anything you set your mind to, including incorporating a baby into your life. And control is one of the natural and inevitable by-products of being organized. In addition to being on top of all the new demands on your time, you'll want to prepare the physical environment. If you are in the habit of living in a swirling mass of clutter, the onslaught of baby-related items heading your way only spells disaster.

We are impacted by the visual. On those days when you are not feeling up to par, one glance around the room is going to make you feel ten times worse. If you have everything related to the upcoming birth tucked away, you can eliminate the stress of "Now where did I put . . .?" That quest is as big a waste of time as searching for house keys or your reading glasses. If you're resting and Dad needs some information, he'll know where to go as well. Organizing cuts down on the noise of unnecessary chatter. You don't have to ask where something is: You know. And so does everybody else in the home.

## WHAT'S IN STORE?

As with all of the books in the *One Year to an Organized Life* series, you can begin this program whenever you receive or purchase the book. Ideally, you'll have this copy of *Baby* early in your pregnancy—the program starts during the eighth week of pregnancy, which is a few weeks after most women learn they're pregnant and when the realization of what's happening is finally setting in. I've charted a logical course that will enable you to take care of all the myriad details that need your attention. I've also taken great pains to schedule things with an eye to where you are in your pregnancy and how you'll be feeling.

For example, you wouldn't want to be painting the nursery when first-trimester nausea had you in its grip, nor would you want to be tackling cleaning out your closet when you can barely see your feet. Each month you'll find a theme. I then break the month down into four weeks with individual assignments. I realize that life can toss a monkey wrench into the most well-thought-out plan, so for the first five months there's a bonus week. Getting ready for baby will no doubt involve more detail and preparation than you ever imagined. If you fall behind with an assignment, you have an opportunity to get caught up. And if you stay on track, you can either forge ahead or rest on your laurels!

Throughout the book you will also find great habits to cultivate and tips that will make your new life easier. You may not wish to embrace all of the suggestions but please at least give them a try. You might just be pleasantly surprised.

Finally, if you are starting this book well into your pregnancy (or even after your baby is born), take heart. It can still serve you well. Start following the book exactly where you are in your pregnancy but be sure to simultaneously read the book from the beginning. There may be material that doesn't pertain to you. For example, not everyone has a pet they need to acclimate to Baby's arrival and not every mom has a career she's interrupting or leaving behind. As for other items you will have to tend to, like assembling the all-important hospital bag or setting up a nursery, you

can make a list, prioritize it, and then schedule tasks on your calendar. Whether it's your PDA, on your computer, or a paper organizer, you can't survive in life without a calendar. Pick a format you enjoy using and leave nothing to chance. "Mommy brain" means you have to write everything down!

Here's a sampling of the projects we'll be working on together while you're waiting for Baby:

- How can you keep track of papers, including your pregnancy- and baby-related research now and the baby's legal and medical documents after the delivery? It can be daunting without direction.
- How are you going to share the news with family, friends, and coworkers?
- Which health screenings and tests are right for you?
- What about maternity clothes? When do you start to purchase them and what do you need? And how in the world will you organize your closet for all these new items?
- What's the best way to prepare the nursery—and when?
- What kind of support do you have lined up for after Baby's arrival? Is your mom coming to spend a few weeks or would you rather use hired help, like a postpartum doula?

Once Baby arrives, a whole new set of challenges and obligations arises. Once again, I've got you covered. Here are some of the items we consider:

- Thank-you notes need to be written. When and how can you fit them in? After all, Baby isn't likely to be sleeping through the night.
- Speaking of sleep, I'll help you organize your sleep schedule before deprivation turns you into someone no one recognizes.
- How are you going to make the transition to the world outside the cocoon you've created for the three of you? And what about the mom who has a corporation or job eagerly awaiting her return? Organized transitions are smoother than ones that are accomplished as you fly by the seat of your pants.
- Does a diaper bag have to drag you down? Or is there a streamlined, necessities-only way to go?
- With increased stuff in the environment, how can you stay on top of everything? What is your partner's role in home organization/maintenance?
- Looking ahead, we'll take a look at keeping your baby healthy as she transitions to solid foods. Will you breastfeed, and for how long? Do you want to purchase commercial baby food or make your own? Best to consider all the options.

## A NEW FOCUS

The early months have more organizing projects than later in your pregnancy. After the delivery you'll be grateful you've got that crackerjack file system, a kitchen that practically hands you what you need, and a bedroom that lulls you to sleep. The time it takes to set these up is minimal when compared to the lifetime of dividends you can reap.

What's that you say? You get organized all the time and after about two weeks the chaos has returned? Allow me to respectfully burst your bubble. You didn't get organized. You tidied up, and that never lasts. Getting organized means taking the time to establish not only a place for every object you own but also systems, habits, and rituals that support the order you created. Maybe this is new territory for you and you're thinking that this just isn't who you are as a person. Or maybe if we were together you'd assure me that you are an artist and creative types just can't be organized. Let me tell you why I know neither of these are real fears.

Here's the bottom line: Organizing is a skill and *anyone* can acquire it. Just because you may not become a professional organizer like me doesn't mean you can't learn the basics. I've never met anyone who couldn't get organized if they put their mind to it. I also know from experience that artists can get organized because I was a professional actress for many years! Being organized will give you a firm foundation from which your creativity can launch into the stratosphere. It gives you unlimited possibilities, allowing you to shift the focus to what you want to accomplish. With the wealth of organizing tools now available, you may be shocked to discover that getting organized is a very creative endeavor.

## NO STONE UNTURNED

There are lots of pregnancy guides that help you understand what's happening in your body. This one helps you understand what's happening in your environment and your life. For example, you don't want to wait until labor is starting to suddenly realize that you and your partner never discussed how to handle the legal and/or medical questions that might arise. In a timely fashion, I'll guide you through the maze. When you drive up to the labor and delivery unit, you can feel secure that everything in your life is ready for this momentous change.

Finally, this isn't a book of boring instructions. If you're going to spend a year with me, I need to be a worthy companion! I promise to make you smile and maybe even laugh out loud from time to time. I will ask you to contemplate things you may never have considered before. And I'm certainly going to keep you busy. Professional organizers have tools—some we buy at the store and some are techniques we use to help you organize your thoughts and the way you see things. Let's take a look at some of the things I use when I Zen Organize your world.

## TRICKS OF THE ZEN ORGANIZING TRADE

If I gave you pages of instruction and didn't offer other tips, tidbits, and tricks I've learned over the years, it might be more difficult to be successful. Here is an overview of the fun things you will find in your Zen Organizing Toolbox.

Baby journal
Healthy living tips
Habits
Product guide
The Magic Formula
The Dream Board (aka Mind Map)

Let's take a look at each in turn.

### The Baby Journal

Let me say it again: An avalanche of stuff is coming your way, matched only by an equally forceful storm of facts. You're going to learn about how your baby is developing in the womb; become familiar with medical tests and technology; learn about baby furniture, toys and clothing; not to mention discover how medical leave works at your company and what kind of tax breaks come with a new baby. Whew! It's exhausting just thinking about it, isn't it? If you are used to having an airtight memory that records items on the spot for easy recall later, you're in for a surprise. Hormones are wonderful things. And during a pregnancy they are wreaking havoc with your brain. You had best get used to writing things down. Enter the Zen Organizer's baby journal. Instead of scraps of paper and a surfeit of post-it notes, keep track of your research in this one place. And, yes, this is totally separate from your baby book where you will record mementos for your child. We'll talk more about how to use each of these journals in the first chapter.

## Healthy Living Tips

It's not uncommon in our fractured world for people to compartmentalize their lives. They think that what happens at home has no relation to their life at the office. How they feel physically is not connected to what they put into their bodies. And so it goes. I embrace a holistic view of life; everything is a part of the whole. It's my goal to help you live an integrated life, especially at this time of transition. To this end, you will find tips throughout this book on things like diet, exercise, basic meditation, taking care of yourself, and more. You have to love and nurture yourself first.

## Habits

Sometimes, for myriad reasons, we get excited about a project like getting organized and then inertia sets in. We become frozen. One of the big fears I hear is that other members of the family won't honor what you create. The easiest way to get motivated and influence others without saying a word is to create positive habits. A habit for our purposes is any *action* that can be repeated for twenty-one *consecutive* days. After that, psychologists say, the action will be an ingrained part of your daily life. Would you leave home with "bed hair"? Would you consider not brushing your teeth in the morning? You get the idea. Our lives are filled with simple, positive habits. Each month I suggest a new one for you to try.

## Products

Talk to any inveterate organizer or experienced parent and they will tell you about the money they wasted on products that proved a disappointment. I hope to steer you in the right direction. It's also important to know which products can be obtained second hand and which can simply be borrowed. You want to save money for the important things in your baby's life. You'll find ideas within the body of the text as well as a full list in the Resources section.

## The Magic Formula

When I first started my organizing career, I presumed that every project would be unique. But soon I realized that all projects in the home or office went from chaos to order in just three steps. What changed were the items in my hand. One day it might be clothing, the next paper, and on the third day I might be handling tools in the garage. Here are the steps guaranteed to bring order:

### 1. Eliminate

One of the basic tenets of Zen Organizing is the understanding that "the whole of anything is overwhelming." As we reduce the clutter, we begin to see what really needs to be organized. This step isn't just about tossing things in the trash. It's actually a varied and highly creative pursuit.

### 2. Categorize

As I make decisions about each item, the ones that are to remain get set aside with related items. Categories are very powerful. They give you automatic inventory control for one thing. Suddenly you know exactly how many white blouses you own and how many cans of chicken soup are in the pantry!

### 3. Organize

Organize your categories in a way that works with your personality. You want to be sure the contents are easy to find. This last phase is also the time to purchase the products you feel you need. If you buy 100 hangers before you eliminate items from your closet, for example, you're likely creating more clutter. But if you make the purchase after you eliminate and categorize, you'll know exactly how many you need. You'll be saving time, money, and energy.

### The Dream Board or Mind Map

I love this project and include it in all of my books. I also understand it's not for everyone. If you love creative memories or are crafty, this will naturally be up your alley. The Dream Board project involves telling a story in pictures of something you wish to create. All you need is poster board, glue, and images from magazines. For example, creating a Dream Board might help a soon-to-be new mom literally see what her baby's room could look like as well as entertain images that reflect the life she hopes to create for him.

Dream Boards are fun to do but especially effective for those who are not visual. It's more difficult to create something if you can't see it in your mind's eye. With a Dream Board, you take an intermediate step that brings your dream closer to reality. If this process seems silly to you, why not give it a try? It only costs a few dollars to make one and you might find you like the process so much you will use it throughout your life. I have several business clients who use Dream Boards to help motivate members of a team. (It's called a Mind Map or a Vision Board in those circles.) These execs very often have team members who can't imagine achieving the stated goals of the company for their group. Once they can see the results, they more easily embrace the possibilities. And so can you!

## THE COUNTDOWN BEGINS

It's time to dive in and start getting ready for your baby's arrival. Most things in life that are of any value take a lot of time, energy, and money to be successful. The very fact that the journey isn't an easy one makes it all the more exciting. Even if you ultimately have a dozen children, each pregnancy will be different. And each will be occurring at a time in your life that will never come again. Why not allow the gift of being organized to give you an opportunity to be fully present?

There is a bonus hidden in this book. You may think you're just getting ready for Baby, but in fact you're streamlining, organizing, and downsizing in order to get ready for the rest of your life! A home that's tidy, clean, and organized nurtures all who live there, encouraging and supporting each family member to do her best in life. I hope you will savor each day before your baby is born and after. As a button I once bought for a friend announced: "This is not a dress rehearsal!"

# PART ONE
# GETTING READY

# CHAPTER ONE

# 8 to 12 Weeks Pregnant

It was the best of times, it was the worst of times.

– CHARLES DICKENS

CONGRATULATIONS! You're having a baby! Now if only you could stop puking. Technically Dickens was describing the French Revolution when he wrote the lines that open this chapter. But I have to wonder. He was, after all, the father of ten children and, therefore, no stranger to the ups and downs of pregnancy and birth.

Nothing less than a miracle is taking place inside you. Dozens of books delineate the week-by-week changes your baby (and body) is undergoing as you move through your pregnancy. These guides are invaluable because they describe a process that is at once under your nose and hidden from plain sight. But this is a time when just about *every* aspect of your life is in flux, not just the size of your belly. Rather than being reactive and dealing with issues as they come along, you can follow the organized journey that I've crafted, which will enable you to easily and logically deal with every change in your life and every

new demand on your time. Change tends to be less overwhelming when we know what's coming.

We'll start at the very beginning this month with your choice of medical practitioner and place of birth. If you've been going to the same OB-GYN for years and wouldn't dream of letting anyone else deliver your baby, then a big decision has been taken off your full plate. Why? Because once you have the doctor you usually also have the hospital. You'll deliver where your doctor has "privileges," that is, where he or she has the right to practice medicine. But what happens if you're new to town, don't particularly like your doctor, or would like to investigate your birthing choices? You'll find the information you need in Week One.

Speaking of information, this month we begin the process of gathering baby-related material. I'll help you focus on what you need to know at the exact moment you need to know it rather than finding yourself buried under an avalanche of books and magazines and newspaper articles or feeling so overwhelmed you can't research anything. In Week Two you'll create a filing system. All of your material will have a place to go rather than piling up on the dining room table, the kitchen counter, or your desk. If you like your existing system, don't panic. I'm not going to ask you to throw the baby out with the bath water. (I couldn't resist!) You can use the ideas to integrate the new baby-related files into your existing system.

Every month, I'm careful to balance out the demands I make on your time. One week you're on your feet doing an organizing project like creating a file system and the next you're sitting quietly doing something like sharing the news of your pregnancy with family and friends. We do that, by the way, in Week Three. (We'll deal with work colleagues next month.) The idea is to enjoy the journey and the process. Have you thought about ways to document this journey for your child? We all know someone whose mom didn't write one word or take a single photo during her pregnancy, right? Your child will have no such complaints. With today's technology, documenting doesn't have to be a chore. It can be creative and fun, even for those among us who aren't the least bit "crafty." I've got lots of ideas for you to consider.

We close out the month with a review of some tests you might consider. Modern medicine can work miracles. The real question is, do you need to take advantage of all these tests just because they are available? I'll help you learn enough so you can

discuss the pros and cons with your physician. You can make the decision as a team.

Assignments change each week but some things are a constant. The basic "musts" during your pregnancy are to eat well and get enough sleep, fluids, and nutrients. When your basic needs are taken care of, you'll be able to devote time and energy to making your surroundings and life more manageable. The nausea will pass and be replaced by waves of high energy. The overwhelmed feeling will give way to a quiet sense of control as you move from assignment to assignment.

## HABITS OF THE MONTH

### Drink Water, and Take a Prenatal Vitamin at the Same Time Each Day

Water washes debris from the cells, boosts your immune system, helps you heal faster from injuries, and helps relieve stress. And when you're pregnant, your need for water increases because your body actually creates and circulates more blood—a total of 45 to 50 percent more! Also, your body needs to be able to replenish the amniotic fluid protecting your baby at the rate of one cup per hour. Not drinking enough water puts you at risk for urinary tract infections, premature labor, and more.

It's best to drink eight eight-ounce glasses of water a day. If you've never been a water drinker, the idea of consuming this much may seem daunting. To make it easier, buy some large bottles of water or get a refillable water bottle. Keep your bottle next to you throughout the day and track your consumption. Make the goal two eight-ounce glasses a day and build up. (If you're used to drinking only soda or caffeinated beverages, this may be a transition for you. But you may not have to cut caffeine altogether; ask your health-care provider what she feels is a safe amount to consume.)

Now that you're gestating new life, you'll also need more nutrients than you did before. And between nausea, fatigue, and just plain old busy-ness, it can be hard to get everything you and your baby need through food alone. A prenatal vitamin is a great safeguard to supplement even the most nutritious diets.

It's easy to forget your daily vitamin amid all the more exciting baby-planning activities. So get in the habit of drinking more water and taking your daily vitamin as early as possible in your pregnancy. Try to take your vitamin at the same time each day. You'll find that the more you ritualize little details like this, the more they become an automatic part of your day. It's one less thing to have to think about.

If nausea is currently your nemesis, try one of the chewable vitamin brands and take them at night. Also opt for a natural, food-based prenatal vitamin you can buy at the health food store. They'll be easier for your body to digest and may cause less queasiness. In just a few weeks the nausea should pass and taking your vitamins will become a lot easier.

Here are some tricks to help make a plain glass of water more palatable and to calm an upset stomach:

- Squeeze in some fresh lemon.
- Add a few springs of fresh mint (if you have a garden, mint is very easy to grow).
- Turn the water into tea! Pregnancy tea blends containing red raspberry leaf are an excellent source of nutrients that expecting women need, and also help get the uterus "in shape" for pregnancy and birth.
- If your stomach is upset, fresh ginger will make hot or cold water more refreshing. If your supermarket doesn't carry fresh ginger, try prepackaged caffeine-free ginger tea.

Grab a glass or cup of your favorite beverage, put your feet up, and let's move on to Week One.

# 8 WEEKS PREGNANT

## Understand and Control the Exhaustion

This week, you can

- Understand the exhaustion that may consume you these days
- Make your first doctor's appointment if you haven't yet done so
- Calculate how many weeks pregnant you are
- Add meditation to your daily routine

IF YOU ARE FEELING under the weather, it may help you to understand what's going on in your body and how best to deal with these changes. These feelings have a purpose, and, thank goodness, they don't last forever. In fact it won't be long before they are replaced with energy. Who said Mother Nature doesn't have a sense of humor?

During the first few months of your pregnancy, your body pours an incredible amount of energy into creating the placenta. This organ literally acts as a lifeline between your body and your developing baby, sharing your nutrients and oxygen with her and removing her waste products.

Until then, you may be amazed at how urgently the need to nap can strike at any time. Don't be surprised if you have to pull your car over on the way home from work because you can't keep your eyes open for one more minute. Or if you find yourself drooling on your sofa cushions when just

a moment ago you were watching your favorite TV program.

The good news is that just a twenty- or thirty-minute nap can prove wonderfully refreshing. Also, many women find that their "nap attacks" strike around the same time each day, which may allow you to do some planning (shut your office door and draw the blinds, or set older children up with some crayons and paper so you can conk out in peace).

If you were expecting a touch of morning sickness, you may be surprised and disappointed to find that actually, pregnancy nausea can strike at any time of the day or night! Some women experience intense nausea; others feel a low level of queasiness all day long. An abundance of pregnancy-related hormones are to blame. The good news is that those hormones will also help you have a healthy pregnancy.

Be kind to yourself. Now is not the time to burn the midnight oil or take on extra responsibilities at work if you can avoid it. Planning for a short nap every day and making sure you get at least eight hours of sleep at night can help stave off sleepiness. Some women also find that exercise helps keep energy levels up. Eating small meals throughout the day to keep your blood sugar levels steady can keep nausea at bay. But the only real cure is time. Early in the second trimester, when hormone levels even out and the placenta is complete, most women start feeling much better.

## IS THERE A DOCTOR (OR MIDWIFE) IN THE HOUSE?

Have you been seeing an OB-GYN or nurse midwife for your routine care? Do you feel completely comfortable with this care provider? If so, she's the first appointment you need to make if you haven't done so already. Call the office and tell them how many weeks pregnant you are (see box). They will schedule your first appointment according to the office protocol. If you're healthy and not having a high-risk pregnancy, you'll probably see your doctor or midwife every four weeks starting in the first trimester through the end of the second trimester. Then you'll have appointments every two weeks until week thirty-six and every week up until you give birth.

If you are new to your city or don't want your current care provider to deliver your baby, start asking friends who are already mothers for referrals and what their experiences were like. Or if you live near a large

### HOW PREGNANT ARE YOU?

A pregnancy is dated back to the first day of the last menstrual period. Let's say a woman starts her period on December 1, but doesn't actually conceive until December 15. She is already considered, technically, two weeks pregnant by that point! By the time you've missed your period, your care provider (and all those pregnancy books) consider you a month pregnant, and you may not figure it out until you're five to six weeks along or more. Some care providers will see pregnant women as soon as they get a positive test; others like to wait until eight to twelve weeks to schedule the first appointment.

hospital and it is one with a neonatal unit in the event of an emergency, call and ask them if they have a referral service.

It's not too early to start thinking about what you hope for in the place you give birth. Some women are reassured by the presence of a high-level neonatal unit in large teaching hospitals. Others prefer the more laid-back atmosphere of a smaller hospital or birth center. Also keep in mind that all hospitals have different policies when it comes to things like eating and drinking during labor, being allowed to move around rather than staying in bed, and laboring or giving birth in water, which may also impact your decision.

If your doctor is part of a large practice, you'll want to ask to meet everyone on staff at some point. Often OB-GYNs rotate who's on call and attending births, so there's a very good chance that the doctor you've been building a rapport with will not be the one who is present when your baby is born. When you call to make your first appointment, ask how the practice handles on-call rotations and who will be your doctor's backup in case she is on call but can't make it to your birth.

Pregnancy is a long partnership with your medical provider. Don't hesitate to ask for a meeting with your top candidates. And remember, you can always change your mind and switch later if it becomes apparent that your care provider or chosen place for the birth aren't a good fit.

## MEDITATION

Add five minutes of meditation to your day. This is a wonderful antidote to the stressful times ahead. Meditation stops the incessant brain chatter that exhausts us during the best of times. You'll find yourself wondering about all sorts of things now, from "what will labor be like" to "will I be a good mom?" Meditation will quiet your mind and enable you to think clearly and make wise decisions. It has countless other benefits, including an increased ability to focus, improved memory, enhanced creativity, deeper sleep, and a lower level of stress hormones in the body.

Why are these important to you? As pregnancy floods your body with hormones, your ability to stay focused and re-member things may well be compromised. You've no doubt heard the phrase *mommy brain,* and it doesn't wait for Baby's arrival to kick in. Finally, all moms will tell you about sleep loss, especially after Baby is born. By that time you'll be meditating easily and perhaps even longer than the five minutes I'm suggesting. Not good at taking catnaps? When you're sleep-deprived, a quick meditation may be just the thing to help you feel refreshed.

The simplest technique:

1. Sit in a straight-back chair with your feet on the floor. Place your hands on your thighs with your palms facing up. Don't let them touch.
2. Close your eyes and pay attention to your breath. Feel it as it enters then exits your nostrils. Breathe normally. Don't do anything fancy!
3. Try to do this for five minutes. Think of nothing else. Simply focus on your breath. When thoughts intrude, *gently* dismiss them. And don't be surprised if you fall asleep. All of these things are normal in the beginning.

Over time it will get easier. If you are too nauseous to sit up straight, you can find a more comfortable position until you are feeling better. Just remember that the classic meditation position as described here is the one you eventually want to embrace. This will be one of the first practices you share as a family. Baby, after all, is benefiting as well!

# 9 WEEKS PREGNANT

## Banish Paper Pile-Ups

This week, you can

- Reduce paper clutter and start a simple file system
- Begin collecting and organizing baby-related information

Don't look now, but with the joy of pregnancy something unwanted is coming to your home: the Paper Monster. The coming months are going to find you inundated with pregnancy and parenting materials. Medical reports, insurance claims, baby books, pregnancy guides, magazines, and clipped newspaper articles from your mother-in-law are going to stack up like planes on the runway the day before Christmas. What's a woman to do? Why, get organized, of course!

If you are like most people, paper clutter is your nemesis. Mail piles up on the kitchen counter. Magazines, catalogs, newsletters, and invitations ooze across the dining room table and tumble onto any available floor space. Projects from work pile up on your home office desk. Stacks of books you hope to read one day create a barricade on your side of the bed.

We need a map showing us the way to a quiet work zone, and this week you'll establish a home for the baby-related information that's key to a successful pregnancy and transition home for your infant. We also need to start implementing *systems*. They are at the heart of an organized lifestyle. You can have the most perfect file setup in the world, but if you never use it, what's the point?

Set time aside to file paper. It has probably piled up in the past because you didn't have a file folder waiting to absorb it. At regular intervals, take out your "To Do" or "Pending" folders (more about those below) and take care of the business of your life. Schedule time in your calendar—don't leave those sessions to chance. It takes some effort to create the system. But then it only takes consistency, not huge blocks to time, to maintain it. The rewards are many and include paying bills on time (one of the best ways to build a solid FICO score), receiving medical and other reimbursements in a timely fashion, and feeling in control of the business side of your life.

## PAPER NEEDS A HOME

The first step is to take a good look around and create a battle plan. Hopefully you have a home office; but if you don't or if your home is small or you live in an apartment, take heart: You can designate any area to function as a de facto office. The key is to have some sort of file cabinet.

If you have a home office, chances are you already have a two- or four-drawer metal filing cabinet. One drawer will probably be all you need for this project. You can make do, however, with a large file box; I'd pick one in wicker or wood. You can plop a vase on it and help it blend into the decor when you're not busy sorting paper. And if absolutely necessary, you can use a cardboard file box. It's not my favorite choice because there's nothing permanent about it; cardboard breaks down over time and eventually the hanging file folders start to fall because the sides are wearing down. So go with a sturdy file solution if possible.

Your designated spot shouldn't involve the kitchen. You want to keep those counters clear. They will soon be filled with baby paraphernalia. The dining room table should also be free of debris. Family members and friends who come to assist you after Baby arrives can have a quiet meal here while you are resting. In fact, it's nice to keep this table clear all year long. Why save the dining room for holiday meals? Eat here every night if you like or make Sunday night supper a new family tradition in this room. Finally, many people work in their bedrooms, but it's preferable that you keep

---

### GIVE YOUR BOOKS A HOME

If you've got a small library of baby-related books, why not get a small bookcase to hold them all? Lightweight portable bookcases are available at The Container Store and elsewhere and do the trick nicely. The sides fold out and release the shelves. Whether it's newspapers, magazines, books, or paper, give everything a designated home. All the time you save not having to look for things is time you can spend with your partner or your baby. There's an old saying: "pennies make dollars." Just so, minutes saved easily add up to hours spent in fun or nurturing pursuits.

---

this space as a place for rest and fun. Televisions, computers, file cabinets, and so on should not reside here. Of course, personal taste and necessity may find you multitasking in this room. Do the best you can. We'll tackle these rooms individually over the next several months. I've scheduled big projects for the time in your pregnancy when the nausea has likely passed and your energy level is high.

### GET READY

When your baby arrives, you'll want everyday tasks like bill paying and receipt filing to be as easy as they can be. Your time and energy will be needed elsewhere. This is a project that takes some time but pays huge dividends. If you don't have a working file system, during your down-time over the next several days you can use the following guidelines to create one.

Here is the first set of tools you will need for this project:

- A few sturdy trash bags (think the heavy-duty black ones earmarked for yard work, not the flimsy white ones used in the kitchen)
- A box for recyclables
- Twenty uninterrupted minutes (i.e., no phones, no e-mails, no text messages, etc.). Use your cell phone's timer to keep track.

## SPEED ELIMINATE

Now we're going to do what I call a Speed Elimination to remove the obvious clutter. The key word is *speed*. Now is not the time to linger over letters from friends, feel remorse for invitations to parties you missed, or stop and read the instructions for your new iPod. It's time to move with resolve and ignore emotion. You'll feel better once this step is taken no matter which room or project you are tackling. The room is going to literally feel lighter and less overwhelming. Don't be surprised if this becomes your favorite area in your home!

The items we're eliminating here are the same ones you'll be searching for when it comes time to clear off the dining room table, the kitchen counters, and any other places you've let paper accumulate. Here's a list of the most likely candidates for the trash or recycle containers:

- Invitations to parties that have passed and store sales you missed
- Magazines older than two months and newspapers older than two days
- Receipts for items that are not deductible on your income tax
- Catalogs
- Expired coupons

There will also be items that you wish to keep that need to live elsewhere in your home. Here are some of the most likely suspects:

- Stale food (think gum and candy for starters; look for dishes that held late-afternoon snacks etc.). Food should be tossed; serving items go back to the kitchen.
- Set aside items that belong to other people. If you don't have a car or the means to return them, make some calls later today so they can be picked up.
- Set aside items that belong in other parts of your home (coffee mugs that need to be transferred to the kitchen are a prime example; if you already have children you may have toys and other items that need to be returned to their rooms).

## CATEGORIZE YOUR PAPERS

Once you have completed this phase, you can go back for another twenty minutes and this time separate out the items you wish to keep. Keep the information in related piles. These are, in effect, your categories. They represent the material that continues to grow over time. We've got to make a home for it. This information will form the basis of your file system; you'll create folders for each category. If you have projects for work or home, they will come to order following these simple guidelines. For example, here are some common categories of paper for the average family:

## Household Expenses
1. Homeowner's insurance
2. Mortgage or rent
3. Phone
4. Utilities

## Automobile Expenses
1. Automobile club Membership
2. Auto insurance
3. Auto loan
4. License and registration
5. Repairs

## Banking
1. Bank of America; personal account
2. Citibank; business account

## Credit Cards
1. American Express
2. Macy's
3. MasterCard

## Medical Insurance
1. Dental
2. Flex spending or medical savings accounts
3. Medical

## Business-Related Expenses
1. Charitable donations
2. Continuing education classes
3. Entertaining clients
4. Gifts for clients
5. Phone calls (depending on the status of your business, you may be able to deduct some of your cell and land line calls. If you don't qualify, "Phones" should most likely be filed under "Household")

While these are among the most common categories I find when I am creating a file system for a new client, the receipts are rarely organized in this fashion. If there is a rudimentary file system in place I typically find all of the receipts relating to a category in one folder. This makes retrieval of a specific piece of information a laborious project because you have to sift through everything related to the topic. You can streamline a category by breaking it down into the parts that make up the whole.

For example, let's say you own two cars and a pickup truck. Each has a title. Your vehicles might all be under one umbrella insurance policy or each might have a dedicated policy. And of course you have your payment record and repair history. Most folks stuff all of this into a drawer or single file folder and struggle when they need to retrieve a specific piece of information. That translates to a big drama before Tax Day on April 15! But if you take the time to create a hanging file folder for each vehicle and a subfolder for each category to house the information, you are set. Why look at the information for the Ford pickup truck if I need to see how much I spent on repairs for the Toyota Camry? Why sift through phone bills when it's my medical receipts that matter? With this in mind, take another quick look at the file examples I gave just above. Break every category down into its parts. This concept is key to your success.

## ORGANIZE YOUR FILES

Now we've come to the next set of tools we need for this project. Here are my favorite items when it comes to creating a file system. You can find them at any office supply store:

- Hanging file folders
- Manila folders (or colored if you wish to designate some of your categories); get the one-third or straight cut
- Long file tabs (the short variety will come with the hanging file folders)
- A label maker (Brother P-touch is my personal favorite) with extra tape cartridges. If you are making a purchase, don't forget to have extra AA batteries on hand.
- Rails for your file drawer if you need to insert them
- One box of two-inch-wide box bottom hanging file folders for the large categories if you anticipate you will have a few

Here's an example of how you use these wonderful tools. I've taken a category from the above example.

### Business-Related Expenses
(This is the title you put on your long tab. Use your label maker so it's easy to read. Attach the tab to a regular hanging file folder and place it on the rails in your metal filing cabinet or in your file box.)

1. Charitable donations
2. Continuing education classes
3. Entertaining clients
4. Gifts for clients
5. Phone bills: cell and land line

Numbers 1 through 5 represent individual file folders. Keep the contents in alphabetical order for ease of retrieval. If the material in the file folders is bulky, use a box bottom hanging file folder instead. You'll have two inches of space to fill instead of a simple sleeve. (Many of my clients think you can fold a regular hanging file folder and make a wide bottom. The lines on the side are for decoration only. If you do fold along those lines, the folders you place inside will sit too high for your drawer to close.)

Box bottoms come with a piece of cardboard you insert to create a sturdy flat bottom. Check your box before you make your purchase. Sometimes folks take the inserts out! And don't purchase box bottom folders that are wider than two inches. The material will be so heavy the folder will eventually rip off the metal rail it's attached to. You don't want to be replacing folders every few weeks.

## CREATE A "BABY FILE"

Now you're ready to take these guidelines and apply them to your baby-related documents. Here is an example list of things you might be researching, broken down into related categories.

**Baby:**

What do I have to have on hand for his arrival home?

Which items are necessities in the baby's room?

When should my friends schedule the baby shower?

**Medical Insurance:**

Will my pregnancy and birth be covered by my policy?

Have I met my deductible?

**Pregnancy:**

What's happening to my body?

How is the baby developing?

What prenatal exercise classes might I want to take? When do they start and where are they? Will I need a note from my doctor or midwife?

When do I need to sign up for a childbirth education class? What is available in my area? (Lamaze, Bradley, birth hypnosis, etc.)

What clothing will I need? When do I start actually wearing maternity clothes?

What kind of birth experience do I want? (medicated, natural, water birth, etc.).

Where will I give birth—hospital, birth center, or home?

If I deliver in a hospital, which one in the area is the best fit for my circumstances and preferences? If I deliver at home or in a birth center, which options exist in my area?

**Work Issues:**

Does my company have maternity leave?

Will I be paid for the time off?

Do I want to continue to work full-time at my current job after the baby comes? If not, what might my options be—work at home, telecommute, flex time, taking an extended leave, or becoming an at-home mom?

The list of items and issues you might want to research is virtually endless. But don't let a feeling of overwhelm settle over you: I've got you covered. All of these issues and more are dealt with within the pages of this book. (If you want even more information, see the Resources section, page 325). However, let's suppose that you wish to research one or two areas in detail. Your files for this purpose might look like this:

## Baby

(Name on file tab, announces a new category)

Baby's Room
Baby Shower
Baby Supplies

(These bulleted items are the individual file names)

## Medical Insurance
Claim Forms/Blank
Claim Forms/Pending
Policy Information

## Pregnancy
Baby Development
Birth Methods
Body Changes
Childbirth Classes
Doulas

The really great news is that in today's world, most of your research will be conducted online. You can easily create folders on your computer and organize this information in the same way. As you go along, you can delete files that are no longer of interest or concern. Suppose, for example, that you are considering several different birth methods. Once you make your decision, only material relating to your final choice needs to be saved. Don't clog up your hard drive no matter how huge it is. It's electronic clutter!

This week may have surprised you. You

As readers of my previous books know, my mom was the Queen of Organization. I never saw piles of anything in our home. If you could clean it or organize it, my mom was your woman. But when it came to research, my mom couldn't stand to read anything medical. In the case of her pregnancy, this refusal to read medical information worked against her. When my mother's water broke, she didn't know what was happening and thought she was literally going to die! Fortunately her mother, who had given birth to eight babies, was with her to reassure her. Knowledge is power.

no doubt want to shop for teddy bears and I've asked you to organize your files. But this simple task will make your life much easier in the months ahead and especially after your baby is born. Soon you'll be dealing with work and insurance issues. Those endeavors as well as all the medical tests and doctor visits create an incredible mountain of paper. I promise that in just a few weeks you'll be shopping for your maternity clothes, planning the nursery, and, yes, picking out that teddy bear.

# 10 WEEKS PREGNANT

## Share the News and Document the Experience

This week, you can

- Decide when and how to share the good news
- Begin a keepsake journal for your child
- Use digital photography to document your pregnancy

IN SOME CULTURES there is a specific time to share the news of a baby's impending arrival. If you have had miscarriages or waited years for this moment, you may wish to hold off on contacting family, friends, and colleagues until more time passes. On the other hand, you may have already spent a week calling, e-mailing, and publishing the news on Facebook. There is no right or wrong, as this is a highly personal bit of news to share.

My only word of caution is to remember that once the cat is out of the bag, the news is going to spread like wildfire. Who isn't excited to hear that a baby is on her way? Unfortunately, it's a given that someone is going to be a little miffed by the way they found out. Uncle Ned is going to be surprised he heard the news from Cousin Melba rather than directly from you. Aunt Edna is going to be shocked you posted on Facebook before calling her. And your brother will wonder why you called your

baby sister first. You can't make everybody happy. Don't try. Just do the best you can!

### GUESS WHO'S MAKING A LIST AND CHECKING IT TWICE?

The first thing you need to do is to write out a list of everyone you wish to contact. Try doing this in Microsoft Excel. It's so easy to delete, cut, and paste. Then, make categories of folks who need to know the news. The most common categories are: immediate family, other family, close friends, colleagues, and other contacts. Between your and your spouse's family, it is probably quite a long list. Do you want to divide the list between you and call everyone on it personally? Or do you want to personally call a few key people (think future grandparents and your siblings) and then let them each make a few calls for you? You and your husband may have very different relationships with your families. What works for one of you may not work for the other. Don't let a difference in family protocol become a bone of contention.

You will probably want to call your closest friends, but don't dismiss the power of e-mail to let the vast majority of your buddies simultaneously hear the good news. Write out something special and include a photo of you and your partner. Do you have a favorite poem? Include anything that will personalize the announcement. If you are a stepparent, you might want to have a photo of the two of you with your stepchildren. This will surely make them feel more a part of the experience.

After the phone calls have been made and the e-mails sent out, then it's an appropriate time to post at your favorite social networking site, provided of course that this is part of the way you like to communicate on a daily basis. I've got friends who post their ultrasound photos on Facebook so their community of friends can all see the first images of Junior. It's your pregnancy. Share it the way you see fit.

## DOCUMENT THE JOURNEY

Go shopping for your journal. You will no doubt pick up a baby keepsake or pregnancy journal. First-time mothers are generally great at recording everything so their child will know exactly what happened when. As the family grows and the novelty of pregnancy wears off, subsequent pregnancies tend to be less well documented. If keeping such a record for your child is going to be fun, I invite you to start a book today. If you are not much of a writer, consider an audio diary. Or you can set up a small video camera on a tripod and speak directly to your child. You don't need to do any of these *every* day! Once a week or even once a month will provide your child with a lovely memento. And don't think for a minute you have to turn into Hemingway or Scorsese to make these interesting for your child. In this case it really is the thought that counts.

Are you at a loss as to what to share? Record your feelings about the changes in your body. Tell him how you feel about his dad. Tell her how much you love to dance and that you can't wait to teach her. You are unique. Allow this keepsake to reflect who you are. Above all, keep it positive. My mother told me the excruciating details of her twenty-five-hour labor every day of my life. Some things are best kept private.

Some women like to document the changes in their body. Stand in the same place once a week and have your spouse take a casual photo. A profile shot can best reveal the more dramatic changes. At the end you will have a fun collage to share with family, close friends, and eventually your child. (But save any nude photographs you might wish to take for your private album.)

If you are a devotee of scrapbooking, you might want to use some of the scrapbooking techniques and special products to enhance the baby keepsake you are making for your child. If this is a new world to you, you can contact a local scrapbooking store like Creative Memories (e-mail listings are in the Resources section) or check the yellow pages for your area. And you don't have to worry about how far your artistic abilities will take you because all stores have classes.

I've had many clients who are very involved in this style of scrapbooking, and it certainly provides an incredible outlet for your creativity. Many women form groups and get together weekly. If you are more of a solitary person, there are extensive guidelines for digital projects. These of course take up no space in your physical home and can easily be shared with family and friends. (For more about photo organization, see page 328.)

This week, explore the possibilities. There are many choices when it comes to documenting this experience. It's easier than ever to instantly share it with those who are far away and relive the memories for yourself for the rest of your life.

## START YOUR JOURNAL

As this week draws to a close, I hope you have picked out your baby journal and keep it handy. If you are a very organized person by nature, you may not want to give up your calendar or your Blackberry. Nor should you. The journal is meant to be an adjunct to any tools you have used up until now to keep your life on track. Some of my clients personalize the pages with doodles or stickers. Many keep them after the birth for reference on the chance they decide to have another child. They won't be starting from scratch. It's also a great source for your friends who may become pregnant in the future. Women are passionate about this experience and the people, books, and blogs that proved useful to the journey.

# 11-12 WEEKS PREGNANT

## Examine Which Medical Tests You May Need

**This week, you can**

- Research the various tests you may be asked to take

In today's world, you have at your disposal an array of tests that can tell you a great deal about your child before he enters the world. The question is, which of these tests do you need? You will of course decide this with your physician, but I believe that being informed can only make your experience better.

### AVOIDING TEST STRESS

Since you won't see your care provider very often during these first few months, it's a good idea to think about all the genetic tests available to you early on so you can research and discuss them with your care provider before you schedule them.

The tests available to you are twofold: screening and diagnostic. Screening tests determine whether your baby is at an increased risk of having a specific condition, while diagnostic tests can actually detect the presence of anomalies and diseases like Down syndrome and spina bifida. You might be inclined to sign up for everything "just because." But there are emotional considerations to take into account.

First let's talk about tests that may have emotional consequences. These fall under the category of screening tests. Even the closest couples who are in sync about everything need to have a conversation about screening tests. Let's take a practical example. The information you get from a test that screens your baby's risk of having Down syndrome is pretty much useless unless you know what you'll do with that information. If you would not then opt to go through with a *diagnostic* test such as amniocentesis, then the results of the screening are only good for creating a lot of worry (or possibly false confidence). Also consider: if you do get a definite diagnosis, will you do anything differently than you otherwise would? All the possibilities need to be considered before you venture down the road of genetic testing. Women

Here's a breakdown of commonly performed early tests, what they're for, and when they happen. The first two are screeners; the latter two are diagnostic.

### The AFP (Alpha-fetoprotein) Test

This blood test screens for the risk for neural tube defects like spina bifida and Down syndrome. It is also called "maternal serum screening," "triple screen," or "quad screen." It is usually performed between the 15th and 17th weeks of pregnancy.

### Nuchal Translucency Screening/ Nuchal Fold Testing

This early ultrasound (done between 11 and 14 weeks) measures the "nuchal fold," a translucent area of skin on the back of the baby's neck. A fold that departs from the "average" size may mean an increased risk of Down syndrome or heart abnormality.

*Note:* It's important to reiterate that both of these tests only screen for risk—they don't diagnose any conditions. For a diagnosis, the parents would have to follow through with the more invasive CVS or amniocentesis.

### CVS (Chorionic villus sampling) Test

This diagnostic test determines whether a baby has a chromosomal disorder. A needle or catheter is placed through the vagina near the uterus or through the abdominal wall to collect a tissue sample. There is a small risk of miscarriage from this procedure and it can cause cramping or bleeding and, rarely, other complications. It's done early—usually between 10 and 12 weeks. It can diagnose Down syndrome, cystic fibrosis, sickle cell disease, and several other chromosomal conditions. It does not diagnose neural tube defects like spina bifida.

### Amniocentesis

This test, probably the most widely known of the four, is done between 16 and 20 weeks. It can detect nearly all chromosomal disorders with 99 percent effectiveness and can also diagnose hundreds of genetic disorders and neural tube defects like spina bifida. A needle is inserted into the amniotic sac through the abdominal wall. (The amniotic sac is the "bag" of water protecting the baby within the uterus.) A small amount of fluid is withdrawn. Amniocentesis also carries with it a small risk of miscarriage and cramping is a common side effect.

In addition to genetic tests, you'll have several mundane blood tests done throughout the course of your pregnancy. These are generally done to check your overall health and are usually not optional. Most blood tests can be done in a care provider's office, though sometimes care providers will send women to the local hospital or lab for routine blood work. This is something women should ask about when they set up their first appointments. For example, is it inconvenient for you to travel to a lab or hospital? Would you rather have everything done in one place? In addition to your comfort and preference, check your insurance coverage. What if the lab or hospital is closer to your home but neither is covered under your plan? There you are trying to be the most prepared mom in the world and the fact that you opted for convenience could cause you to have an unexpected bill to pay.

These issues take the romance out of being pregnant, don't they? And you thought nausea and touchy relatives were a pain.

over thirty-five or those with previous histories of specific genetic/chromosomal disorders in the family are more often advised to get the tests.

## REWARD YOURSELF

What a first month! You probably thought you were going to research fun things like cribs and strollers. Now I've plunked odd-sounding medical tests on your plate. But don't panic—we're taking this journey one step at a time. By the time you go into labor, you'll be an old pro. (And the volume of medical jargon you've learned will sim-

ply amaze you.) And instead of having information on scraps of paper strewn about your home, you have it organized all in one place!

It's time for you to have a reward. Why not plan a romantic evening out with your spouse? His life is changing at lightning speed along with yours. You both deserve some R & R. If you're a single mom, this is a good time to start making a habit of caring for yourself. Join a book club or go see a movie with a friend. Make sure you're building relationships with people who will act as your "village" once your baby is here!

# CHAPTER TWO

# 13 to 17 Weeks Pregnant

We must not, in trying to think about how we can make a big difference,
ignore the small daily differences we can make which, over time, add up
to big differences that we often cannot foresee.

—MARION WRIGHT EDELMAN

THIS MONTH IS THE TIME to take care of "the business of pregnant life." Whether you work outside the home, are self-employed, or will be a stay-at-home mom, there are details to be ironed out. You don't want to be surprised in any way regarding finances. Additionally, you'll need to start thinking about the days when you return home from the hospital. What kind of help will you have? If you are a mom who works outside the home, child care will ultimately be a long-term concern. On the other hand, if you plan to resume working at home, a new baby will complicate your usual routine. Safeguards need to be built into your day so that clients don't have to be put on hold so you can tend to your baby. (Clients may get as cranky as newborns when you do that!)

Of course all planning and no activity will find you crawling the walls. Therefore, this month you get to organize your bedroom closet. It's critical for you to have a true sanctuary during the coming months. And because your wardrobe is about to change, we need to rearrange your closet. And then you can reward yourself by buying maternity clothes!

This month you will begin to fully experience the ongoing pleasure of a well-organized file system and the convenience of your trusty baby journal. I can wax poetic about these tools, but your direct experience is the best barometer of success. Please continue to drink water and build up to your eight glasses a day. This month, as promised, I have another habit for you to cultivate.

**HABIT OF THE MONTH**

## Do Some Form of Light Exercise Like Walking, Yoga, or Swimming for at least Five Minutes Each Day

Exercise releases chemicals called endorphins in your body. These are the "feel good" hormones. In addition, exercise builds strength. As your baby grows, added strength in your legs, buttocks, and back will be a natural counterbalance to your baby weight. You'll find you have more stamina, stand straighter, and feel better. Childbirth experts agree that strength, flexibility, and endurance can help women have easier and shorter labors. Finally, a strong body is likely to get back to normal faster than one that hasn't been gaining strength and stamina. You don't have to become an Olympic athlete to reap these benefits! Walking is easy and will do the trick. If you already have a regular exercise program, ask your doctor how to modify it during your pregnancy.

Check your local YMCA, hospital, gym, or yoga studio for classes tailored to those who are pregnant. This is a great way to make friends with other new moms.

If you are not an exercise person at the moment, there's a pleasant surprise waiting for you. Exercise can become something of a positive addiction. And the benefits can extend to your baby—throughout his life—without your having to say a word. My mother loved to walk. She pushed me for miles in my stroller all over Brooklyn. As soon as I could walk, she held my hand as we walked all over town—to stores, Prospect Park, and the zoo. Today, I still knock off three to four miles every morning.

Like drinking water, exercise is something you can incorporate into your life forever. Be sure you get clearance from your physician before you start any new program, no matter how simple, especially if you have any preexisting medical conditions and/or have never exercised before now.

# 13 WEEKS PREGNANT

## Take Care of Business

**This week, you can**

- Inform your boss that you are pregnant, then check with the HR department to find out if and to what extent you are covered during your maternity leave
- Research your state's disability coverage in the event that you do not have private insurance or coverage at work
- Be sure your work flow is systematized to help your coworkers and clients in your absence
- If you're planning to be an at-home mom for a while or a long period of time, look beyond your weekly budget to the long-term effects of leaving the workforce

MY CLIENT SANDY is a people person. Turn her loose in a store and within minutes she'll know all the sales staff and most of the other customers. When Sandy found out she was pregnant, she couldn't share the news fast enough. And because she is gregarious and open by nature, she never looked back or regretted one shared moment. At the opposite end of the spectrum is my client Dale. She's a career corporate attorney determined to make partner before she turns forty. When she found out she was pregnant, she carefully planned when and how the people in her life, from her parents and family members to her colleagues at work and her postman, would find out. Do you hold things close to the vest? Or do you follow the old saying "If it's on her lung, it's on her tongue!" Wherever you fall in the personality spectrum, there is no right or wrong.

Just as people are different, so are corporate cultures. The bottom line is twofold: you want to follow company-mandated protocol to telegraph to your superiors that you are a team player. You also want to control the news so that you are always in charge of who knows what and when. If any of the advice here doesn't sit well with you, chat with some trusted colleagues who have been down this road before you. Tailor a program that's just right for you. That's the goal.

## TELLING YOUR BOSS

Unless your boss is the character on whom Michael in the TV show *The Office* was patterned, you should have no problem letting him or her know that you are having a baby. As happy as your boss may be for you, the reality of your position being vacated for any period of time is likely to cause some concern. Before you go in to share the good news, take some time to outline a plan. For example, your boss will want to know:

- Who will cover for you during your leave? Does that person need training or do they now work so closely with you that you are already an effective team?
- Is there someone you'd like to nominate to cover for you? What makes this person qualified? When and how will you train her?
- What are your projects, listed from highest priority to low? Let your boss know how each will be handled in your absence.
- What are your thoughts on informing clients, vendors, and colleagues about this blip on their business radar?

I am not suggesting that you have a *detailed* plan worked out at this moment in time. I am suggesting you let your boss know that you are on top of the transition and will cover all the bases in a timely fashion. Change, whether positive or negative, makes most people a little nervous. Even if you don't intend to return to this job after the birth, it would behoove you to take the same precautions for a smooth transition. You never know when a few good words from this boss about your performance will be important in the future. As you take your leave, tell him your next step is to visit HR. Be sure he knows that you would like to be the one to share the news with your coworkers.

## THE HR APPOINTMENT

One of your big tasks this week is to speak to HR. Something as important as a pregnancy needs to be discussed in person, not via phone or impersonal communication forms like e-mail or voice mail. Your leave has ramifications for the company, whether it's the local fast food joint or a big corporation. There is a lot to be discussed. Some HR offices have an open-door policy, while others require an advance appointment. Very large corporations will often assign a specific HR rep to a division. With any luck, you already have a relationship with this person.

### Investigate Your Maternity Benefits

Chances are that when you were hired at your company, you received a packet full of information delineating your medical and other benefits. Few of us take the time to study the details. If a baby was not anywhere in your consciousness at the time, I'm sure you didn't race to read the section on maternity benefits! Did you file those booklets and updates? Take them out now and read the sections that apply to you.

Don't panic if you tossed them. Your HR rep will most likely hand you an updated maternity packet that outlines current company protocol and benefits policies, including your eligibility for maternity leave and, if you are entitled to maternity leave, whether all or a portion of your leave will be paid. In certain circumstances, the Family and Medical Leave Act will protect your job for an unpaid twelve-week leave after the birth or adoption of a child. For specific details, see the Web site, http://www.dol.gov/whd/fmla/index.htm. Be sure you understand exactly what your benefit package and applicable law guarantee for your position. With the recent financial upheaval in the world, benefit packages are changing all the time. You don't want to make assumptions based on old information.

Here are some items to check:

- Am I entitled to maternity leave? If so, how long is the period and will I receive my full or partial salary?
- If the company provides medical insurance, are maternity benefits covered? If so, are these for a certain number of checkups and the delivery?
- What about tests? And more to the point, what about tests recommended by your doctor that are outside the norm? Will there be full, partial, or no coverage?
- When will your leave begin?
- When will you be expected back?
- What if you intend to return to work

but there is a medical complication with the birth or the baby that delays your return? What happens to your benefits?

Your spouse should take a variation on these questions to his HR department to see if there is any coverage available to supplement what you are to receive from your medical policy through your place of employment. You will need to find out from your doctor's office exactly what her charges are for care and delivery. What will the hospital charge? How much for the anesthesiologist? Are these projected fees in keeping with your policy's coverage? How much do you need to have for out-of-pocket expenses for everyone on the medical team? Remember that if you have your baby via cesarean section—which about one in three women do—the costs will be much higher and your hospital stay will be longer. Once you have ironed out all these details, it's time to make some adjustments to your budget. By the way, doctors and midwives are usually pretty good about giving a ballpark assessment of their specific fees, but hospital estimates are often wildly inaccurate. Tack on an extra 20 to 30 percent just to be on the safe side!

Some employers and states offer short-term disability coverage to pregnant women for a period of time after they give birth. Every state has its own rules regarding disability payments. To further complicate matters, every disability program has its own definitions regarding how a pregnancy might qualify. Whether or not you have medical insurance, you need to check out the disability benefits available to you from your state or employer.

Armed with the information from your medical providers and HR, you'll be able to ascertain how much extra cash you'll need out of pocket for the delivery. Ask about payment plans if that will help you. This is an area where you want to minimize the chances of any surprises. You want to enjoy your child from the moment she enters the world without having to worry about unexpected medical expenses.

## LET THE OFFICE KNOW

You need to decide exactly how you want to do this. If you have any close friends among your coworkers, you'll want to tell them in person. After that, in today's world, a clever e-mail announcement would be acceptable. However, before you hit Send, there is another group who should be notified at the same time: your vendors, your suppliers, and, most important of all, your clients. You don't want anyone in this group to hear from another source that you are pregnant. If your contribution to a particular project is vital, for example, a client may panic if he finds out you are going to be gone for a few weeks or months. Share the good news and assure everyone that not only will your projects be up to speed when you leave but talented people in the office will be covering the projects in your absence.

## THE "B" WORD: BUDGET

For even the most financially responsible couples, having a baby may mean tightening your financial belts. If you have been a free-spending, credit-card-dependent duo, now is the time to create your first budget. For some reason, people hear the word "budget" and recoil in horror, thinking it will rob them of all the fun in their lives. This is far from the truth. I want to be sure you can afford your lifestyle and safely incorporate the good times and splurges that make life worth living.

Creating a budget takes a little time and effort. People tend to stumble in their quest to manage their money by not paying attention to their everyday cash expenses. Track them for a week and you may be surprised how fast they add up. Those fancy coffee drinks consumed multiple times a day can ding your budget. What about the casual cash you take from the ATM or the grocery store? Do you sometimes forget to note it in your checkbook? It can add up to a loud ding! And speaking of the grocery store, do you pick up several magazines every week? How many do you actually read? Could you check them out online, get a subscription to enjoy a lower rate, or perhaps share a subscription with a good friend? These impulse buys give a temporary high but like the crash that comes with a sugar rush, it's not worth it in the long run.

To create your budget, you can work in Excel or use grid paper. (There are also Web sites and software that provide you with budget templates.) Make two columns: Income on the left side and Expenses on the right. You won't forget your mortgage or your cell phone bill. You might overlook those expenses that occur only once or twice a year, like dues to a professional organization or payment on your safety deposit box. List everything.

Then, look at your discretionary income, what is left over, and give yourself a weekly allowance. Have that cash in your pocket to get as many lattes and magazines as you can afford. When your allowance runs out, you'll have to wait till next week to start over.

If you find that you have been spending more than you make or cutting it close, it's time to have new financial goals. Look around for ways to save money. Here are five tips to get you started:

- Check your phone plans (land line, dedicated fax, cell, etc.). Call the companies and see if you can eliminate some perks that you aren't taking advantage of in order to save every month. Consider eliminating a phone.
- Check your cable package. Do you really need the entire premium package? Do you need cable at all?
- What about meals out? That really adds up. Check out your local Farmer's Market. Brown bag your lunch and get a Crock-Pot so you have a hot dinner ready when you get home. You'll have fresh produce, support the local economy, and save money over the chain store prices. Start planning meals a week in advance. And never go to the grocery store hungry.
- Do you have too many credit cards? Take some of the money you're saving each month and pay off the highest interest-bearing card first. If you always pay on time and have a high FICO score and your debt ratio is in line, call your credit card companies and ask if you can negotiate a lower interest rate. If they refuse and you have no big-ticket items on the horizon, consider transferring your balance. Read the fine print to be sure it's a good deal. Your score may be lowered, but only for a few months. Contrast that with the amount of money you are saving each month. (When you're out from under this debt, start saving to have three to six months' worth of living expenses set aside for emergencies.)
- Were you left any antiques by Uncle Henry? Did Aunt Gladys leave you jewelry you will never wear in this lifetime? It may be time to sell these items and use the money to finance your future. I'd also be willing to bet your family would be happy to help your baby start out life in a secure financial setting.

## FINANCIAL CARE OPTIONS FOR YOUR PREGNANCY AND DELIVERY

It's scary being without medical insurance. I am a cancer survivor with no health

Financial planner Russell Wild has these tips for new parents:

- Write up a will that stipulates not only what happens to your money but, more importantly, who becomes guardian of the children if both parents should die. If you don't name your guardian, the court will and it will likely be your next of kin.
- Start a college savings account, also known as a 529 college plan. It allows you to sock away money that can grow tax-free. But don't invest in a 529 plan until after you've accumulated six months of living expenses as an emergency reserve and after you've maxed out your 401(k) contributions at work (making sure to get the full employer match). When you're ready, start your shopping at www.savingforcollege.com. Invest directly in a good, low-cost plan. You do not need to go through an investment adviser or brokerage house.
- You should have home insurance and health insurance before you become a parent, but life insurance becomes a good idea only after you've become a parent. Look for a twenty-year term policy on each parent's life. As a general rule of thumb, the death benefit might be in the ballpark of eight to ten times your annual expenses.

coverage, and I know from firsthand experience that there are indeed ways to "work the system" and get the care you need. If you lack insurance, here are some avenues for you to investigate:

- Check with your state about Medicaid coverage specifically for pregnant women and babies. Even if you wouldn't usually qualify for Medicaid, many states have special programs for pregnant women with more lenient guidelines. They will also cover your baby for a period of time.
- Ask at the county health department about prenatal care for women without insurance.
- If you are losing your job, you need to check out the possibility of unemployment benefits. And losing your job because of a pregnancy is illegal. If this happens to you, consult with an attorney right after you file for unemployment.
- Your physician and your hospital should be willing to negotiate a lower cash price than the ones quoted to patients who have medical coverage. If these entities will not consider a reduction in fees, find a physician or hospital that will.
- Consider a midwife. Certified nurse-midwives, or CNMs, often work in the same medical practices as doctors but tend to have lower fees. That's quite a bargain considering a nurse-

midwife will generally stay with you throughout your labor and birth, not just show up for the delivery like most obstetricians.

- If you have a freestanding birth center in your region, that may be another option. These centers are generally run independently from hospitals and are a much less expensive option than a hospital birth.

- If you and baby are healthy and you want a natural birth, consider having your baby at home. Midwife's fees for home birth are generally between $3,000.00 and $4,000.00 and are all-inclusive. That's a huge savings over hospital delivery and you'll get very personalized care.

- Teaching hospitals very often have clinics where patients without insurance can be treated for less money. You'll have to check with them to see exactly how you can qualify. It usually involves an in-person interview, the completion of a long form, and the presentation of two years' worth of income tax returns and pay stubs.

- Finally, if you live in a large city, see how many county hospitals there are. These vary in quality depending on where they are located. After a phone call to see if you could indeed go there for care, you'll want to make an in-person visit to see how comfortable you are at the hospital. Your physician must have privileges at the facility or you will be required to see a different doctor. Ask whether your regular doctor has any contacts.

If all of the research required is starting to overwhelm you, why not consider hiring a "Virtual Assistant" for a few hours to help out and do the legwork for you? These are men and women whom you will never meet. They are found through friends and agencies. (Check the Resources section.) It's worth remembering, especially if research of any kind isn't your forte or if you're simply too overwhelmed with nausea to sit at a computer or be on the phone for hours.

If you prefer to hire someone in person, check out the job referral department at your local college or university. It's a great way to help a student and secure inexpensive assistance. You can probably find someone who loves research and is practically a professional at it. You know what they say: Where there's a will, there's a way.

## PREPARE YOUR OFFICE FOR YOUR ABSENCE

Even though it may seem like you have plenty of time before you'll be going on maternity leave, now is a good time to start preparing your space and thinking about how your workflow will be handled in the coming months and during your absence. Leaving an organized space with projects up to date is another sign you are a team player. When your colleagues can easily locate data, they are less likely to be calling you at home during your maternity leave. When you're sleep-deprived and sore, this silence will be an appreciated blessing. If your vendors and clients are up to speed, they won't have to rattle your colleagues' cages during your absence. But don't think for a minute you're doing this work solely for the benefit of others. You are doing it for you! No one wants to return to a chaotic nightmare. You want a seamless transition to the team that will be covering for you and back to you upon your return.

Let's face it: Some people subconsciously love to create complicated "systems" so that no one else at work can figure out what they do, much less how. Their file systems (I use the term loosely) appear to have been created by someone at the CIA. And their physical spaces are a maze of stuff. Today's projects are buried under a sea of coffee mugs, family photos, plants that leak water, and stale gum. But of course this doesn't describe you! Or does it?

This week, start preparing your physical space for your absence. You don't have to spend hours and completely overhaul your files. Make that a goal when you return and get caught up. For now, try my "fresh eyes" exercise: Set aside some time to work on your office or cubicle. Enter and pretend you have never been here before. How do you feel? What do you know about this person? The space will speak volumes without ever uttering a literal word. Trust me. If you open yourself to this exercise rather than dismiss it as silly, you will be surprised by what you discover.

Next, if you realize you have a lot of clutter, do a speed elimination. Be sure you have bags for trash, a way to recycle, a way to shred, and a box on hand to hold items you need to take home. Most companies have a procedure for handling large amounts of material that must be shredded.

Set a timer for twenty minutes. The guidelines will be familiar to you from last month.

- Toss or recycle paper that no longer needs to be saved. This includes newsletters, memos, receipts, outdated HR materials, old health care benefit booklets, newspapers, and magazines. If you're on the fence about something your company produces, like a newsletter, find out whether a copy is always available online, in the company library, or with another employee.
- Toss old candy, gum, food, condiment packages, and plastic silverware.
- Take real plants home if they are small enough to carry. Have large plants moved to a plant-friendly coworker's space or ask a coworker to water your plants in your absence.
- Personal photos should be kept to a minimum. Take the overflow home now. Why not instead have personal photos rotate as your screensaver? You'll have a friendly face in the office without your workspace looking like your family room at home.
- If you live in a four-season climate or an office with a wayward thermostat, you may have collected a number of sweaters, shoes, and boots over time.

Take the excess home long before you go on maternity leave.

- Return items to the company kitchen or supply room.
- Do you have enough pens to last a lifetime? Remember, they dry out. Toss those that are no longer useful, return excess to the supply room, and bag the overflow. If you pass a school, see if it could use any supplies. Too much of any item is what I call "fake prosperity." It looks like you have a lot when in fact all you are doing is losing valuable space to debris.
- Pull aside old projects that need to be archived. If your company has offsite storage, take advantage.

A pregnant woman's due date is calculated for week forty, but it's considered within the realm of normal to have the baby anywhere from week thirty-seven through week forty-two. That's more than a month during which you could possibly have the baby, which might throw off even the best-laid plans. The moral of the story: Make and execute your exit plan early. You don't want to be in the labor room holding a stopwatch in one hand and a Blackberry in the other trying to help your colleagues find important papers!

Now it's time to get your projects streamlined. Make a list (Excel would be the easiest format) of every project on which you are working. In the next column, please note the due date for its completion. Along the way there will be interim due dates for various phases of your projects.

Which projects will be completed before you leave?

Which are due long after your return?

Which have critical dates during your leave?

This timeline will give you a bit of mental control over the amount of work to be done. Are there any projects due during your absence that are not critical? Perhaps you could negotiate a change in due dates with your clients. If necessary, clear this with your supervisor. Once you have these due dates set in stone, be sure you note them on your calendar. These are important markers and you can't afford to lose sight of them.

For filing purposes, every project can be broken down in the same manner we used for your personal information in the previous chapter. It's going to be crucial that those who cover for you in your absence can find key papers. Spend some time setting up these files. It's really helpful if you copy the list onto an Excel sheet and send it to your coworkers, noting the location of the files in your office. Should they need to access this information, they won't have to rifle through your drawers or stacks of wayward papers on your desk.

If you don't wish to create a list in Excel, make an appointment with your coworkers to show them the lay of the land well in advance of your departure. You won't be able to take any frantic calls about due dates and the location of key papers while you're in labor!

Finally, be sure your clients know well in advance not only of your pregnancy but who will replace you during your leave. You need to reassure clients that you have systems in place that safeguard their projects and that the transition will be seamless. And it will be if you take some time now to organize everything. You may of course have paper waiting for you upon your return. However, with this experience under your belt you'll be able to quickly eliminate what you don't need and file away what you do want to keep. If it doesn't have a waiting file folder, add one to your system. If you continue to streamline in the future, you will never again be faced with the task of decluttering your space. I think that's motivation to start eliminating now!

## THE SELF-EMPLOYED MOM

The good news is that all of the above instructions apply to your workspace at home. Now is a great time to clean it out and streamline your procedures, practices, and projects. If you have someone who works with you, it's going to be easier for her if this work is done now. Just as an organized home cuts down on the barrage of questions like "Where are my shoes?" an organized office means your assistant can leave you in peace except for emergencies. If you work alone, be sure your clients are up to speed on your plans and that all project due dates have been shifted to adjust to your schedule. I think you'll find that every relationship you have will thrive

with open communication. We all learn this over time, very often the hard way.

Even with several file cabinets full of information, most of us deal primarily with a few key folders every day. There are file totes that give you complete portability. You can find them in inexpensive plastic at the local big box office supply store and in elegant leather at a site like www.seejane work.com. You'll be able to set up your laptop, file case, and portable phone just about anywhere in the first weeks after the birth.

You have other options as well. Should you wish to stay in your home office, you can use a baby monitor. Test it to be sure its range connects you to Baby's room before the birth. If your office is large, you can set up a sleep/play area for your newborn. There is no right or wrong solution. See which works best for your personality as well as for the needs of your business.

## IF YOU WILL BE AN
## AT-HOME MOM

You may opt to become a full-time mom, putting your career on hold for a few months, a few years, or indefinitely. While this can be a beautiful choice, it's a good idea to give it careful consideration to avoid common pitfalls and to ensure you're making a financially sustainable choice. My mother, the queen of sayings and proverbs, said this to me every single morning as I left for school: "Regina, think with your head, not with your heart." Let's take a look at some of the issues you need to consider:

- If you are not going to return to work, how will you transition out of your current job? A replacement needs to be hired and trained. Will they want you to be a part of that process? After all, it's good karma to leave your place of employment in the best shape possible. You never know what the future holds for you. Someday you may need to petition them for a return position or a recommendation, and you want them to remember you fondly.
- Can your family survive on your spouse's income alone? Run those numbers!
- Consider that you will not be paying into Social Security. That may not seem like a tragedy if you are twenty-five or thirty, but one day if you are lucky, you will be older and wish to (need to?) draw on that account. Do you have other sources of retirement funding set up?
- Are you working in corporate America? Have you been on the fast track as a professional woman (doctor, attorney, financial planner, etc.)? Keep in mind that by leaving you will miss out on automatic raises.
- You may have a problem jumping back into the workforce later if you don't do anything to keep your résumé fresh and stay in touch with the working world while you're at home. You have no idea what the future holds. How can you keep as many options open to you as possible?
- How will you protect yourself and your child against the chance that you will be left a single mother via death or divorce?

You and your spouse need to have an open discussion about how you'll handle the budget and discretionary income now that you'll be doing the important work of staying home with your child. If you've each been treating your own income as "your" money, drastic changes will need to be made. Being an at-home mom can be a wonderful thing, but you need to be brutally honest with yourself about the challenges that may lie ahead should you decide to re-enter the work force.

## BE OPEN TO CHANGING YOUR MIND

My former client Autumn welcomed her son Josh to the family via international adoption. While most new moms are tired because of labor and birth, at the beginning of Autumn's motherhood journey she was exhausted by a trip halfway across the world to bring her child home!

Though Autumn wished at first that she could stay at home with Josh, by the end of her maternity leave she was quite ready to get back to the office. Other women I know have had the opposite experience: They assume they'll be chomping at the bit to get back to work, but as the maternity leave comes to an end, they find they're willing to give up the office, the title, and even the paycheck in order to stay home for as long as possible.

Like these women, you may be surprised later at how differently you feel about being a working mom when it's time to drop your baby off at day care . . . or you may rethink your plan to stay at home after a few weeks of 24-7 baby duty. There are plusses and minuses to both situations, but neither is more right. Follow your gut, and feel free to change your plan if it seems to be a better fit for you and your family.

Also consider that there is a lot of middle ground between full-time working mom and full-time at-home mom. If neither arrangement seems right for you, with some planning and creativity you may be able to create a hybrid situation that gives you and Baby the best of both worlds.

## A BUSY WEEK COMES TO AN END

You must be exhausted from all I've asked you to consider. Don't worry if you have to spread some of this work out over the month. Just be sure to stay on track. When you are in your last trimester, growing large and feeling uncomfortable in your own skin, you'll feel relieved that you took the time to address these issues well beforehand.

Finally, why not try delegating tasks this month? It's a surefire way to reclaim some energy. Here are some guidelines to help you learn how to delegate well:

- Give tasks to someone who is capable of doing the assignment. If he hasn't

had a chance to prove himself, start out with inconsequential items. Is this an idea person or someone who likes detail? Is this a big-picture thinker or someone who loves to be a part of the literal process?
- What is this person's work ethic? Does she dive in and work on everything as if this were her own business? Or does she just do enough to get by?
- Set false deadlines for your helper. Build time into the project for you to check over material and do triage if it's needed.
- Learn how to explain exactly what you want. Very often people do not deliver what we asked for because our instructions (not their abilities) are at fault.

These are the same guidelines you can use when you are at home directing your spouse, family members, a doula, a housekeeper, or anyone else present to help you. Over the years I've learned that work ethic is perhaps the most important ingredient in the mix. Which is the most important for you? Be sure your helpers are equipped to meet your needs.

Next week you'll be on your feet working on your bedroom. Physical activity will be a nice contrast to this week of intense planning. If you need to sneak in a reward as the week draws to a close, I think that's a wonderful idea. Just be sure it's within your new budget!

# 14 WEEKS PREGNANT

## Organize Your Closet

**This week, you can**

- Clean out and reorganize your closet
- Make a space for your soon-to-arrive maternity wardrobe
- Designate items for charity donation and/or giving to friends

CLOTHING TENDS TO BE an emotional issue for most women. I often see clients hanging onto multiple-sized wardrobes in the same closet. Hormones can cause some women's bodies to blow up and shrink down faster than tires in a tack factory. And that's just during menses or after a heavily salted meal! Now your body is expanding for a different reason. This is the perfect time to clean out the space so it will be easier to use for the next year or so.

After your pregnancy, even if you return to the exact same weight you were before, it's likely that your body is going to redistribute your weight differently. So it might be time to take a second look at those teeny tiny T-shirts you've been saving since college. We need to make room for a fabulous new wardrobe. In a few weeks' time, we'll tackle the rest of the bedroom. You'll have a true sanctuary by the time your baby comes home from the hospital.

### STEP ONE: GETTING READY

First things first: see if a girlfriend (who isn't pregnant) can volunteer to help be your hands and feet today. Don't feel guilty if you need to sit down during this process. You've got the toughest part to play: making decisions.

It doesn't help if you are ready to let go and your partner isn't. You've got to make unfettered decisions about your stuff. Let me say that again for emphasis: *your* stuff. No one should toss another person's things without permission unless the person in question is five or under.

It's time to gather your supplies and get started. You'll want several heavy-duty garbage bags to hold clothes for donation as well as items to be tossed. Most people also find things that need to be returned to loved ones and friends. And of course we're likely to encounter a few items that were surely meant to live elsewhere in the home. Set aside a few hours one day for eliminating and distribution; a few hours of shopping on another day to pick up any supplies you need; and a final day to put the pieces of the puzzle together. You can also shop online or send a friend out to shop for you. Be sure you have healthy snacks on hand and lots of water. If you are feeling at all nauseous, be sure the food isn't highly aromatic.

## DAY ONE: ELIMINATE & CATEGORIZE

You have two main objectives today. You want to create space in the front of your closet for the maternity clothes you need to purchase. (I'll have guidelines for you next week covering every aspect of the process: shopping, borrowing, and of course organizing.) And you need to keep nearby the items that will serve you from your current wardrobe until you get to the "final expansion." Think billowy sundresses, for example. Your other objective is to get the clothing that you weren't even wearing before you became pregnant out of the house. You don't want to live with the clutter. Nor do you want to be tempted to sneak a few items back into the closet. Trust your instincts.

The most creative and expansive step in the Magic Formula (eliminate, categorize, organize) is eliminating. Don't be surprised if you're more tired than you anticipated when you're done today. It won't be from the physical labor involved. Decision making wears all of my clients out. It's an important skill to have and there's no better time to practice than today in your closet.

Of course the Magic Formula isn't just about tossing things out permanently or setting them aside for several months. It's also about putting the items you are keeping back in your closet in related categories. When I teach the Magic Formula in my seminars, I always use the closet as an example because we all have at least one and clothing categories are pretty universal. To wit: tops, sweaters, jeans, slacks, suits, shoes, and so on. Wondering how to make the clothing categories functional and beautiful? Read on! I've got the tips and tricks professional organizers use listed below.

Before we start, an important note. Do not remove items on hangers. If you pile them on your bed, you will only succeed in wrinkling the ones that return to the closet.

Immediately pull off and throw away the plastic covers that have come home from the cleaners. They seal in the chemicals, some of which may be carcinogenic. You don't want to breathe in those chemicals the next time you wear that item, especially if it has been covered for several months.

Now look for empty hangers and remove them all. Throw away the cheap wire ones that come home from the cleaners with you. They destroy clothing over time.

Next, I want you to work one section of your closet at a time. Mark off about a foot of hanging clothes with your eyes and pretend that whatever hangs in that area is all your closet holds. Look at one item at a time. Most things you will have an immediate reaction to; when you aren't sure, ask yourself some questions. When was the last time I wore this? Is it still in style? Does it look good on me? Does it represent a special time now past?

There are organizers who will tell you the "rule" is to toss one item when you purchase something new. Still others will say if you haven't worn something in six months or a year, it should go. I think these rules are arbitrary. If they work for you, that's great. Use them. But the *reason* you haven't worn something is usually lodged in something emotional. You can make a better decision if you figure what bonds you to this item. If it's an experience or a special time in your life, for example, do you have a photo of yourself in the item? Why not put that photo in a scrapbook or a small shadow box instead. Attach a swatch of the fabric. You'll have a fitting memento without clogging up your closet.

Items that are frayed, hopelessly out of style, torn, or stained should go into the trash bag immediately.

Items that are decade-specific and in good condition can be donated to the local community theater (gigantic shoulder pads or wide bell-bottoms, anyone?)

After you are finished with the hanging clothes, go through your shoes. This is usually a big task for most women. Be fearless when it comes to eliminating items

like sky-high heels. Your feet are likely to grow larger over the course of your pregnancy. And unless you are in politics, the entertainment industry, or the upper echelons of business, glamorous evenings out are probably over for a few years. They will be replaced by days at the park and the zoo. Hang on to the shoes that offer good support.

The next big category in your closet will be handbags. Do you really need twelve black purses? You're on a roll. Don't hold back now!

Most women have large sweater and scarf collections, especially if they live in a four-season climate. Check for moth holes, stains, and other signs of wear. If you have expensive cashmere, consider taking some items to a tailor for repair. If these are inexpensive garments that are past their prime, pass them on to a charity. By the way, if you don't already have a favorite charity, call around and see if there is a women's shelter in your city. You'll be helping someone start a new life.

If you have been working in corporate America, you probably have a collection of suits. Are you going back to work soon after the birth? If you plan to take several years off, consider donating your suits to Dress for Success. You will help a woman enter the workforce by giving her a beautiful suit to wear for her interview. When you are ready to return to work in a few years, you'll probably want a new wardrobe. Save one or two suits at most if you have several.

After clothing has been eliminated for charity donation or set aside for friends and family, you can start categorizing. Go back to your closet and look at the items you wish to keep but know you won't fit into for quite some time. You might as well put these away for a bit. You need the space for that maternity wardrobe you'll be creating soon. Space bags are a wonderful way to store these things. Place your clothes in the bag and suck out the air with a vacuum cleaner. Your clothing will literally shrink before your eyes. When you need them again, just open the bag. It has the same type of closure as a zip-top food storage bag. Voila! Nothing has been ruined. It has been waiting to serve you again.

There are space bags that hang in the closet and others that are flat and can be stuffed on a high shelf. The only item that doesn't work well in a space bag is one that is designed to "puff up." Think comforters and pillows and you'll get the idea.

Alternatively, if you are blessed with a large walk-in closet, you might simply store items you wish to keep but won't be using in the far back. Perhaps you have a large home with a guest room closet you can commandeer for this purpose?

## STORING OTHER ITEMS

In the best of all possible worlds, no closet would house anything except clothing. In reality, I usually find a mishmash of all sorts of items. The most common are fans,

small weights, memorabilia, and photos. What's a new mom to do? If there is no other logical place for such items to be located, store them in your closet as discreetly as possible. Most closets have a huge space between one existing shelf and the ceiling. Create a second shelf by placing a brace on each side and laying a piece of lumber across. Your local home store will cut the lumber to your specifications. You can leave it plain, cover it with decorative contact paper, stain it, or paint it. I vote for plain. This high shelf will enable you to put miscellaneous items away until you are ready to deal with them.

Try and break the "I'll just shove this here" syndrome. It's not something you want to teach your child. Rather, cultivate the art of making decisions. Use the Magic Formula when deciding the fate of every item that enters the home. Ask yourself, "Do I really need this?" If the answer is "Yes," the next question is "Do I have other related items?" When you identify the right category, work the new item into the system. It seems huge to you now because it's a new way of thinking. Give it a few weeks and you'll find it will become quite simply how you process information, whether it's a new purchase, the incoming mail, or that thingamajig in the back of your closet.

## REGINA'S TOP 12 CLOSET ORGANIZING TRICKS

What do professional organizers do in a closet? I'm going to give you our top secrets to help you make your closet more functional and beautiful. Decide which ones you'd like to employ. If a purchase is necessary, The Container Store is my favorite source for products (and I'm not a paid spokesperson!). First, their quality is outstanding. If you purchase cheap or flimsy products, you're going to have to replace things frequently, and over time you'll be wasting money. Second, if you discover you need more of a particular item, you can bet The Container Store will still carry it in six months or a year. A mishmash of organizing tools in a closet can make it as crazy as an unorganized one.

Here, in no particular order, are a few of my favorite things when it comes to closets.

1. Use one type of hanger throughout the closet for uniformity and visual appeal. Wood hangers do the least harm to your clothes. There are other great choices: hangers (originally from the Home Shopping Network and now in stores) that have a sticky fabric that prevents garments from falling off, tubular hangers, and thin, clear plastic ones.

2. Face your clothes in the same direction, preferably facing the door if it's a walk-in closet. This is how department stores make their apparel appealing and easy to find.

3. Group related items: Shirts, slacks, jeans, suits, and shoes all go together. This cuts down on time when you know what type of garment you need.

4. Arrange all groups in color order. This gives the closet a restful appearance and makes finding items within a category a snap. If something isn't where you expect it, try the laundry or the dry cleaners. I use the following order: white/off white; beige/brown; blue/purple; pink/red; yellow/green; gray/black.

5. If you really want a closet that looks like a pro did it, within the colors arrange by "style." For example, with blouses I do sleeveless, short sleeved, then long. I keep patterns behind solids. If your head just exploded at the idea of giving this much attention to clothing detail, don't worry. Just keep those colors together!

6. Shoes need to be off the floor. Over-the-door canvas shoe bags are great for sneakers and exercise shoes. Expanding shoe racks are great for shoes with any kind of a heel. Those evening shoes you're going to save for the next time you get to dress up like Cinderella can go into an acrylic shoe drawer and sit on a high shelf. Or, if you have several pairs, you can stack several shoe drawers on the floor of your closet.

7. Avoid hangers that hold multiple pairs of slacks. When you are in a hurry, you will reach for one and three will fall to the floor.

8. Sweaters can be stored in stacks on the shelf or in acrylic sweater drawers. Some people like sweater bags. If you go that route, be sure you get the ones with a clear front so you don't have to unzip the bag to view the contents.

9. There's a wonderful item called a shelf divider that will keep your categories separated. But you need a wooden shelf to snap it onto!

10. I like my purses lined up in color order and I use tissue paper so they keep their shape. I keep the tissue inside a cloth bag (the kind that some shoes and many purses come with). The tissue goes in and out in one piece.

11. If you don't have a light in the closet, try one or two of the battery-operated, portable lights you can stick on the wall. It's so important to be able to see your clothes. And if you are blessed with a light, use a good-sized bulb. Black and blue look an awful lot alike in a dim light!

12. Finally a word about closets with sliding doors. They are a nightmare, aren't they? You would best be served to remove the doors and put up a simple bamboo shade. You can lower it when you expect company and keep it up the rest of the time. This will give you added incentive to stay organized as the closet contents are clearly on display. If you must keep the sliding doors, arrange your clothes in the order you put them on. That way you won't be returning to a section over and over. Each door will slide once.

## PUT THE PUZZLE TOGETHER

I've had many clients walk in to see their newly organized closets and burst into tears. They tell me they wish they could sleep that night in the closet because it's the most restful place in their home. It may sound lofty, but you'll have the same reaction when you have followed these simple directions. Again, please do ask someone to come and help you. This project is exhausting even when you aren't pregnant.

But in a few months when your baby has arrived and you need to move like greased lightning, you'll be so grateful you took the time to organize your closet. The time you save will quickly outstrip the time you spent working on this project. And there's another perk hidden in this project. Children aren't born organized. They learn the skill from their parents. You will organize your child's closet using the same guidelines and techniques. And she'll just naturally grow up an organized person. Now doesn't that just make you want to jump up and switch out hangers?

# 15 WEEKS PREGNANT

## Build Your Maternity Wardrobe

**This week, you can**

- Go through your existing wardrobe to decide which of your clothes to pack away, which you might be able to get more wear out of during your pregnancy, and which you should keep close by for after the baby's birth
- Make a list of clothing items you'll need during your pregnancy, and decide whether to borrow those items from a friend or relative, raid your spouse's closet, or buy your own
- Come up with a system for circulating clothes as they are outgrown
- Shop for items you'll need in the coming weeks, with an eye to the future
- Make a plan for replenishing your maternity wardrobe as your pregnancy progresses

CONSIDER YOURSELF LUCKY! When Meagan was pregnant with her first child in the late '90s, there weren't nearly as many options in maternity wear as there are now. Stores usually carried just a rack or two of maternity clothing. What was available was often cheaply made and featured prints as infantile as a newborn's layette, complete with unflattering details like ruffles and bows in all the wrong places. It was as though pregnant women were expected to dress like babies themselves. Many tears were shed in department-store dressing rooms during that first shopping excursion.

Things have certainly changed since then. From high-end to discount, there's a huge array of maternity clothing available that's stylish. Better still, some compassionate genius finally realized that women don't stay the same size throughout their pregnancies. Now you can buy clothing specially made for the first, second, or third trimester. You'll also find a variety of fitting options to choose from, from drawstring waists to elastic panels that firmly hug a growing belly instead of falling down.

While choices are great, they can also complicate things a bit. Do you run out and buy clothes for the entire pregnancy early on? Or wait and see how big you get? Do you need a pair of pants with each type of waistband?

I recommend shopping for maternity clothes slowly and deliberately. Yes, it can be tempting to run out and load up on those adorable shirts. But every pregnant woman develops differently, and carries her baby differently, too. Surely you've seen a pregnant woman who looks as though she swallowed a basketball—no weight gain in her rear or hips. If you're less lucky, you'll add extra "padding" throughout your entire midsection. You'll need to make decisions about which styles are most flattering and comfortable based on which category you fall into—and you probably can't know that yet.

Also, a word of caution: Don't leap into maternity clothing too early in the pregnancy. Yes, many women start outgrowing their jeans almost as soon as they see the pink lines on the pregnancy test. And by now, several months in, you're almost certainly bursting out of some of your pre-pregnancy clothes. But while you may feel like you look just huge, chances are good that your "baby bump" isn't very noticeable to others yet. At this point, maternity tops or jeans may just hang on you and look sloppy—or worse, make that cute baby belly look more like a case of bloat.

What to do while you're waiting for your midsection to grow a little bigger? Some tricks to try:

- Shirts with gathered sides. Whether you get them off the maternity rack or from the regular department, gathered shirts hold nice and snug against your figure early on, then expand with you. They make a great postpartum top because they are forgiving without looking like muumuus.

- Crisp, tailored cotton tops. Don't shy away from fitted clothes early on in your pregnancy. A shirt with just a bit of "give" will accommodate your growing form but still look pulled together.

- Work with what you've got. With some ingenuity, your existing pants can work for a few more weeks. Try threading a rubber band through the buttonhole on your favorite jeans and use it for stretchy closure. Or buy a Bella Band—a stretchy tube of fabric you wear over your unbuttoned pants to hold them snug against your body while giving you a smooth look under shirts.

- Raid your husband's closet. If he's not much larger than you, you may find that his T-shirts or even his pants fit for a while.

- Think yoga and dance. Companies like Gap Body, Capezio, and Lululemon make yoga and dance wear that easily go from studio to home, and, depending on your dress code, maybe even the office. Plus you'll get a lot of wear out of a well-made pair of yoga pants in your early months of motherhood. Look for pants with firm enough waistbands to support your growing body and smooth out lumps and bumps.

## PLANNING YOUR MATERNITY WARDROBE

I know you're still dying to get to the fun part—shopping—but we need to go through a few important steps first. You just got done organizing your closet. The last thing you want to do is stuff it full of clothes you won't really need.

What I want you to do first is to think about your unique clothing needs. Many pregnancy books will give you a checklist of items to buy for your maternity wardrobe—for example, three pairs of jeans, two skirts, two leggings, and so on. I'm not going to do that because I don't know how you dress on a regular basis. The point is that your maternity wardrobe has to work for you. The only way for you to know that it will is to look at what you actually wear and then try to figure out wardrobe solutions for your new body.

Think back over your last typical week and write down the items you wore each day. For example, maybe you work in a professional office. This week you may have worn two skirts, two button-down shirts, two blazers, two sweaters, two pairs of dress slacks, one dress, one pair of leggings, two pairs of jeans, three casual tops, and two sets of workout clothes. On the other hand, if you work from home or in a casual office, your particular wardrobe may have been much heavier on the jeans and casual tops. Either way, the best way to get a feel for what your needs might be throughout the pregnancy is to take a look at what you wear in your actual life.

### A NOTE ABOUT BRAS

It's likely that the first clothing purchase you'll need to make is a good, supportive bra. For many women, added girth in this area is one of the first symptoms of pregnancy. And while you're gestating, your breasts may continue to grow.

A good bra that fits your new figure is a must, but there's nothing magical about maternity bras. If you already shop at a lingerie store whose products or employees you trust, feel free to go back there to get fitted for your pregnancy bras. Just make sure that whatever bra you choose, it has a supportive cup and a wide, adjustable strap that's not too stretchy.

Some so-called maternity bras double as nursing bras, but I think this is a potential waste of money. Your breasts may grow again by as much as a cup size or two in the early days of breastfeeding. Don't spend a lot of money on maternity/nursing bras now expecting to use them later. You may have very different needs when you're actually breastfeeding.

The same goes for maternity underwear. Many women find that they can wear the same bikini underwear throughout their pregnancies. You might be tempted to buy a few packages of those "granny panty" maternity briefs, but consider this: They have a nasty habit of rolling down over your belly. This is very uncomfortable and not too attractive either.

Now think about how often you do laundry or take your clothes to the dry cleaner. Are you willing to attend to laundry more often throughout your pregnancy so that you don't have to buy as many clothes? Or will you do the laundry with the same frequency—or even less often? Also, how hard are you on your clothes? How many times do you wear a garment before you toss it in the hamper or the dry cleaning bag? Be realistic. With this information in mind, map out a list of what you'll need to get you through your pregnancy.

Using grid paper, regular notebook paper, or an Excel spreadsheet, make a list of each item you'll need down the left-hand side of the paper. List each item separately (i.e., if you need two pairs of jeans, write "jeans" twice). If you want specific styles or colors of each (e.g., "black slacks" or "white button-down shirt"), also note that in your list. Working in Excel will allow you to easily update this list throughout your pregnancy as your size and needs change. I've included a sample checklist for you to copy.

Now go through any clothing you may have already purchased or that friends or family have lent you and figure out what fits into which category. If you've got an item, mark an X to its right. Again, be realistic. If your best friend loaned you a maternity sweater and you hate it, it doesn't count. You won't wear it. If you are lucky enough to find in your stack of loaner clothing a few "bonus" pieces (e.g., a fancy dress you love even if you aren't sure

you'll need it yet, or three sweaters when you only need two), add them to the bottom of your list. You want an accurate picture of what you have on hand, so if a wedding or other special event comes up, you can tell at a glance whether you're ready.

| Clothing Item | On Hand |
| --- | --- |
| Jeans, boot cut | X |
| Jeans, skinny leg | X |
| White button-down shirt | |
| Leggings, black | X |
| Cardigan, casual cotton | |
| Cardigan, dressy cashmere | X |
| Work jacket, black | |

When you've finished with this exercise, you'll have a pile of clothes that you know you'll need and a list indicating exactly what you still have left to purchase. You may also have some items that have been loaned to you that you aren't sure whether you'll need or not. Read on for some ideas to help you prevent a "donation explosion" in your home!

## GETTING A HANDLE ON HAND-ME-DOWNS

People love to give pregnant women unsolicited stuff—especially advice, books, and clothes! Chances are good that the minute you tell the world about your baby-to-be, friends start showing up at your office or front door with bags and totes full of maternity and baby clothes. Sharing clothing and baby gear is a wonderful way to save money on things you'll only use for a short time. But it can also be a pain to keep track of, and one woman's taste (or size) may not match another's. If you live in a small space and Susan is dying to bring over a tote full of baby clothes, you may not know where you'll put them. And of course, if both Kelly and Jenny lend you maternity clothes, it can become tricky keeping them all separate as you grow out of certain items and into others. Here are a few simple guidelines to help you keep track of donations.

Realize that most women hold onto their pregnancy outfits for sentimental reasons. *Your* pregnancy, however, offers them a completely guilt-free way to clean out their closets! Consider accepting only those clothing items that are being given, rather than loaned. You won't have to worry about rips, tears, or stains. You can also donate the items as soon as you outgrow them, or sooner if they're not your style.

If you are part of a large circle of family and friends who are planning multiple births over the next few years, you may wish to keep these items rotating in your group. This is fine provided you have the space to store everything while you wait for the next birth announcement. Garage shelves are ideal for this. Divide the items by trimester (or size, for baby clothes) and store them in clearly labeled, heavy-duty plastic tubs. If you aren't the one with the garage, find the gal in your circle who does have the space!

If you do wish to accept items that are only on loan, get permission to ID them. You can keep a written log, but this can be easy to lose track of, especially if you aren't feeling your best throughout your pregnancy and/or are inundated by stuff. Instead, assign a color to each friend or colleague who makes a donation. Placing a slight color mark or initial on the inside sewn-in tag will remind you who gave you the item. You can find a cheap ten-pack of fabric-safe markers at fabric stores like Joanne's.

If you simply don't need or have space for items, steel yourself for those well-meaning souls who want to foist their castoffs on you. Don't be afraid to gracefully say no!

## SHOPPING FOR SUCCESS

Finally—you can go shopping! Armed with your list, head to a few of your favorite stores and try some items on. Maternity boutiques often have "pregnant belly" prostheses you can try on under your clothing to get a sense of how an outfit will look as you grow. This may or may not be all that accurate for you, but it will at least give you an idea.

A few things to think about as you shop:

- Keep seasons in mind. If you live in an area with four seasons, your pregnancy will span at least three of them.

If you're going to buy clothes you won't fit into for a while, be sure the seasons will work.

- Better yet, don't buy ahead. In general, just try to focus on the next few months of your pregnancy. As you grow out of certain items, you can come back with an accurate idea of what you still need.

- You're still you. While it can be tempting to splurge on romantic, fluttery dresses or hippie skirts while pregnant, if you didn't wear those styles before, you probably won't wear them now. Pregnancy doesn't change your sense of style. If anything, you'll probably feel even more conspicuous in a fashion that isn't "you" when you've got a twenty-pound lump sticking out of your front.

- Look carefully at waistbands. You'll see simple drawstrings, two-inch firm elastic waists, belly panels that come about halfway down to the crotch of the pants, and full-belly panels. The drawstrings and two-inch elastic waists are great for early on, but many women outgrow them fairly quickly. The half-belly panels often work well into the third trimester and will probably be what you will wear for the first couple weeks after your baby arrives. At this point of your pregnancy (three months in), you'll definitely want to avoid full-belly panels. They'll just let your stomach "pooch" out and look baggy and lumpy. Only

buy them later, if and when you need them.

- Store all your maternity clothes by the stage of your pregnancy. Hang as many of the items in your closet as you can, then keep them sorted on hangers by type (pants, tops, or jeans for example). Use color as we discussed last week to help you find things in a flash. But whether you're putting these clothes in your dresser drawers, closet shelves, or a storage tub or two, just be sure you keep everything separate! If you have the bathing suit for your first trimester in with the tops for your final weeks, it's going to get crazy-making.

As this week draws to a close, I'm going to bet you are feeling a bit overwhelmed by the clothing issue. Remember the Magic Formula? When in doubt, "eliminate, categorize, organize."

"Eliminate" can mean something shouldn't even cross your threshold. Bring into your life only what you really need. Resist impulse spending. A top may be adorable, but how many times are you going to wear it? Continuously send back out into the world the donated items you will no longer use.

Keep related items together. You will find that categories make you feel powerful and in control. From soup to T-shirts and screws to paper towels, you'll be aware of exactly what you have in every household category imaginable because you will then automatically know exactly what you need.

Think of the time, energy, and money you'll be saving. Practice keeping your categories organized. If you can control your wardrobe, you can control the other large categories that are about to descend on your life, from toys to books and beyond. In organizing, the items change, but the principles stay the same.

Finally, if you share a closet with your spouse, don't forget to give some thought to how his clothes will be arranged, too. He's watching his partner grow and the environment change right before his eyes; be sure he doesn't feel displaced. I worked with a woman once who had usurped every closet, drawer, cupboard, and cabinet in the home as she grew great with child. She felt she was all set and so was their soon-to-be-born baby. But her husband felt like he was being squeezed out of the house. Don't let that happen in your home. Include your husband in everything from the start. It will develop into a natural habit. The story of a marriage isn't told in the grand, sweeping events that mark its history. It's created in the day-to-day details like making sure he has enough space for his clothes. You're teammates after all in this great, once-in-a-lifetime adventure.

# 16-17 WEEKS PREGNANT

## Plan for Your Baby's Care after the Birth

**This week, you can**

- Consider the differences between a home day care, a child-care center, or a nanny/in-home caregiver and decide which is best for you
- Research different child-care options in your area
- Ask friends for references and recommendations
- Narrow the list down to a few top contenders
- Call and make appointments to tour/interview child-care providers

IF YOU'LL BE RETURNING TO WORK within the first few months to a year after giving birth, now is the time to start thinking about choosing a child-care provider. If you will be staying at home with the baby for the foreseeable future, if your spouse will be the at-home caregiver, or if you will be fortunate enough to have a relative or friend caring for her, you can take the week off! It may still be worthwhile to read over the chapter, though, just so you have a good idea of what to expect from the child-care search should your circumstances change.

Compared to last week's clothes-shopping mission, scouting around for child care may seem like a bit of a downer. Your baby's not even going to be here for months, and already you have to think

about who else might be taking care of her one day?

It can be overwhelming and maybe even a bit sad to consider, but of all the decisions you'll need to make during your pregnancy, perhaps none is as important as choosing your child's care provider(s). When your pregnancy and delivery are just a memory, your baby's care provider will be an extremely important person in his life. Whomever you choose will have a close relationship with you and your child for months or even years to come.

It's also something you need to start thinking about now. Depending on where you live, the best facilities may have long waiting lists and nannies are already making their plans for months down the road. Between doing your homework ahead of time, calling around for details, and interviewing or visiting a few centers, this process can take a while—so don't delay. If you won't be returning to work for months after your baby's birth or even longer, it's still worth thinking about this topic and making some phone calls now. Then you'll be armed with accurate information to help you make future plans.

If you live in a medium-sized to large city, you probably have an array of child-care choices. Moms in small towns often have fewer options, but you'll probably still find a day-care center or two, several in-home day cares, and nannies. Sometimes it's harder when you live in a large city with many choices. You may feel obligated to keep searching for the "perfect" arrangement or caregiver. But in reality, no situation is ever perfect. The trick is figuring out what is most important to you so that you make a decision you can live with.

First, let's talk about the three most common kinds of child-care options and the differences between them.

one person and may also employ a hired assistant or two. Different states have different licensing or registration requirements for home day cares, but in order to be licensed the day-care provider usually has to pass a background check and will be allowed to care for a limited number of children at a time.

The home day-care experience generally offers these qualities:

- Multi-aged group of children
- Home environment
- Exposure to fewer children (and their germs) than larger day-care centers
- Less expensive than larger day-care centers
- Often less structured than larger day-care centers
- One consistent caregiver
- Rules and policies may be flexible
- May not be licensed with the state
- Educational background and experience of care providers may be inconsistent

## HOME DAY CARE

These small, privately owned businesses go by many different names depending on whom you're talking to and what part of the country you live in. You may also hear them referred to as "family day care" or "in-home child care," but for the purposes of this book, we'll refer to this option as "home day care" just to avoid any confusion.

Home day cares are generally run by

## CHILD-CARE CENTERS

A child-care center, for the purposes of this book, refers to a larger, more institutional facility. It may be run through a local college, church, YMCA, YWCA, or other organization. Or it may be a for-profit business. Some child-care centers are franchises, like Kindercare. Though they use the same marketing materials and share a logo, the experience may vary greatly from location to location.

A child-care center experience generally offers these qualities:

- Usually a fairly structured day, with "school-like" surroundings
- Children divided up into classrooms by age or ability
- May be more turnover of staff
- May be more expensive
- Generally, policies and procedures are fairly "set in stone"
- Usually licensed
- Staff generally has clear requirements for education or other credentials

## IN-HOME CARE (NANNY)

The most personal and private—but also most expensive—option, the in-home caregiver, is considered your employee. That means you'll have to pay taxes on her wages, and most likely she'll expect paid vacation and other benefits.

An in-home care provider or nanny generally offers these qualities:

- One-on-one care
- Consistent provider
- Child stays home in his familiar surroundings
- Parents will need a backup plan in case the care provider is sick or has an emergency
- Usually most expensive option
- Less exposure to other children
- Not as much oversight from outside agencies or a supervisor

There are other options. For instance, if you plan to work part time, you may be able to swap care with another mom. Sometimes two groups of parents will get together and plan to "share" a nanny, either switching off hours to create one full-time position or having the nanny care for two children at once (this works best if the children are not both needy newborns).

You'll notice I didn't arrange these different qualities into "pro" and "con" lists. In my experience, one mom's con is another mom's pro! Consider two women I know—I'll call them Carol and Stacy. Carol chose a home day care for her six-month-old son, Ryan, when she returned to work. Carol liked that the home day care was less structured and that there weren't any other babies her son's age there to "compete" with Ryan for the caregiver's attention. It reminded her of being at home with siblings rather than being in a formal "institution." To Carol, having Ryan experience relatively unstructured days with a small group of kids of different ages was a plus.

Stacy considered the same home day care for her eight-month-old daughter, Erica, but ultimately chose a larger child-care center instead. She was looking for something more akin to a preschool experience for Erica, with lots of structured activities done with other babies her age. She liked that the facility felt like a school, with very clear routines, policies, and procedures. To Stacy, the more structured, more social feel of the day-care center was a plus.

There is no right or wrong here—only what is most important to you. Most likely, you'll have to make trade-offs somewhere, so pick your two or three top priorities and narrow down from there. The choice you feel the best about is usually the right one. And that can be said about almost every other parenting decision you'll ever make!

You should also know that it's OK to change your plan later. Some parents start out with an in-home nanny when their baby is very young and needy, and move to home day care or a child-care center when the baby gets a little older. Others realize that the higher cost of a nanny is not so stark when they add a second or third child to the family. As your child grows, you may also find that her specific needs or personality are better suited to a specific type of care. Or you may just find that the things you think will matter to you aren't as important when your baby is really here.

In the meantime, don't feel like you have to have her care figured out from the day you go back to work until she's a teenager! Just make a plan to get you started, making the best decision you can based on the options available to you and what your instincts say right now. If it works, you can stick with it indefinitely; if not, change it up later.

## NARROWING DOWN
## THE OPTIONS

Now that you have a sense of what your options may be, give it some thought.

---

### PRE-INTERVIEW CHECKLIST

Education level of caregivers \_\_\_\_\_

Cost \_\_\_\_\_

Proximity to home \_\_\_\_\_

Proximity to work \_\_\_\_\_

Rate each factor listed above on a scale of 1–4: 1 = Not a factor; 2 = Somewhat important; 3= Very important; and 4 = Deal-maker or breaker

---

Imagine you're heading back to work and are about to start leaving your precious baby in someone else's care. In your imaginary scenario, do you feel drawn much more strongly to one type of care or another? Other factors, like cost and location, will also help you rule out some options and focus in on others. Use the checklist above and the journal questions below to help you explore the child-care experience you want your baby to have and determine how much weight to give other factors as you narrow down your list.

Imagine it is your first day back to work, and you are leaving your baby with a child-care provider you feel comfortable and confident with. Describe the caregiver here. Is she older or younger? Energetic or calm? Which qualities make you feel good about her?

_____

_____

_____

_____

_____

_____

_____

_____

Now consider the surroundings. In your fantasy, does your baby spend her day in your home, in another home, or in a classroom-like environment? Describe the environment, and be specific. Is there art on the walls? What kind of toys do you see? Are other children there? How many, and how old are they? Is the room cheerful and noisy, or calm and quiet?

_____

_____

_____

_____

_____

_____

_____

After the previous exercise, you should be starting to get a handle on what's really important to you in a child-care provider or center. Of course, it's very unlikely you'll find your fantasy environment right down to the color of the carpet! But imagining your absolute best-case scenario will help you sort through the things you think "ought to" matter to you and hone in on what you feel really strongly about deep down.

For instance, maybe you're finding that you're most drawn to an image of a grandmotherly woman who will rock your baby in the chair she rocked her own babies in. In that case, a home day care run by a veteran mom may be just what you're looking for. Or maybe you envision your baby spending her days playing with other babies in a clean, brightly lit classroom, with an energetic, well-educated teacher. In that case, a child-care center may be the right choice for you. While checklists and pro/con lists can be great tools, I think the child-care decision is best directed by instinct. If you feel good about your baby's caregiver, it'll come through loud and clear to your baby, who will sense your confidence. You'll be able to relax and engage more fully at work and at home when you feel really good about your baby's care. A happy mom makes for a happy baby!

Of course, even within these three broad categories, you'll find a lot of variation from caregiver to caregiver and from center to center. So do your homework. Ask friends and family and professionals like your OB-GYN or midwife for recommendations, and keep your ears perked up during childbirth classes and moms' groups. And use the Internet. If you're considering a specific center, try entering the name into a search engine and see if any rave reviews—or rants—come up. Many baby-related Web sites, like Baby Center.com and Mothering.com, have local forums where you can ask questions about raising kids in your city or town. These forums are often a great place to get

Before you can start narrowing down your caregiver options, first you have to find out what's in your area. Try these strategies:

### Home Day Care

Since these are very small businesses, they often don't advertise in the Yellow Pages or have a Web site. Word-of-mouth and referral are the best way to get connected with home day-care providers. You may also find flyers for home day cares on the bulletin board at your local grocery store, toy store, or wherever mothers congregate. Check Craigslist, Angie's List, and local news sites for ads and classifieds listings. Or see if your local college or your county have child-care referral services.

### Child-Care Centers

You'll find larger centers advertised in the yellow pages, and they'll likely have Web sites, particularly the franchises. Universities, hospitals, churches, YMCAs, and other large service organizations very often have affiliated child-care programs.

### Nannies and In-Home Caregivers

Word of mouth and referrals are great ways to find somebody you can trust, but if you don't luck out there, you'll have to do some digging. Since you'll be hiring this person as your employee, it makes sense to advertise in the newspaper or on Craigslist. Colleges and universities often have listings of students and former students looking for nanny positions. You can also try Web resources like SitterCity.com or ILoveMyNanny.com. Finally, consider trying a nanny referral service or agency in your town. They will do background searches and initial interviews and make a match for you, but it'll cost you: You'll pay an up-front fee, plus a percentage of the nanny's salary, to the agency for their services—12 percent is standard.

the no-holds-barred scoop on a particular center or caregiver.

## HITTING THE PAVEMENT

By the time you've gotten to this point, three or four of the choices should be emerging as top contenders. Call and make appointments to go tour the centers or homes and/or interview the directors or care providers. This request should be met with an enthusiastic "Come on in!" If any child-care provider doesn't want you to interview her in person or any center seems hassled by a tour request, that's a big red flag. Are they hiding something or just annoyed by parents? Either way, run!

You'll want to bring along questions to ask the caregiver. Don't neglect this step—it's easy to get overwhelmed by information and forget important questions! But don't feel like you have to hammer her with a 100-question multiple-choice test! Many caregivers and centers will provide a lot of written information at the interview.

You'll also learn a lot just by looking around and listening to what they have to say. Hone in on the issues that are most crucial to you. Here are some possible questions you may want to ask:

- What is your discipline policy?
- What, where, and when do older babies and children eat?
- Are you supportive of breastfeeding?

This is a very important question to ask if you plan on nursing. The center or caregiver should be willing to store your breast milk in the fridge and feed it to the baby. And if you want to stop by during the day and nurse your baby yourself, they should accommodate that wish.

- What is your sick day policy?
- Do you take vacations? What sort of backup do you provide in that case?
- Do you charge late pick-up fees? What are they?
- What is your staff turnover like?
- What are your security procedures?
- Do you have a philosophy about child care?
- Is your staff required to have a specific level of education, training, or experience?
- May I visit my baby during the day?
- Is your center or home licensed?
- What is the caregiver-to-child ratio?
- Are you and your staff trained in infant CPR and other lifesaving and emergency techniques?
- Can you describe a typical day in your center or home?

Now here are some questions to ask yourself as you view the home or center and/or interview caregivers:

- Does the environment seem clean and bright?
- Are the toys in good repair? Do they seem to be age-appropriate?
- Do I like this person (or people)? Can I see myself having a long-standing relationship with her? What is my gut saying?
- Do the caregivers seem nurturing and engaged?
- Are staff members up front about policies and procedures?
- Does the center seem to be well run and organized?
- Do the babies seem happy? If there are other parents coming in and out, do they seem to have a good relationship with staff?

If you're lucky, one of the centers or caregivers will emerge as the clear victor after the initial round of interviews. Or you may find yourself with a two- or three-way tie. Worse, you may find yourself back at the drawing board! You may also find that the things you thought would be deal-breakers didn't matter so much if you loved the caregiver, or that an unfriendly or condescending center director killed what would have otherwise been your top choice. This is a great introduction to parenthood! Just when you think you've got something figured out, you get thrown for a loop. Don't worry—you will find the right care provider well before your child goes to kindergarten.

If you're stuck, use the "post-interview checklist" following this chapter to help you work through the factors that are keeping you from making a choice or sealing the deal. I've included some things you should keep in mind while making your decision and left blank rows for factors that you may personally feel strongly about.

For example, perhaps you plan to use cloth diapers and are hoping to find a caregiver or child-care center who will also use them on your baby. Or maybe you feel strongly that television and small children don't mix and are looking for a low- or no-media center. Or maybe you're hoping for a nanny who will go out of her way to prepare healthy, fresh meals when your baby's big enough to eat them. Whatever the issue, if it's important to you, it should go on the list.

Photocopy the checklist, and create a clean copy for each center or caregiver. Plan on keeping the information—whether a hard copy or an electronic one—until after your baby comes along. That way, if you ever need to make a change to your arrangements, you won't have to rack your brain trying to remember which caregiver it was that reminded you—in a most unflattering way—of your mean aunt Edna.

## THE BOTTOM LINE

Although this week is the time to start exploring your options, don't be surprised if the search for child care spills across sev-eral weeks. It will all depend on the care choices available in your area and how much assistance you're going to need. One of my clients, for example, is married with a baby and a toddler. Sally works long hours outside the home, as does her husband. Her mother lives with them and her mother-in-law comes several times a year for extended visits. Another mom I know, Grace, needed to have a lot of non-family help lined up. She's a single mom, and her parents and siblings live out of state, meaning she needed to line up paid child care for work as well as any "after-hours" events.

Finally, when it comes to child care, remember that *you* know best what's right for your baby. Even if your best friend loves having a nanny, it's fine if you're more comfortable with a large child-care center. And if you've ever had a hard time asserting yourself in the past, prepare to be amazed by the mama bear inside you. I once knew a mom, Erin, who had always been a bit of a people-pleaser and had a hard time standing up for herself. But one day she encountered a potentially unsafe situation at her baby's day-care center, and was amazed at how quickly and confidently she flew into action. Never underestimate the power of a mother protecting her child! That instinct will serve you well if issues large or small come up with your child-care provider. As this week draws to a close, remember Lao-tzu's wise words: "The journey of a thousand miles begins with a single step."

# POST-INTERVIEW CHECKLIST

Name of Caregiver/Childcare Center: _____

Initial Impressions of Caregiver/Center: _____

_____

_____

_____

Discipline Policy/Childcare Philosophy _____

_____

_____

Friendliness of Staff _____

_____

_____

Atmosphere _____

_____

_____

_____

_____

_____

_____

_____

_____

_____

_____

_____

_____

_____

_____

Rate each factor listed above on a scale of 1–4: 1 = Bad; 2 = Not Great; 3 = Okay; 4 = Good; and 5 = Great

# CHAPTER THREE

# 18 to 22 Weeks Pregnant

*There are two ways to live your life. One is as though nothing is a miracle. The other is as though everything is a miracle.*

—ALBERT EINSTEIN

As you move into the second trimester of pregnancy, it's likely that you'll be experiencing an increase in energy. Your skill as a Zen Organizer is growing by leaps and bounds!

This month you can consider which birth plan you're going to follow. When my mother gave birth to me, the local hospital was virtually the only option. But in today's world you have many options for where you give birth, including a hospital-based birth center, a freestanding birth center, or even your own home. There are also many different techniques and birth methods you'll learn about, from birth hypnosis to the Bradley method.

You've also reached the point in your pregnancy when it's possible to learn the sex of your baby. For some couples this will be a no-brainer; for others it's a time of reflection. In the second week of this month we'll be pondering the pros and cons to help you make the decision that's right for you. (I remember one husband who assured me that he and his wife did not want to know the sex of the baby. In fact he was quite adamant about the fact that only the doctor knew whether they were having a boy or a girl. He and his wife had agreed to find out in the delivery room. Over his shoulder his very pregnant wife smiled at me and mouthed the words "It's a boy!")

Of course a month with no organizing projects would be boring, right? In week three, we tackle the kitchen. You will be spending a lot more time there and I want you to feel super efficient and in charge. My goal is for you to have a well-organized kitchen where every tool, pot, pan, and plate has a designated spot. When you're sleep-deprived or Baby is fussy, you don't want to have to go on a quest for the colander or the Crock-Pot. And keep in mind you'll often be holding Baby while trying to locate those kitchen items. Ever tried to rifle through a cluttered lower cabinet to find the right saucepan lid with a newborn in your arms? I don't recommend it!

Good nutrition helps Baby's developing body. It also helps you avoid excess weight from consuming food that's loaded with empty calories. Gone are the days when you flew through the supermarket hoping you remembered everything you need. It's time for menus and shopping lists. The time you had the luxury to fritter away will soon belong to your baby. We're saving minutes every chance we get.

People are frequently afraid that having created order, they won't be able to maintain it. It's as if they believe that little gremlins will sneak in while they are asleep and cause havoc. But in weeks 21 and 24, you'll learn how to *stay* organized—even when your life is busy or when you're functioning on three hours of sleep! I'm going to show you how to make full use of routines and rituals so all your hard work will be respected, maintained, and appreciated.

## HABIT OF THE MONTH

### Start These Small Routines and Improve Your Environment in a Big Way!

Here are my all-time favorite new daily routines to start if you don't practice these already. You'll be amazed at how these simple yet powerful little efforts will transform your physical space, build your self-esteem, and positively influence those with whom you live. These dovetail with the work we'll be doing in week four; if you start at least two of them this week, by weeks 21 and 24 you will be ahead of schedule.

- Make the bed every morning.
- Wash dirty dishes immediately rather than letting them pile up in the sink.
- Put clean dishes away rather than leaving them to languish on your drain board.
- Place your keys in the same place every time you enter your home. Do this with reading glasses as well if you require them.
- If you live in a large household and generate a lot of trash or recyclables, check the cans daily to see if they need to be emptied.

# 18 WEEKS PREGNANT

## Think about Your Birth Plans and Preferences

This week, you can

- Research different birth philosophies and techniques
- Read several books to get an idea of how you'd like your ideal birth experience to go
- Start to create a birth plan
- *Birth* plans? But I'm still twenty-two weeks away from my due date!

I HEAR YOU. Finally, you can keep down an entire day's worth of meals and aren't falling asleep at random times during the day. Can't a girl enjoy her newfound energy for a while without thinking about how this rapidly growing baby is going to somehow get out? (Unfortunately, it doesn't involve getting "beamed out" a la *Star Trek*. . . .) While you don't have to have your birth plan set in stone yet, it's still a good idea to start thinking about your birth options now. For one thing, if you want to labor or deliver a certain way—for example, maybe you want to avoid an IV or hope to have a water birth—your doctor or midwife and the hospital or birth center you deliver in will determine whether or not it's a possibility.

Researching birth philosophies may lead you to the discovery that the practice you're currently seeing for prenatal care just isn't a great fit for you, or that you'd be better off giving birth at a different hospital than you'd planned on. The sooner you know that, the better. When pregnant with her first child, Stacy actually switched care providers at thirty-two weeks of pregnancy after having an enlightening conversation with her obstetrician. When she asked him about avoiding certain interventions, he all but patted her on the head as he told her, condescendingly, "Well, we'll just see about that when you're in labor." Stacy bolted and was able to find a good care provider she liked even at her late state of pregnancy. Still, it would have been much less stressful if she'd asked those questions and made her switch earlier on.

For many women, the best way to learn about the process of labor and birth and figure out what kind of delivery they'd like to have is by taking a series of childbirth classes. These classes most commonly meet weekly, starting in the second trimester, for six to eight sessions or so (though occasionally you can take a single-day workshop or even take your birth classes online).

But before you go around town signing up for classes, I think it's wise to do some reading. Birth classes can vary wildly in philosophy and scope of information, and they require a commitment of time and money from you. Simply reading a bit more about a specific type of class can give you a sense of whether it could be a good match for your philosophy or comfort level. Alternately, you may learn as much from reading some books as you would from an entire class series of less-comprehensive classes. Here is some information about the most common types of childbirth philosophies and methods you may encounter:

## Lamaze

Probably the first thing that comes to mind when you think of Lamaze is the exaggerated "Hoo-Hoo-HEE!" breathing style made famous in sitcoms and movies. But Lamaze, the first "active" birth movement and method to attain popularity in the United States, has moved away from its hallmark breathing techniques and now embraces a more holistic view of natural, normal birth. In a Lamaze class you'll learn about a variety of relaxation and coping techniques to help you have a natural birth. You'll also learn how to make edu-

cated decisions should you want or need to pursue medical intervention during your labor or delivery. Lamaze teachers have a lot of control over how their courses are taught, so you might find a significant difference in curriculum or length of a series from instructor to instructor. Some series may include information on pregnancy exercise and nutrition, postpartum care, and baby care. Visit www.lamaze.com for more information and a directory of teachers near you.

## Bradley

The Bradley Method focuses on complete relaxation in order to achieve a natural, medication-free birth. Many women find its focus on slow, deep breathing to be very effective at helping them cope with contractions and avoid interventions. You'll also learn a lot about nutrition and health during pregnancy and after your baby is here, and much of the course is geared toward helping spouses and partners become effective "coaches" during labor and birth. Keep in mind that the Bradley Method is extremely pro–natural birth, and their classes may not feel like the friendliest environment if you aren't completely sold on the idea. The Bradley series includes twelve classes, which cover early pregnancy, nutrition, exercise, labor and birth, newborn bonding, and breastfeeding. All Bradley instructors must be certified and must recertify each year to be able to continue teaching the classes. Bradleybirth.com is where you can find more information.

## Birthing From Within

Taught as a series of classes or as a workshop, the Birthing From Within method focuses on helping women conquer fears through a combination of information and spiritual and creative projects like art and visualization. Birthing From Within may appeal to you if you're artistic or creative, or if you see pregnancy and birth as a spiritual journey. More straightforward women may find the class a bit too touchy-feely for their liking. (If the idea of "caging your birth tiger" makes you cringe, look elsewhere!) While natural birth is definitely supported in the Birthing From Within environment, the classes do not promote any one sort of birth experience and the information is useful no matter what kind of delivery you're planning. Check out www.birthingfromwithin.com.

## Birth Hypnosis

Several trademarked brands offer birth hypnosis classes, including Hypnobabies (www.hypnobabies.com) and Hypno-birthing (www.hypnobirthing.com). These classes teach hypnosis techniques specifically tailored to help laboring women remain calm and in control. Birth hypnosis isn't about being "put out" or not knowing what's happening during your labor. On the contrary, women who study hypnosis learn to train their minds to interpret pain differently so that they can be active participants in their births without anxiety and fear, and without a need to dull any of the sensations involved. Birth hypnosis will require a lot of practice, but women who devote themselves to it report great

success in the way the method helped them experience birth in a relaxed, joyful way—and often, they report, without pain. If you can't find a birth hypnosis instructor in your area, you can also take a few sessions with a licensed hypnotist, or look into a program on CD.

## Hospital Birth Classes

The hospital where you will be giving birth most likely offers a class series of its own. Topics covered are likely to run the gamut from which procedures you can expect as part of a typical hospital birth to your postpartum recovery and new-baby care. You will probably also get a tour of the labor and delivery unit and a rundown of the registration and check-in procedure, as well as other details you'll need to know, like what to pack in your hospital bag, what personal items you may bring to the hospital with you, and hospital policies on visitors and the like. Having all that information is definitely useful, but some hospital classes seem to focus mostly on teaching expecting moms and dads to "be good patients" and aren't as supportive of choices that challenge hospital protocol. So be sure to supplement the information you get from hospital classes with reading of your own or maybe even by taking a second set of classes.

## Other Birth Classes

This is just a sampling of the different types of birth classes you might encounter in your region. A variety of certifying bodies train and certify educators to teach birth classes, and while they may all have slightly different philosophies, generally they are geared toward helping you be an active participant in your birth process. There are many machines, drugs, medical procedures, and interventions that have become part of the typical modern birth experience, but it's important that you see yourself as more than just a patient. Even if you plan on using many or most of these interventions, it's a good idea to have a full understanding of what each procedure or process is for and any possible drawbacks. Any good birth class will help you go into the hospital with the information you need to make empowered choices. Some organizations that train childbirth educators include the International Childbirth Education Association (www.icea.org), the Childbirth and Postpartum Professional Association (www.cappa.net), and the International Birth and Wellness Project (www.alace.org).

Much of your choice of childbirth class may be limited by what's available in your region. If you live in an area that doesn't offer any classes in your preferred method, see if the organization you're interested in offers any virtual or distance-learning classes. The organization may also be able to connect you with a student who has completed the book-learning portion of her training, but hasn't yet taught enough hours to be certified. A mother I know, Kara, was lucky enough to connect with a childbirth educator who had completed her training but needed to teach one more class to gain certification. She was also earning "contact points" to receive her doula certification (more on doulas in the

## DO I NEED A DOULA?

Every laboring mom needs someone on her side to advocate for her needs. Unfortunately, against the hectic backdrop of a labor and delivery unit, you can't always count on getting the information and support you need from your busy nurses and doctors. And while dads-to-be are often great at providing their wives and partners love and comfort, they can't really be expected to translate complicated "medical-ese" or be true advocates under stressful, new circumstances. That's where a doula comes in. A trained and knowledgeable professional who knows an "epidural" from an "episiotomy" (and how to help you avoid both if you want), a doula will stay with you throughout your labor and delivery, providing hands-on support and helping you make informed decisions about your care as labor progresses. You can also hire a postpartum doula to help you adjust after your baby is born by providing a listening ear, light housekeeping support, and instruction on caring for your baby.

Studies have shown that women who have support from doulas tend to have shorter labors with fewer complications and are more satisfied with their birth experiences over all. Dona.org and Cappa.net are two places to get more information or start your search for your own doula. You can also ask your doctor, midwife, childbirth educator, or mom friends for recommendations.

box on page 71). The educator was grateful for the opportunity to work with a real, live, pregnant woman to complete the certification process, and she gave Kara an excellent deal on her fees for both education and doula support. Less-experienced teachers can still have a wealth of knowledge and are often the most passionate about their subject. Be open to alternative arrangements if cost or availability are an issue for you!

No matter what style or method you find yourself gravitating toward, once you've done your research, you should call and register for classes now. Though your birth still seems a long way off, you'll want to give yourself plenty of time in case the classes fill up fast.

Of course, even if you live in an area that offers childbirth classes of every stripe, there's a lot to be said for educating yourself as well. If you find the offerings in your city lacking or simply want to learn all you can about the birth process, you'll want to do some reading. See page 325 for a list of trusted resources to check out. Don't feel like you have to read every single book or Web site listed! Feel free to flip through them at the bookstore, read a few paragraphs, and see if the author's tone and point of view speak to you. Much of this will depend on your personality—if you're a "just the facts, ma'am" type and want to see cold data and hard research to help you make decisions, Henci Goer's *The Thinking Woman's Guide to a Better Birth* might satisfy your science-loving mind. On the other hand, if you gain more confidence from reassuring stories and

spiritual affirmations, Pam England's *Birthing from Within* might be more up your alley.

All this reading could take several weeks (if you're an information junkie you've likely already read some of these and I bet you'll be reading throughout your pregnancy!). Make time for birth research every day, even if it's just five minutes. Pour a cup of pregnancy tea or a glass of water, put your feet up, and read! In your pregnancy journal, jot down terms you want to research more fully or quotes you find inspiring. The more educated you become, the more you will likely feel yourself drawn toward certain birth methods or philosophies.

## YOUR BIRTH PLAN

Likely your childbirth class will help you create a birth plan—a written document detailing your preferences for labor and birth. Many women give their birth plans to their doctor or midwife and bring copies for nurses and other hospital staff to inform them of their wishes. Others use the birth plan for their own purposes, to help them remember what is most important to them when they are losing focus during labor and to use as a reference tool while in the hospital.

You'll find lots of boilerplate birth plans online, but I encourage you to avoid going by somebody else's idea of what a good birth plan looks like. Instead, let your personal birth plan grow organically from what you learn from your readings and how you feel about what you learn. Doctors and nurses are not likely to respond the way you'd like to a long list of demands printed off the Internet. They've seen those dime-a-dozen plans a hundred times before.

Instead, dig deeper and prioritize. Think about what really matters to you, and why. Maybe all you need is a simple paragraph stating your overall philosophy of birth and asking hospital staff to check with you before they deviate from it. Then you can consider each possible change or intervention on a case-by-case basis. Or maybe you'll find that you are OK with most of the interventions that are part of hospital protocol. In that case, you may want to focus more on the postpartum part of your experience than the labor and birth portion. This is your birth, not anyone else's. Listen to your own gut.

You'll have plenty of time for creating a formal birth plan. For now, just let the information you're taking in percolate a bit as you think about how you'd like your own birth experience to go. Here are some questions to keep in mind as you consider this issue:

- Do I plan to have an unmedicated birth, or will I opt for an epidural or other pain relief?
- If I plan to "try" for a natural birth, how important is it to me?
- What are my reasons for wanting medication, or for wanting to *avoid* medication?
- What coping techniques seem like they'd be most helpful to me?

- Are there any interventions I absolutely want to avoid?
- Are there any procedures or medications I absolutely want as part of my birth?
- Who would I like to have at my birth? (These should be people you are absolutely comfortable around.)
- What would I like my husband or partner's role to be in the birth?
- What kind of support and attention would I like from the nurses and my doctor or midwife?
- How do I hope to spend the minutes immediately after my birth? Is it important to me that I have time to bond with the baby before he is taken away to be checked out?

Remember, birth is unpredictable. You can't control how it will go, and no one can guarantee a specific outcome. Letting go of illusions of control over your body or the birth process can be very difficult for some women. This is where meditation can come in very handy. Are you remembering your five minutes a day?

This week, we packed in a lot of information and you may be feeling overwhelmed. That's okay. You don't have to commit to any style or birth method right now. In fact, you always have the right to change your mind—even (maybe especially) while in labor. But the more you think about the process of labor and birth in advance, the better a position you'll be in to make decisions you're satisfied with.

Of course, the ultimate goal of any birth is a healthy mother and a healthy baby. But the way you give birth is your passage into motherhood, and how you feel about that journey may have a huge impact on how you feel about yourself as a woman and a mother. It's important that you feel educated and empowered so that no matter what surprises come your way, you are prepared to deal with them and work through them. After all, if you don't know about your options, you don't have any.

# 19 WEEKS PREGNANT

## Is Pink or Blue in Your Future?

**This week, you can**

- Think about the practical and emotional considerations that go into finding out your baby's gender while you're pregnant
- Research ways to build a nursery and wardrobe that will work for either sex

YOU'RE PROBABLY only a week or two away from your mid-pregnancy ultrasound—the one where you can possibly learn your baby's gender. Will you find out whether your baby is a "he" or a "she"?

There are those who will passionately argue that it shouldn't matter to you whether your baby is a boy or a girl. They act as though a mother caring one way or the other whether her baby is a boy or a girl is somehow frivolous or selfish. Of course, a healthy baby is the most important thing to any expecting mom. But I'd argue that gender is important, too! There is a lot wrapped up in the decision of whether—or when—to find out if you're expecting a boy or a girl, so don't make that decision lightly.

For example, whether you're having a boy or a girl could make a big difference in the relationship you have with this child down the road and how you adjust to motherhood. If it's a girl, you may find

that you're terrified of passing on some of your less-than-perfect qualities or excited about sharing the things that made your girlhood special. If it's a boy, you may worry about how you'll relate to him or revel in the chance to bring up a strong, sensitive man. Your background, childhood, relationship with the baby's father, and even long-standing fantasies about what your first child will look like all come into play as you're contemplating. And if your husband or partner has a strong preference one way or the other, that will also affect how you react.

Finding out the baby's sex can also make the whole pregnancy seem a lot more real, and that can be rather mind-blowing. Up until now, the baby has probably seemed more like a vague concept than an actual living person. Knowing that the baby is a boy or a girl suddenly makes him or her so much more human and specific. And it can be jarring to find out that your baby is a different gender from what you had anticipated or fantasized about. Though mothers have no control over who our babies are or who they will become, it's hard to resist pouring a lot of wishes and hopes into that growing fetus and thinking that you can somehow create it in your image. If you've been dreaming about a little Elizabeth, finding out your baby is actually an Ernie may be the first step to crushing that illusion. And that can be painful.

Meagan, who had four sons before giving birth to her only daughter, loves her boys dearly and can't imagine girls in their places . . . now that they're actually here and in her life. It was a different story when she was pregnant and didn't "know" her babies yet. She'd always wanted a daughter, and each pregnancy represented the possibility of a little girl. As she had boy after boy it began to seem less likely that her dream would be fulfilled. Meagan never felt that wishing for a girl was the same as wishing away the boy baby she actually had. But still, she needed a bit of time to mourn the *idea* of the girl each of those babies turned out not to be. As a side note, by the time she got to her fifth pregnancy Meagan was so comfortable with the idea of having a family full of boys that she didn't believe the ultrasound technician's report of "Mom, you got your girl!" So no matter how disappointed you fear you might be if your baby is not the gender you hope for, don't worry—once you see your actual baby in your arms, you will love him or her just as he or she is.

If you are likely to be disappointed by the news that the baby is a different gender

> ## HOW RELIABLE IS AN ULTRASOUND FOR DETERMINING GENDER?
>
> With today's technology, a technician should be able to tell you your baby's gender at twenty weeks or later with *close* to 100 percent reliability. As with anything in life, there are no guarantees. Your baby's age, her position, and the age and condition of the equipment will factor in, as will the skill and experience of the technician. So keep in mind that even if you've been told "It's a boy!" or "It's a girl!" there is still a slim chance . . . that it's not!

than you'd hoped, consider when you'd like to receive that bit of news. Meagan, who had four boys and then a girl, always felt it was better to know halfway through the pregnancy and get past any pangs of disappointment early on, then go through the rest of the pregnancy embracing the actual baby rather than the dream baby she'd been fantasizing about for the first twenty weeks. Amanda, a first-time mom I know who was hoping for a boy, decided she'd rather find out after the baby was born because in all the excitement of the birth she'd be less likely to feel disappointment if "he" turned out to be a "she." There is no right or wrong approach, just how you feel and how you are likely to react.

Of course, some parents truly have no preference for one gender or another, and in that case, it's just a matter of deciding whether waiting or finding out ahead of time will bring you more joy! Some parents love finding out early on because it allows them to start thinking of their baby as a real, concrete person. They can refer to the baby as "he" or "she" and even start calling the baby by name if they wish. Others find that the surprise of finding out the baby's gender just after giving birth adds to the happiness of the moment. Karen, a first-time mom I know, asked the doctor and nurses to not announce her baby's gender after it was born. Instead, the doctor handed Karen the baby immediately after birth, and she and her husband Keith made the discovery together: Their baby was a little girl. Both Karen and Keith say they'll treasure that moment forever.

Besides the emotional concerns that will help shape your decision, there are some practical questions, too. Lots of women would rather know the baby's gender because it makes choosing a layette, nursery theme, and baby gear easier. On the other hand, there are ways around the issue. If you aren't sure whether you want to find out your baby's gender ahead of time, but are afraid you won't be able to prepare properly, consider these tricks:

## NURSERY

Navy blue, yellow, green, brown, and cream are great colors for either boys or girls. Try tie-dye, rainbow, plaid, or animal prints. Check Target, Pottery Barn Kids, or the Land of Nod (www.landofnod.com) for beautiful unisex bedding and decor.

Alternately, you can only purchase (or register for) items that aren't usually gender specific (strollers, cribs, etc.) and wait until after Baby's here to go all-out in decorating the nursery. This is also a smart move if you plan to have more children down the road, since it's more likely you'll be able to reuse your gear then. If you can't bear the thought of a bare nursery, try just investing in small items like lamps, wall hangings, crib or bassinet sheets, and a pretty, light blanket in a color like cream or apple green. Later, you can layer more bedding on top. Since heavy crib bedding isn't considered safe for young babies, you probably wouldn't be using a comforter at this point, anyway.

Look for strollers, car seats, and other "on the go" gear in black, gray, brown, or navy blue. These are stylish, gender-neutral options, and they won't show dirt as readily as pastels.

And chuck the idea that your diaper bag has to "coordinate" with your baby's gender. *You* are not an infant, and your baby isn't going to be carrying the diaper bag. There's just no reason to accessorize with a bag decked in pink hearts or blue teddy bears (unless that's what you like, of course). Pick something that appeals to your sense of style—you have to live with it, after all, and the baby won't care. Due-Maternity.com has a great selection of diaper bags that look like designer purses, not cartoon nightmares. Or you can just carry a purse that has enough room for baby stuff. Believe me, you will not lose any "mom points" if you never buy a diaper bag!

## Going Gender-Neutral

Newborn babies really don't need to be equipped with full four-season wardrobes! In fact, many babies outgrow those newborn outfits within a couple of weeks. Consider waiting until you know how big he or she will be until you invest in much clothing. For now, purchase a very limited layette of gender-neutral colors. You can shop again a month or so after your baby's born, when you know how big she is or how fast he's growing.

Whether or not you find out your baby's sex, raising him or her in a "gender-neutral" manner is another possibility. In fact, there is a growing movement of parents who believe that avoiding "pink for girls, blue for boys" as a general rule helps children discover who they are, rather than who society says they should be based on their gender. Even if you don't embrace this idea fully, don't be afraid of buying dolls for your baby boy or trucks for your baby girl. Not only will it broaden his horizons or show her that she can be anything she wants, but it's practical, too: If you have the opposite-sex child later, you won't have to worry that you don't have anything to hand down because all the gear and clothing is too "girly" or "boyish."

Here are some tips for building a gender-neutral wardrobe that will work now and for future babies to come.

- Gender-neutral clothing is pretty easy to come by for little babies, who mostly live in sleepers and nightgowns. You won't notice much of a difference between the "girl" and "boy" versions of these items except that some will be blue and some will be pink—but you'll also find plenty of other colors to choose from.

- Unisex clothing is harder to come by in bigger sizes, where the difference between "girl" and "boy" styles becomes more and more pronounced. T-shirts (long- and short-sleeved), bodysuits, and pants are the staples of a gender-neutral layette. Look for colors like navy blue, brown, purple, gray, light green, and orange, in solids, stripes, or fun prints that don't scream GIRL or BOY.

- When buying pants, look for a fit that's not too tight or loose, without details like ruffles or hearts. Little jeans or corduroys are great, if you can find them without "boy" detailing like hammer loops and side pockets, and without "girl" detailing like appliqués and bows. Stay away from bell-bottoms and capris, which look decidedly girly no matter what you pair them with.

- Shirts can be a challenge, too, as "girl" shirts tend to have puffy sleeves, gathers in the neck, and other details that just don't meld well with a unisex wardrobe. Try the boy's department instead. You'll have to flip past a lot of bears playing baseball and driving trucks, but you should be able to find a few plain T's that will make great layering basics for either a girl or a boy.

- Go online. Do a search for "gender-neutral baby clothing" or "unisex baby clothing" and see what comes up. Many boutiques and specialty stores are now catering to the parent looking for unisex fashions.

- Once you've pulled together Baby's "base" wardrobe of shirts and pants, you can use layers and other accessories to make it more girlish or boyish. Think hoodies, button-down shirts, or cardigans over those T-shirts. Many baby and toddler dresses look adorable worn over a pair of pants. Hair bows, cute socks, or rugged boots go a long way toward adding a "girl" or "boy" vibe to that otherwise neutral outfit.

I didn't give you much to do this week (after the way I've been working you, that should be a relief!) but there is a lot to think about, isn't there? Don't worry. If you still can't make up your mind whether or not to find out at your ultrasound appointment, you have another option. Ask the technician to write down the baby's gender and fold up the piece of paper. Place it in a sealed envelope (so neither you nor your spouse can peek without getting caught) and put it somewhere safe. The two of you can talk it over at leisure until you're either comfortable opening the envelope . . . or maybe even throwing it away. After all, sooner or later you're going to find out for certain whether this baby is a boy or a girl. Maybe you'll realize that you don't need to know until he or she is in your arms.

# 20 WEEKS PREGNANT

## Organize Your Kitchen

This week, you can

- Clean out your kitchen cupboards, counters, drawers, and the refrigerator
- Move the items you wish to keep into "zones"
- Consider the things you want to duplicate with your child if you have any childhood memories that revolve around special meals.

IT'S AN OLD SAW BUT TRUE: Where do we all gather in the home, whether it's for a party, on a holiday, or simply for a quiet gathering of a few friends? Right. Even if it's the size of a matchbox, everyone will crowd into the kitchen. You would think that such a popular room would be organized to the nines. Sadly, this is not the case. I could count on one hand the number of organized kitchens I've encountered over the past twenty-plus years. Why is that, you may ask?

Think back to moving day. You probably had a few family members or close friends stop by. Boxes were everywhere. You were all in a hurry to get things put away. People slammed items into any available cabinet space. They shoved things into drawers. And when they were done they said: "I just wanted to get these boxes out of here. You can organize later." But later never comes, does it? And the reason is twofold. Many people have no idea how a kitchen should be organized so they simply get used to the current, albeit chaotic, placement. Or you feel like the only way to get organized is to pull just about everything out and start over—and who has time for that?

### WHY BOTHER NOW?

But it's easier than you may think to get your kitchen in tip-top shape, and there's never been a better time to do it. For one thing, nutrition is more important in your life than ever. After all, you're eating for two, and what you need are nutrition-rich calories. Learn to pick your foods not only for how they taste and look but for the nutrients they provide.

For example, to avoid constipation be sure to get fiber each day. In addition to fruits and vegetables, consider whole-grain breads, cereals, and legumes like beans and lentils. Fluids also help reduce constipation so now you have even more incentive to keep drinking your water. Calcium helps your baby develop strong bones. You don't have to drink gallons of milk—consider the wide variety of yogurts and cheeses available today, not to mention dark leafy greens, broccoli, and almonds.

Finally, let's look at how important iron is in your diet. It makes red blood cells, which carry oxygen. The baby needs iron to make her new blood and you need as much as 50 percent more blood during pregnancy. Without enough iron, you can find yourself anemic, exhausted, and having trouble concentrating. The remedy is delicious and varied: meat, poultry, salmon, soy products (tofu and tempeh), nuts, and eggs. Cereals, dark leafy green vegetables, and beans also supply iron. Pregnancy may usher in an entirely new way for you to look at food.

You have a child to nurture and love. One day she will be in your arms and you can sing her lullabies to coax her to sleep, or toss your son in the air to hear that wonderful laugh. The body you hold will have been created by the very nutrients you supply during these crucial months of pregnancy. If your kitchen is a mess, it's less likely you'll want to spend time there. Instead of whipping up a good meal or a healthy snack, you'll be running out the front door for a burger and fries.

In addition, it's never too soon to plan ahead. Your baby is going to grow quickly, especially during his first year, and you'll be racing to keep up. Organize your kitchen now and you'll be ready to whip up homemade baby food when he graduates from breast milk. It will be a snap to find Baby's bottles and later his plates and cups. It's better to be organized from the start than to find yourself in the kitchen around 2:00 a.m., wondering where the heck is that bottle you clearly remember washing earlier in the day. Once you're organized, all the gizmos have a designated spot! And as your child grows, he'll learn from your well-organized example.

Grab your journal and go into your kitchen. Take a minute to look around. Peer into the cupboards and drawers but don't touch anything just yet. Now sit for a few minutes and make some notes. Here are the questions I'd like you to answer. But don't spend more than thirty minutes on this exercise—it's meant to pinpoint your needs and spark your motivation, not rob you of an entire afternoon.

## THE PRESENT

- What do you like about your kitchen? Perhaps you have a window and you enjoy the way the light streams in. Or maybe you painted it a sunny yellow and you think the room is cheery to be in.
- What do you not like about this room? Make two columns: On the

left, list what you don't like that could be fixed, and on the right side, list the things you don't like but have to live with. As an example, you might feel that with a baby coming you'll need a bigger refrigerator. You have to run the numbers to see how much you can spend and look for a good bargain, but it's not insurmountable. On the other hand, if it's a tiny space and you lament the absence of room for a table and chairs, well, you'll just have to eat in the dining room.

- When you opened the cupboards and drawers, were the contents a mess? Or did you have areas that were organized? What bothers you the most in terms of the current setup?
- Would you be happier if you could function better in your kitchen?
- Do you have a few hours you can devote to this organizing project?

## THE PAST

- When you think about your childhood are there any special memories you have about the kitchen? Did you come home to freshly baked cookies? Was coloring Easter eggs a tradition for your family? Did you have Sunday dinner each week?
- Was the kitchen in your childhood home organized or thrown together?
- Did you have chores that revolved around the kitchen, like setting the

table, doing the dishes, taking out the trash, or cooking any of the meals?

## THE FUTURE

What types of activities would you like to do with your baby as he grows up? Do you like to bake? Are you a great cook?

You'll want a kitchen that makes preparing nutritious meals a pleasurable experience rather than a homework assignment. The first set of questions helps you get a realistic idea of what needs to be done. A battle plan ensures success. Flying by the seat of your pants can be momentarily exhilarating but in the end you'll only wind up depleted physically and emotionally. People who follow this method usually abandon projects about midway through the process. Imagine how much easier it will feel to grind up some fresh carrots for Baby's meal or reach for a healthy snack for yourself when you don't have to push aside the contents of some cupboards that you left sitting on the countertop several months ago.

I've asked you to look at the past to help uncover any special memories you'd like to duplicate in the not-too-distant future. Perhaps you'll be reminded of a few things you want to avoid at all costs. It would be interesting to compare notes with your spouse. If you grew up in a home where everyone sat together for dinner at 6:00 and his family ate dinner together just once a week on Sunday, you may have different expectations about the future. It's nice to uncover and discuss them now.

We're going to break this task up so you only need about two hours a day for three days this week. Focus on what works. Take care of what is under your control to change. And if you feel overwhelmed as you organize the space, think about the fun you're soon to have in this kitchen: feeding your baby in his high chair, the cookies you'll one day be baking with your child, or the meals you'll whip up together.

## DAY ONE

First, it's time to divest your kitchen of anything you aren't going to use. You know what I'm talking about, right? There's that fancy coffeemaker you got for Christmas five years ago. It takes up too much room on the counter and you need a degree to learn how to operate it. It has been a space hog since you got it. And there's that fancy Panini maker you dreamed about but never took out of the box. I think that was for your birthday about three years ago. And don't forget to look in the drawers. You went to a cooking party at your best friend's house last year and got all those great kitchen gadgets. Of course, you don't remember what they are for, but you liked them when you saw them. And what about those threadbare dish towels? Don't be embarrassed. I didn't sneak into your house last night. This is everybody's kitchen.

Set your timer for twenty minutes. Start at one end of the kitchen and work your way around to the other side. Do only the upper cupboards the first time. Move on to the lower cabinets and finish with a third and final round to examine your drawers. The maximum time allotted for this is one hour. You'll probably have the following categories:

- Items you can give to a family member or friend.
- Things you can donate to charity.
- Tools, pots, pans, etc., that have seen their best days and belong in the trash.
- Items you only use once a year, like the Thanksgiving turkey roaster. If you have a small kitchen, park that baby in the garage. If your kitchen is large, stash it in that deep cabinet above the refrigerator. You know, the one you need a stepstool to reach. (Don't avoid using the highest shelves if you are short. A two-step stepstool is one of the best investments you can make. My favorite folds up and slips into that sliver of space between the refrigerator and the cabinets.)

Make sure before you wrap things up for today that all of these items are on their way to their new homes. Give everyone a deadline for pick up if you don't have a car and can't do drop-offs yourself. If cousin Melissa doesn't pick up that coffee maker by Friday, on Saturday it's going to Goodwill or the local women's shelter.

You probably noticed I didn't mention the counter space. Since you organized your papers a few weeks ago (page 17), I hope you've stopped using the counters in the kitchen as an adjunct office! We're going to address using the counters for maximum effect on day two.

## DAY TWO

I want to keep these work sessions short so today we have just two areas to consider: the dark cave under the sink and your counters. Since cleaning products are usually stored under the sink, I'd play it safe and ask your spouse or best friend to help you. I want to keep you away from toxic chemicals, and soon enough you'll be wiping down the counters with a baby in your arms. That brings me to an option you have: Consider replacing your household cleaners with "green" varieties from companies like Seventh Generation or Meyer's, or make your own cleaning products. With regular household supplies like vinegar, baking soda (is there anything you can't do with that stuff?), and lemons, you can have inexpensive, toxic-free cleaning agents in your home. As with any new cleaning agent, test all of these concoctions on a small area to be sure they work in your home without damaging surfaces.

### Mission Possible:
### Misadventures under the Sink

Ready to begin? Your job is to sit on a chair and direct the operation. Have your helper sit on the floor and pull out items one by one. Be sure a sturdy trash bag is handy to catch the debris. You might want to spread out a garbage bag on the floor so you have a safe staging area. If one of your containers has a leak, you don't want to damage your floor. As always, put all related items that you wish to keep in categories. The most common for this area are:

Household cleaners
Polishes
A bucket
Sponges (soft and for scrubbing)
Hand soap and dish detergent
Poison for critters like ants and roaches

One by one examine the items. Here are some guidelines to help you keep this process moving quickly.

If the container is old (check for an expiration date) or leaking, toss it.
If you don't use this product any longer, toss it or give it to your helper.
What about the condition of sponges and cleaning rags? If they have reached the disgusting stage, let them go!
If you bought several items in the large economy size, can you better store those containers elsewhere? For example, if you have a garage, place an inexpensive shelving unit right inside the door for these large containers as well as for overflow paper towels and toilet paper. In the absence of a garage, do you have a walk-in pantry? Paper products can be kept here, but

## HOMEMADE HOUSEHOLD CLEANERS

Let me tempt you with four easy cleaning product recipes. The minimal expense is in your base ingredients like vinegar and baking soda as well as in new spray and storage bottles, which you will want to have on hand.

**Vinegar:** Mix one part water with one part vinegar and you've got an all-purpose cleaner you can use all over your home. (Don't use it on marble.) Before store-bought household products became a big industry, women traditionally cleaned with vinegar. Did you know it disinfects and deodorizes in addition to cleaning? And don't worry about that distinctive aroma: It dissipates in a matter of minutes. Your home isn't going to smell like a salad! Try it full strength in your toilet bowl to remove the ring that all bowls acquire over time. And, last but not least, you can save on fabric softener because a half-cup of vinegar will soften your clothes and effectively break down your detergent. If Baby turns out to be sensitive to detergent, vinegar in the wash will help her skin stay soft and irritation free.

**Lemons:** You can mix fresh lemon juice with vinegar to make a cleaning paste. Who could have imagined that the tart and tasty lemon, so lovely in sparkling water, tea, and salads, could also clean your home? A paste can be more effective than liquid cleanser in those hard-to-clean areas of your home.

You can use straight lemon juice to dissolve soap scum and hard water deposits in your shower and around the sink. Imagine how lovely the area will smell when you're done! Speaking of clean-smelling, don't toss your lemon rind away after extracting the juice: Put it in the garbage disposal. Lemon juice is safe on copper and brass and if you mix a half-cup of lemon juice with a cup of olive oil, you can polish your hardwood furniture.

**Baking soda:** You can brush your teeth with it (my dentist suggests adding a little peroxide to make a paste), bake with it, and keep a container in the refrigerator to absorb odors. (You can use it in your diaper pail for the same purpose.) Guess what else you can do with it? Add a little water (or lemon juice) and use it the way you would a commercial abrasive cleaner.

**Lavender oil:** This popular oil has antibacterial properties and a lovely, relaxing fragrance. In your kitchen and laundry room, you can clean with fresh lemon because the citrus fragrance seems appropriate in that room. In the bathrooms and bedrooms, you can slightly reduce the amount of vinegar you're adding to your water and add a few drops of lavender. (Use the pure oil, not a synthetic version.) You can also mix up plain water with lavender or lemon to keep in the nursery. Use it to spray around after diaper changes to freshen the air.

I don't like to store cleaning products near food. Better to keep them under the sink with a secure lock to be sure your baby can't access the items.

If you are storing items under the sink that you use in other parts of the home, transfer those items to the more appropriate location. As an example, toilet bowl cleaner should live in a bathroom and laundry detergent should live near the washer.

After you whittle down, take a look at your categories. There are all manner of containers that are designed for under the sink to help keep these items together. You might want to take a break with your helper or send her out to shop while you move on to the counters. The most important thing to keep in mind is the configuration of the pipes. If the most popular under-the-sink organizer doesn't fit, it can't serve you. Remember, you can mix and match your product solutions or use items designed for other areas. And sometimes nothing is more beneficial than a simple zip-top storage bag for loose items like sponges. Just be sure you benefit from the container. I don't want to add to the clutter!

## Counter Clutter

Some people get nervous when they see space. They feel more secure when objects fill the area. In the extreme, you might find it's literally hard to breathe in their homes. "Stuff" seems to literally suck the oxygen out of the room. The great Vietnamese Buddhist monk Thich Nhat Hanh says

> One of my pet peeves as an organizer is American packaging. The smallest items come buried in five pounds of cardboard. It's best to remove items and store them without all that cardboard and plastic! You'll be surprised how much space you will save.

that sometimes his cup is full of tea but when the tea has been consumed the cup is full of space. Wrap your mind around that for a minute. I'd like to see your counters full of space rather than full of clutter. I'd like to have the visual of space bring clarity to your busy day and to those sleep-deprived nights on the horizon. Let's take a look.

During the first month we were together, you created a file system. If you didn't gather the papers off your kitchen counters at that time, I want you to make short shrift of them today. First, you can speed through and eliminate what you don't need. Next, take the remaining material to your home office or wherever you have designated as your workspace. Sort the items into categories and then file the material away in the folders you created two months ago. And you thought this was going to be a complicated process, didn't you? You laid the foundation, now you can reap the benefits.

The way you have used your counter space is going to change. I want you to stop and think for a few minutes about the equipment, decorative items, and tools you now have out. Are they on display or do they get used? I have clients who can't boil water but who keep top-of-the-line kitchen equipment on the counter because it speaks to their prosperity, or so they think. On the other hand, your countertop equipment might be a lifesaver. When I was into cooking and dinner parties, my food processor lived on the counter. Why put it away every night only to haul it out the next morning? I was so into cooking during that phase of my life that I literally wore out the motor on one processor and had to replace it!

If coffee and toast are part of your morning ritual, I can easily see you dedicating an area on the counter to them. When my clients want those items out, I take the cabinet just above to store the items that go with coffee like mugs, sugar, powder creamer, etc. It's creating a category by using all the related space to make breakfast preparation as easy as possible. Personally, although I do drink a cup of coffee each morning, I put the coffeemaker away after I use it. I could leave it out and not fear a demerit from the Organizing Police, but I'm into space these days. The moral of the story is clear: There is no right or wrong. There is clutter, but then there is convenience.

Only you can design your counter space. Every woman and every kitchen are unique; make this space serve you. Here are some questions to help you create your design:

- Do you have plants everywhere? Could they do just as well if not better in another room?

- Are bowls or other serving items piled high and attracting dust?
- Is there equipment out you never use? Can you donate it? Would a relative like to have it? Can you pack it away in the garage for another time in your life?
- Is there equipment out you wish to keep but aren't going to be using for the foreseeable future?
- Is there anything in your cleaned-out cupboards that should now live on the counter?

Here are some suggestions for items you *may* want to have out over the next year and beyond:

**Blender.** Everyone needs a good blender. You can whip up food for your baby and simple, nutritious smoothies for yourself. If your blender has seen better days, get a new one. There are inexpensive and compact versions out there. Watch the newspapers for a discount coupon to a store like Bed Bath & Beyond.

**Baby food maker.** Many baby food recipes don't require the purchase of a special baby food maker (see page 325). But again, it's a matter of taste and temperament. If you know that making that purchase will cause you to prepare more fresh food for your baby because you like the machine, go for it. By the way, start making a wish list for your baby shower. This item is a perfect addition.

**Steamer.** I like to pop a steamer into a pot. But many of my clients insist on

There is one piece of equipment you can purchase that will function as your blender, food processor, and juicer. It's called a Vitamix. It's expensive but guaranteed for life. It also takes up less counter space than three separate pieces of equipment. You can go online to www.vitamix.com and view some explanatory videos and recipes.

purchasing special steamers to prepare rice and/or veggies. Make the choice for the item you will use religiously.

**Juicer.** There is no doubt that using a juicer is a super healthy choice. It will provide creative, healthy drinks for you and every member of your family. It's also an expensive piece of equipment and a space hog. Be sure you are going to make use of it before you make the purchase and dedicate the space.

**Crock-Pot.** The Crock-Pot has really come back into vogue. What easier way is there to have a hot, nutritious meal at dinnertime? If you love it and use it regularly, by all means, keep it out. But if you know in your heart that you are the last person on planet earth who will prepare food in a Crock-Pot, again, all you are doing is dedicating valuable space to a dinosaur.

By now, your kitchen probably feels very different to you. One more day and your work here is done. If you are wondering which cabinet should house which equipment, don't fret. We take care of that tomorrow.

## DAY THREE

The traditional way to organize a kitchen involves creating zones. In every kitchen you'll find the dishes to one side of the sink and the drinking glasses on the other. The pots and pans will be in the cabinets closest to the stove. Do you have that in place? This isn't going to be as difficult as you thought! Now you need to look at the space and the items you decided to keep. The goal is to create categories so that when you wish to prepare a meal, everything is at your fingertips. When you need to clean up, your tools are in one central area. And if you like to bake, that too is all located in one section. Designate the areas before you get up and start moving things around.

Here are some ideas to help make the inner life in your cupboards work better:

If the shelves are deep and you lose items in the back, you can put in sliding drawers. You can find them at a store like The Container Store and in catalogs like www.Solutions.com.

If you don't have a separate pantry and have to store food in your cupboards, try using a shelf creator for your canned goods. This unit can be found in wood, plastic, and mesh. It elevates your cans, creating three levels. You won't lose that treasured can of chicken soup ever again. And if you create categories, your soup and your veggies can live in separate areas.

Not able to put in sliding drawers? Make use of dead space in corners or in the back of a cupboard by storing items you rarely use there. Keep your everyday tools in front.

Are there any items that could be stored in your dining room hutch? Very often I find a set of Grandma's china in the kitchen. It's only used on holidays but it takes up several shelves in the kitchen. Get china holders at any home store (I like the padded ones that zipper close) and tuck the china safely away in your hutch.

If you want to keep items in a drawer from exploding the first time you shut the drawer quickly, use thick drawer liner (it's washable and comes in colors and designs should you wish to coordinate with your kitchen decor) and drawer organizers. They come in plastic, wood, or mesh, but the clear acrylic has my vote, as they are the easiest to wipe out and keep clean.

Finally, if you are blessed with a lazy Susan–style organizer that makes the corner of a cabinet really useful, keep in mind that you don't want to weigh it down with extremely heavy equipment. They are fragile units and break easily. They are great to hold common lightweight food prep items like colanders or mixing bowls.

The overhead kitchen light may prove especially jarring during the middle-of-the-night visits on the horizon. Put a small lamp on the counter and use it to cast a soft glow in the room. Those late nights will be less painful on your psyche and your eyes.

## Food, Glorious Food!

Take a few minutes more to clean out your refrigerator. Why have fresh veggies, chicken, and a can of opened peanut butter clustered together? Instead, create zones on your shelves so that it's easier to prepare a meal or find a snack. You organized categories of related items in drawers, inside cupboards, and on the counter. Now you can do the same inside the refrigerator. At The Container Store or in the kitchen department of your local home store, you will find an interesting array of products designed specifically to make your refrigerator more organized. Take a look at what's available and see if there is anything you need.

When it comes to the food itself, you'll want to get in the habit of purchasing more fresh fruits and veggies now, if you aren't already. Skip the fast food, the processed fake food, and the deep-fried, artery-clogging treats. Keep the fresh food in the foreground. When you're attacked by a case of the "ravenous pregnant hungries," or you've got a toddler hanging on your legs or a baby on your hip, healthy food will be at your fingertips rather than something processed or laden with fat or sugar. Try coming up with a list of snacks that are healthy, easy to prepare (or that can be prepared ahead of time), and appeal to you. Then create a place in your refrigerator—front and center, not hidden behind the milk!—for those "go-to" snacks. Soon it will become second nature to reach for that hard-boiled egg or carrots and hummus when you're hungry instead of the chips and dip.

## The Big Freeze

Make sure your freezer is organized, too. If you live in an area where fresh fruits and veggies are hard to come by during parts of the year, you may be surprised to hear that frozen veggies are a healthier choice than what's in your produce section. Those "fresh" veggies and fruits have often been shipped from someplace so far away they're two or three weeks old by the time they get to your table. And during that time they've lost a lot of flavor, not to mention nutritional value. Freezer veggies are frozen within hours of harvest, sealing in the vitamins, minerals, antioxidants, and flavor. You can also freeze your "fresh from the farmer's market" veggies to last you year-round.

One of the strangest things human beings do is to fill the freezer with packages of "mystery meat." I know a lady who keeps these things for years. When she offers to thaw one of these relics and make dinner for me, I politely decline and remind her I am a vegetarian. In truth, after six months those items should be tossed. Label your packages so you know what's inside. And be sure you note the date.

On that note, you'll also want to make sure to clear out some space in your freezer and fridge close to your due date. Friends and family often bring food to a new family as a way to help out. You'll want to have a place to put it.

Adapt these solutions to your specifics and you'll come out with one organized kitchen.

When you are done, please do one thing for the Zen Organizer: Be sure your

---

### EXPAND YOUR CULINARY WORLD

Now is a great time to expand the variety of food you're accustomed to keeping on hand. What pantry doesn't have white rice and pasta? My friend Chef Tanya suggests you open yourself to the world of grains and experiment with barley, oats, and soy. Don't forget the delicious grains with exotic-sounding names: quinoa, basmati white or brown rice, kamut, couscous, and spelt.

If you are interested in experimenting with soy, tofu is a great source of protein. It's versatile because you can steam it, sauté it, or toss it in the blender. Aside from being a substitute for meat in main dishes, tofu makes great desserts, salad dressings, and soups.

In your market near the tofu you may see a product called tempeh. That's another soy product with a meatier texture. Get a "simple" tempeh you can steam or sauté at home. Don't go with the one that's been saturated in soy or some other salty sauce. Not all tempeh is created equal, so experiment a bit with different brands.

---

newly organized, streamlined kitchen isn't marred by a refrigerator that has too many photos, ads, notices, and general debris all over it! You are about to bring a baby into your home. Create an Emergency Contact list and post that for all to see. Include all key names and contact numbers. I'd make this sheet the only decoration for your refrigerator. This week is about embracing the beauty of empty space.

# 21-22 WEEKS PREGNANT

## The Magic of a Routine

This week, you can

- Learn how routines help you stay organized
- Decide to create a few routines that make today easier

As I prepare to exit their homes, my clients often fret that whatever we created will not last. It is as if they expect that an evil spirit will suddenly inhabit their bodies, preventing them from performing maintenance tasks. Do you feel this fear deep inside you? Perhaps you envision the newly decorated nursery descending into chaos. Or maybe you have never liked doing laundry and fear Baby's soiled onesies will pile up to the sky. This week I am going to demystify the art of maintenance. It isn't the scary, pain-in-the-neck series of burdensome tasks you think it is. In fact, you are already an expert organizer!

### TRADING PLACES

When I teach a seminar I usually begin by saying, "You know what they say: There is good news and there is bad news. Which do you want first?" Inevitably the audience wants the good news first: I tell them that they are already organized. More than just being organized, they are devoted to the systems they have in place. "You are like religious zealots in your devotion and zeal." You can hear the buzz in the audience. "Oh no, Regina! You haven't seen my home!" I assure the audience I am correct, which of course brings me to the bad news: Not all systems are created equal. While some bring you peaceful, calm environments that literally nurture and support your best efforts in life, your current system may assure that you exist in a bastion of chaos. The environment seems to sabotage you at every turn. Instead of being calmed, you are constantly agitated. And now that you're expecting a baby, life is about to get more complicated and stressful than it's ever been before. Even if you have been able to get by with dysfunctional systems so far, why make your adjustment to motherhood harder than it has to be? You need to figure out a way to create new routines that work for you instead of against you.

How do you make the shift? Is there some big psychological hurdle? Do you have to practice for weeks and weeks? Is there any hope? Wait until you hear how *easy* it is! Here's the secret. Every action takes some time to perform. Whether it's a few seconds or a few hours, it's a finite amount of time. In order to maintain the order you create, you don't have to expend any extra energy. You have to redirect the energy you are already expending. Here are a few examples.

Let's say you habitually walk in the front door and toss your keys somewhere. Later a drama ensues. I like to say that "Where are my keys?" is actually THE most popular soap opera in America! And when you have a baby, the drama becomes that much more intense.

Imagine this scenario, a year in the future. You come into the house with a baby on one hip and a bag of groceries in your arm. You pitch your keys on the closest flat surface you see and go about your business of putting away the groceries. Two hours later, you and the baby are late for an appointment. She dirtied her diaper at the last minute—as babies are prone to do—and you had to change her. Now you're running behind, but you can't remember what you did with your keys. The seconds tick by as you run around the house searching in vain. Your arm and shoulder are starting to cramp up from holding your baby, who now seems to weigh about fifty pounds. The baby's fussing; you're sweating and on the verge of tears. Why does it have to be so hard to get out and about as a mom?

Guess what? It doesn't have to be. Imagine that same scenario if you had walked in the door and placed your keys in one designated spot. Later, when you and your baby were on your way to your appointment, you could have just grabbed your keys from that one spot and been on your way. It wouldn't have taken any longer to deposit them and you would have saved a lot of time and emotional energy. As a mom, there will be plenty of unpredictable events—a dirty diaper, a tantrum, or an unexpected nap—that can throw your day off course and cause stress. Eliminate the unnecessary stress of searching for your keys by making their location something you can always count on!

Let's take another example. You walk into your bedroom at the end of the day. You toss your clothes onto the easy chair. You do this for several days. Your clothes get wrinkled. Maybe the cat or the dog decides to periodically sit on the growing pile. Now the clothes are covered with hair and wrinkled beyond repair. You could have worn some of those items again but now you'd look like a homeless person. Somehow, the fact that your clothes have been gathering fur on a chair has seemed to turn that chair into some kind of junk magnet. Now your husband's socks and belt are there, too, along with your baby's diaper bag and a toy or two. You're irritated with your husband, the dog, the cat, and maybe even the baby; and to make matters worse, now you have a dry-cleaning bill to contend with. Wouldn't it have been easier to just hang the clothes up to begin with, wear them again, hug the dog, kiss the cat, and embrace your spouse?

Finally, let's look at your office. You open the mail. There are some things to be tossed, a few sheets of paper to shred, and several items to file. You say you are tired and it all sits in a jumble on your desk. After several days, it looks like the Tasmanian devil blew through. Now you have to set aside time to get caught up. If you think it's bad now, imagine that incoming paper doubling or tripling after you have your baby. Hospital bills, insurance statements, immunization records, reminder notices from the pediatrician . . . you're going to have a lot more paper to manage once this baby enters your life, and you need to create habits now that will help you stay on top of it. It takes a few seconds to put a piece of paper in its proper place right this minute. It will later take the same amount of time but there will be additional aggravation, guilt, and shame layered onto an activity that should have taken a few minutes and raised your self-esteem.

## DID YOU REALLY GET ORGANIZED?

Another lament I hear is this: "Regina, I get organized on a regular basis but it never lasts! Two weeks after I expend all that energy, the chaos is back. Why should I bother?" People are astonished to learn that they did not in fact get organized. They tidied up. Things got shoved into cupboards, drawers, and closets so the *appearance* of order might reign for a few

days. Being organized means that you designate a specific spot for every item in your home. When you see that item out of place, it gets returned to where it belongs. These are two very different activities with two very different outcomes. Which one have you traditionally done in your home?

Another sad song I hear is: "Regina, I can't throw anything out. What if I need it later? I don't want to be wasteful!" This speaks to me of what is called in metaphysical circles a "poverty consciousness" or a "consciousness of loss." It means people are ruled by fear. They are afraid they will make the wrong decisions so they find a few noble words to give them a pass. They fear they won't have the money to replace an item if indeed that need should arise. What they fail to embrace is that they are being wasteful, not with stuff, but rather with space, time, and energy. The space is so crowded they can't function. Somewhere along the line they were taught that this is the way life is, and freedom and ease feel foreign to them. If you relate to this, I ask you to face this issue head on. Along with a new baby come a lot of extra things. You need to get comfortable with getting rid of items your child no longer uses or needs, or you will find yourself drowning in stuff in short order. And if you let your fear of lack keep you from exercising healthy control over your belongings, you'll be passing this fear on to your child. I have a story that perfectly illustrates how a poverty consciousness can rule us. I tell it in all of my seminars and classes. I hope you see yourself in this dramatic story and find the key to your own personal freedom when it comes to the bondage of stuff.

I once participated at an event for young executives. We would each respond to questions from our field of expertise, the goal being to communicate how we felt the questioner could improve her life. A successful young woman entered the room I was in with two friends. She walked up to me and said, "Well, Regina, I find that two weeks after I give something away, I inevitably need it. So, tell me, what do you think about that!?" She crossed her arms across her chest. I wanted to know her story. There's always a reason these things happen. It's never chance or "bad luck." She was going to be a tough nut to crack, so the first thing I did was give her permission not to change.

"I would say that as long as this is your belief, it's going to continue to happen. My advice would be: Don't give anything away!" I asked her if she knew where this "consciousness of loss" came from. Were her parents Depression-era babies? Had she ever been robbed or lost luggage on a trip? No matter what hypothetical possibility I tossed out, she shot it down. I had never before been unable to get a client to reveal the underlying cause for such a belief. She would undoubtedly go down as my first failure. Then, as if by magic, my colleague, a Feng Shui practitioner, elicited this story from her.

When she was five years old, she packed a tiny suitcase and went off on her first sleepover. That night there was a tragic accident: Her brother burned down the house! The next morning she had no home to return to and all of her belongings were now in that one tiny suitcase. I was stunned. I asked if she had ever seen the correlation between her fear and this horrific experience. "No," she said. I invited her to investigate the possibility. How could a child not be scarred by such an experience? Although the connection may not always be so clear, it's within your grasp as well. All it takes is a period of honest reflection.

## RITUALS AND ROUTINES

Every day you perform a series of comforting actions without giving them any thought. Let me give you an example from my own life. I get up and do the following without thinking: go to the bathroom, light incense on my altar, put on the coffee, start breakfast, and bring in the paper. If the series gets interrupted I feel off kilter for a few hours. Let me give you another example: I create my grocery list all week and shop on the *same* day. When it's time to have my car serviced, I tie that into a visit with another provider in that part of town. I usually go to the dentist and the dealership twice a year. You get my drift.

Likewise, you probably already have some routines in place. Alas, in the established mix there may also be some routines that cause great distress. Here's a common scenario. You check Facebook right before bed. You don't set an alarm and time gets away from you. Instead of ten minutes, you spend two hours. Now you crawl into bed exhausted. Traditional

Chinese medicine says that the sleep you get before midnight is the most restorative. You can forget that noise because it's now 2:30 a.m. and you have to get up for work at 6:00. But you don't get up at 6:00, do you? You hit the snooze button several times and run the risk of being late for work. You grab a food bar or donut and eat it on the fly. You spend money for a designer cup of coffee because you didn't have time to make any. And you play catch-up all day. Sound like you or anyone you know? It's a ritual gone awry!

You'll find it completely untenable to live this way once you have a baby. Sleep will be at a premium and more important than ever. You won't be able to hit the snooze button for a half hour, then jump out of bed at the last minute and still make it anywhere on time. Your baby will need to be fed, diapered, and dressed before you can leave the house. You will need to get adequate sleep or you'll never be able to deal with the demands of motherhood. Don't panic! As the person who created these inadequate, quasi self-destructive habits, you are completely free to replace them with ones that nurture and uplift you in your new situation.

## THE POWER OF THE PEN

Right about now a few journal questions will help you clear the cobwebs from your mind and set you on the road to creating your own positive rituals and routines.

Sit quietly in a nice comfortable chair and think carefully about each question before you start writing. The goal is to uncover the unconscious sabotage behaviors that are perhaps ruling at least a part of your life. Once you identify them, you are free to change them. This exercise isn't about guilt; it's about empowerment.

Can you identify two or three positive routines you have established like the morning ritual I described above? Some of you may be hard-pressed to name one.

What about time-wasting routines: Do you have any of those you could list here? Don't be surprised if this is a long list! Ah, now we know you're human.

What parts of your life don't work as well as you'd like? Are you always late for work? Do you not get enough sleep? Do you habitually shop at the market without a list? Identify five things you'd like to work on. What is the payoff for making each change? It's important to identify the payoff. That knowledge will help keep you motivated when the going gets tough. For example: If you don't get enough sleep, why do you want more? Your response might be something along these lines: *If I got more sleep I wouldn't be as tired during the day. I could accomplish more and enjoy the day. I'd also like to banish those dark circles under my eyes.*

Can you identify at least three good habits you have now? Is it possible to string them together in a way that creates a positive, productive ritual?

Keep in mind the way your life is going to change in just a few short months. Are the routines and rituals you're creating conducive to life with a baby? Can you create a system that allows you to make your morning coffee with one hand? Or read your morning paper in a room where you can keep your eye on the baby? Creating habits that take your baby into account now will help make the transition much smoother later.

What habits could you cultivate to achieve this same goal?

Once you understand the concept of routines, you can create new ones and revise the old as the demands on your time change. Remember that getting organized takes time and a little old-fashioned elbow grease. But *staying* organized is really about directing your energy in a positive way. It doesn't require more of you; it just requires something new. After Baby is born, I'll have some suggestions for baby-related routines (page 268). Children and animals thrive on structure. Perhaps they have something to teach us!

# CHAPTER FOUR

# 23 to 27 Weeks Pregnant

The best and most beautiful things in the world cannot be seen or even touched. They must be felt with the heart.

—HELEN KELLER

WHAT IS CUTER than baby toys, baby clothes, and baby furniture? Nothing, except maybe Baby! Right about now you are probably feeling the desire to feather your nest even more intensely. Let's capitalize on this hormonal phenomenon with well-timed organizing projects. (You might as well be focused in your quest rather than finding yourself scrubbing walls at 3:00 a.m. because it seemed like a good idea.) This month we move to what is perhaps my favorite organizing project: getting your baby's room ready. Even if there will not be an entire separate room for your child, you can adapt the tips to whatever space you are turning over to him or her. From paint for the walls to finding the best changing table, I've got you covered—in ways that can save you time and money.

This month you'll also be out in the world looking at many items that your emotions will urge you to buy. Don't do it. After all, I'm sure there's a baby shower in your future, not to mention a few friends who could loan you some key items. You don't have to purchase everything you need. And if the item isn't on your list, press the pause button and wait forty-eight hours. See if you still want it two days later. Ask your experienced mom friends if they know anything about this item. Is it worth the price? Work on your budget and shop within the sane parameters it sets for you.

In 2008 the United States Department of Agriculture calculated it would cost a family $221,190 to raise a child born that year to the age of eighteen. This figure did not include college. And of course you'll have to adjust for inflation. But don't panic: About $70,000 of this study was housing expenses and you'll have those with or without Junior. You are in control of how much you spend in many areas, like toys, clothing, and entertainment. You don't have to fall down this slippery slope.

In fact, that's why I chose the quote from Helen Keller for this month. Yes, Baby needs "stuff," but more importantly, he needs many intangible things, like a loving home that's filled with peace and calm. You can create a sanctuary for Baby without going overboard. I promise you'll have the right furniture and enough onesies and diapers.

Baby isn't the only one who deserves a sanctuary. Mom and Dad do as well. Sometimes I enter a bedroom that's a chaotic mess; I'm never surprised when everyone tells me they have trouble sleeping at night. Now that we've cleaned out the closet, we end this month with a return visit to your bedroom. We need to be sure it functions perfectly, welcomes you at the end of the day, and is dedicated to sleep and fun. Ideally your home is your sanctuary from the world—and your bedroom is the ultimate respite from the turmoil, trouble, and strife you may encounter from time to time.

## HABIT OF THE MONTH

### Keep Romance Alive

Are you shocked to see a note about romance in a book designed to keep you or-ganized? Remember that Zen Organizing isn't just a system of tips and tricks to get organized. As a philosophy it goes much deeper than that. The goal of Zen Organizing is to help you create an environment that nurtures and supports you at every turn so you can fulfill your life's purpose. When the home is calm, organized, and peace filled, it's easier to consciously nurture your relationship with positive words and actions. When hormones are flowing, tempers can flare. And then there are all those unconscious fears floating around: Will I be a good parent? Do we have enough money for a down payment on a house? What about college? We drive ourselves crazy with "what if's" during normal times. Now everything is heightened.

Remember to embrace the person who made this journey possible. It's so easy to take the people we love the most for granted. Say please and thank you. Leave surprise "I Love You" notes around the home. Plan a regular date night, and aim to keep this tradition alive after the baby is born. (Interview prospective sitters now, and plug their numbers into your speed dial.) In the not-too-distant future you will be teaching your daughter or son the importance of manners. Start now to consciously demonstrate what manners look like. They are, after all, a way of expressing love.

# 23 WEEKS PREGNANT

## Make Baby Feel Welcome:
## Transform His Room or Living Area

This week, you can

- Become more aware of contaminants in common household products and items, and investigate healthy options
- Clean out the room intended for Baby
- Decide on what improvements are necessary

THE GOOD NEWS about this week is that most people won't be saddled with a big, renovation-style makeover of a room for Baby. For most of you, it will involve simply moving some types of furniture out and purchasing a few baby-geared pieces in their place. But while you're doing so, it's good to consider the pros and cons of various types of paint, carpet, wood flooring, and area rugs, especially when it comes to environmental toxicity. The goal this entire month is to help you create a welcoming space for Baby that will adapt to his needs over time without breaking your bank. Let's get started.

### CREATE A NONTOXIC ENVIRONMENT

Before you purchase paint and furniture, be aware that some new materials may emit toxic volatile organic compounds, also known as VOCs. The issue is called "off-gassing"—but Beano can't rescue this situation!

The fumes we smell, like those from fresh paint, varnish, or wood stain, tell us that VOCs are present. The volatile organic compounds being released can be hazardous to your health, especially if the area in question is enclosed (new car smell, anyone?). Breathing the chemicals in, as well as absorbing them through the skin, are the big concerns. Keep in mind, however, that some harmful compounds may emit no odor.

I had never been really conscious of this phenomenon until a few years ago when I painted my apartment, got new carpet, and purchased new furniture. Because I rent my apartment, unfortunately I had to go with the carpet the management wanted. The fumes were toxic and noxious. As far as new furniture, the smell coming from the mattress and box spring alone was overpowering. There are petroleum-based by-products used in the manufacture of these products.

At the time, I had an old golden retriever and several birds. They were all shipped to a friend's house until it was safe to come home. I was with the various workmen all day but slept at my friend's house with my pets. When I came home, I bought an air purifier, which saved the situation.

Your baby is developing quickly and every day counts. Over the next month, his brain development will be particularly rapid. According to the Natural Resources Defense Council (NRDC) and the U.S. Environmental Protection Agency among others, the gases that paint and other solvents release over time can cause a variety of problems. The list is long and includes nausea; eye, ear, and nose irritation; damage to the liver, kidneys, and central nervous system; and of course cancer (http://www.epa.gov/iaq/voc.htm and http://www.nrdc.org/thisgreenlife/0905.asp).

While no studies have been performed to date to determine the possible effects of exposing pregnant women to VOCs, I think it's safe to assume that the less off-gassing you're exposed to, the better. Let's keep your home environment as clean and pure as we can.

Read the labels of any new products you plan to use, especially during preparation of your baby's room. The first line of defense is to purchase products that are as pure as possible, such as paints marketed as "low VOC" or better yet "zero VOC." Begin with a visit to your local paint store and use your favorite online search engine to find the latest in these products. Famous makers like Benjamin Moore and Sherwin-Williams each have lines of low-VOC paint. I also found a company called Baby Safe Finishes (www.babysafefinishes.com) that specializes in safe products for you and your baby.

Next, be sure to keep the area well ventilated. Wear protective clothing including gloves, a mask, long pants, and a long-sleeved shirt. If you begin to have any unusual symptoms like burning eyes or difficulty breathing, leave the area immediately. If you aren't able to purchase non-toxic furniture or low-VOC paints (yes, they can be expensive), consider going out of town for the weekend while the painting is going on and/or while new furniture is being installed. Leave windows open if possible and/or run an air purifier to eliminate some of the gases from the air.

## PLANNING THE NURSERY

### Phase One

There are two common scenarios when it comes to Baby's room: The first involves turning a guest room or home office into Baby's room and the second is adapting an area in an existing room because space is at a premium. Let's start with the first one. I'd like you to go into that room now and have a seat. Be sure you have your baby journal with you, as we need to do some planning.

# AVOID COMMON INDOOR CONTAMINANTS

## Mattress and Box Springs

Petroleum by-products have found their way into the manufacture of these products. The typical mattress and box spring are soaked in some combination of fire-retardant chemicals, formaldehyde, and other toxic glues, stains, and coatings. These chemicals can release carcinogenic gases. If you don't have an air purifier, order your baby's mattress well in advance and let it air out before she ever comes in contact with it.

## Rugs and Carpets

The issue here is simple: Do you get a wool carpet or rug or do you go with synthetic? Natural wool absorbs chemicals, while synthetic fibers will contribute to the chemicals in the room. Wool, unlike synthetic fibers, rapidly absorbs common contaminants in indoor air like formaldehyde, nitrogen dioxide, and sulphur dioxide. Not only does wool keep the air free of many harmful pollutants, it will not re-emit them, even when heated.

Carpets (and rugs) also absorb something else: sound. This is a benefit to consider if you live in an apartment and have crotchety neighbors right under your designated nursery or if you live in a home and a sibling lives downstairs. Noise is after all another form of pollution, isn't it?

## Paint

As noted above, you want to purchase paint with low or no VOCs. There is, however, an additional consideration: When was your home built? If it was built prior to 1978, there may be lead paint somewhere in the house, even if it's below several layers of newer latex paint. This is a concern because the paint can chip (particularly in areas like on windowsills), creating dust, and if the dust is ingested or breathed in, it can pose a danger to your baby's health and development. But don't panic! This is a very common situation and the health department for your city or your state will have guidelines for safely removing or painting over lead paint.

The low- or no-VOC paints are also good for the environment, as they are not designated as hazardous waste. (You should contact your local sanitation department to find out how to correctly dispose of all chemical products used in your home. You may not simply dump them in your regular trash!) These new and improved paint products also reduce ozone-depleting contaminants. Your choice may cost a bit more but you have the solace of benefiting the planet as well as your new baby. And yes the coverage is just as good as the less-expensive VOC-producing versions and just as easy to keep clean.

## Wood Floors

The 411 on wood flooring is that it's safe and doesn't off-gas. Of course nothing in life is easy so you still have to be a Sherlock Holmes wannabe when you shop. Why? Because the adhesives used during installation might contain formaldehyde and VOCs! You need to shop with a reputable retailer you trust and request formaldehyde-free adhesives and finishes. These are water-based, are solvent-free, and do not off-gas. As you might expect, they are a bit more expensive but worth it in the long run.

*If the room is currently a guest room:*

If the room is now used as a guest room, are you going to divide the room in half, move the guest bed to another area, or donate the guest bed and use a futon when you have visitors? An inflatable bed works well unless of course your visitors are elderly and can't sleep that close to the ground.

If the bed or any other furniture needs to be removed, what are you going to do with it? Common options include donating it to charity or someone you know; selling it through a service like Craigslist or your local consignment shop; putting an ad on Freecycle so someone will pick it up; or putting it out on the street (be sure you call your sanitation service so the items don't languish on your sidewalk!).

Take a second look before you eighty-six any furniture: Could you paint something and use it for the baby? For example, let's say you have an old dresser from your childhood home. You could paint it a lovely pastel color and use the top as a changing table.

If you have a garage, is there any room to store some pieces you are attached to and wish to use later?

With my clients, I've found that losing a guest room, a craft room, a workout area, or any other type of nonessential room tends not to be so hard. The difficulty arises if you are transforming a home office into the nursery and need to find new spaces for your office-related pieces.

Clearly, if you work from home or run a business, you can't share the space with a baby. Just as he falls asleep, you'll be answering the phone and dealing with clients. It sounds like a scene from a Will Ferrell comedy, doesn't it? If this room has been where you came to pay bills and run the business of family life, you can find ways to set up a work zone elsewhere.

*If the room is currently a home office:*

Are there any pieces of office equipment that you don't really use? Pack them away for now, or sell them or donate them as is appropriate.

If your family room or living rooms are large enough, you may be able to create a work corner. Do you have hardwood floors? You are in luck, as you can use an area rug to mark off the office zone. If you can't use an area rug and you like to entertain in this room, you can always use a decorative screen to keep the room's functions separate.

No matter how many files we create, we usually use only a few on a daily basis. The decorative file box is best if you are going to be using a public room. Put a lamp or a decorative vase on it and no one will suspect its true purpose.

The last place to commandeer for your office is your bedroom. That room really is for rest, sleep, and fun. Introducing a computer and the energy of work invites you to wake up in the middle of the night to check e-mail. If this solution is the only one, use the trick of the area rug or screen.

Your assignment is to decide what stays and what goes. Make calls and be sure everything that is scheduled to leave has a pick-up date. If a relative says they want something but can't come for months to retrieve it, apologize profusely, but you need the space now. Don't hesitate to donate the item to local women's shelter or thrift store instead. If furniture has to be moved to other parts of your home, call in some burly guy friends to assist your spouse. Don't try any heroics! You aren't to do any heavy lifting.

After the room has been rearranged or emptied, return with your journal and let's make some notes.

### Phase Two

Now the room should feel very different. The energy of its former identity is giving way to something new. One day soon you won't remember it as anything but a nursery! Let's take a minute to examine the room.

Does the room need to be painted? Or are you going with wallpaper? You and your spouse should schedule a time to shop of course, but never underestimate the value of perusing magazines and online sites for inspiration. If you have some direction, the stores will be less overwhelming.

Before you make any final decisions, bring home paint chips and fabric swatches. Your paint store should have small cans of your favorites. Put a few patches of color on the wall. How does the light at different times of day play on the colors?

What about the floor? Do you need new carpet? Perhaps you have a hardwood floor that needs to be polished? Or did you want to use a few area rugs to make activity zones in the room? Rugs make it so easy to demarcate space.

How will you dress the window?

Is there a closet? Will you share with Baby or is this his territory?

Does the room have its own bathroom? If not, is one close by?

What is the light source in the room? Do you need lamps? They certainly create more ambience than overhead lighting.

Does the room have enough electrical outlets? If you bring in an electrician to add a few, be sure she adds a light to the closet if it needs one.

### WHEN BABY MAKES FOUR

If your first child is about to be asked to share her room, even if she is very young, you may find out it isn't the most popular idea, unless you adequately prepare her. Think how you would feel if I marched into your bedroom and started rearranging your personal items and furniture because you had to share the space. Wouldn't it be nicer if I talked to you first, invited you into the process, and perhaps even asked for your input? A friend of mine had her second child when her first was three years old. Throughout her entire pregnancy she and her husband told their daughter that the role of a big sister was an important one. Mommy was going to need her help. This little girl never missed a step. Her role as big sister made her feel proud, and she was excited to share her room and her things with her new sibling.

## LIGHT AT THE END OF THE TUNNEL

As this week draws to a close, remember to have fun with all of these assignments. You are, after all, creating your baby's first sanctuary, even if he will most likely be set up in your bedroom for at least the first few weeks. If you feel stuck as to how to transform the room, go through some magazines for inspiration. Cut out some pictures you gravitate to and make a Dream Board just for this room. This is a wonderful tool for anyone who isn't highly visual by nature. Seeing can be inspiring! All you need is some inexpensive poster board from your local stationary supply store like Staples or Office Max along with a stick of glue. Paste the images that capture the look or feel of the nursery you'd like to create onto your poster board. You don't have to have multiple nurseries on view. You might simply have eight or ten images of various aspects of the room as you'd like to create it. It's nice to cut out words or phrases and add them as well. You might find them in ads or you could purchase a sheet of letters when you pick up your poster board. Use glitter or stickers if you wish. Just remember this isn't a homework assignment. The idea is to have fun and unleash your creativity.

# 24 WEEKS PREGNANT

## What Does Baby Need?
## Shopping and Registering for Baby Showers

This week, you can

- Determine what you need to have on hand before the baby arrives, what can wait until after he's here, and what you might not need at all
- Register for baby gifts

I'VE GOT GOOD NEWS for you. Despite the shopping frenzy you might feel obligated to embark on, babies come into the world with pretty simple needs. They don't pay any attention to the commercials that constantly barrage expecting parents with the idea that babies need a bunch of gadgets to be happy and healthy.

First, let's consider a newborn baby's needs. Babies need to be warm, they need to be dry, and they need to be fed. If you're breastfeeding, the third need is already taken care of. While bottles may still serve a purpose for a nursing mom, you probably won't need any for a while. And even bottle-feeding moms don't need an arsenal of nipples and bottles right away, especially since the hospital will provide them during your stay. That leaves "warm" and "dry," and it doesn't take too much to provide for those needs.

While it's good to be prepared for "wants," there are relatively few things

you'll absolutely *need* to have on hand before the baby makes her arrival. So don't panic or feel like you have to have everything you could ever want already purchased ahead of time. Your baby will be just fine if he enters the world without a fully stocked nursery. And remember, you can always send a spouse or family member on a quick trip to a discount store or pharmacy for a forgotten item.

If this is your first baby (and possibly if it's your second or beyond), a friend or family member is likely planning you a shower. Baby stores and department stores like Target offer you the opportunity to register for gifts you'd like to receive by walking around and "shopping" with a little scanner. It can be difficult to keep yourself in check as you wander the stores zapping the barcodes on this adorable blanket or that oh-so-cute outfit. So I recommend you make a plan before you ever set foot in the store. Here are two lists you can consider while planning your shower strategy. The first is the list of items you'll want to have on hand while your baby is very small. The second is a list of items you can probably wait to purchase.

## GET IT NOW

### Clothing

As with maternity clothes, consider your lifestyle before you decide how many of each different item of baby clothing to purchase. How often will you (rather, your spouse, friend or family member, or hired help) do laundry in those early weeks? That will help you determine how many of each of the following items to have on hand:

**T-shirts or bodysuits (i.e., "onesies").** You can expect a baby to go through at least one undershirt per day; often two or more if she's the type to "blow out" her diaper.

**One-piece sleepers or gowns.** Your baby will probably live mostly in one-piece sleepers or gowns for the first few weeks; be sure to have at least two on hand for every day you'll go before doing the laundry, plus a couple extra just in case laundry plans don't go as expected.

**Baby socks.** You can never have too many of these elusive little items, since they will go missing like crazy (did you know washing machines actually do eat socks? It's true—small items occasionally spill over the top of the drum in top-loading machines.) A small mesh bag for keeping them all together in and out of the laundry will help, but still expect a few to go missing. Buy several pairs in the same color and style.

**Receiving blankets.** Great for everything from mopping up milk to wrapping up babies nice and snug, you'll want at least four or five of these soft, lightweight blankets on hand. Look for a couple of extra-large ones for swaddling.

**Burp cloths, pre-fold or flat cloth diapers.** Babies create an awful lot of liquid of all sorts, and burp cloths and cloth diapers are easy to fling over a shoulder or lap for extra protection. Have several on hand.

**A few "cute" outfits for photos, visits with Grandma and Grandpa, etc.** Don't go overboard here. You have no idea how big your baby will be when he's born nor how fast he'll grow. Some babies stay in the newborn or "0-3 month" size for quite a while. Others will outgrow it practically before they leave the hospital. You don't want to invest lots of money (or space) in adorable newborn outfits that never have a chance to be worn!

**Diapers.** Just get one package of the newborn size—they are often outgrown really quickly.

**Cloth diapers** are a great ecologically friendly choice and can be handed down from baby to baby. The cloth diapers of today are not the fold-and-pin nightmares your mother probably wrestled with!

Nowadays, there is an array of cloth diaper options that are just as easy to use as disposables—promise. And laundering them is no big deal as long as you get a system in place. No need to spend a mint on fancy "designer" diapers (yes, they exist!). A couple dozen high-quality prefolds with four to six covers with snap or Velcro closures will get you started. For more information on different styles and brands and where to buy, visit thediaperpin.com.

### Furniture and Gear

**A place to sleep.** Perhaps you'll be receiving a crib and/or bassinette or cradle as a gift, or maybe you'll be purchasing Baby's bed yourself. If you're looking at cribs, consider purchasing one that converts into a toddler bed later so you get more mileage from your purchase. Another option is borrowing or finding your baby's bed second-hand on Craigslist, on eBay, or at a rummage sale. Just investigate the model, brand, and serial number online before you use it for your baby—many cribs have been recalled over the years because they have been found unsafe.

**Somewhere to hang out.** Babies love to be held, of course, but you will have to put her down occasionally so you can use the bathroom or take a shower. She'll need a place where she can be near you while she's awake and you can't hold her. A Moses basket, a bouncy seat, a swing, or even an extra car seat can fit the bill. If your budget is tight or space is limited, get something portable so you can move it from room to room.

**Other furniture for the baby's space.** We'll talk more about specifics next week, but it's a good idea to get the baby's area set up ahead of time if possible. Whether he has his own room or will be using a corner of yours, having a place to put all the stuff you get at the shower will help you feel ready for his arrival.

**Medicine-chest tools** like nail clippers, thermometer, and a bulb syringe. Little babies' fingernails grow amazingly fast and can be sharper than you'd think. And you'll want to have a thermometer on hand when they're little—newborns aren't good at regulating their own body temperatures, so if there's any question of whether Baby's too hot or cold, you can reassure yourself. A note on the bulb syringe: The two-piece models you can get in the baby aisle at the store are all but useless. Get the one-piece blue kind you'd find at the hospital from the pharmacy section.

**A good carrier.** A well-made sling or supportive, soft infant carrier is a must-have for new moms. Not only will it allow you to keep Baby close while going about your business during the day, but it's usually a more convenient way to get around with a small baby than pulling out a bulky stroller. Meagan loved her Moby Wrap or Ergo Baby carrier for longer trips, and opted for a Mod Mum pouch sling for just puttering around the house. There are endless options for slings, front packs, hip carriers, and backpack carriers, so be sure to read reviews before you buy. A good resource to help you choose is thebabywearer.com.

# CO-SLEEPING

Throughout the ages and still today in many cultures, the idea of a baby sleeping in a crib would seem very odd. In the West, it's the other way around: Babies sleeping alongside their parents has come to be regarded as strange and even dysfunctional. But a growing movement of parents and experts embrace the idea of "co-sleeping," "bed sharing," or "the family bed." Benefits include easier breastfeeding, better sleep for both Mom and Baby, and more opportunity for bonding.

Though there have been some highly publicized cases of babies dying while sleeping with adults, it's important to note that babies also die in cribs and other baby beds. Any sleep space has the potential to be unsafe, and experts believe that when done safely, co-sleeping is no less safe than crib sleeping.

Even if you don't plan on co-sleeping, you may change your mind when your baby is here. You may think you will "never" take your baby into your bed, but until you've spent half the night walking the floor with a screaming baby who finally falls asleep in your arms (but won't stay that way in the crib), it's hard to know exactly what you'd do!

I believe it's important for all adult beds to be baby-safe zones because you never know when you may decide you need or want to sleep next to your baby, even if it's just for a night or two or a nap now and then. Here are some things to consider when setting up a baby-safe adult bed:

1. The surface should be flat and smooth. Waterbeds and very soft mattresses are not safe for babies.

2. The sheets should be snugly fitted. Yank the corners to make sure they won't come out and cover the baby's head.

3. The bed should be pushed up against a wall, or have a mesh guardrail on one side to keep the baby from falling out.

4. Keep pillows and blankets away from Baby's head. Give Mom and Dad each their own blankets. Baby can sleep in a "sleep sack," which is a built-in sleeper and blanket in one. (This is also recommended for crib sleeping.)

5. Only mothers should sleep next to their babies. Extensive research conducted by James McKenna, Ph.D., at the Mother-Baby Behavioral Sleep Laboratory at Notre Dame University has indicated that mothers and babies share breathing and movement patterns and move in and out of sleep cycles at the same time. That is, moms seem to have an instinctive sense of their babies as they sleep next to them. Other adults—even dads!—may not have the same instinctive sense of where the baby is at all times.

6. Moms who are under the influence of alcohol or medications that make them sleepy should not sleep next to their babies.

7. If you want to have Baby at arm's reach but aren't comfortable with having her in your bed (or don't feel your bed is safe enough) consider the Arm's Reach Co-Sleeper. It's a "sidecar" baby bed that sits flush with your bed. You'll have easy access to your baby at night, but you'll both be in your own space.

Even if you plan on co-sleeping full time, you'll want someplace where you can safely put your baby down for naps when you aren't holding her. This may be a crib or bassinette. Or you might opt for a portable playpen, which is convenient for taking to Grandma's house on the weekends, too.

**A car seat.** You'll need one of these before they'll let you leave the hospital with the baby, and it's nice to get it far in advance so you can practice putting it in and taking it out of the car. It's best to buy these new or borrow one from a trusted friend or family member who can tell you about its history. If an infant safety seat has been involved in a car crash (even a minor fender-bender) in the past, its integrity could be compromised and it's not considered safe to use. If you do borrow or buy used, be sure to check the model for recalls.

**A breast pump and/or bottles and formula.** If you plan on breastfeeding, you don't necessarily need to buy a breast pump or bottles. Many women never use them at all. But if you'll be returning to work while your baby is still small, or want to have a stash of milk on hand for emergencies or outings, you'll want to either buy or rent a pump. Sometimes your health insurance will pay for the expense, particularly if your baby is small or has a hard time getting started with breastfeeding, so you might want to put this purchase off until later. In either case, don't waste your money on battery-operated pumps from the big-box store. They aren't effective and can be uncomfortable to use. Avent makes a good manual model for once-in-a-while pumping, but if you plan on using the pump regularly, you'll need to invest in a high-end electric pump. Medela and Ameda are brand names to keep in mind.

As for bottles, if you'll only be giving them occasionally, one or two is plenty. You can always purchase more later if or when there is a need. Opt for glass bottles or BPA-free plastic ones like those found at www.newbornfree.com. Regular plastic bottles have been shown to contain chemicals that can interfere with your baby's hormone levels and have been linked to certain cancers. Now that your kitchen has been cleaned out, you will no doubt have space on a shelf you can dedicate to these products. As your needs change, the bottles will one day give way to sippy cups and some dishes for the baby.

If you won't be breastfeeding, you'll need to have infant formula on hand as well as bottles and nipples. You'll be giving eight or more bottles a day in the early weeks, so purchase accordingly. I wouldn't recommend purchasing formula in bulk just yet. Sometimes babies have sensitivities to certain formulas and you may need to switch brands or types. Formula is expensive, so it's wise to wait and see whether the type you've chosen is a winner before you invest in a lot of it.

**A humidifier.** Your baby probably won't need this right away, it's true, but for little babies, who can't take cold medicine, a humidifier is one of the most highly recommended comfort measures. And if your little one is unlucky enough to get a cold in his first month or two of life, *your* life will be a whole lot easier if you already have one of these tucked away in the closet. Eventually you'll need it, so you may as well put it on your list (or pick one up) now.

A small table-top water fountain produces moisture in the air and a soothing sound that may help Baby relax. He has, after all, spent nine months in a water environment. At the very least it may calm you on nights when you're both in the rocker in quest of sleep!

**Mom stuff.** Don't forget about your own needs when you're purchasing and registering. In the early days of motherhood, some items can make your recovery a lot smoother. This includes nice, absorbent breast pads if you'll be breastfeeding, a heating pad or rice pack (nice for soothing post-birth cramps), and nipple cream. A nursing pillow is a nice investment and can make breastfeeding much more comfortable. Meagan loved her organic Nesting Pillow from blessednest.com. The buckwheat filler adjusts around the baby, creating a supportive surface to lift her up and hold her in place. That way Mom doesn't have to hunch over or struggle to keep the baby still while she's getting the hang of breastfeeding.

## WAIT FOR IT

### Clothing
**Snowsuits and coats.** These items are an investment and you want to be sure they'll fit. Think about it this way: Newborns often come out weighing six pounds. They also often come out weighing closer to ten pounds. That's a pretty big difference in size!

**Shoes.** Same reasoning as above. Yes, there will be adorable little shoes you'll have a hard time resisting. Just don't go overboard.

### Furniture and Gear
**A stroller.** This may seem counterintuitive. Strollers are one of those items that usually end up on the gift registry or purchased way in advance. But until your baby is here, it's not going to be easy for you to know what you'll really value in a stroller. These are big-ticket items, and I think there is a lot to be said for waiting until the baby is here and you see what your new life as a mom is like before you shell out several hundred dollars. If you do opt to purchase or register for a stroller before your baby is here, do your research. Read reviews online, and consider your lifestyle and what features are really important to you. Ask friends for recommendations. Stop other parents on the street and ask them what they like and don't like about their strollers. This is also a great way to make new friends and tap into the mom community.

**Toys.** Your baby will not be playing with much other than his fists and feet for several months. And despite what clever marketing ploys may suggest, the toys or videos your baby is exposed to at this age aren't going to turn him into a baby genius (that's where you come in, Mom—talking to and interacting with your baby is the best way to build smarts, naturally!).

Whether or not you register for toys, people won't be able to resist buying them for you (and let's face it, you won't be able to resist some of the adorable ones yourself) so believe me, you'll have some on hand when Baby starts showing interest. Toys can take over a baby's room (and the rest of your house) very quickly. I don't recommend you put them on your registry. Instead, wait until Baby's here and seems interested in them to start—slowly and carefully—amassing his collection.

**All the rest.** While there are some gadgets parents swear by for helping to soothe, comfort, and entertain babies, there's no way to know until your baby is on the outside which ones of these she'll need or want. Once she's here, you can start figuring out whether she might sleep better with a white noise machine or whether you can improvise with the fan you already have.

## RE-THINKING THE TRADITIONAL SHOWER

Sometimes expecting parents find that all their immediate baby needs are covered from family hand-me-downs. You still want the baby celebration, but really can't think of a thing to register for. What to do?

One option is not to register at all and just let people give you what they really want to. As a person who loves to give thoughtful gifts, I always enjoy the freedom that "no registry" parties allow me—I can pick up that beautiful handmade baby blanket or picture frame at the local boutique without guilt. You may end up with far more beautiful and unique items than you ever would have found at the baby superstore.

Another idea is to throw a themed party rather than a traditional shower. Some ideas:

- **A diaper shower.** Figure out what type of diapers you'll be using (cloth or disposable) and then ask for a variety of sizes of that type of diaper. You may find yourself set for months.
- **A freezer meal shower.** Ask guests to cook you a healthy meal that can easily be frozen and heated up after the baby's here. By the time the party's over, your freezer will be stocked with foods you can pull out, heat up, and eat when you're too busy or tired to cook.
- **A book shower.** One guest (probably one of the grandparents) gives a beautiful bookcase for your child's room. The rest of the guests bring books. No need to stick to baby books—this is a gift that can last your child a lifetime. Ask guests to bring their treasured childhood favorites or books they wish had been around when they were kids. Personal inscriptions are welcome!
- **A blessingway.** This celebration is actually geared more toward honoring the expecting woman on her journey to motherhood than it is toward filling her house with baby stuff. But if you want to celebrate your baby's upcoming arrival without getting a bunch of new stuff, it's a wonderful alternative.
- **Feel free to come up with your own variation** on this idea. Think about your values and goals for your child: What are things you won't mind her having a LOT of? What will stand the test of time and see her into the

future? What kind of party fits with your family culture—and what will be just plain fun for you and your guests? This is your pregnancy, and you're allowed to call the shots. Think outside the box.

When my friend Donna was pregnant, after the traditional shower festivities, we gathered in a circle. Each guest in turn told the story of how we met Mom and Dad. After that, we went around the circle again, this time offering the baby (we knew her name) our personal wishes for her future. She's a teenager now who treasures this piece of family history. If you offer to be the videographer, you'll be giving a gift that will last longer than any stuffed animal. To paraphrase the commercial: Stuffed toy? $5.00. Baby diapers for a month? $30. Video of Baby's shower? Priceless.

The registration and baby gear–buying process of course is, and should be, a lot of fun. You just want to make sure that the fun you have now doesn't lead to regret down the road. When your baby isn't here yet, it's easy to fall into the trap of getting everything under the sun because she "might" need it. But those infant months are fleeting and all babies are different. The last thing you need to do is clutter up your house with expensive stuff you never wind up using—and then have to unload later. Don't worry, if you decide later that your baby simply *must* have that bouncy seat that plays music, jiggles, and creates a light show at the same time; you can always send your spouse out to pick it up at the nearest discount store—or just buy it online.

# 25 WEEKS PREGNANT

## Set Up the Nursery

**This week, you can**

- Set up your baby's room (or area)
- Consider the ancient wisdom of Feng Shui

WHEN IT COMES to children's rooms, I've seen it all. Is it an odd shape? Is there a cathedral ceiling or are there heavy wooden beams? I remember one young girl's room that was essentially a converted attic. When she got into bed at night, she could touch the sloped ceiling with little effort. (My claustrophobic soul would never have had a moment's rest in that setup!) To make this week as universal as possible, I'm going to assume you have a small room in the shape of a square with a window. You can revamp for any peculiarities your situation presents.

### RECONNECT WITH YOUR OWN CHILDHOOD ROOM

We are great at replicating what we know. When it comes to children's rooms, I've sometimes seen parents go overboard to compensate for what they didn't have when they were young—giving kids hundreds of stuffed animals because they did-n't have any, for example—or replicate the unsavory aspects simply because it's what is comfortable for them. These questions are designed to shed light on our own experiences as children. I'd like to ask you a few questions about the room you had as a young child. You never know what you might discover. You can of course jot down your answers in your trusty baby journal.

Did you have your own room? Did you enjoy spending time there or was it an uncomfortable experience?

Whether you savored or avoided your room, can you give specific reasons for those feelings? Perhaps you had to share the space and felt your brother's stuff took up too much of the room. Or perhaps you loved to read and spent hours in the window seat going off to foreign lands with your books. Specifics here will help you replicate the good and avoid the uncomfortable in the room you are about to set up.

As you grew up, were you allowed to express yourself here or was decorating the province of your mother?

Are you excited about decorating a room for your child? Or is decorating an activity that leaves you feeling inadequate? If it's the latter, can someone help you?

Does your husband defer to you when it comes to the home or he is a Nate Berkus (Oprah's decorator) wannabe? Will you clash over this room? How can you achieve compromise?

A little baby is coming here soon who will grow up and reveal herself along the way. It's far better to consciously set up your child's room in a way that is welcoming, organized, streamlined, and has the ability to grow as he does. Keep these ideas in the back of your mind as you organize this room.

## SETTING UP THE NURSERY

As you think about where to place items, consider these principles from Feng Shui, the art and science of placement. Feng Shui comes to us from the Chinese, but the principles are universal. It includes all aspects of how we set up a space: design (everything from paint color and furniture placement to art selection and imagery), function (making sure everything has a proper home and not living among clutter), and energy (the "feeling" of a space.) Ideally Feng Shui is a balance of these three different aspects of spatial design.

Why consider its principles when you are putting together your baby's room? Each of us has an inner guidance system that can tell us if a space feels good to us or otherwise. Babies have an instinctive response to whether a space feels safe, restful, or stimulating or whether it feels off somehow. Wouldn't you want to know if your environment was affecting your child in some way that you weren't intending?

Most Feng Shui principles just make a lot of practical sense to people, and therefore give you more tools to set up a space that will allow your baby to be healthy, happy, and supported. Other aspects of Feng Shui require a bit of a leap of faith, but the intentions behind these other aspects can add beauty, peace, and good feelings to a space and, when embraced, can add a new layer of possibilities into your life and the lives of those you love.

For this chapter I went straight to my Feng Shui expert, Ariel Joseph Towne (www.thefengshuiguy.com), an old friend and a respected colleague. Here are his top suggestions for placement of items in Baby's room.

### What are the most important things you would absolutely do even if you knew nothing about Feng Shui?

I would not place the baby's bed in the path of the door.

I would place the baby's bed in a corner near two walls so that the baby feels safe.

I would not place a baby's bed in the path of a mirror. If I had to have a mirror in the room, I would cover it with a curtain or shawl at night. (Some would say that the energy that a mirror creates in the room is too stimulating; covering a mirror helps a room to feel smaller, more intimate, and safer so that your baby will rest and rejuvenate through the night.)

I would not place the baby's bed underneath a window.

If I had to have the baby near a window I would check for drafts, I would lower a screen to act as a "solid wall," and I might hang a crystal in the window or a soft baby mobile up above.

I would not put fluorescent or LED lighting near the baby.

I would use full-spectrum lightbulbs to simulate natural light.

I would not paint colors that are hyperstimulating (bright yellows, oranges, pinks, and reds). I would also not paint colors that are too dark and could feel scary, sad, or depressing (no blacks, dark purples, or dark blues).

I would paint in colors that are soothing and calming (soft pastels, earth palates, and natural tones).

### What are some additional things you would do for someone who does embrace Feng Shui?

I would check for electromagnetic frequencies (EMFs) in the room. Unplug things, and don't have the baby's room next to the wireless router or satellite dish. Counteract the effects of EMFs with soft-edged live plants, Himalayan rock salt lamps, or an ionizer.

I would not put the baby's bed on the other side of the wall from a toilet, sink, elevator, or garbage shoot. Movement, even behind walls, can be disruptive to deep rest.

I would not place furniture with sharp edges near where the baby sleeps. Besides being a dangerous thing, sharp edges create energy that can be disruptive to health over long period of time.

I would not place the baby near wall edges or under overhead beams. The same principles apply as above; sharp edges create disruptive energy that can affect people over time.

I would consider blessing the nursery before bringing the baby into the room. The energy from whatever took place in there before can linger, so it is better to create a clean slate. You can do this with your good thoughts and loving intentions or you can use natural aromatherapy sprays or dishes of sea salt to absorb old stuck energy from the room. If you feel that something deeper is afoot, I would not hesitate to call in an expert (a priest, rabbi, shaman, or Feng Shui expert) to perform a blessing.

### LET THE SETUP BEGIN!

### The Crib

Placement of the baby's bed should be first. Whether or not you embrace Feng Shui, I would follow Ariel's guidelines for placement of the bed because they simply make good sense. I'd keep Baby away from a window even if I didn't know a thing about Feng Shui.

Instead of buying a crib and then a bed, why not buy one piece of furniture that converts and grows with your baby? Check out the Catalina 3-in-1 from the Pottery Barn Kids Catalog. (You can see it online and get an idea of what is available before you hit any stores.)

### Chair or Rocker

Be sure you have a comfortable chair or a rocker for times you and your baby will be cozy and together in this space. Children are hard on furniture. They aren't born with an appreciation of fine wood and craftsmanship. Don't give Junior the rocker that's a family heirloom. Give him one that he can be comfortable with as he grows. If you do get a new rocker for this space, consider passing it on to another mom and baby once your child is at the age of playing in his room independently—and replace it with a toy chest or kid chair. I don't think rockers are particularly kid-friendly furniture to begin with—they are too easily flipped over—but you may have your heart set on one. Next month when we work on your bedroom, I'll have another idea for you.

If you can, try to keep any chair from being in line with the entry door, as Ariel recommended for the baby's bed. It will be more calming for both of you.

### Bookcase

A bookcase is a must, as is reading to your child each evening. It spawns a love of learning that is natural, inviting, and will grow over time. I'd bolt it to the wall so that as he grows in strength and begins to explore the room, Baby won't pull it down on himself. In the beginning, you may have books on the upper shelves and a few stuffed animals on the bottom. The top of the bookcase can hold a few containers of items you need to grab all the time. By all means bolt furniture to the wall if you live in earthquake country.

### Dresser

Now and in the future your baby will need a dresser. One with many and deep drawers is worth its weight in gold. If you use a dresser with a wide top, it's easily converted into a changing table, thus saving you some moola. There is a sweet catalog and store called The Land of Nod that will show you the pads you can purchase to convert the top. In fact, they have the perfect dresser should you need one. (This is a sister company to Crate & Barrel.)

If you're on a budget, a well-made solid wood dresser from an antique, consignment, or thrift store may give you much better bang for your buck than a particleboard prefab one from Target. (And it's been around so long, you don't have to worry about off-gassing!)

When you organize your baby's clothes, keep items in groups within a drawer or in separate drawers. When you need a onesie in a hurry, you don't want to be on a fishing expedition through receiving blankets, cloth diapers, and socks! There are inexpensive items that keep clothes sorted in a drawer. They are made for adult T's, underwear, socks, and bras, but you can use them for anything you like. They come in an inexpensive plastic you literally fold together or in elegant wood and cloth varieties. If you want to invest in the latter for Baby now, you can use them later for yourself. (How sneaky of me!)

## Storage Bins

Let's face it: From the moment you announce your pregnancy, stuffed animals are going to start arriving at your home, along with DVDs to turn Baby into Einstein and toys to stimulate her creativity. What this does early on is stimulate your panic: Where the heck am I going to store all this stuff? It's never too early to introduce a baby to the concept of categories: Like items go with like items. Stuffed animals should live in one area and DVDs and CDs in another, and toys of differing types can also be corralled in unison. Again, check out catalogs like Pottery Barn Kids and The Land of Nod for storage ideas.

I love the soft, handwoven cubes called The Roper Collection because you can buy them in different colors. A holder in a specific color for specific items can help your baby learn. After all, you won't be using labels for a few years. Containers in rattan and canvas are also wonderful. You don't want to use heavy storage or items with a sharp edge. Remember too that it's what you give your baby and your attitude that are paramount. If you complain about having to pick up and put away, no matter how cute the containers are the message is clear: This organizing thing is a burden.

### TOY TIPS

When it comes to toys, don't limit your baby's creativity. A little girl can play with classic boys' toys and have her horizons expanded beyond the world of dolls. And a little boy can get in touch with his feminine side if he does have a doll or two. One day she may have to haggle over contracts in a boardroom while her brother helps his wife change diapers and do housework. Skip the stereotypes. It can't hinder; it can only help.

Now when it comes to creative relatives and friends who want to give you life-sized stuffed animals, just say no if you don't have the space. (And how many parents do live in a house that big?) You'll have to put your foot down and explain the house rules to these generous individuals. If they send such items, you will be forced to donate them to a charity or preschool. The best idea is for family and friends to hold onto these items so that the baby will be enchanted when he comes to visit. Of course they will scream about the lack of space, but then that's the whole idea, isn't it? You don't have room either!

One of the sweetest visuals in a baby's room is to put a mesh hammock above his bed and fill it with his soft toys. The key here of course is that you can reach them but your baby cannot. He could suffocate under the toys or choke himself in the mesh. A hammock can be a nice organizing solution, but you simply have to be conscious and careful when and where you use it.

Finally, I love the idea of a toy box, provided the lid is hinged and stays open without a child having to hold it. That's an accident for small fingers and hands just waiting to happen. You won't need one for a year or so but keep that hinge in mind when you do. And do get one with a soft padded top so it can become a place to sit and read.

You'll be choosing your baby's DVDs and CDs for quite some time, so try album storage. You can purchase anything from a fancy leather binder from www.exposures online.com to a utilitarian one from a big office supply store. The inserts that hold the discs can be purchased from places like Exposures and The Container Store.

## THE PUZZLE COMES TOGETHER

As you put the finishing touches on this room, something magical is likely to happen. The reality of what is happening will hit you. I think reality comes in waves for all life-changing events like a birth.

Over the next few months, come into this room frequently. Begin to invest it with the hope and love you feel inside you. Talk to your child. Play music for him. Carly Simon said that when each of her children were born, they instantly related to the music she had been writing while she was pregnant. I have no doubt that your child will feel comfortable in this room because you have crafted it with such care for his enjoyment, his safety, and his growth.

# 26-27 WEEKS PREGNANT

## Go from Bedroom to Sanctuary

**This week, you can**

- Complete the organizing of your bedroom
- Decide on any decorative changes you wish to make
- Schedule time for research or projects
- Consider some organizing solutions for this room

CAN YOU GUESS what the most common visual I encounter is when I enter a new client's home? I find a seemingly organized, clutter-free appearance in the public rooms. If there's clutter, it's hidden away. When I enter the bedroom, however, the mask is off. A swirl of chaos envelops me. Now I wonder how this couple can possibly ever get any rest. If the home is meant to be your sanctuary from the world, your bedroom is your respite from the demands of daily life that may surround you in the home. It's a place for sleep/rest and sex/fun. I know I've said this before but it bears repeating because it's so difficult to find in this busy world of ours. In lieu of a bedroom sanctuary, we so often inadvertently invite the daily chaos into our most private space.

I'm going to share another secret from my life as a professional organizer. Every so often I meet a client who says she wants her entire home to be organized. Can you guess where Mom wants me to start? In her child's bedroom! I try to talk her out of that choice and start with her own. Children need to see that you do what you are asking them to accomplish. Otherwise the organization of their room will be a futile exercise. Why not show your child from day one what an organized bedroom looks like?

On the day I was writing this week's material, I received the following words of wisdom from a Web site I subscribe to called Daily Om (www.DailyOm.com). "It often doesn't occur to us that the best way to create change is not to try to convince others to change but to change ourselves. When we make adjustments from within, we become role models for others, and leading by example is much more inspiring than a lecture or an argument." Changing from within is the best way to positively influence everyone in our lives.

While I am revealing secrets from the professional organizing trade, here's one more: Whenever young children and teens come home from school and see an organized bedroom and closet, they ask if I can do that in their room. Children are drawn to order and want it for themselves. Frankly, I think it's those color-coordinated closets that hook them. And it's never too early to start—you are in the prime position to welcome Baby into an organized world.

Let's look at different issues that may be plaguing your room. Check off the ones that pertain to you. We'll take this one step at a time. And do have your baby journal nearby for any notes you wish to take.

### DECORATING ISSUES

- The room is due for a fresh coat of paint.
- The drapes or blinds are old, flimsy, and in need of repair or replacement.
- The bed linens are frayed, yellow with age, and/or completely uninviting; the mattress offers no support.
- The dog or cat's claws have shredded the bedspread or duvet cover.
- There are stains on the rug from when Fido was a puppy. And that was five years ago.
- There is a huge flat-screen TV in the room and a computer on a desk. There's enough electrical stimulation to take your mind off the fact this is the sole source of fun in this room.
- The walls in any room tell a story. Yours may be full of photos from the past, artwork you had in college, or decorative items you regretted buying

as you exited the store. But worst of all are bare walls! They always speak to me of a couple who have not yet taken emotional ownership of the space. It's as if they are perpetually living in just-moved-in status. I call this "hotel syndrome" because that's what the room looks and feels like.

### ORGANIZING CHALLENGES IN THE ROOM

- A stack of books blocks easy access to the bed.
- The nightstands have miscellaneous items piled high and the drawers are equally stuffed.
- Clothes are draped over the one easy chair in the room. The clothes get wrinkled and it's impossible to enjoy the chair.
- Don't look to the dresser for solace: The drawers are stuffed to the gills. Who knows what's lurking in the bottom layers?
- If there is already a child in the home, this room looks like an annex for Toys "R" Us. Wait! Maybe those toys belong to Fido or Fluffy?
- There is so much stuff scattered everywhere, you can't dust or vacuum.

### WHERE TO BEGIN?

As we have done elsewhere, there will be items you know must be tended to; however, the time may not be right. New window treatments may have to wait for a year. On the other hand, if you are going to have your baby's room painted, why not ask the painter to do both rooms? You may be able to negotiate a better rate.

The key is to decide what you are going to tackle immediately and then schedule it on your calendar. Break the end result down into the steps that will bring it to completion. For example, you might note that on Thursday you will shop for paint samples/chips and tomorrow you have to find a painter. Before you call anyone, select a few dates that will work in your schedule. Check everything with your spouse on the chance he has a lead on a painter or plans for the days you think might work. Hormones may now be giving you "mommy brain" and keeping details in your head is asking for trouble.

Have you ever noticed that after a move to a new home your furniture and decorative items look different? You get to appreciate them in a new way. You can have that experience just by moving your furniture. (My housekeeper says she's sure that if I could put my furniture on rollers it would be in different positions every time she came to clean.) Last week I introduced you to Feng Shui. Go back now and re-read Ariel's notes with your bedroom in mind. For example, are you sleeping with your head in line with the entry door? You might want to rearrange the furniture in this room for a different experience. No one has to know it's for better Feng Shui!

## MIRROR, MIRROR ON THE WALL: WHAT THE HECK DO I NEED HERE AFTER ALL?

Let's look at some common solutions to the organizing challenges I presented above:

**A bookcase.** Do you have a virtual library next to your bed? Does it spill from the nightstand onto the floor? You need a bookcase. There are folding, portable ones; fancy ones that match the wood in your bedroom set; or inexpensive ones from the home store. Corral those books!

**A nightstand.** Your nightstand should be something of a mini-command post. But that doesn't mean that it's going to hold everything except the kitchen sink. Here are some key items you might need: medications, glasses, pen or pencil and paper, tissues, and the book you are currently reading. You might fancy a framed photo and certainly a good reading lamp. One of you will have the remote should a TV be in the room. What have you crowded onto and into your nightstand?

It's wonderful to line these drawers with the thick liner I suggested for the

Old towels and sheets are always needed at your local animal shelter or animal hospital. Even if you don't have a pet of your own, consider donating these items to help abandoned and sick animals in your city. You don't need to make an appointment; just drop them off with a smile.

kitchen. And do make use of drawer containers; in this room you might want wood containers and a liner with a design rather than plain. You'll find the former in any kitchen department and the latter at The Container Store. Don't worry if these drawers go from crowded to relatively empty. Baby items will soon fill the void. Here are some examples of the items you may want to have close at hand: pacifiers (they are always getting lost, and it's nice to have a spare tucked away in the bedroom), a burp cloth for those messy little emergencies, and maybe even a diaper and a small container of wipes in case you've just gotten comfy in bed when Baby decides to mess her diaper. Keep a bottle of water here. You never know when you might get stuck in bed under a sleeping or nursing baby and suddenly realize you are desperately thirsty! Meagan tucked stationery and pens into her bedside drawer so that when she found herself stuck, she could keep her hands and mind busy writing thank-you notes.

**A chair.** If you are lucky enough to have a chair in your room, I invite you to enjoy it! You will really want it available to you after Baby comes so you can sit here and breastfeed. If you have continued to toss clothes here even after you organized your closet, ask yourself why. Perhaps you need to make the action of hanging up your clothes the new habit you cultivate?

If you have a glider/rocker already in your home, your room is now probably the ideal place for it. Perhaps the comfy chair you currently have in your room could be re-covered with some baby- or child-friendly motif and go into the baby's room. Getting ready can be more a matter of moving furniture than buying new pieces. Don't think of your furniture as set in stone wherever it is currently placed. Consider giving some pieces a new life in a different location.

**A dresser.** Pity the poor dresser whose contents are so crammed it's a treasure hunt every time you open a drawer. You'll need to attack these drawers one at a time. Toss the junk. Donate what you can. Are there items you could hang in your closet? Many of my clients fold their jeans and put them in a dresser. Items like this are bulky and take up too much room. It's best to hang them. When it comes to the surface of your dresser, do you have too many knickknacks and photos out? Let's keep all the surfaces in this room as clear as possible for now. You want to make way for items like a baby monitor. You don't want to add them to the clutter.

**Storage.** If you have CDs and DVDs in this room, consider putting them into albums. Divide your collection by type. When you want to see the latest James Bond release or listen to the Rolling Stones you'll know just where to go.

If you have a young child at home already, why not have one or two special items (including books) in your bedroom for him to enjoy when he shares the space with you. Keep toys and stuffed animals in a basket. Make a special section on your bookcase for his books. It won't keep the romance alive in your relationship if you and your husband feel like you're living at F. A. O. Schwarz! Nor will it do much to teach your child about boundaries and how special a bedroom can be.

You'll want to corral your pets' toys as well. When you get to the point when you can't see your feet, you will be grateful there are no bones or fake mice to trip over on this floor.

## WHAT YOU DON'T NEED IN THE BEDROOM

**Miscellaneous items.** I'm not a fan of under-the-bed storage; however, sometimes I understand it's necessary. Please don't store memorabilia, photos, seasonal decorations, or other miscellaneous items here. There are under-bed storage containers meant for this spot. They become in essence extensions of your dresser (or a replacement for the one you don't have) and can hold seasonal items like heavy sweaters and long johns when it's summer.

**Electronics.** If the computer has to live in this room, we've previously discussed marking off the territory dedicated to work with an area rug or decorative screen. Power down at night so you won't be tempted to check e-mail at 3:00 a.m.

Does your TV hold a position of honor in your bedroom? Different strokes for different folks, as they say. I am a purist who prefers to have no modern technology in my bedroom. If you can, place items like the TV, DVD player, and others, inside a cabinet. During the day and when you are

### COMMUNICATE

You and your spouse will be busy this month getting your home ready for the arrival of your son or daughter. During this time, I have no doubt you'll be entertaining fantasies of one day doing things with your child that your parents did with you. Dads play catch on the lawn with their sons while moms introduce their daughters to makeup. Many families also have traditions. But I can't stress the idea of communication often enough. How does it tie in this month? Let me tell you the story of Tony and Brooke.

Tony comes from a big New York Italian family. His parents kept an open-door policy when it came to their bedroom. Everyone piled in at will to talk, share, and comfort each other. They watched movies in their pj's on Friday nights. They left toys strewn on the floor. If you had a problem to discuss or a joy to share, you piled on Mom and Dad's bed and all was made right.

Brooke, on the other hand, was raised in a prim and proper Midwestern home by parents who kept their bedroom off limits to their children. You see where this is headed, right? Tony wanted to replicate his parents' open-door policy and Brooke was horrified by the very idea. It took some time and a lot of communicating but I'm happy to report a compromise was reached. Now they have their own family tradition and it's a nice blend of the two extremes.

What assumptions do you have about the master bedroom?

ready to sleep at least you can literally close the door on these activities.

**Heavy wall hangings.** If you live in an earthquake-prone area, don't hang heavy items above your bed. You'd be amazed by what I have seen. In the event of a big quake, you don't want a heavy mirror to fall on you while you sleep, or worse, have Baby hit when she's sleeping with both of you.

If the room itself is overflowing with "stuff," it's time to get real and make some decisions. What is this stuff? Do you have too much furniture? Are suitcases from your last trip still open and littering the landscape? Has it been forever since you got on the treadmill? You'll have to go item by item and be brutally honest about the usefulness of each thing in your room, especially the big-ticket space hogs.

## EMBRACE THE CHANGING LANDSCAPE

You are about to start a new phase in your life. Let the relics of the past move on to new homes and new adventures. It's not uncommon to look around this room and realize you have outgrown it. It no longer reflects who you are. Set the old free and create something new in its place. Just remember that it's your room as a loving couple; it's not an extension of the baby's room. Everyone deserves a space of their own in the home.

# CHAPTER FIVE

# 28 to 32 Weeks Pregnant

We should notice that we are already supported at every moment.
There is the earth below our feet and there is the air, filling our lungs
and emptying them. We should begin from this when we need support.

—NATALIE GOLDBERG, *WRITING DOWN THE BONES*

THERE WILL BE more and more moments now when you say to yourself: "Wow! This is real!" No matter how much we prepare for something, choose it, and intellectually understand the parameters, reality still sets in slowly. I had a friend who was in such panic and denial that he was about to become a father that we gave him his own shower! The baby is growing inside you and you're still adjusting to the reality. Imagine how it might be for Dad, the rest of the family, and your friends.

This month is dedicated to some important details that will set you up for support. I don't want you to be blindsided by any of the myriad decisions you may be asked to make. Forewarned is indeed forearmed. To this end, we'll spend the first week making sure your birth plans are fairly foolproof. Did you know, for example, if you have chosen a hospital birth that you'll likely be spending more time with

the nurses than with your OB-GYN? I have a friend who is an OB-GYN and he tells me the head of the department at his hospital misses just about every birth. He does, however, sail in the next morning with a dozen red roses and a well-rehearsed apology. Your doctor isn't likely to behave like this one; however, you still want to be sure you'll be surrounded by the professionals of your choosing, and that includes the nurses. Ask your obstetrician or midwife about who will provide backup care if she is unable to make it to your birth. Will another care provider in her practice fill in? Ask about meeting other medical staff who might be involved in your care.

In the following week, we zero in on how you can stay connected to others after the birth. Motherhood is a blessing and a joy. It can also be isolating and lonely. But not for you! You need to take conscious steps to stay connected. Let's start now. Make your wishes known. After the excitement dies down, everyone goes back to their same old/same old lives. They may be so caught up in their own realities that they either forget you for the moment or assume that you will call when you need them. Don't play the time-worn "If you really loved me, you'd know" game with anyone. Even if you come from a family of professional psychics, assume they are off duty and need to be told what you need!

Of course, no month would be complete without a little on-your-feet organizing project and this month we're going to work on the laundry and the pantry. Have you ever noticed that moms have an unconscionable amount of laundry to do? We need that room to be in tip-top shape. And personally, I find that pantries are one of my favorite areas in any home. There's something nurturing about an area devoted to food. I don't want you in there after the baby is born asking, "Now I wonder if we have. . . ." I want you to know exactly what you have and where it's located. We end the month with a look at those first weeks Baby will be home. The way you handle this critical juncture will very likely predict the way your careers as parents will be spent. Take this week to consciously communicate with your partner and create an equitable division of labor.

## HABIT OF THE MONTH

### Practice Self-Care

What's that refrain all pregnant women utter? Oh yes: "I feel like a beached whale" or "I'm as big as a house!" If you're eating properly you might stay the size of a small whale but, still, adding twenty-five to thirty-five pounds to your frame is usually part of the process. That doesn't mean you can't have pretty fingers and toes. Make yourself a cup of tea and use a favorite teapot. Get the latest issue of *Vogue* and start dreaming about what pieces you'll add to your wardrobe after you lose the baby weight. Why not create a Dream Board showing a stylish mom having fun with her baby and her husband? Take an aromatherapy bath while your favorite music plays. Wear a piece of jewelry you forgot you have. Read a book while you're in the tub or dim the lights and daydream about the future. Take a nap. Call an old friend you haven't connected with in a long time. Grab your baby journal and list five ways to care for yourself that are unique to you.

# 28 WEEKS PREGNANT

## Finalize Your Birth Plan

**This week, you can**

- Create a more specific birth plan
- Talk to your care provider to make sure you're on the same page

BY NOW, you've had a chance to do some serious reading about labor and delivery. Now that you have some data about common hospital procedures and interventions, take a few minutes to go through this list of common birth-related procedures and ask yourself how you feel about each one. Remember that every goal, whether it's getting labor started or making contractions more comfortable, has several alternative methods you can try to get there. Thinking about each option separately will help you tease out exactly what it is you do or don't like about the idea of each medication or procedure. Knowing the choices available to you means you'll be armed with the information you need to make the choice that's right for you. If the need to take action arises, you can usually start with the option you are most comfortable with and then work your way down the list.

Here's an example of why I think it's so important to have a real handle on the different medications and procedures you'll

likely be confronted with in the delivery room. A mom I know named Heather went through her first pregnancy with only a basic understanding of the medical side of labor and delivery. She wanted a natural birth and had a general idea that she would try to avoid an induction. However, some test results close to her due date concerned her doctor, who wanted to get labor started. Heather didn't realize that there is more than one option for getting labor going, and checked into the hospital early the next morning to start her Pitocin drip. Since Pitocin causes stronger-than-average contractions that come on much faster than a typical labor would, Heather found that the rest of her birth plan was thrown out the window as she struggled to cope.

During her next pregnancy, Heather again had troubling end-of-pregnancy lab results and her doctor wanted to induce. This time, she understood that there were a few things they could try before they skipped right to the Pitocin, and she asked her doctor if they could start with a prosta-glandin gel and stripping her membranes. It worked! Her contractions started that night and by the next evening she'd had her baby . . . without pain medication. Heather never had Pitocin and her second labor was much easier to handle.

Following is a chart that will keep each of these topics separate and give you a way to define which procedures and interventions you're just fine with, which you'd rather avoid, and which ones you want to discuss more with your care provider, both now and as they come up during labor. This chart includes the most common procedures and medications, but it's not exhaustive, so I also left blank spaces at the end of each section for you to fill in if needed.

With your chart in hand, you'll be prepared to talk to your doctor or midwife about your concerns without forgetting any details. You don't have to bring up every single thing on the list. Instead, use it as a tool for determining your priorities and areas of greatest concern. Ultimately you'll be able to use the information you've gleaned to have a frank discussion with your care provider about your birth plan, and make sure the two of you are on the same page. I recommend doing this in week twenty-eight of your pregnancy because you'll be able to tell a lot by the conversation you have with your care provider—and if it doesn't go well, there's still time to switch practices. If your doctor or midwife is thoughtful and respectful and takes time to go over each of your concerns and come up with compromises, that's a

> If you'll be delivering in a teaching hospital, student doctors and nurses could have a large involvement in your care. Think ahead of time about how much of your care you'd like to turn over to them. For example, you may be just fine with a student taking your vitals but would prefer they didn't perform internal exams. You may be just fine having a room full of people you barely know watching you push your baby out . . . but you may not. Speak up! It is your right to determine who will perform your care and be present at your birth.

good sign even if she ultimately thinks some of your wishes aren't likely to happen. If she brushes you off, condescends, or, worse, seems put out or offended that you'd state your preferences, that's a huge red flag. You need your care provider to be on your team. If this isn't the case for you, strongly consider finding another one. The third trimester is not too late to shop around, but you'll want to do it quickly, as many practices won't take on new patients who are very close to their due dates.

After you've spoken to your doctor or midwife, it's time for possibly the most important part of your birth plan—the hospital tour. Why is this so important? Most of the time, the nurses on duty at the hospital have much more one-on-one contact with a laboring mother than does her obstetrician, who checks in with nurses (often from home) during the bulk of labor and then comes in as Mom's getting ready to push. What does that mean? Your nurses have a huge amount of say over the care you'll get while in labor, and the hospital's procedures will determine whether or not some of your wishes are do-able. For example, your OB may think it's a great idea for you to walk around during labor, but if it's the hospital policy that moms must be constantly tethered to a monitor, it'll be much harder for you to make that wish a reality. Whether or not you'll be allowed to eat and drink, walk around, have guests, or skip the routine IV is largely determined by hospital protocol.

Just as you have preferences for how you'd like your birth to go, nurses have their own opinions as well. Some have a decidedly "birth is a medical event" mind-set, while others view it more as a natural process best left unmanaged. When you check into the hospital in labor, take a moment to tell the nurse about your preferences.

Certain nurses may be more willing than others to "bend" the rules, but if the labor and delivery unit is always very busy, you may find it more difficult to have things your way. That's because straying from standard operating procedure takes more time and effort on the nurses' parts—and if they're already stretched thin as it is, they may not be able or willing to do the extra work. Don't forget to ask about your postpartum care and newborn procedures as well—too many moms focus on the birth and forget about the environment they'll be getting to know their new baby in. It's important! Will you be allowed to room in with your baby? Is there a board-

certified lactation consultant on staff to help with breastfeeding issues? If it turns out that your baby has to spend time in the neonatal intensive care unit (NICU), will you have close, regular access to him? The NICU is a reality for many babies, even if it's just for a brief time, so factor in how "mother friendly" it seems.

Ask questions, and if you have concerns, don't be afraid to research other hospitals and birth centers in your area to see if there's a better fit. Visit www.motherfriendly.org for a list of hospitals deemed "mother-friendly" by the Coalition for Improving Maternity Services.

As you look around at hospital options and talk with your doctor or midwife, you're likely starting to see how complicated this birth plan business is. Even if your care provider is 100 percent on board with your wishes, you can't guarantee your nurses will be. And vice versa. You also can't predict what your body or baby will do while you're in labor, which throws another wrench of unpredictability into the whole process. Try to relax, and if you haven't strongly considered hiring a doula yet, now may be the time to start looking. She can help you make sense of what you've learned through talking with your care provider and touring the hospital, and can work with you to figure out how to get the best possible experience you can. Hiring a doula is the first big step you'll take in setting up your support network, which we'll be working on next week. For now, take a deep breath. Don't worry—one way or another, this baby is going to come out!

| | SURE | LET'S TALK | NO THANKS | NOTES |
|---|---|---|---|---|
| *Induction of Labor* | | | | |
| Induction using prostaglandin gel | ☐ | ☐ | ☐ | _____ |
| Induction with Pitocin | ☐ | ☐ | ☐ | _____ |
| Stripping membranes | ☐ | ☐ | ☐ | _____ |
| Breaking bag of waters | ☐ | ☐ | ☐ | _____ |
| | | | | |
| *Pain Relief* | | | | |
| Narcotic pain relief such as Demerol or Nubain | ☐ | ☐ | ☐ | _____ |
| Regular epidural | ☐ | ☐ | ☐ | _____ |
| "Walking" epidural | ☐ | ☐ | ☐ | _____ |
| Laboring in water | ☐ | ☐ | ☐ | _____ |
| | | | | |
| *People Present During Labor* | | | | |
| Student doctors/ nurses present | ☐ | ☐ | ☐ | _____ |
| Student doctors performing procedures | ☐ | ☐ | ☐ | _____ |
| Doula | ☐ | ☐ | ☐ | _____ |
| "Non-essential" hospital personnel | ☐ | ☐ | ☐ | _____ |
| Older children, friends, relatives Describe: | ☐ | ☐ | ☐ | _____ |
| | | | | |
| *Other common procedures* | | | | |
| IV fluids | ☐ | ☐ | ☐ | _____ |
| Antibiotics during labor | ☐ | ☐ | ☐ | _____ |
| Constant electronic fetal monitoring | ☐ | ☐ | ☐ | _____ |

|  | SURE | LET'S TALK | NO THANKS | NOTES |
|---|---|---|---|---|
| Internal fetal monitoring | ☐ | ☐ | ☐ | _____ |
| Episiotomy | ☐ | ☐ | ☐ | _____ |
| Forceps | ☐ | ☐ | ☐ | _____ |
| Vacuum extractor | ☐ | ☐ | ☐ | _____ |

*Mother's Freedoms*

| | | | | |
|---|---|---|---|---|
| Upright/walking in labor | ☐ | ☐ | ☐ | _____ |
| Ability to change positions during labor | ☐ | ☐ | ☐ | _____ |
| Eat and drink during labor | ☐ | ☐ | ☐ | _____ |
| Labor and give birth in my own clothing | ☐ | ☐ | ☐ | _____ |
| Push in a standing, squatting or other non-reclined position | ☐ | ☐ | ☐ | _____ |
| Deliver in water | ☐ | ☐ | ☐ | _____ |

*Postpartum Plan*

| | | | | |
|---|---|---|---|---|
| Hold baby immediately after birth | ☐ | ☐ | ☐ | _____ |
| Breastfeed the baby immediately after birth | ☐ | ☐ | ☐ | _____ |
| Bonding time before sutures/ newborn procedures | ☐ | ☐ | ☐ | _____ |

*Baby*

| | | | | |
|---|---|---|---|---|
| Rooming in with Mom | ☐ | ☐ | ☐ | _____ |
| Bottles in nursery | ☐ | ☐ | ☐ | _____ |
| Pacifiers in nursery | ☐ | ☐ | ☐ | _____ |
| Circumcision | ☐ | ☐ | ☐ | _____ |

# 29 WEEKS PREGNANT

## Make New Friends and Keep the Old

**This week, you can**

- Start making concrete plans for a post-baby social life with other moms
- Be sure your old friends ride the baby wave into your new life with you

PICTURE THIS SCENARIO. It's six months from now, on a cold, gray, rainy (or snowy!) day. Your baby's mood seems to match the weather—she's been fussing for hours. You've had your fill of daytime talk shows since about two months ago. You feel like climbing the walls, in fact. Between sobbing bouts, your baby just stares at you and eats her toes—she's definitely no conversationalist yet.

You're bored. And it's just occurred to you that you have no one you can call. All your friends from your "old" life are at work right now. As for other mom friends? Well, you don't really have any.

Sounds awful, doesn't it? New motherhood can be wonderful, life-changing, and fascinating. Sometimes, it can also be boring as all get-out. It's too easy to find yourself stuck at home with only soap opera heroines for friends. Unfortunately, too many moms wait until they're walloped with the isolation that can be life as a new

mother before they try to do something about it. And when the weather's rotten, you aren't sure where all the other moms are, you're sleep-deprived, and maybe you have a touch of the baby blues, it's not the best time to *start* the process of seeking out friends and things to do.

This six-months-from-now scenario can look quite different if you start working on setting up your post-motherhood social life while still pregnant. Maybe you'll send a message to the moms on your local e-mail list, asking if anyone wants to meet up at the coffee shop to chat over a latte. Or perhaps you'll call that mom you really hit it off with during your childbirth class to check in. The two of you can congratulate each other and have a nice chat. Or if you're really organized, you'll know when and where there are a variety of different mom's groups happening in the area and you'll be able to say to yourself "Oh, it's Tuesday at noon—at two o'clock, there's a La Leche League meeting across town! I think I'll go."

If you'll be returning to work post-baby, don't just think you'll pick up your old social life where it left off and everything will be back to "normal." You're heading toward a new normal now, and you need to seek out other mom friends. Mothers in your community are a rich resource. Through them, you'll learn about the best preschools and pediatricians. Other moms have the scoop on different put-baby-to-sleep methods and will give you the unvarnished truth about teething and ear infections. If you already have a lot of mom friends at work, you may be covered here. But it can't hurt to branch out, and it's best to organize your efforts ahead of time to make the transition to motherhood as easy as possible.

After all, being organized doesn't just help you find the right place to put your things. It's also about how you keep track of information and manage your relationships. When you have a baby, your relationships will change. You won't be able to rely on comfortable old habits for sustaining the friendships you've already got. And you'll have to come up with a plan for nurturing potential friendships as new people enter your life via your child. Knowing where you put the phone number of that mom you met at the playground last week could mean the difference between a long, lonely afternoon and the beginning of a wonderful new friendship. Remembering to schedule in a twice-monthly lunch date with your oldest and dearest friend could mean the difference

between a relationship that grows distant as your lives change in different ways and a relationship that weathers and even benefits from those differences and stands the test of time. The choice is yours. Put yourself on the path to strong post-pregnancy friendships now.

## NEW FRIENDSHIPS: WHERE DO I FIND THE OTHER MOMS?

One of the biggest questions, of course, is where exactly to track down other moms with whom you can forge a friendship. After all, since the baby isn't actually here yet, it might look a little odd to show up at Gymboree and start clapping along with "The Wheels on the Bus." So you may have to get a little creative in order to find and befriend pregnant women and mothers.

If you're very friendly and outgoing, this may be no problem at all. You're probably the type who seeks potential buddies everywhere you go, easily striking up conversations and exchanging contact information. But the less bold might crave a more formal venue for getting to know other expecting moms. Here are some ideas:

**Pregnancy support groups**. You'll find them in most big cities and many smaller ones. They may be run through an organization or church, or may meet informally in someone's home. Pregnancy support groups give you an opportunity to talk over the ups and downs of pregnancy and impending motherhood with other women in the same place as you. Some possibilities to track down pregnancy support groups:

- Check the catalog of your local YMCA or Parks and Recreation Department
- Ask the owner of the local baby boutique
- Check with your hospital or birth center, yoga studio, health club, or any mom- and baby-related business or organization
- Ask your childbirth instructor, midwife, doctor, or doula
- Look at the bulletin board at your local coffee shop, library, or bookstore
- Search Craigslist or other online venues like mommyandme.com
- Start your own! Let moms in your area know about your group by hanging flyers in local stores and cafes, and posting at Web sites like mommy andme.com and mothering.com. The local library or toy store might let you use their space, or you can rotate the group through participants' homes.

**La Leche League**. This is an organization devoted to supporting breastfeeding women, and pregnant women are always welcome. The group meetings can be a great way to make new friends as well as to get information you'll need to get off to a good start breastfeeding. Check www.llli. org for a searchable directory of groups near you.

**Mom's groups**. Many of them are especially welcoming to pregnant women and will enjoy the opportunity to help initiate you into the "club" of motherhood. Try Mothers of Preschoolers (MOPS) at www. mops.org.

**Social media**. Over the past few years there has been a virtual explosion of "mommy blogs" in which women chronicle their adventures and thoughts on motherhood. You'll also find a rich array of blogs that can help tie you to your pre-motherhood self, whether your passions include crafting, politics, art, music, cooking, gardening, or any other imaginable topic. Jump in and comment! Soon you'll find that you're getting to know other readers and maybe even considering starting a blog of your own. Blogs and other social media, like online forums, Facebook, and Twitter, can provide ready-made community whenever and wherever it's convenient for you to log in . . . there's no need to drag a baby out on a blustery day. Just be careful: While online community is great, it can't replace the immediate, hands-on support of in-real-life friends. Don't forget to get off the computer and go out and find people in your own community (or better yet, use the Internet to help you find them, as my next paragraph will illustrate!).

**Online**. A variety of Web sites help bring together people with similar interests in the same community so they can take their relationships to the third dimension. Try moms.meetup.com and momslikeme.com to get started. You can also search Yahoo!

Groups (groups.yahoo.com) and Google Groups (groups.google.com) for mom gatherings in your area.

## KEEPING TRACK OF POTENTIAL FRIENDS

If you're not great at remembering names or linking them with faces (and possibly even if you are!), it won't do to simply plug your new acquaintances' names and contact details into your iPhone or address book. Pregnancy and early motherhood is going to, in a short time, throw you into many new experiences and places with a lot of people you've never met before—and may never meet again, unless you put forth some effort. In your previous experiences making friends at work or school, you probably worked with or near the same people for months or years and had ample opportunity to develop friendships based on proximity. This is different. Pregnancy is short, new moms are busy and often overwhelmed, and your exposure to these potential new friends could be limited.

To make matters more complicated, "mommy brain" is not just a stereotype—it's a scientifically studied phenomenon. Pregnancy and early motherhood have a funny way of turning even the sharpest brain as fuzzy as a Monet painting. You'll find yourself thinking of that wonderful, funny woman you met in your childbirth class and wondering if she had her baby yet. Wouldn't it be great to get together one of these days? And then you'll realize

you have no recollection of her name. It's simply leaked out of one of the holes that the demands of motherhood has punched in your memory. And where did you put that scrap of paper where you scribbled down her phone number again?

Don't let that happen! Instead of mixing all these potential new friends in with your business contacts, old friends, and family in your existing address book, try keeping a small notebook in your purse where you can jot down their names and pertinent information . . . as much information as possible, as it will help you keep them straight later and will also give you some fodder for conversation. Your notebook might look like this:

**Name:** *Paige Johnson*

**Contact Information:** *555-3334*
*paige@mail.com*

**Work Info:** *Freelance graphic designer*

**Children?** *2 year old, Thomas*
*Pregnant with baby girl, due in June*

**Identifying information:** *Lives in Uptown neighborhood, long brown hair, very sarcastic*

Months from the day you meet Paige, when you read her entry in the notebook, you'll immediately remember her brown hair and biting wit. You'll know her older son's name, when she was due, what sex baby she had, and her name. Best yet, you'll be able to get in touch with her because all this information is at your fingertips and easy to find. Maybe it seems a little silly now to keep these kinds of detailed notes, but you won't regret it later. However, you may want to wait until Paige has walked away before you start documenting her personal details!

If you do elect to use your usual Rolodex system or PDA to keep track of new friends' information, make sure to include some identifying bits of information you can use later in the "notes" area, for example, "Met during prenatal yoga. She wore pink top and had red hair. Is a nurse at Memorial Hospital. Likes wine." Include any notes that will jog your memory later. It may help to group your new acquaintances together in one place, wherever it is you keep track of them. For instance, in your address book, you could alphabetize them all under "M" and give them each a title, for example, "Mom Friend: Kristy," "Mom Friend: Wendy," and so on. That way, when you're struggling to remember the name of that potential soul mate you chatted with in your Hypnobirthing class, you can pull up "M" for "Mom Friends" and flip through the entries until you find the right one. Much easier than searching your entire address book!

## PLANNING FOR FUTURE ACTIVITIES

When you have a new baby in the house, it's easy for time to take on a whole new meaning. Your baby will be waking up to eat 'round the clock, you'll probably be napping during the day to catch up on lost sleep, and it's easy to lose track of what time it is . . . okay, what day it is, too. Those early weeks of motherhood are not the time to be filling out registration forms or trying to juggle scheduling. Plan ahead now by looking at the calendars of different groups and other classes in the area and try to form a basic plan for which ones you'll attend, and when. Flip your calendar or PDA to a month or two after your due date and pencil (or punch) in classes and activities that interest you, along with times, locations, cost, Web sites, and any other necessary information. That way when you're starting to feel like it's time to get out of the house with your new baby, you won't have to go looking for all that information again.

Don't over-commit yourself . . . in fact, don't commit in stone to *anything* just yet. Getting used to life with a baby may be more challenging than you expect, and if your little angel decides she's going to take a nice solid nap from noon until three every day, I strongly encourage you to enjoy the peace and time to yourself rather than interrupting the nap just because you feel like you're "supposed" to go to Baby Yoga classes at 1:30! If you have to sign up for something in advance to hold your spot, go ahead, but never be afraid to change your mind . . . particularly if your sanity is on the line.

## HOLDING ON TO OLD FRIENDS

Now is the time to give your dear old friends their own special place in your calendar. If you have a friendship that's always been freewheeling and unscheduled in the past, have a talk with your friend. Explain that from now on you're going to need a little extra planning time to go out so you can coordinate your schedule with your babysitter, spouse, or partner. And let her know that for the first few outings you may want or need to include the baby. Sit down with your friend and schedule out regular "dates" for the first six months or so of the baby's life . . . long enough to make your new arrangement a habit. Be sure to share your calendar with your spouse or sitter so everyone knows the plan. You may not see your old friend as much as you did pre-baby, but as long as you both make a regular effort to spend time together, your friendship can weather the changes.

It seems to me there are two kinds of mothers in the world: those who socialize exclusively with other mothers and those who maintain contact with their old friends while making new ones in the mommy world. I hope you'll toss your hat firmly into the latter ring. Over the years my friends who made no distinction between the friends who had children and those who did not have told me it was refreshing to spend time with someone who didn't want to discuss diapers, school grades, or the SATs. Remember that the next time you think to yourself: "Oh! I can't call Mary Jane. She doesn't have children; she wouldn't understand." Mary Jane may not know the best brand of diaper to buy but she just might keep you connected to the latest news from your favorite baseball team or television show. Even if the days when you could return calls right away or go out at a moment's notice are over, you can still keep the lines of communication open. E-mail, IMs, text messages, snail mail, voice mail, and carrier pigeons give you a lot of options. Give them all a chance to love you. In the end that's what friendship and communication are all about.

When your baby is here, we'll revisit your social life to help give it a nudge in the right direction. Right now, it's hard to know just how you'll be feeling when you've got an infant to care for. Many women find themselves turning inward, feeling more introverted and introspective, when they have new babies. That's normal. But it's still a good idea to set yourself up now for a rich social life. That way, when you're ready, you can jump right in . . . instead of wasting time searching the bottom of your purse for that lost phone number.

# 30 WEEKS PREGNANT

## Organize Your Pantry and Laundry Room

This week, you can

- Clean out your pantry
- Organize your pantry for ease of retrieval and maximum use of the space
- Streamline your laundry room or laundry area
- Create a shopping list in Excel and post it
- Discuss the chores that will keep these areas organized

WHEN IT COMES to food stockpiles at home, people seem to be divided into two groups. The first are what I'll call the "fly by the seat of your pants" folks. They wing it in the kitchen and pretty much in life. Why spend time making a shopping list, they muse, when you can live dangerously and never know exactly what's in the pantry? They find themselves at the grocery store several times a week. "Gosh, I hope I got everything I need" is their mantra. You hear them chant it to the cashier at checkout. Later you can hear their screams as they discover that the missing ingredient for tonight's impromptu pasta primavera is . . . pasta!

In the other group are the "I gotta be prepared" guys and gals. They shop once a week with a list and they never, ever enter a food store when they are hungry. Fre-

quently, they are recipe collectors. The world is full of food adventures they hope to have one day. There isn't much to say about this group. They are rather dull, really, always saving money, time, and energy. The latter have an easier time in the world in general, and certainly when it comes to eating at home. However, membership in the former group is huge. Which group are you in?

### DAYS ONE AND TWO: WHAT'S IN YOUR PANTRY?

For our purposes, I'm going to help you organize a walk-in pantry. I realize not everyone has one, but you can easily adapt the tips and tricks to your situation. Even a small area devoted to food storage should be an orderly space. In fact, you'd think it would be easy to organize and maintain. But there is a pantry gremlin who routinely invades the space, making it almost impossible to find anything. If you create and maintain food categories, however, the gremlin is guaranteed to move on to a new home. He'll think yours is a big bore.

Let's start with another speed elimination. Depending on how you are feeling at this moment in your pregnancy, you might have to enlist the aid of a friend. Again the key in choosing your assistant is that he or she be someone willing to do your bidding. They can offer an opinion but they are not welcome to take over and run the show. I'll let you decide if your mother-in-law is right for this assignment.

Set a timer for twenty minutes. Peer into your pantry and pretend you've never seen it before. Going shelf by shelf, I'd like you to look for items you can discard: food items that have expired, items you know you will never use again (you might be able to donate them to a food bank or shelter depending on the packaging), and items that don't belong in a pantry. A good example would be your cleaning supplies: Chemicals shouldn't be stored near food. Even in the supermarket they have their own aisle. Another example: Do you keep kitchen equipment or serving pieces here? If you don't have any other place to keep these items and they aren't robbing you of food storage space, you get a pass. OK, ladies and gentlemen, start your speed elimination engines and meet me back here in twenty minutes.

I don't want to continue until you clean up any mess that was created during this activity. Bag or box the expired food and take it out to the trash. Bag or box any food items you wish to donate. Place them in your car or call a friend and ask him to make the delivery for you. Do you have to move any items to the dining room or the garage? When you organized the kitchen, did you make room for some of the cooking tools you had stored in the pantry? Be sure you tend to any items that need to be moved at this time.

The next step is a bit tricky because I can't see the size of your pantry or how much counter space you have in your kitchen. But it's rare not to be able to take the next step with ease and a little elbow grease. I'd like you to take out what's in the pantry but not in a wild frenzy. Please organize the items into categories on your counters. You need to know how many cans of soup you have, how much pasta there is, and whether you need any tomato sauce.

After that phase is complete, the pantry needs a good cleaning. This poor area usually gets swept and wiped down on move-in day and then ignored. Take a damp cloth to the shelves and clean the floor. Clearly your helper has to be a good sport to do this for you! While she's doing that, I have an assignment for you.

### Kitchen Tools to the Rescue

Once you see your food in categories on your counter, you may be amazed. Who knew you had twelve cans of chicken soup hidden in the debris? Did you remember those lasagna noodles you got a month ago at the gourmet food shop? And what about that Texas hot sauce you picked up in the Dallas airport last Christmas when you were changing planes? I'm going to give you the tools, tips, and tricks I use to organize a pantry. You won't lose track of food ever again. Read through this list. If you're near a computer, check the items out online. Create a shopping list so you and your helper can head to the store right after lunch. It doesn't take long to put the puzzle back together when you have the right tools.

Remember the shelf dividers I suggested for your closet? They can work wonders in a pantry. You want to be sure the categories stay divided.

To that end, label the shelves. No one needs to remember the setup; all they have to do is read. When relatives come after the baby is born, you want them to know exactly where to place things; otherwise today is an exercise in futility.

There are wonderful containers called grid totes at The Container Store that work well to hold different types of food. I suggested you research them when we were looking at the area under the kitchen sink. They are easy to grab, come in two sizes and many colors, and are easy to keep clean.

What would you store in these totes? All of those wonderful food packets people collect like instant salad dressing, mix for Sloppy Joes and instant soups can be tucked into a small, square tote. Otherwise they tend to pop up on every shelf like weeds. Do you have small packages of

food? The long grid tote will hold them nicely. Very often multiple food items like Ramen noodles come packaged together. Once the packaging is torn open and one is removed, it becomes a free-for-all to keep the others intact. Your grid tote will prevent that from happening.

Many types of pasta come in bags rather than boxes. If you don't corral them, the spirals, the shells, the bow ties, and the tubes will have tumbled on top of each other like puppies in a dog pile. You get the idea!

If you have a large pantry and prefer the look of baskets you can use them instead. Or simply integrate them holding items like onions or garlic.

Shelf creators give you different levels so that your cans of soup or vegetables are easier to spot. They come in different materials and different widths. Baby food (should you elect not to make your own) works perfectly on these shelf creators, as do cat and dog food cans. It's the handiest tool in the pantry!

If you have items like flours and sugars that languish on a shelf after you open them, do invest in airtight containers to keep them fresh. If they are used infrequently and you have a pantry, this is the ideal place to store them rather than a countertop, unless of course you have designer canisters and feel they add a decorative touch to the room. The Container Store as well as the kitchen department of your local home store will carry a variety of types and styles. Rubbermaid makes many of these containers.

Foods like flour and nuts are ripe for pantry moths and other pests, even in sealed packaging. Keeping these foods in glass containers will prevent this problem. Transfer the inviting items to glass the minute you get home from the store and those moths won't be your new tenants! Trust me: It's very tricky to evict them once they move in. Another trick is to place flour and bread in the freezer for 15 minutes; that kills any potential moths. In fact, if you have a large separate freezer, you can store the items in the freezer rather than on a pantry shelf and take them out on an as-needed basis.

### Design Your Pantry

It may not be decorative in your mind, but a well-organized pantry will not only look different, it will feel very different from a tossed-together one. You'd be surprised how attractive, restful, and enticing the space can be. (By the way, do you have a light in the pantry? Be sure the bulb is bright enough for you to see. Very often I'm in a home where the bulb burned out and no one bothered to replace it.) Here are the most common food categories I see:

- Pastas
- Tomato products: cans of whole tomatoes, sauces, paste, and others
- Soups
- Vegetables
- Flavor enhancers like olive oil, vinegar, salad dressings, mustards, salt and pepper (large containers), and those packets I discussed above

- Side dishes or items for garnish like olives, chutneys, capers, and salsas
- Cereals and pancake mix
- Snack items like popcorn, chips (be sure you have a supply of clips to keep those bags closed; otherwise the contents get stale), crackers, and candy
- Fish (cans of tuna, sardines, and salmon are common)
- Water
- Sodas
- Paper products like paper towels and napkins (Keep toilet paper in the bathroom area or the linen closet if you don't have a shelving unit in the garage. TP isn't the right visual for a pantry, if you catch my drift.)

What categories would you add from your personal stash of food items? And which would you eliminate as not being a part of your diet?

As you look at your categories, which are the ones you most frequently use? Those should go toward the front of the pantry shelves. You want to be able to reach in and grab. Items that are less frequently accessed can live in the back or on the shelves behind the door. You'd be surprised how much time you can save over the course of a year if you can just reach in and grab what you need!

Keep sodas and water in separate areas on the floor. Liquid is heavy and you don't want to tax a shelf and hear a big crash in the middle of the night, above all after Baby arrives.

The top shelves, especially if they are very high, are great for party items you rarely use, like the Fourth of July margarita mix or the large bag of holiday cookie cutters that were clogging up a drawer. You can tuck your new two-step step stool in the pantry or kitchen corner (traditionally there's a space between the refrigerator and the cabinet closest to it) to keep these items at your fingertips.

Once you have your battle plan and a list of organizing tools to pick up, you're on the home stretch. If you can't shop today, put items away in the spot you wish them to reside. It will take a second to pop them into or onto containers in a few days when you have made the purchase. Placement is the most important end result for today's endeavors. Unless you have a palatial kitchen with a huge walk-in pantry, you should be able to accomplish this task in one or two days max.

## DAYS THREE AND FOUR: THE LAUNDRY ROOM

With the arrival of a baby, every day will be laundry day. It's amazing how anyone so tiny can have so many things to keep clean. Remember when you are faced with mountains of laundry that this too shall pass. One day Junior and his sister will be doing *your* wash!

Once again I'm going to assume you have a separate room for laundry. (Many of my clients who live in large homes have a washer and dryer upstairs as well as downstairs, but most of us aren't so lucky.) However, if you have to go to a laundry room outside your apartment or condo,

it's very important you have a hamper on wheels. Carrying a heavy sack of dirty laundry over your shoulder while holding a newborn in your arms is a prescription for disaster. Pick up a hamper and make your life easy. There are hampers with multiple canvas bags on wheels and they fold for easy storage. You can have the laundry sorted before you start a wash. Some hampers even have a bar across the top so you can hang up shirts and other items destined for a little pressing. But before you buy, gauge how much storage space you have. The greatest container in the world is a nightmare if you can't put it away when it's not in use.

While you are shopping for hampers on wheels, you might consider a small shopping cart. You can place your canvas laundry bags inside it and transport them to the laundry room. You can also use your cart to transport heavy groceries to and from your car or from the store. They are available for as little as $40 and will save your back, neck, and shoulders. It's an inexpensive and versatile solution.

Another word about hampers: If you need to have a hamper in your room, there are attractive ones in wicker that won't be a total eyesore. You can put a canvas bag inside and just pull the bag out on laundry day.

Guess what we're going to do first? You guessed it: A speed elimination is on the horizon. I'm always amazed at the junk I find in the laundry room. It's a great place to dump items you can't make a decision about, or so you think at the time. Set your timer. Here are the common culprits I find:

Detergent and fabric softener you no longer use is still sitting in the room. You tried it once and didn't like it. Guilt prompted you to hold on to it. Toss or donate it now.

If you have multiple containers of detergent and fabric softener, keep one of each out on the dryer and put the rest away on a shelf. If the room doesn't sport any cabinets, is it big enough for you to add some? You might put up a few single shelves or pop in a baker's rack depending on what space you have. No space? Try the shelving unit you added to the garage when you organized the kitchen. Keep your extra stash out there.

Miscellaneous tools often find their way here. It's OK to have a simple toolbox with the basics here. House the lion's share of the specialty items in the garage or the back of the hall closet.

While it's wonderful to save paper bags and plastic bags you got from the supermarket for recycling, it's absurd to have so many they are eating up valuable space anywhere in your home. Keep about ten paper and twenty plastic bags and give your helper a bonanza—or recyle the overflow. You have to be careful your good intentions don't backfire. You need your space. Use every inch wisely.

Do you keep mops and brooms here? Secure a unit for the wall so you can hang them up. It will keep the brooms and mops cleaner and you won't be tripping over them in a few weeks when you can no longer see the floor or your feet. Besides, a sloppy visual will make you feel tired every time you enter the room.

Is there a window in this room? Is it time to replace the curtain? Or does it need to be washed and ironed? Speaking of ironing, be sure your ironing board is secured behind the door and off the floor if at all possible. You might even be able to downsize to a mini-tabletop ironing board and save some real estate.

Very often if this room has a lot of cabinet space, my clients will use shelf space for shoe polishes and specialty polishes like those for silver, brass, and jewelry. This is clever as it frees up the area under the sink. Put those small items on a shelf creator or use a small grid tote. Great organizing products can be used all over the house, not just in the departments where you purchased them. Think outside the literal box.

If you have a big room and some wall space, you could hang a poster or put up a chalkboard. Or you could hang a plant to take advantage of the natural light from the window. I'm into clean, clear, Zen-like spaces; however, that doesn't translate to austere and without personality. You'll be spending a fair amount of time here over the next several years so you might as well enjoy it.

## DAYS FIVE AND SIX: DIRTY DIAPERS BE GONE!

Let's face it. Diapers are a part of your future. And they get dirty. The easiest way is to use disposable ones. But is that fair to the local landfill? And what about your pocketbook? Cloth diapers are a gentler, kinder, more economical solution, but without a system you might get overwhelmed. What do you know? We've hit upon yet another way to make systemized behavior serve you. Let's take a look.

1. Be sure you have a diaper pail in the changing area. You needn't get anything fancy. A medium-sized garbage can with a step-lid will do. This is a great place to have some baking soda on hand to absorb odors. For cloth diapers a liner will keep the inside of the pail from getting yucky and will make getting the diapers in and out of the pail a snap. Just make sure it's a washable one so you can toss it right into the washing machine along with the diapers.
2. You'll want several diaper liners ready to use in rotation. When one or two are hanging up to dry, you'll still have a clean, dry one ready for Baby.
3. With a mere flick of the wrist, toss any solid poop into the toilet and flush. (It will be a few months before you have to deal with that!) Rinse the diaper cover and let it hang to dry. You can wash it when the need is great if you catch my drift. Put up a portable indoor clothesline or hang the liners from clips you hang on your shower rod. It all depends on where you are doing diaper duty.
4. Remember those plastic bags I asked you to whittle down to twenty? If you plan on using disposable diapers, you have a built-in way to recycle those bags. (I presume you are using reusable canvas bags to do your grocery shopping.) Keep them around and use the plastic for disposable diapers. Tie the bag securely so that the, uh, aroma won't overtake your home in between trips to the outside garbage can. There are special cloth storage bags that hang on a hook or doorknob to hold plastic bags and others that attach to the inside of a cabinet door to house plastic bags. I stored mine near my golden retriever's leash so I never left the house for a dog walk without one. It was the ultimate recycling! Keep your bags contained so they don't spread like a fungus all over the house and take up space you need for more important items.
5. A bit of experimentation will be required to find the perfect cloth diaper laundering solution because everyone has access to different types of washing machines. Additional factors are the hardness of your water, the make of the diaper, the detergent you use, etc. Trial and error will lead you to the formula that works best for your situation. Here are some tips and tricks that will help you get started:

- Wash dirty diapers first in cold water; hot will set fecal protein into the fabric.
- Add baking soda to the wash (yes, you'll be buying the large economy size!).

- Follow a cold wash with hot and add your favorite detergent.
- Give the diapers an extra rinse.
- Are your diapers getting smelly? Add some vinegar to the first rinse.
- Don't use fabric softeners in the dryer, as the diapers will become less absorbent over time. Bt the way, if you can, avoid the dryer and let everything hang dry. And if you can, let the sun do its magic. The sun will remove stains but either way you'll save on electricity.
- Finally, avoid detergents with additives as they can leave a residue that may leave your diapers smelling not-so-fresh, reduce absorbency, or even eat through the material.

I'd be remiss if I didn't mention that there are other methods for dealing with dirty cloth diapers. Your experienced mom friends will no doubt sing their praises. It's a matter of personal taste. For example, the "wet pail" method leaves me literally breathless. You keep a wet pail around ready to catch the dirty diapers before laundering. What can I say? A pail of stagnant poopy water in Baby's room doesn't work for me. Your sense of smell may dictate otherwise. Of course, there are diaper services that do the work for you. They tend to be expensive, however, so be sure and check your budget before you enlist one. Once you get a system going, I think you'll find dirty diapers don't deserve the bad rap they tend to get. Be creative, but above all be consistent.

## USE EXCEL TO EXCEL!

The products in the pantry and the laundry room get used up quickly. You've got to have a system to note when a purchase needs to be made. A well-stocked pantry is one way to express how much you value yourself, your family, your time, your energy, and your finances. There is something comforting about knowing that what you need is at your fingertips. Once your baby arrives, this is critical. Gone are the days when you could fly to the store at will for one or two items. What if your spouse or a friend can't respond immediately to bring some items you need desperately? It's time to streamline, stock up, and stay organized.

The easiest way to accomplish this goal is to have a list and post it where it can be instantly accessed. I like to keep my master list in a drawer next to the refrigerator. It's always there with a pencil so I can make notes throughout the day. Some people like to post the list on the refrigerator. Placement isn't as important as consistency (if the list starts moving around the room or home, it will be abandoned in short order). Create your master list in Excel and you'll be able to tweak it as needed and print out a fresh copy each week. There are several ways to organize your products. Let's consider a few.

If you shop at several stores, list the items you purchase at each. When you shop you won't have to scan the list to see what you need at this location. You did the work when you set up the master list.

Make a master list that groups items by type. You'll have all frozen items in one section, for example, and you can check that section in every store you shop in.

Take this idea a step further: List the items you purchase in the order you will encounter them in the store. Most of us take the same route through a store each time we go. If you are a "wandering the aisles" kind of shopper, I would suggest you consider a change. Wandering will lead to more impulse buying.

If you have a laptop, you can curl up in your favorite chair today and crank out your list. If you put the words "shopping list" in your favorite search engine, you'll find lots of premade choices online. You can copy, paste, and edit to your specifications. One of my favorites is at www.grocerylists.org; they have a list for meat eaters and one for vegetarians.

## CHORES TO THE RESCUE

Making decisions is the heart and soul of getting organized. And maintenance is the engine that keeps the organizing train on track. Remember, it isn't about adding work to your busy schedule; it's about shifting your energy to a different action. If you are organized in this arena and do the shopping but your spouse is a bit lax, have a talk. A baby brings sleepless nights, frayed tempers, and a need for lots of new products in the home. Having a fight over food or diapers is wasted energy. If you are

the "fly by the seat of your pants" partner when it comes to grocery shopping, it's time to change. You may be surprised how comforting a well-stocked pantry can be! And I know you'll be grateful for a cheery, well-organized, welcoming laundry room because you're going to be spending so much time there.

Remember when I asked you to create new routines? Here are my top three ideas for habits that will keep these rooms tidy. You can string them together if you wish to create a personal ritual. After you read my list, come up with three ideas of your own. You want to walk into an organized room and leave it that way when you exit.

As you finish work in an area, wipe it off to keep it clean as you go. Having all the kitchen counters dirty at one time can be overwhelming; wiping as you go keeps you in charge.

When you open a package of multiple products—say, that six-pack of sponges—don't leave the torn wrap there looking like a gaping wound. Put the products on the shelf. Recycle the cardboard and plastic wrap. When you are stressed, calm shelves will positively influence you.

Open containers of powder laundry detergent tend to spray their contents. Over time the top of your dryer and the floor start to crunch and look dirty. Wipe this area down after each use. Don't think of these actions as a pain in the neck. Think of them as a gift you give yourself (or your spouse) the next time you need to work here.

## FATHER SOMETIMES KNOWS BEST

I'd like to close with a piece of advice I got from my father. My parents shared home maintenance. My mother cleaned every square inch of our home with precision and on schedule—it was her passion—while my dad did the grocery shopping and the laundry. My mother cooked (I use the term loosely) and put the laundry away. My father never embraced the idea that chores were to be divided by considerations of male and female. He said the most qualified person should do/get the job, whether it was in the boardroom or the home. Those are truly words to live by.

Now is an excellent time to have a talk about chores with your partner. How the work in the home is divided sends early messages to your child about gender equality and how a home is run. If Mom and Dad are both keeping the home tidy, it will be a natural transition for Junior to participate. We women have wonderful nesting/nurturing instincts. We want to care for those we love. Sometimes that very natural desire causes us to take on the entire task of maintaining the home. We turn ourselves into housekeepers and nannies. We infantilize our children and our partners. Don't set yourself up now to feel taken advantage of down the road.

As your child grows and wants to be a big boy or girl, don't forget that maintenance of the pantry and the laundry room present great chores!

# 31-32 WEEKS PREGNANT

## Planning for Co-Parenting

**This week, you can**

- Consider the practical implications of certain child-rearing decisions
- Come up with a plan for sharing parenting with your partner in those early weeks

THERE ARE A LOT of parenting books on the market. And most of them have definite opinions about things like where your baby should sleep, what he should eat, and whether he should have a pacifier or not. I will try not to add to the burden of "shoulds" or "should nots." Instead, I'd like you to consider the practical implications of different choices and make sure you and your co-parent are on the same page for rolling out a parenting plan after the baby's born.

No matter how you'll divide up the parenting burden later, keep in mind that the early weeks of caring for your baby will be exhausting and confusing. You'll be recovering from labor and delivery. You'll be short on sleep. You'll need to take it easy! Even if you're going to be a stay-at-home mom and therefore caring for the baby during the day is "your job," your partner will need to share the load . . . especially

in those first few weeks. Plan for it now so nobody gets an unpleasant surprise later.

**Who will make medical decisions for the baby in the hospital?** If there are any emergencies or if your baby needs special care, will you make decisions together? What if Mom is getting stitches in the recovery room or Dad is down at the snack machine when a decision needs to be made? Talk about the possibility that you will be faced with unexpected surprises and decisions during your hospital stay, and come up with a plan for communicating and handling decision-making together.

Not all decisions will be high-stakes emergencies, but they still warrant discussion beforehand. For example, babies routinely receive Hepatitis B vaccinations while in the hospital. Some parents prefer to wait until the baby is a little older or in a risk group for this disease before giving the shot. Circumcision is another issue that often throws parents off guard when it comes up. Their precious baby boy is only a few hours old and they haven't really discussed the topic—and suddenly there's the nurse, ready to take him away for the procedure if only the parents will sign on the dotted line. Talk about this ahead of time! Circumcision is surgery and cannot be taken back. It's not an emergency and your baby does not have to have it done before he leaves the hospital. If one of you has questions or doubts, you can always have it done later on an outpatient basis.

**What will be each parent's role during the postpartum hospital stay?** Ideally, Dad will be doing most of the baby care that requires fetching, carrying, and walking, while Mom stays put and recovers. Fortunately most newborns sleep through most of the first couple of days of life (and sometimes beyond). Pacing the floor with a fussy baby is likely days or weeks away. Still, there are considerations to be made. Will Dad accompany the baby for any medical procedures or tests? What if Dad needs to go home to check in on pets or care for other children? There will be nurses on duty to care for Mom and help with the baby, but they will likely be busy and might not be able to immediately respond if Mom needs help getting to the bathroom or would like somebody to hand her the baby for a feeding. If your partner or spouse can't be with you during your postpartum hospital stay (or if you aren't in a relationship), is there another person who can step in?

### IF YOU ARE A SINGLE MOM

Whether your baby's father is completely out of the picture or plans to be very involved in his child's life, the issues I'm posing this week will look very different for you than they will for a married or partnered mom. Remember that your first obligation is to take care of yourself and your new baby. Any legal arguments regarding your baby's care or custody can wait until you've been home for a while and have had a chance to recover. Despite what the hospital staff may tell you, even birth certificates and paternity paperwork can be put off for days or weeks. If your baby's father is AWOL, or if you have made a conscious decision to be a single parent, ask a close friend to be your stand-in "dad" for the first few weeks so that you can navigate this new world of parenting without being alone in it. If your baby's father wants to be very involved with her care and the two of you have a cordial and friendly relationship, by all means, discuss all these issues ahead of time to come up with a plan the two of you can agree on. On the other hand, if your relationship is contentious or if you feel anxious or stressed out around him, you are within your rights to hold him at bay until you're feeling more settled in with your baby. If need be, get a friend or family member to act as go-between, giving him vital information and facilitating visits. If you are uncomfortable with any decisions he's asking you to commit to at this point, stand your ground. That is what the court system is for.

**How will you feed the baby?**

**Breastfeeding** is recommended by pretty much every health organization, and for good reason—it's good for Mom, good for Baby, and good for public health. It can also be extremely convenient, once you get the hang of it: no bottles to wash, no formula to purchase, no water to sterilize . . . your milk is always ready, and always at the right temperature. If you plan to nurse your baby, here are some issues you'll want to think about:

- How will you share the burden of nighttime feedings? Some moms pump and leave a bottle so that Dad can get the first feeding while they sleep through. Other moms find that pumping a bottle is almost as much hassle as getting up in the middle of the night, and you may experience a drop in your milk supply if you don't breastfeed every few hours in those crucial early weeks. One nice compromise is for Dad to be the one who gets out of bed and brings the baby to Mom for the feeding.

- Will Dad feel left out if he doesn't get to feed the baby? If so, brainstorm ways to help him feel involved in the process. One nice idea—he can "feed" mom nutritious, healthy food so she can keep making that milk without overtaxing her own body.

- Is Dad really on board with breastfeeding? Does he understand the level of support he'll need to provide to help you succeed? Some reading ma-terial or even a special "breastfeeding 101" class geared toward expecting couples may help him see the light.

- How does your spouse or partner feel about breastfeeding in public? If he's squeamish, educate him now. Babies shouldn't have to hide away in dirty bathrooms to eat, and moms can learn to breastfeed so discreetly you'd never know they were doing it.

- Make sure you plan to bring your spouse or a good friend (the kind you don't mind being a little immodest around) with you the first time you make a public outing with the baby. When you're getting the hang of breastfeeding in public, an extra set of hands or just a body to block you from view can make it much easier.

**Bottle feeding** can be comforting to the mom who wants to know exactly how much milk her baby is getting from day one, and moms who know they'll be re-turning to work soon after the baby is born often see bottle feeding as the more con-venient option. Here are some considera-tions to keep in mind before you choose the bottle:

- Will you give formula exclusively, at-tempt to alternate breast and bottle, or pump breast milk for your baby? Some mothers who are uncomfort-able with breastfeeding because of a history of abuse or other body issues are able to pump and give breast milk. Regular pumping will require quiet time every two to three hours and active help from your spouse, since it's pretty difficult to pump and hold a baby at the same time.

- Have you budgeted for formula? It can be very expensive. If your baby does not tolerate the kind of formula you've chosen, can you afford the special type?

- How will you and Dad share feedings, especially nighttime feedings? Will you split them fifty-fifty or come up with some other system? Talk about it now so you're both on the same page later. If you have a cesarean birth, it'll be especially important that you have a lot of help with bottle feedings. Remember, you'll need to measure and mix the formula, heat the water, pick up the baby, and put her back down. That's a lot of activity for somebody who's recovering from abdominal surgery.

## Where will Baby sleep?

Once you're home, will your baby sleep in her own room, in her own bed in your room, or in your bed? Consider these potential issues:

- If she's sleeping in her own room: She'll be eating around the clock for the first several weeks of her life. Who will listen for the sounds that indicate she's waking up and hungry? (It's usually easiest to calm a baby who hasn't worked herself up into a full-fledged cry.) Will you use a monitor?

Who will go get the baby and bring her to the bedroom? Don't make any assumptions. Talk about it in advance.

- If she's sleeping in your room: How will Dad assist with nighttime waking? If the baby is sleeping in your bed or very close to your bed, it might seem there's no point in your husband getting up for feedings— you'll have it covered easily. But if he can take over all or some of the nighttime diaper changes, that will ease your burden.

## What kind of diapers will you use?

**Cloth Diapers:** Some dads seem almost afraid of cloth diapers. They envision pin-pricks and poop flying everywhere. If you're leaning toward cloth, take a moment to show your spouse how simple the new systems are to use (see the cloth diaper tips on page 143). In those first couple weeks postpartum, you will need to rest, not cart heavy loads of diapers to the washing machine. Make sure your spouse knows what he'll have to do to get the diapers where they need to go. Some couples who know they'll be using cloth diapers down the road opt for disposables for the first few weeks to make things easier. If chemicals and the environment are a concern, you can buy unbleached, eco-friendly disposables from companies like Seventh Generation and Tushies. Or try flushable diapers, a relatively new product that's more environmentally friendly than regular disposables but doesn't have the same laundering requirements. You can find out more at GDiapers.com.

**Disposables**: How will you dispose of dirty diapers? Some people are fine tossing newborn baby diapers right in the regular trash. Even the poopy ones generally aren't any smellier than other food waste. Other folks aren't comfortable unless the diapers are triple-wrapped and stamped with a biohazard symbol. Where do you fall on the spectrum? Where does your partner or spouse?

**No matter** which option you choose, diapering requires developing a comfort level with your child's bodily functions, not to mention fluids! Yes, I am afraid sometimes you will get poop on your hands, no matter how careful and sterile you try to be. Unfortunately, society seems to give men a pass in this department (ever noticed there aren't nearly as many diaper-changing stations in the MEN'S restrooms?), and too many women let their partners squirm out of really taking responsibility for diapering because the guys play squeamish. Along with children come years of pottying accidents, blood, and vomit. If Dad can't handle a little innocuous newborn poop now, he needs to get over it! Making the lion's share of the diapering his job in the early weeks will help.

### Who will take Baby to her first doctor's visit?

It's a cruel truth: You've just gotten home from the hospital and settled in with your new baby, and the very next day, your pediatrician is probably expecting you to show up in her office with the baby. I highly recommend that your spouse or partner attend this appointment with you. Not only will it be good for the two of you to both develop a working relationship with your child's doctor, but you're going to need help getting out the door on time with a new baby!

This is only the beginning of your co-parenting relationship with your child's father. Most decisions you make now can be changed later as you get a real taste of juggling life with a baby and all your other responsibilities. But I encourage you to involve your spouse or partner heavily in your baby's care (and in the early weeks, *your* care) because this may influence how involved he is comfortable being down the line. As your lives get busier and busier, it will be only too easy for both of you to fall into the familiar gender roles that were likely reflected in your home growing up, and for his involvement in his child's life to be downplayed or relegated only to stereotypical "male" areas. Begin as you mean to go on. Get Dad on board early, and in a meaningful way. This is such an important topic I'll revisit it after Baby arrives. In the meantime, open the lines of communication with your partner. It's bound to reap rich rewards in every area of your relationship.

# CHAPTER SIX

# 33 to 36 Weeks Pregnant

Sometimes I go about pitying myself, and all the time I am being carried
on great winds across the sky.

—CHIPPEWA, TRANSLATED BY ROBERT BLY

A CLIENT OF MINE, Rachel, had a six-month-old daughter when I started working with her. She admitted that there were things she had let go during her pregnancy because she was too tired to deal with them and didn't want to ask for help. Before the baby, she was still able to stay relatively on top of things, and she didn't want to put anyone out or admit she couldn't do it all. And then her baby was born, and she realized she really couldn't! Rachel finally did reach out to friends and family, but by that point she was buried under mess and disorganization, not to mention clutter. After that, she promised herself that she'd never hesitate to ask for help again (which included hiring me).

By now, I trust that your environment is taking shape. This month, you'll want to devote more time to getting your team in place. I want you to feel supported and nurtured as you begin this journey. There are many times in life when an experience

demands we have a village of supporters around us. Never be afraid to ask for help. After all, now you've opened the door for the other people to ask you when they have needs. This is the essence of family and community.

One safeguard is to have several relatives and friends available who can each do a few things, rather than dumping everything on one or two good-hearted folks, especially your spouse. It's also wise to give each person an assignment he is going to enjoy and actually be good at. You'd want chef Tanya to cook a meal for you and you'd ask me to organize the nursery. It could work the other way around, but neither one of us would have as much fun. You also want to stock up on a reasonable number of supplies. Sending your spouse or a friend out for diapers at midnight isn't the best use of anyone's time or energy.

As you make final maternity leave arrangements at your place of employment this month, keep that advice in mind. Be sure the coworker who is covering for you is capable of keeping the ball rolling on your projects, making all your clients feel secure, and in general keeping your office/project systems in place. You won't be open to receiving frantic calls when you are in labor (although I do know one working mom who wanted to take her Blackberry into the delivery room).

## HABIT OF THE MONTH

### Never Leave a Room Without Making It Better (This will keep items where you have designated them to be)

This month at home, we bring order to all the bathrooms in your house. I'm always amazed how a room that's dedicated to cleanliness is almost always a mess. It doesn't take much effort to introduce order, just cooperation and attention to detail to maintain your work. (But then, you and your spouse are experienced Zen Organizers by now, so tackling one more room should be a breeze!)

As time goes by, you will develop an uncanny sixth sense about all the rooms, cupboards, drawers, and closets in your home. You'll be able to tell in an instant when something is out of place. Please understand that I don't want to turn you into a "space Nazi" who never allows anyone to relax. I want you, your family, and your guests to enjoy themselves; but enjoyment need not be synonymous with sloppy, chaotic, or messy. My goal is to turn you into someone who has control over her environment. It will bring you peace and calm, restoring you especially on days when you feel battered by emotional storms.

Once you organize a space, take a mental snapshot of it. This month, whenever you're about to leave a room, take a quick look around first to see what's out of place and return items to their designated areas. Do CDs and DVDs have to be returned to a media album or jewel case? Did someone leave the throw for the couch in a lump on the floor? Did magazines and newspapers get taken out of their respective holders? Are they now abandoned on the coffee table? It doesn't take Sherlock Holmes to do this. One big thing that happens with children is that items get left all over the home. Babies and toddlers have to be taught to be tidy. You are their teacher and the one who must set the example. Late-stage pregnancy is a great time to practice this life skill.

# 33 WEEKS PREGNANT

## Create Your Team

**This week, you can**

- Think about the people who will play an important part in your life before, during, and after the birth of your baby

You're just about two months away from your baby's expected arrival date, and only *now* am I asking you to arrange your support team? That's right. My late timing for this topic was quite intentional, and here's why: The people you might think you want to be in the delivery room, visiting you in the hospital, or staying in your guest room as you welcome your baby to the world might be very different at the end of your pregnancy than they were in the beginning. A woman I know named Alison invited her two closest friends to be part of her birth experience within hours of getting the double pink line on the pregnancy test. By the time she was six months pregnant, however, the two friends had had a falling out, and the tension between them could darken any room. Plus, one of the women had turned into a control freak when it came to Alison's pregnancy, giving her constant unsolicited advice. Alison became so annoyed that she started avoiding the friend . . . who still fully expected to be called when

she went into labor! Alison finally told a white lie, informing both friends that her hospital policy only allowed family to be present for the birth. But she went through a lot of stress leading up to it.

When your pregnancy was new and your baby's arrival seemed far off, you may have had some ideas about who would be involved in her welcome . . . and you may find that those ideas aren't weathering so well now. Maybe you have come to realize that your mother, whom you'd planned on having in the delivery room, is driving you crazy with advice you don't want or need and that doesn't agree with your birth plan. On the flip side, you may find that somebody you never thought of as a birth attendant—like your child-free aunt—has turned out to be so warm, encouraging, and helpful that you'd love to have her there. Give yourself time to think about the birth experience you'd like to have before you give anyone a definite invitation—and even then, let them know that you may change your mind, and if you do it's nothing personal. As you get larger, slower, and more uncomfortable, it's very normal to find yourself drawing inward and focusing on the life within you and the big event and transition about to take place. You may find you're a lot more selective about how many people you want to share this time with than you thought you would be.

See what I'm getting at?

As you think about assembling a group of people that will be with you during this eventful and life-changing time, I want you to be very selfish. This is not the time to worry about not hurting feelings or trying to include everyone. This is also not the time to be dealing with old baggage or wounds that have yet to heal. You are welcoming a new life into the world and you need to be nurtured and surrounded only by people who make you feel comfortable and safe. Visits from your toxic aunt whom you have decided to tolerate twice per year for your mother's sake can wait until your baby is a bit older and you've gotten your groove back. And that cousin who never lifts a finger to help when she visits? Forget it. You will be too busy playing Mommy to your actual baby to worry about people who can't or won't help out.

Every person you invite to be part of this event should have a clearly defined role. A woman in the late stages of pregnancy or caring for her newborn should not have to play hostess. People should not be hanging around the delivery room or your house just to get a shot at holding the baby—they need to have some helpful purpose for being there! Sometimes it can be hard for friends and family, no matter how well meaning, to know exactly how they can help you. So I recommend having a clear plan ahead of time of all the different support roles you may need, and who will fulfill them. That way everybody will have a clear sense of direction and will know exactly how to help you. Here are some questions to think about:

## Home

- If you have last-minute shopping needs when you go into labor, who can take care of them?
- Do you have friends who could make you a meal ahead of time that you can put in your freezer?
- By the end of a pregnancy the simplest tasks—such as bending over to load the dishwasher or sweep dirt into a dustpan—can seem impossible. Do you have any friends who would come over and tidy up for you?

## Pets

- Who will care for your pets while you are in the hospital?
- Who will walk your dog when you're home from the hospital but resting and/or busy with the new baby?

## Labor and Birth

- If you are single or if you go into active labor and your husband isn't at home, who can drive you to the hospital or birth center?
- Who will care for your older children when you go into labor? Have you thought about the logistics? If possi-

ble, your sitter should plan on coming to your house. If you go into labor in the middle of the night, you don't want to have to worry about waking the kids and loading them into the car, not to mention the hassle of adding another stop on the way to the hospital.

- If you plan on having your kids at the hospital or birth center with you, who will look after them? You need to have a support person on hand besides your husband. If your child isn't handling the situation well and needs to leave your hospital room, you don't want your husband to miss the birth! Your support person doesn't have to come into the delivery room—she can sit in the waiting room, and your husband or doula can bring the kids out to her if needed.
- Who will be in the hospital room with you while you are in labor? Why will these people be there? What role can they fill? Will these people all stay for the birth? Why or why not? Would you like them to have an active role in your birth, or simply be present?

## Back at Home

- Who will visit you in the first few days after your baby is born?
- Who is coming from out of town? Where will they stay?
- Do you have a plan "B" in case your plans to have a houseguest don't work out?
- Who can do laundry?
- Who can keep your dishes clean?

- Who can cook or bring you meals?
- Who can hold your baby while you shower or take a nap?
- Who can look after older kids?

## THE DELIVERY ROOM

Deciding whom to invite into the delivery room can be a loaded issue. Before you allow anyone to be part of this event, I would like you to be very honest with yourself. Why are you inviting this person? Anyone you invite to your birth should be there because they are helping you and *you* want them there, not just because they want to be. Keep in mind that emotional support counts as help.

If you feel like you need your mother there because she will keep you calm and strong, great. If you're having her there only because her feelings will be hurt if you don't, you may be surprised by how anxious or resentful you feel about her presence once you're actually in labor.

Childbirth professionals have long observed the relationship between a laboring woman's sense of security and relaxation and the way her body responds to the hard work of labor. We are all animals deep down, and our instincts will only allow us to give birth to our babies if we feel safe and secure. If you're stressed out, your labor may actually stall or stop and lead to more interventions . . . and more stress. The cycle isn't good for you, and it isn't good for your baby.

If necessary, there are ways to graciously get out of an invitation you've already extended and now regret. You can be direct and honest, or ask your spouse to do it for you. If that's out of the question, you can blame hospital policy ("Oops, just found out I can only have one person in the delivery room with me!") or you can just wait and "see how it goes." Heather, a first-time mom I know, was in labor for twelve hours before her husband put in the call to his mother—and by the time Mom made the three-hour drive, the baby had arrived. Truth be told, Heather had a pretty good idea that her labor was picking up by about the sixth hour, but decided at the last minute that she just couldn't deal with her generous yet overbearing mother-in-law while in the throes of contractions. Nobody seemed surprised that Heather had "misjudged" her baby's arrival time, and Mom was never the wiser. The details of your labor are nobody's business but your own, and babies often come more quickly than laboring moms—and their nurses!—expect. Make the decision you are most comfortable with and decide how much information to divulge later. Just be sure you don't put up a conflicting birth story on Facebook!

Also give some consideration to which people you will invite to visit in the hospital after the baby is born. Don't overbook your schedule, and reserve the right to change your mind. You may be exhausted, sore, or just not feeling up to visitors. Again, you can always use hospital policy as an excuse. Or if there's a visit you feel obligated to keep but would like to be short, you can time it for just before some planned event, like a visit from the lacta-

tion consultant. My guess is that most guests won't want to hang around for that!

Now that you've done some brainstorming, you may be getting a clearer picture about the specific needs you'll have before, during, and after the birth of your baby. Likely some people have already given you a vague offer of help or asked if they can visit after the baby is born. You may have other people in mind that you'd like to ask to fulfill a certain role. Take a moment and write their names down on a piece of paper.

Now, I'd like you to make a chart with five columns. You can do this in Excel or on a page in your baby journal. Down the left-hand side of your chart, you're going to list all the different tasks you will need help with. Create three more columns for the person's name who will fill the role, when they'll fill it, and their contact information. The final column is for notes. You can use the example I've created below as a guide.

Armed with your chart filled out with the list of tasks, go through your list of friends and family members. You can either call or e-mail each one personally or send out a group message via e-mail or Facebook letting people know what your needs are and asking them to respond with a way they might be able to help you. Ask them to be specific. For example, if they can watch your kids on weekend nights but not weekdays, you'll need to know. If they are willing to take your kids to the park for an hour to give you a break but can't commit to an entire day, you'll need to know that, too.

| ROLE | PERSON | WHEN | CONTACT INFO | NOTES |
|---|---|---|---|---|
| *Walk dog* | Mike | Mornings, as long as I need him | 222-555-1111 | |
| | Wendy | Evenings while I am in hospital | 222-555-5029 | Can't do Thursdays |
| *Laundry* | Sharon | Call her when needed | 222-555-6464 | Can help until 8:00 p.m. |
| *Care for older kids* | Cindy | While in hospital | 222-555-1212 | She will come to us; call as soon as labor begins. |
| | Aunt Melanie | Will take kids to park daily after Baby is home | 222-555-5495 | Can't do Sundays |
| *Bring dinner* | | | | |
| *Baby holder* | | | | |
| *Shopping* | | | | |

As friends and family respond, you can fill in the columns with pertinent details. Use the "notes" column for any special limitations or information you will need to keep in mind. I've started filling out my pretend chart so you can get an idea of how to do yours. For simplicity's sake, notice how I've created just one row for each task, and then broken it down by more specifics within the row. You may want to organize this information differently in a way that makes sense to you.

Not everyone is fortunate enough to have a large, nearby group of friends and family ready to jump in and help. You may find a lot of gaps in your chart. If that happens, go back and ask some of your closer friends if they can fulfill a specific role. You could also consider tapping into a larger circle of acquaintances—say your mom's group or church. At the very least, you'll have a good idea of what you can count on others for and what you'll have to do yourself—or pay somebody else to do.

## VISITORS

You may be wondering what you need to do to get ready for visitors. Again, I would like you to get out of the mode of thinking of the people who will be staying in your home as guests. Whether they'll be there a few hours or a few weeks, they are coming to help you. While you'll need to figure out some kind of arrangements for them if they'll be staying for a night or longer—for your comfort as well as theirs!—they can handle many of the details of the trip, such as making their flight arrangements. And I don't want to hear about you getting up early to cook them breakfast!

If you will have guests in your house for more than a night, keep in mind that everybody will get along best if there is a place to retreat. You may be getting the hang of breastfeeding, something that requires less modesty than your father-in-law may be used to. The baby will probably cry a lot, and the last thing you want is to be worrying about keeping your houseguests—er, I mean *helpers*—awake.

All in all, I urge you to keep visitors to a minimum during your transition to motherhood. Limit those people you invite into your home to the ones you feel most comfortable with and those who will be most helpful to you—those "can-do" souls who will gladly jump in and help out where needed without needing a prod.

I don't want to sound stingy or unreasonable. You are about to have a beautiful baby, and of course you will be very proud of her and want to show her off. But you will also be entering a very sensitive time of your life. Hormones will be flying, various body parts will be leaking, you may doubt your parenting skills, you'll be running on little sleep, and your baby will probably spend most of her time either pooping, wailing, or snoozing. A month or so after your baby is born you will be feeling much more human, and she'll have transformed into a cute, chubby little person who can charm everyone's pants off. It'll be the perfect time for visits from your bossy Aunt Alice or that casual friend from work who you'd really rather didn't see you with breast milk stains on your shirt!

If you have a separate guest room, by now it's surely organized. The instructions for closets and bathrooms are fairly universal. But if you didn't get around to getting this room ready to receive guests, here are some guidelines to make it functional, fast:

- Have a set of clean sheets on the bed and a fresh set of towels for anyone who stays here. Ask them to wash these items and replace them so that the next set of helpers will have the same consideration. If the laundry isn't done in your home but elsewhere in the complex or at a public laundromat, be sure one of your helpers is assigned to laundry duty if your guests are elderly or not capable for some reason of handling laundry.

- If the closet is full of off-season clothing, rarely used sports items, or memorabilia, be sure your guests have about five inches of hanging space per person and a few hangers. Clear the floor space in this section for their shoes.

- A luggage rack is nice if you have one. If not, clear a space on the floor and have one empty dresser drawer per guest.

- Pull together a bathroom basket of basic items like shampoo, conditioner, and body lotion and leave it on the bathroom counter.

- Is there a TV or other form of electronic entertainment in the room? How close is it to the baby's room or your room? Decide what the ideal volume setting is and educate your guests. This isn't a request; it's a house rule.

- If you do not have a guest room, set up an area for your visitors. If your couch folds out, decide ahead of time whether it can stay open while your guests are here or whether it should it be put away each morning. Again, this isn't a social visit, and house rules that ensure you will not be unduly disturbed are to be established. (This goes for laundry rules and entertainment etiquette as well.)

- If it's just for a few days and your guests are young, ask them to sleep on the couch rather than the pull-out bed.

- Anyone on the couch will probably be living out of a suitcase. Make some room for items that need to be hung in your child's closet, the baby's room, or your room. Ask your guest to enter these areas under the circumstances you designate.

- You can of course give a toddler's room to your visitors and have your child sleep in your room. It's imperative that you explain to the child what's happening and why he is being asked to make this sacrifice. Ask him to cooperate. No one likes to be kicked out of his room without being consulted.

## HELP YOUR PETS ADJUST

Consider your pets and decide how you'll incorporate them into your new life with a baby. Whether it's getting your dog used to being around babies, training your parrot not to shriek during naptime, or just planning for who will take care of them while you're at the hospital, it's a good idea to give your pets some thought and plan now to keep stress to a minimum later. Ask your friends with pets and children how they made the transition. Consult with a trainer or animal communicator if you need outside help (see the Resources section).

Andrea was very careful to include her pet pug in her plans when she was pregnant. She left her baby's first car seat on the floor of the living room. Chewy, the pug, frequently slept in it. When Andrea's son Jonathan was born, she had her husband bring home items from the hospital with Jon's scent. The baby smelled Chewy in his car seat and guess what? They have been devoted to each other since day one.

Studies show that babies who grow up around dogs and cats usually have fewer allergies in adulthood than kids who don't. Dogs and cats provide an experience of un-

conditional love for the child. They also give your child an opportunity to learn responsibility through chores: fresh water, food, and walks are daily requirements.

Cats are solitary creatures by nature, but in general they have an easier time adjusting to what they surely view as an interloper. Dogs are pack animals; your dog wants to protect you and your baby. He needs to be with you. If you're considering tying him up and leaving him in your yard for hours on end, think twice. You are only creating a problem. Your dog is likely to become depressed and destructive and start barking. If you feel overwhelmed, find someone to help you.

As a last resort, relocate your dog or cat. Start your quest for a good home by consulting with your vet, family, and friends. *Under no circumstances* should an animal who has been a part of your home and your life be relegated to the pound and certain death. There are general rescue groups and, if your pet is a pedigree, you'll find rescue groups for each of the major breeds. Fido and Fluffy were your first children. Don't neglect them during this time of transition.

# 34 WEEKS PREGNANT

## Stock Up on Postpartum Supplies

**This week, you can**

- Stock up on the supplies you'll need to take care of yourself after your baby is here

You've given lots of thought to your baby's layette, securing her all the clothes and other supplies she'll need for a comfortable and cozy newborn life. But have you thought much about the items you'll need to have on hand for yourself after you give birth?

As you can probably imagine, giving birth to a baby causes some physical aftermath. You will probably be sore after delivering and you may have healing stitches to contend with. You'll probably experience some cramping as your organs contract and return to their original "homes." The extra fluids your body has created to support your growing baby will now need to be eliminated. And the physical pressure of carrying a baby in your body may have caused some other issues, like hemorrhoids or varicose veins, which you'll now be trying to relieve.

So don't forget to head to the drugstore and stock up on supplies for yourself before the big event. Here are some of the things you'll want to have on hand:

**Peri-bottle.** This is a little plastic squirt bottle that you can fill with warm water. It serves a variety of purposes, including helping keep stitches clean, and warm water can be soothing on sore nether regions. The hospital will probably send you home with one, but I'd pick up an extra couple at the medical supply store or pharmacy. Keep one in each bathroom you might find yourself using in the early days after giving birth.

**Ibuprofen and acetaminophen.** Even after delivering her babies without the use of drugs of any kind, Meagan reached for her bottles of Tylenol and Motrin to help with postpartum soreness. Ibuprofen acts as an anti-inflammatory, which helps to ease the pain of cramping and keeps swelling at a minimum. And acetaminophen can be alternated with ibuprofen around the clock for even more soreness-fighting protection.

If you have your baby via cesarean section, your doctor will probably prescribe you stronger drugs to use in the first few days after giving birth. Most women who've had uncomplicated vaginal deliveries can get by with over-the-counter pain relief. Prescription pain meds may interfere with your ability to initiate breastfeeding and make some women feel loopy and out of it while they're trying to get to know their new baby, so try to use the OTC drugs if you can. Maybe you'll find that you have no need for medical pain relief at all, but it's a good idea to have it on hand just in case.

**Holistic Medicines.** Over the course of your pregnancy, your uterus has been stretching and expanding to accommodate your growing baby. Then suddenly, in a matter of hours, the baby exits his first home and leaves it more or less vacant. Your muscular uterus will start to contract shortly after birth to restore itself to its original size and location. This can result in cramping that can be anywhere on the spectrum from similar to a mild menstrual cramp to worse than labor pains.

The herbs Crampbark and/or Motherwort can help with the discomfort. Pick up a tincture (an extraction of an herb in liquid form) from a health food store. Five to twenty drops in a small amount of water every few hours will help ease cramping. You can also buy a prepared mixture called After-Ease that is a little harder to find but can be purchased online. And of course you can always take the wonderful homeopathic remedy arnica, which can help with bruising or tissue trauma you may experience when you give birth. An-

> If you've never taken homeopathic remedies before, here's a word to the wise. Shake the pellets into the bottle cap and then pop them into your mouth rather than touching them with your fingers.

other great homeopathic remedy that promotes healing and, like arnica, comes in both tablets and a cream is Traumeel.

You may also wish to pick up a product called Rescue Remedy at the health food store. This is a flower essence that many swear by to help calm anxiety. Perfect for those moments of stress when you have a new baby in the house! (You can also safely put a few drops in your cat or dog's water bowl to help them adjust to the commotion.)

**Heating pad or rice pack.** Remember the cramping I told you about? Heat is one of the most effective ways to ease the pain and is also great for sore muscles. I recommend having several rice packs on hand. Take a clean tube sock, fill it with rice, and tie off the end—voila! You've got a portable heating pad. Just toss it in the microwave for a minute or two for lasting heat.

**Tucks medicated pads,** or cotton pads and witch hazel. These are good for soothing the hemorrhoids that can often result from late pregnancy and delivery. Some moms also opt to use Preparation-H or another hemorrhoid ointment after giving birth. If 'roids run in your family or if you're already suffering from one now, be prepared!

**Absorbent underwear and pads** for after-birth bleeding. Many women use Depends or other absorbent underwear for the first day or two after giving birth, then switch to extra-absorbent maxi pads. You might need them for as little as a couple of weeks or as long as six weeks or longer . . . all women are different. You won't be able to use tampons—they can cause infections as you heal, and besides, yow!

Here's a cool trick: Soak a couple of maxi pads in water, gently squeeze out the excess, and stick them in the freezer. You'll have perfectly shaped ice packs for your tender parts in case you experience post-pushing soreness or bruising. You can also fill rubber gloves with ice blended with a bit of water and tie the end to create a flexible, soft ice pack that will move with you.

**Nipple cream and nursing pads**. The first few days of breastfeeding can be tough going. Never before have your breasts been so busy, and they can get pretty sore. You will probably also experience some leaking as your milk comes in. Soft, absorbent nursing pads (you can get thick washable ones or thinner cotton disposables) and nipple ointment or lanolin can be life-savers. Lansinoh, found at many discount stores and pharmacies, is a safe, approved pure lanolin ointment that can soothe sore nipples and help them heal.

**Nursing pillow**. I mentioned nursing pillows in an earlier chapter, but they're worth another mention. Not only can they make it easier for you to get off to a good start breastfeeding, but you can use them to prop your arms up while you hold the baby or as extra support for your back.

**Reading material, water bottles, MP3 player, etc.** You'll be laying or sitting down a lot while your baby is small. It can get boring! Have some things on hand to help pass the time and to help keep you hydrated.

Once you've got all those postpartum supplies on hand, don't just leave them sitting in a bag somewhere. In addition to your baby, you'll probably come home from the hospital with a bunch of stuff. That won't be the best time for trying to track down the supplies you need to be comfortable!

I recommend creating several totes stocked with supplies and keeping them in the rooms you'll be most likely to spend time in when you come home from the hospital. Simple plastic dish tubs will work fine, as will one of those famous grid totes that now populate your bathrooms and your kitchen . . . there's no need to be fancy, as you won't be using most of these supplies for long. Group these supplies by purpose and place of use. If you will be splitting your recovery time between the bedroom and the sofa, you might want to have a tote stocked with maxi pads, Tuck's pads, and a peri-bottle in the master bathroom and one in the hall bathroom. In the living room and bedroom, you could have totes with nursing pads, nipple cream, reading material, a heating pad, and pain medication. Once you've sorted your supplies into their proper totes, there's no reason to hang on to packaging. Get rid of it, and it will be one less piece of clutter to worry about when you come home with your baby.

This has been a short week. Shopping for all these supplies will take some time and I don't want to overwhelm you with a long to-do list at this late state of your pregnancy. You have a lot to think about and dwell on right now. Once you've got your supplies, put your feet up and relax!

# 35 WEEKS PREGNANT

## Beautify Your Bathrooms

**This week, you can**

- Create order in all the bathrooms in the home
- Purchase a few organizing tools
- Become conscious of the simple chores that keep these rooms in tip-top shape
- Clean out and organize the linen closet

PITY THE POOR BATHROOM. It helps you get clean but in most homes it's left in habitual disarray. Towels start life on a bar and end up in a damp heap on the floor. Cabinets and drawers are stuffed with products that are used and those that serve as monuments to past beauty and cleanliness experiments. The trash can is usually decorative but woefully inadequate. The medicine chest houses prescriptions from years ago. And multiple bathrobes are piled on top of one hook on the back of the door.

In taking care of the general debris, you'll need to consider the size and function of your bathroom. I've been in postage stamp–sized bathrooms and one so large the couple had a small refrigerator for late-night snacks. No matter the size or the number of bathrooms in your home, you don't want to scatter your energy and run from one to another in a wild organiz-ing frenzy that yields poor results. I'll divide the process into steps over the course of three days.

You most likely have one bathroom in your bedroom and with any luck, Baby has his own as well. Very often the guest room has a bathroom nearby, although it's likely your guests and Baby may have to share. Many homes and some apartments also have a guest powder room near the entry. This is a lifesaver on many levels. You'll want to tackle them all, but one at a time. I would work in the order I mention them here so the most difficult is taken care of first.

While organizing the bathroom, we're also going to take a look at your linen closet. The linen closet is meant to serve the bathroom and the bedrooms. If yours is large and the bathroom is small, we might be able to sneak in some organizing totes and make the linen closet more useful. Are you ready to begin? Depending on your physical size and energy level, you may want to call in the organizing sidekick you've been using throughout the past few months. Don't forget about the possibility of hiring a professional organizer. A week of physical activity is a nice balance to the weeks of research, phone calls, and e-mails you've been handling.

## DAY ONE: DEBRIS, BE GONE!

Yes, it's true. You knew in your heart it was coming. I want you to grab a few sturdy trash bags. We're going to fearlessly whittle down the debris that collects in this room. There is nothing as useful as a speed elimination in a situation like this. Let's go into the master bath with your trusty timer. Set it for twenty minutes.

Now a word to the wise: Moving quickly is essential. Women get stopped in their organizing tracks by two things: emotional items, like photos and old love letters (think boyfriends prior to your hubby), and purchases they made for the bathroom. There is something in our estrogen that makes us feel tremendously guilty if we use a mascara, shampoo, or moisturizer once or twice and decide we don't like it. We want to toss it but we hear a voice in our head saying something along these lines: "You are so wasteful!" "Keep it. You never know when you'll need it." "Maybe you'll feel differently later on." You know the drill. There is a certain reality you have to face. There is a shelf life to beauty products. They don't sit there for years hoping

you'll give them a second chance. Check every product for an expiration date. If you're past it, toss it. If it's still viable but you know you don't like it, set it aside for a friend who might like to try it. You can ask your girlfriends to do the same and have a swap party. One final caveat: If you used a product one or twice and the container looks clean and inviting, put it in a bag or small box for a swap party or to give it to a friend. Maybe your helper today would like these lotions 'n' potions? But if you used half and the item looks extremely uninviting, please toss it. Not even your best friend wants your sloppy seconds!

Here is a list of items you might want to eject from your bathroom:

- Get rid of threadbare towels and washcloths. (Donate them to your local animal shelter or vet.)
- Toss expired cosmetics, lotions, oils, etc.
- Remove items you know you won't use; give them away as discussed above.
- Toss brushes, combs, hair clips, etc. that are no longer used.
- Do you have any broken small electronics like hair dryers, curling irons, or electric toothbrushes? Toss 'em. You need the space.
- Eighty-six the shower curtain if it's old and coated in mildew.
- Go through the drawers looking for worn-out toothbrushes (I've seen spare change in the same drawer as a toothbrush: Toss it!) and other small items you no longer use.

## SHOULD YOU TOSS IT?

Women tend to think of their beauty products as "evergreen," when in fact most have a short shelf life. Keep that in mind the next time you want to pick up some makeup items you really don't need in your kit. They will probably expire before you have a chance to get your money's worth! Here are some guidelines direct from my client Sarah Garcia, the director of Product Development at Jouer Cosmetics. These first appeared in *One Year to an Organized Life*.

**How to find out how old it is:** It is FDA law that all manufactured makeup has a "batch code" or "lot code" on or under the label; for tubes this is crimped into the tube crimp. This code is usually three to five digits or letters and is a record of when the makeup was produced. Each brand and lab has a different system, but this code can easily be used to call up customer service of any brand and ask the age of the makeup. For example: F61 in Jouer language would stand for June 2006, first batch that month.

**Anything SPF** (powders, gloss, lipstick, foundation, etc.): Toss after two years! Most SPF chemicals are only good for two to three years in cosmetics and you don't want to use anything that is expired. Most SPF-containing products in bottles or tubes have expiration dates; tubes usually have this date crimped into the end of the tube.

**Powders—eye shadow, blush, etc.:** These last much longer then we'd think. Most are good for up to five years, but pigments can change over time or oils used in the powder can dry out, making them chalky and dry. They are not harmful if old. I say, test it on your skin. If it applies nicely, keep it; if not, toss it.

**Wax-based products like lipstick and cream blushes:** These tend to have a nice long shelf life, I'd say often up to three to five years. Same advice. Test it out . . . some formulas dry out and get clumpy.

**Wet lip gloss and liquid foundations:** These should be tossed after one to two years! The ingredients often start to separate. You don't want to consume or allow your skin to absorb old ingredients.

**Mascara:** Older than six months—toss it. Unless it's new and has never been opened. If it is still sealed, it can last a few years on the shelf.

- Toss the threadbare throw rugs.
- What about the walls? Are they bare and in need of some decoration? Or does it look like a crowded wing of a museum? Less is more.
- Are there too many items on the counter? Perhaps you have a decorative bottle perfume collection or you like every lotion and potion you use throughout the day to be on display.

If your items are decorative, whittle them down to a precious few and then rotate them rather than re-creating a cosmetics counter in your home. The items you use daily will be dealt with on day two.

- Do you like to stay well stocked on some items? It's wonderful to have backup supplies but it's cumbersome to have them all in your environment at once. Let's set aside the extras and see if we can't find a better storage solution for them.

- Did you buy two large economy-sized bottles of shampoo and put one in the shower while the other was left in the original packaging taking up space under the sink? Just as you did in the kitchen and pantry, eighty-six the packaging. Cardboard and plastic eat up space you need.

- Call your pharmacy and see if they have a drug-recycling program. If they don't, try other pharmacies in your area.

- Expired prescription drugs are classified as hazardous waste. Call your local hazardous waste facility and follow their instructions. They may ask you to deliver the meds to them, do a pickup, or simply give you instructions for the safest at-home disposal.

- You can contact the drug manufacturer to see if they can connect you with an organization that donates expired medications to third-world countries. Each medication is different and you'll have to rely on the experts if you select this option.

While your assistant is hauling the trash bags and the donation box to the next bathroom, take a look around and see if you need to do any of the following before the birth:

- Paint the bathroom. Can this be done before the baby's arrival? Will you be able to leave the apartment or home until the paint is dry and the smell has vanished? If so, schedule a shopping trip for paint samples. Call a painter and put a date on your calendar. (Be sure you tell your spouse!)

- Purchase new throw rugs, shower curtains, towels, and/or washcloths.

- Do you have any grid totes, drawer liners, or small containers for the drawers left over from your kitchen-organizing project? Could you use some in this room? Add them to your list.

- Do you need any additional towel bars or hooks? There is a sturdy, plastic hook that goes over the door and offers several inches of hanging space. If you keep your bathrobes on hangers, several will hang here nicely. This hook is available in the closet or bathroom section of any home store.

- Did you install any items like an over-the-toilet tank organizer that actually eat more room than they supply? Remove them.

- Conversely, do you need any organizing tools of this nature? What about shelves on the wall for towels?

- What about the size of your trash can? Is it too big for the space or much too small?

• Is lighting in the room adequate? Did any overhead or vanity lights burn out months ago? Replace them today.

Let's move to the baby's bathroom. I realize that in many homes this will also be the guest bath, so we have our work cut out for us. Today our task is merely to eliminate. Follow the exact same guidelines you used for the master bathroom. If this is going to be your baby's bathroom, you may want to paint or put up some decorative wallpaper. Just be sure it's done well in advance of his arrival. You don't want your baby wearing a HAZMAT onesie!

If you have a separate guest room with its own bath, you're in the catbird seat because you have an area that's ripe for storing the backup supplies everyone needs. You may also find that Dad decides to use this bathroom so he's got a bit more room for his grooming items. Some couples do everything together, while others need a bit of breathing space. There is no right or wrong and I would bet the need for sharing or for space grows out of your individual childhood experiences. Meagan has five children. When they grow up, the rough-and-tumble sharing that goes on in a big household will be the norm for them. It will probably feel comfortable and familiar. I, on the other hand, am an only child; space and privacy are the norm for me. In other words, if Dad migrates down the hall to a different bathroom, don't push the panic button. Rather, make this room as organized as possible. Use storage tools made of wood or dark colors so it feels more masculine. Get him some towels in

> If the good folks in your home can't seem to keep the linens separated, try this trick: Put the sheets and the extra pillowcases inside one of the pillowcases. You'll keep the entire set together. This is a great way to help toddlers. Try to purchase colors or patterns that identify the set for a specific bed size or room. All-white linens in every room will drive the best of us crazy.

his favorite color. Here is another example of the need for communication and an opportunity to nurture and love through the space itself and not just with words. You know the old saw: "actions speak louder than words." And you thought the bathroom was a big bore, didn't you?

Finally, it's time to look at the linen closet. Your old, frayed, faded, torn, and stained sheets and towels will be welcome at the local animal hospital. If your linen closet is stuffed, remember that you need to make room for the baby's linens. If you have an area with shelves, you can use shelf dividers to set apart the areas for different rooms. You can also label the shelves. Keep in mind that your home may be flooded with relatives and friends all eager to help after the baby arrives. You don't want them trashing the order you create this week. It really saves time if the linens for a specific room reside next to each other on a designated shelf. It also saves you from opening folded sheets and asking yourself: "Is this for the king in the master or the queen in the guest room?"

### If You Don't Use a Linen Closet

Some people don't have a separate area for linens and clear off space on a closet shelf in the room where those linens are used. Usually it's one set on the bed and a spare in the closet. This works well and it certainly prevents any mix-ups. In the absence of a linen closet, some of my clients store all of the towels for a particular bathroom in that room. This only works well if you have cupboard space or if the room is large enough to put shelves up or perhaps bring in a small storage unit to house linens. In today's world there are myriad tools in all manner of designs and materials. You can find wicker, rattan, and wood, just to name a few. There isn't any reason the bathroom can't have a touch of style.

## DAY TWO: BATHROOM ORGANIZING TOOLS

Once the bathrooms have been cleaned out, it's time for lunch. Be sure your helper takes out the trash and finds a spot for the products you wish to share. My best advice is to share it with her so it all leaves today. Discuss with your helper which organizing items you think you need. Get her feedback. Make a list. Take a day to shop for these items yourself if you enjoy this process. Or you can ask your helper to shop for you and schedule a return date. The final option is to order what you need online. It's all going to depend on your individual needs, your interest level in products, your area, and how you are feeling. Don't forget to add up the projected total and be sure we're honoring your budget. Here is a lit of organizing tools:

- Shelf liner for the drawers; use the thick washable liner you got for the kitchen.
- Small containers for the drawers; use acrylic here as it's easy to keep clean.
- Grid totes to keep all related products corralled in one area. Look at your categories of products and decide whether you need the small square or the rectangular size.
- Possibly a container for cleaning supplies under the sink. You can use a grid tote or one of the containers designed for toting cleaning products. The big concern, as it was in the kitchen, is your pipe configuration. Take note!
- If you and your partner use towels only once, is there room for a hamper in the room? It's certainly preferable to the floor.
- Clear, acrylic countertop organizers for items you feel you must have at hand like makeup and cotton balls.
- If you like lots of perfume bottles out, keep them on a tray so there's no bleed-out over the entire countertop.
- If you have shelves that will hold supplies but they will be on view, use small wicker or rattan containers. Be consistent. Different styles, colors, and fabrics will give you a less-than-restful visual.

Some bathrooms have shallow drawers and you can store an entire category there

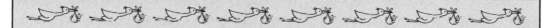

## BABY BATH ITEMS

While you are out shopping for containers, don't forget to have some for baby-specific items. Here's a list to help you get ready to greet Baby in organized style:

In a small grid tote keep:

- 1 bottle baby shampoo
- 1 bottle baby lotion
- 1 container baby powder

(You can of course keep the shampoo in the shower caddy if you want it with the ones you and your partner use.)

You may need to purchase a baby bathtub in the event you didn't receive one at your baby shower. This item takes up room but is a necessity for Baby until he can sit up unsupported. Store it in the tub or lean it against the shower wall. (Many parents bathe their baby in the kitchen sink.)

If you intend to bathe Baby in your regular tub, have a pair of kneepads on hand. You can buy a special mat in baby stores that's specially made for protecting Mom's and Dad's knees next to the tub.

Purchase a few baby washcloths. You can have one in the bathroom and the rest in the linen closet or wherever you store your towels.

You'll want a few containers for inside the baby's bathroom drawers. Start with one to hold his fingernail clippers and his hairbrush.

Have two hooded towels: one for the linen closet and the other for the bathroom. You can hang it on a decorative hook so it's handy.

Finally, don't forget to create a staging area near the area where you'll be bathing Baby with someplace to sit down and all the supplies you'll need to dry off, groom, and dress a slippery naked babe who just got out of the bath. A note: Sometimes you may prefer to wash your baby on the counter and other times the bathtub may be the most appropriate place. For example, the kitchen counter is a great place to put Baby's bathtub because you won't have to stoop over to use it, but sometimes the kitchen might be drafty or you might be in the middle of cooking dinner when Dad wants to give Baby a bath. The tote will give you the flexibility to bathe Baby wherever it makes the most sense.

with ease. In most cases you'll have deep drawers, and inserting grid totes will make your storage more efficient. For example, let's say you have beautiful hair and every day you deal with mousse, gel, spray, etc. Instead of constantly bending down for each product, take out a grid tote that has everything you need to do your hair. Use this for any large category of item that gets used each day. Grid totes are easy to wipe out and keep clean, which is why I like them so much for the kitchen, laundry area, and bathroom. They also come in many colors, which means your products can be in white totes, your spouse's can be in blue, and your baby's supplies can reside in green. And you thought organizing by color only worked in the closet! Organizing is really part of design. Have fun with this part of the process.

You'll want to line Baby's bathroom drawers and have some small drawer containers to catch the miscellaneous items that will be stored here. Keeping related items together saves you time and energy. It also makes you feel very powerful. Just as fumbling and searching make you feel demoralized. I'm repeating myself I realize but until you experience this for yourself you are likely to doubt the importance of categories. By the time you get to the last page of this book, however, I'm going to bet you will be a true devotee!

## DAY THREE: CONTAINER FUN!

What can I say? Putting things away in an organized fashion is a great joy to me. I think about the time, money, and energy my clients are going to save and it truly makes me happy.

As you organize, work in two phases. First, put related items into the containers or drawers, or onto the shelves, you feel are the most convenient. Next, make decisions about your backup supplies. If you

have a large bathroom with lots of storage space, it makes sense to have all such items here. If you need to use a hall closet or the linen closet, keep one thing in mind: As a product gets to the end, you want to transfer the backup supply in a few days early. (Standing soaking wet in a shower is not the time to remember you need the shampoo that's down the hall in the linen closet!) If you are using a guest bathroom for storage you still need to be mindful of your waning products in the master. Knocking on the door and waking Grandma because you need a roll of toilet paper isn't the best way to start any day.

Over the course of about a week, you may move your categories around a bit in order to find the perfect placement. Be sure you keep whatever is stored under the sink in containers. Why? On that inevitable day when you need a plumber, it's going to be a breeze to take out a few containers rather than a chaotic mound of products. Your plumber will be impressed. By the way, were you able to put in a shelving unit in the garage for paper products? Overflow of sanitary supplies, toilet paper, and bathroom cleaning supplies can be stored here before they have to migrate upstairs. Be consistent with your placement and you will always be in charge.

## GRANDMA, HOW LOVELY TO HAVE YOU HERE! WHEN ARE YOU LEAVING?

Whether it's Grandma, Auntie, a cousin, or your best friend, if a guest is sharing a bathroom with Baby, you need to set parameters. What, for example, happens if Grandma or Grandpa gets up frequently in the night? If the baby is in your room, there's no problem. But if he's in his room and it took two hours to get him to sleep, you don't want flushing or fumbling to wake him. The ideal solution is for your guests to use the entry powder room at night and during the day when Baby is asleep. As a last resort, your bathroom is the likely target. It's concerns like these that will help dictate how much live-in family help you have and for how long.

## KEEPING IT CLEAN

It takes as little time to refold a towel or put it in a hamper as it does to toss it on the floor. It takes less than a minute to wipe off a counter with a sponge so that any sticky residue from a beauty product won't cake on the counter. It takes no extra time to place your products where they belong rather than toss them willy-nilly on the countertop.

Some tasks each person using the bathroom must do. Most of my clients, for example, use a squeegee on the shower glass just before they exit the shower to keep the soap scum under control. Here is a list of bathroom maintenance tasks each person can do to keep this room pristine between cleanings:

- Wipe off the counter with a sponge or a pop-up cleaning wipe as you prepare to exit.
- Squeegee the shower when you are done.
- Rinse the bathtub to avoid a ring around the tub.
- Check the garbage. Does it need to be emptied?
- Put products away.
- Fold your towel or put it in the hamper.
- Spray the mirror and wipe off the spray of toothpaste and other debris that inevitably collects on the mirror just above the faucet.

If this seems like a lot, remember that you don't shower or take a bath every time you are in the bathroom. Neither do you take out all of your products during each visit. Very few things are done each time. These small actions make the bathroom an inviting place for you and for your partner. If one of you habitually leaves towels on the floor, you have a choice. Either that partner grows up and acts like a responsible adult or the other person becomes the maid or the butler. Which of these do you want to offer your baby as an example of the ideal way to share space? Let me close with this bit of advice: Never leave the bathroom knowing that there are two squares of toilet paper left on the roll. We've all been there. I rest my case for this week!

# 36 WEEKS PREGNANT

## Wind Down at Work and Prepare for Maternity Leave

This week, you can

- Take a look at the role procrastination plays in your life
- Make final arrangements at your place of employment
- Wrap up things around your home office

LET'S SEE how clairvoyant I am. I predict that you had one of three reactions to the initial material on getting your business life ready for your departure:

- You are a gold-star student who did everything I suggested. You have been ready to leave for a long time. Everyone at work has been coached. Clients are happy. Vendors feel secure. The space itself is pristine.
- You're a dabbler. You did some of the things but not all. But you've been planning to get with the program this week and finish so you can have your baby and be truly present with the experience.
- You read the material and said as they do in my hometown of Brooklyn, New York: Fuggedaboutit. You have a deep sense of panic as this week dawns and another month draws to a close. Nothing is in place for your departure. Worse-case scenario, your

coworkers think you're on top of things! Won't they be surprised?

Take a deep breath. There's no reason to panic. Remember one of the basic concepts of Zen Organizing is that the whole of anything is overwhelming. You need to break projects down into the parts that make up the whole in order to gain control. No one exits her mother's womb and runs a marathon. We crawl. We walk. We run. We work in stages. And that's what we're going to do this month. The difference is, you'll need to buckle down and really do the work. Let me ask you a few questions to see if we can't shed some light on which choice you made a few months ago when this material first presented itself.

## THE NATURALLY ORGANIZED

If you took the first route, you're probably a naturally organized person. You thrive on order. You are wired very much like me. You use this book as a guide not a teacher. Motherhood will be a time you train your own child how to be organized. (I'm going to guess you learned from your mother.) Of course, the universe has a sense of humor so don't be shocked if you have a child who is a free spirit and rebels against you in this area. My parents didn't want a child who was an artist. They wanted a doctor or a lawyer. Very often in life we get what we most need, not what we want.

## THE DABBLER

Were you the dabbler? It is more than likely that you are in the majority. It takes several months before the idea of the impending birth really takes hold as a reality. Is there a part of you that is reluctant to leave your job? After all in this arena you may be very successful and in control. You're leaving this world for one that is unknown and that's always scary. Never fear. About two weeks after the birth you will feel like an old hand. In reality, organizing is organizing and what changes are the items in your hands, not the concepts behind the work. One day it's file folders and the next it's diapers.

## THE QUEEN OF FUGGEDABOUTIT

If you are the Queen of Fuggedaboutit, let's see if we can't find out *why*. That's the

great thing about life: There's always a reason. I love helping my clients find out why they are so reluctant to get organized. If we can understand the root cause, we're free to set something more productive in its place. Please take twenty minutes and answer the following questions in your baby journal.

- Are you always doing things at the last minute?
- Is that the behavior you observed as a child? Is it "the norm" as far as you're concerned?
- When others have to wait for you to go to dinner or deliver a project at work, do you secretly enjoy the extra attention?
- If you gave this up, would there be another way for you to gain the attention you enjoy/crave?
- Do you ever worry about being a mom? Do you wonder if not being able to do things in a timely fashion will adversely affect your child?
- Were you always on time and super organized until a specific event occurred? What was that?

As you can tell from these questions, I'd like to uncover the reason you tend to procrastinate. It's going to make life as a mother more complicated if you are always late, harried, and in chaos. You don't have to solve this issue today; just keep your thinking cap on after you complete this exercise and see what inspirations come to you. Let me share a story that may help you feel less alone.

## Connie Makes the Connection

This lady is one of my favorite clients. Connie is warm, funny, entertaining, a great mom, and an accomplished businesswoman. She called me in to assist her because she has trouble getting rid of things. Her home is small and she didn't want chaos to be imprinted on her children's DNA as the norm. It was also no secret that her husband, Jeffrey, was at his wit's end. Connie decided we'd work in her home office to jumpstart the changes she wanted to make. As always happens, Connie and I chatted away and almost by magic the past revealed itself. Here is what she shared with me.

Connie is the product of a broken home. Her father died shortly after the divorce and her mother remarried a few years later. Connie never liked her stepfather and from all accounts he was jealous of her relationship with her mother. The family made two significant moves during Connie's school years. She was never consulted or informed. One day she would just come home from school and a few key possessions would be packed into suitcases. The rest would have been dumped. Was it any wonder that as an autonomous adult in charge of her own world, Connie had difficulty parting with her possessions? See whether you have a traumatic experience like this in your childhood. You want to disconnect from it, if you can, before your baby arrives. A few sessions with a therapist might work wonders. It certainly made all the difference for Connie!

## THE RELUCTANT BUT REFORMED

Yes, it's true. There is another path to organization. Maybe you'll be like Meagan as the reluctant but reformed organized person. You weren't born with a penchant for organization and routines. In fact, for a long time you rebelled against anything in your life that resembled structure. But then you began realizing that when you make small, orderly changes to your environment, you feel better and it is easier to get things done. Organizing may not be second nature to you, but you can still exert control over your surroundings. You can be just as disciplined and orderly as the naturally organized—as long as you give yourself plenty of time to create a new, healthy habit.

## LEAVING THE OFFICE BEHIND

### Projects

The first thing we have to do is make an assessment of your projects. What has to happen with each one while you are gone? Do you have competent people covering for you? Are your clients aware that in the not-too-distant future they will be dealing with someone else at your company? Now is the time to check to see if there are any details that need your attention. If you will be returning to your job post–maternity leave, it is especially important that you provide for smooth sailing. Otherwise you'll be a sore, sleep-deprived new mother who has to deal with unnecessary chaos at work.

## Information

The second question is: Do you have all your papers in order should anyone wish to check out the status of a project? There's no time now to overhaul your file system. If it's in disarray, at the very least you can pull the files your colleagues will need to access and put them in one drawer. Let's say you have the ABC, the XYZ, and the DEF projects. There are about five files for each that contain volatile information that someone will most likely have to access. Empty a file drawer (preferable the one in your desk), and place the projects in alphabetical order with the files for each in box bottom file folders (if the material is large enough to fill one). This emergency step will short-circuit complaints about your lack of organization. It will remain your dirty little secret. After your return you can revamp the system as you make room for the new information that has accumulated. Remember to ask whoever is collecting your mail to leave it all in a box in your office. You don't want to walk in and see mail, memos, newsletters, magazines, and other communications sprawled all over your desk. It will be *Little Shop of Horrors* without the music!

## Communication

Some women will want to be out of the loop while they are away. Others will want e-mail and/or phone updates so that they can stay current and save time when they get back to the office. It depends on your personality and the type of job you do. If you fall into the latter group be sure and set boundaries. You don't want calls, e-mails, or IMs being sent at all hours of the day and night. At the same time you set boundaries for others, set parameters for yourself. When and how you respond is up to you. If you have an assistant, ask everyone to run their communications through him. And give your assistant specific instructions about what information can be shared with others. Do you really want *everyone* to know when you go into labor?

## Physical Space

Finally, what does your physical office look like? If it will be closed up while you are gone, don't think you're off the hook. Remember that sleep-deprived, sore, cranky mom I referenced above? She deserves to walk into a space that is at the very least devoid of extraneous debris. I'm not asking you to organize the space now; it's really too near to your due date. I am asking you to divest the space of junk. You know what I'm talking about. Here are some ideas for you to consider:

- If you have lots of office supplies, return them to the central area. Let others use these in your absence. You can restock later.
- Now is a good time to take home personal mementos, photos, and plants (real or fake).

- Take home the shoes, sweaters, umbrellas, and boots that clog this space.
- Check your drawers and files for anything relating to your personnel file or any personal information you have stored here.
- If you have sensitive information about other employees be sure it's left under lock and key.
- If you have food items like condiment packages, take them to the communal kitchen or toss them. Don't leave *any* food in your office.
- Did you stash items here that needed to go to the post office or be returned to a store? Dispense with these tasks now.

As you gaze around your office, what would you add to this list? Pretend it's a few months or weeks after the birth. What visual do you want to be presented with upon your return? Create that this week! You want to walk into this space after your baby arrives and feel welcome. It's possible with the work you do this week. And if you are leaving your job for good, clean out your space and set up those key files I mentioned above to honor the person who follows you. It's funny the way life works: When we take the time to care for others the very same energy returns to us multiplied. In fact, why not take a few extra minutes and divest the space of all extraneous files. Send off to archives any material that must be part of the company record but doesn't concern the next person working here. And finally don't forget that your computer and your physical space mirror each other. Be sure they are both streamlined before you walk out for the last time.

## THE HOME OFFICE

Please read the material for the mom working outside the home (page 32). If you skipped that material, I assure you there are many parallels. And the key is communication. By now, everyone who is involved in your work, from clients to vendors, knows you are pregnant. The most important things you can take care of this week are twofold: First, make sure all projects are on schedule. Secondly, make your post-baby plans clear to everyone. You don't want anyone to assume you are going to shut down your business after your baby arrives and take the precautionary step of taking their business elsewhere. If you need this income to support your lifestyle and your baby, safeguard it with care and clear communication.

Working as a freelance writer, Meagan had a challenge when deciding how to handle her maternity leaves with babies number three, four, and five. She didn't want her clients to feel anxious about her ability to handle her workload, but she also didn't want to find an unexpected "emergency" issue in her inbox a few days after giving birth! So Meagan took a few minutes to contact each of her clients about four weeks before her due date, either via e-mail or phone (whichever the client seemed to prefer). In this communication, she'd tell her clients that she was just a few weeks away from her due date, and ask them to come to her as soon as possible with any questions or concerns . . . or else to shelve them until a few weeks after her due date. Her clients were always grateful for the heads-up and usually either let her know there was no hurry on the project, or else came to her right away with last-minute concerns. She never had to field a question or problem during her self-created maternity leave!

## AS THE MONTH DRAWS
## TO A CLOSE

For a long time we were inching along, weren't we? Now time is flying and your progress needs to be swift. Baby may not follow the proscribed timetable and may decide to arrive early. Next month the assignments won't be as time consuming, I promise. But they will be important. Next month is the last mini-rest you'll have before your new life begins. Savor it. And if you are berating yourself for not doing more office organizing earlier, remember that everything happens when the time is right. Instead of guilt and regret, make this a teaching moment. For those of you who are prone to these feelings, I'm closing out the month with a quote:

*Mistakes are the portals of discovery.*
—James Joyce

Maybe this is the week you leave procrastination behind for good.

# CHAPTER SEVEN

# 37 to 40 Weeks Pregnant

*For so many, life is a battle. For so few, life is a dance.*

—RAMAKRISHNA ANANDA

THIS MONTH IS DIFFERENT from all the others in this book. I'd like you to read it through once before you set out to do the assignments. I want you to take care of the tasks in the first two weeks. If Baby should arrive a bit early, it's really important these items (your hospital bag and contact list) are crossed off your to-do list. And there is information in the last two weeks that you can make use of all month long. I don't want you to wait!

Grab your favorite drink and put your feet up. Take a few minutes and read the chapter. As promised, there are no big organizing projects this month. Your sidekick can retire. You're free to float around your home admiring your handiwork as a Zen Organizer. Stop often in your baby's room and daydream about the future. If you find there are some daydreams you particularly enjoy, embrace, enhance, embellish, and repeat them. Daydreams become creative visualizations when you do this!

This month we're going to be sure you have every last detail handled. If you have a computer, once again Excel will be your new best friend. It's a snap to create documents that you can keep accessing long after the baby's birth. You will, for example, need an updated contact sheet for years to come. Start it now and tweak it often. And with e-mail you can share this information with key members of your family and friendship circles. Our other big task for this month is to have the all-important hospital bag ready to go. You don't want to be fumbling around your home between contractions mumbling: "Gosh, I hope I have everything!"

When the hospital bag is by the door and the lists have been created, our major focus will be on you. Taking care of yourself enables you to keep your physical, emotional, and mental storehouses full. Otherwise you won't have anything to give your baby. You can draw water from a full well, not a dry one. Many of my clients feel guilty when they plan a reward or spontaneously do nice things for themselves. It's time to embrace healthy self-care as an expression of high self-esteem. What a wonderful gift to give your child: the ability to nurture herself, something she will learn by observing how skilled Mom and Dad are at the process.

I've worked in apartments that were so tiny a hobbit would have been right at home. Conversely, I've worked in huge homes that took days to unpack. And in every home, from studio to mansion, there always seems to be one special place. It's usually a little nook where you can curl up and be at peace. I've always dreamed about having a window seat where I could watch the world go by. Cats have the right idea, don't they? Let's consciously create such a place for you and your baby. Ancient yogis said that it was best if you meditated in the same spot every day. On those days when you didn't really feel like meditating, the energy of past experiences would draw you in. I've adapted that concept to my organizing philosophy.

Part of Zen Organizing is dedicating each room to the function for which it was designed. It's why I feel that bedrooms shouldn't have computers, DVD players, or TV sets. Bedrooms are meant to be for sleep and fun. And now you can create a special nook for you and your baby. Sit there now and dream about the future. Imagine your baby in your arms. What will you say to her? What songs will you sing? Will this be your favorite breastfeeding spot? If you don't have a place already, this month has tips to help you create one. My hope is that your baby will feel comfort the minute you two settle into this spot. After all, she was with you when you designed it, wasn't she?

## HABIT OF THE MONTH: PUT YOUR FEET UP FIVE MINUTES A DAY

Now tell me, isn't this the most delicious habit? On the horizon is a time when you will wish you could do this, so take advantage. And what will you do during these 5 minutes? Let's see, here are some ideas:

- Take a cat nap
- Start a new book
- Reacquaint yourself with a favorite book
- Meditate
- Call an old friend
- Call a new friend
- Surf the Internet for baby blogs
- Watch a funny movie

Now let's go crazy, OK? You can enhance any of these choices. How? I'm so delighted you asked!

- Wrap yourself in a new shawl when you nap, read, chat, or meditate. Make it a soft cashmere or fine cotton or silk. There should be a tactile pleasure the minute you touch it.
- Have your favorite drink at your side: hot tea or mineral water with a twist of lemon or lime. Drink out of a beautiful glass or mug that's just for you.

- Be sure you are completely comfortable and use some decorative pillows in strategic places. Make fluffing and placing the pillows part of the ritual.
- Have a healthy snack on the table by your chair. Put it on a beautiful dish.

Make your five-minute breaks something you look forward to and savor. And if they extend beyond five minutes, so much the better for you and Baby.

# 37 WEEKS PREGNANT

## Prepare the Final Checklists

**This week, you can**

- Be sure you're organized and ready to deliver
- Create a master list and then distribute versions of it as needed

YOU'VE COME A LONG WAY, Mama. This week we cross our t's and dot our i's. If you're like me and you adore lists, I've got some ideas for checklists that are right up your alley. I trust you've been walking around your home admiring all the order you created. It's more than likely you've also gotten attached to Baby's new toys. I mean, who doesn't love stuffed animals? You have a right to be proud.

Getting organized for your baby has surely taken you into territory you didn't expect to visit. Over the course of the next few months you are going to be grateful you did this work. The organized kitchen, bathroom, and bedroom will be much easier to navigate. Just think, when Aunt Ellen asks where something is, you will be able to pinpoint the exact location with remarkable speed. And those labels you took the time to put up will ensure that all of your helpers honor your handiwork. You won't waste a second with your baby looking for an important piece of paper. No one will ask you for a contact number because they will have a copy of the reference list you created for yourself.

Let's wrap up and get ready for the joy, upheaval, and sleep deprivation to come!

### EXCEL: A MOM'S BEST FRIEND

I've suggested you use Excel several times during the course of the past six months. This week, if you don't have a computer I'm going to ask that you borrow a laptop or work at the library. Some smart phones also come with Excel or a similar spreadsheet application installed, which is great because you can take your information with you when you're mobile. You have a lot of material to pull together and Excel will make it a snap to tailor checklists for different groups of people working from one master. First, we'll create our categories. Next, we'll fill in the pertinent information. We'll wrap up by grouping the information for specific family members and friends. You and your spouse need to access the master list; everyone else will have the sections they need. Yes, I know, Aunt Ellen likes to think she knows it all. When you send her list, don't tell her that there's more information out there. It will make her crazy.

## FAMILY MEMBERS AND FRIENDS

When it comes to notifying the army of well wishers who are waiting to hear the birth news, don't saddle your partner with the task of calling a bazillion people. He's likely to be as worn out as you are. Why not create a list with everyone put into groups. Each group has a "captain" who will notify everyone on his list. Dad only has to call the captain. And if your list is large, let him call one captain who can in turn alert the other team leaders it's time to hit the phones. You'll want to include name; home, work, and cell phone numbers; and e-mail addresses. The latter is for those captains who are tech savvy and may want to send a written message in lieu of a phone call to save time.

## GOOGLE YOUR GUESTS

Around the time your baby is born, you'll likely have several out-of-town guests coming to stay. Since nobody knows exactly when a baby is coming until she arrives, some of the travel plans will probably be last minute. You'll want a way for family and friends to stay connected, but of course you'll be in no position to oversee all the details yourself. This is a perfect situation for Google's menu of free products and services. You can set up a Google Group where loved ones can discuss travel plans with one another. They can use Google Calendar to create a schedule they can all see. And using Google Docs, one relative can create an Excel spreadsheet with details like cell phone numbers, flight arrival times, and more, that all the other members of the group will be able to access and edit. You'll have given your family and friends a useful way to stay connected and informed of one another's travel plans without having to go through you. You'll have enough on your mind!

## CHILDCARE, PET CARE, AND YOUR HOME

Back to your master list. List whoever is taking care of your children, your home, and your pets while you are in the hospital in a separate section; include their names, phone numbers, and e-mails. I would also indicate the schedule so that everyone from family and friends to all the various caretakers know who is to be on site when. They will also be able to call each other in the event that one of them has an emergency.

If you have small children at home, be sure their caregivers have the pediatrician's contact information. You will want to create a simple document with your child's insurance information and birth date along with a statement allowing their caregiver permission to seek emergency medical treatment on their behalf. Be sure to sign this letter. If they take any meds, clear instructions should be written and the secure location shared.

If you have animals, don't forget to leave your vet's phone number and his address as well as the nearest animal emergency center. No one ever gets sick during regular business hours, do they?

Have you distributed house keys? Does everyone know the combination to your security system? Did you alert the security company to the fact that you have an impending delivery and a lot of new people will be coming and going? They will most likely give you a temporary code for use during this period. In most cities false alarms generate a fine. Ask for some leniency in the event that Uncle Harry inadvertently screws up! Do you have lights on timers? Is someone bringing in your mail? What about your newspaper? Who is going to take out the garbage cans and bring them back down the driveway? The devil really is in the details.

## LEGAL

This section of your list includes the information that is truly for emergencies only. List your attorney if you have one. Did you draw up your will? What about the childcare document specifying who will raise your child in the event both you and your husband have a fatal accident? And what about your life insurance policy information? I know you have an organized file system and that this information is easy to find. I also know that there is only a remote chance you'll need this during the delivery. I just like to be prepared.

## MEDICAL AND BENEFITS

Everyone will want to know the name and address of the birth facility. I would include the phone number as well as contact information for all medical personnel assisting you, especially your OB-GYN and doula. Family and friends are most likely to reach a service and have to leave a message. But at least they won't be flying blind if they are trying to find out your condition in the event of an emergency. With that said, we all have Nervous Nellies in our family tree. And that's the beauty of Excel. Aunt Tilly and Uncle Tony don't need these numbers, right?

Be sure you have your medical ID card with you. (You'll be packing your hospital bag next week.) Is there any other information the hospital will need for admission? (Pre-registering at your hospital can help you save time while checking in.) I would have your ID number and the name of your insurance company and agent (if applicable) on hand as well as contact numbers on this sheet for added security. In the event you lose or forget your wallet, you can access your list.

Keep a hard copy of the contact list with you, and if you have a smart phone, keep it there too so you'll be able to access the document easily. Does your phone have these functions? Great! Do you know how to use them? Take some time to learn and be sure your partner has the same information on his phone.

## SO MANY DETAILS, SO LITTLE TIME

I'm sure it feels a little overwhelming when you read this material. I think you'll be amazed how quickly this will go because you have been so organized over the past seven months. You can always beg your sidekick to return and do this for you. Promise to make her a nice pot of tea. You can snuggle into a chair and dictate names and numbers to her. I bet you feel better already!

# 38 WEEKS PREGNANT

## Pack Your Hospital Bag

**This week, you can**

- Prepare your hospital bag

IN SOME WAYS, packing for your hospital stay can feel like preparing for a lengthy voyage. Your hospital stay will usher in a huge change in your life. In many ways, it will be very much like visiting a foreign country! What do you need to have on hand for this journey?

In most hospitals, the bulk of your postpartum stay will happen in a separate room —sometimes even on a separate floor!— from where you labor and deliver. Some of the items you'll need for each portion of your stay are different, but you'll want to have some of your items in both places.

I'm going to split this list into three sections, in case you'd rather pack your items separately. This will also keep you from having to dig through a lot of items you won't need while in labor and vice versa.

Keep in mind that if you are planning a cesarean birth or end up having one unexpectedly, your hospital stay will be several days long. You can either pack for those extra days or plan to send your spouse home to get you extra changes of clothing during your stay.

### LABOR AND DELIVERY

- Your birth plan.
- Music you might like (many moms like to make their own playlist. Check with your hospital to see if you need to bring your own CD player or MP3 player).
- Snacks and drinks for labor. Keep it light: fruit juice, herbal tea, an electrolyte replacer like Gatorade, granola bars, fruit, etc. If you're hiring a doula, bring snacks for her, and for Dad, too. Some women like hard candy, mints, or gum while in labor.
- Heating pad or rice pack.
- List of people to call to announce the news.
- Any reference materials you think you might need—for example, your childbirth educator may have given you illustrations of different positions to try in labor or descriptions of massage techniques. Don't rely on your memory! Labor and delivery will take you to a more basic and primal place

in your mind. Written instructions are often necessary to remind you of what you've learned.
• Massage oil.

---

If you're giving birth at home or in a freestanding birth center you may have a different list of supplies you will need to have on hand and/or bring along with you. Your midwife will supply this information. Don't wait until the last minute to track down the supplies you'll need—some of them may be tricky to find.

Some women who are planning a hospital birth still like to have an emergency birth kit at home or in the car (or in both places!) just in case things go much faster than planned. You can buy kits online that contain all of the supplies plus an instructional sheet helping you know what to do in the event that your baby decides to make a surprise appearance. At minimum, you'll want to have some clean, dry towels, a blanket big enough to cover Mom and some receiving blankets for wiping/swaddling the baby, hand sanitizer, a flashlight, a bottle of rubbing alcohol and cotton pads, and a hospital-quality suction bulb on hand in your car and at home. Many birth kits will include scissors and cord clamps, but in most cases you can leave Baby's cord intact until emergency help arrives. If you are unable to make it to the hospital and your baby is on her way, call 911. The dispatcher will send help and talk you through the process.

---

• Whatever nightgown or other outfit you plan to wear when you give birth. Bring an extra just in case.
• If you'll be laboring or giving birth in the water, bring something to wear in the tub. (Some moms prefer to go nude, while others like to wear a bathing suit top or bra). Don't forget swim trunks for Dad in case he wants to get in the water as well.
• Don't forget your insurance information and master list!

## POSTPARTUM

• Nursing bras. If you'll be having your baby via cesarean section, pack several of these to last your whole stay.
• Nursing pads. The washable ones are nice but how will you launder them in the hospital? Disposable cotton pads may be more convenient until you're home.
• Something to wear in the hospital—perhaps a pair of soft pajamas with a nice loose top for breastfeeding. Nursing gowns are nice, too. Bring an extra pair or two.
• Rescue Remedy, arnica, crampbark or After-Ease tincture.
• Going-home outfit and blanket for Baby.
• Going-home outfit for Mom. Remember, most women are not going to fit back into their pre-pregnancy jeans yet . . . or any time soon. It takes a long time to lose pregnancy weight, so give yourself a break and

pack something very forgiving and comfortable to wear home. That doesn't mean you have to go home in pj's or sweats. What about a nice pair of yoga pants or some of those second-trimester jeans you haven't been able to fit into for a while?

- Bella Band or maternity support garment. For the first few weeks after giving birth, your internal organs will literally be shifting around and trying to find their way back to where they used to be. Wearing something that provides gentle support to your abdomen can help make this a lot more comfortable—and you'll look smoother under clothes, too.
- Maxi pads, Depends.
- Tucks Pads, hemorrhoid cream (even if you're confident hemorrhoids won't happen to you—better safe than sorry!).
- Phone number for lactation consultant or La Leche League.
- Baby journal, birth announcements, reading material, and other things to keep your mind occupied while you're resting.

## DELIVERY AND POSTPARTUM

These are the items you'll want in both rooms. You can pack a separate bag for these or double up on them in each of the other two bags.

- Toothbrushes for you and your partner and toothpaste.

---

### DON'T FORGET THE CAR SEAT

Remember, you'll need to bring your infant car seat with you to the hospital. Most hospitals will want to see the car seat before they will let you leave with the baby! Now is a great time to read the instructions and practice installing and removing the seat so that it's second nature by the time you're leaving the hospital. You might also practice with a doll so that you can figure out how all the clasps work ahead of time. Car seats are often more complicated than they look.

---

- Your own pillow. Use a recognizable pillowcase so you don't get it mixed up with the hospital's pillows.
- Camera and/or video camera. Don't forget batteries, film, and if it's a digital camera, a way to download pictures for showing your baby off!
- Cell phone or laptop. After the baby's born, you may want to share news via social media, ask your virtual friends for baby advice, and/or look up information on breastfeeding or baby care. And if your labor slows down, you may welcome the distraction of your favorite applications or Web sites. You know what they say about a watched pot. . . .
- Lip balm.
- Toiletries like deodorant, shampoo, and soap. You'll want this with you in both rooms. Sometimes labor goes

longer than you'd expect and a nice shower can help you refresh.

This list is by no means exhaustive. If there is an item I've left off that would bring you comfort while you're in the hospital, by all means, bring it. Just remember that while it may seem like you're packing for a North Pole expedition, anything you may forget will be as close as your home or the nearest pharmacy. The last thing you'll want to have to worry about while caring for a new baby is unpacking an enormous suitcase.

Every woman I know has two items that will come in handy at this time: cosmetic bags and zip-top storage bags. Keep related items in separate containers so you (or your partner, doula, or best friend) don't have to rifle through a big duffle bag every time you need something. Ziploc makes a really large bag now that will come in handy for the bulkier categories. Lay everything out on your bed per each master category above and then divide them into (what else?) related categories. For example, you might place your "comfort items" for labor, like massage oil and heating pads, in one bag, while items you'll need to use during a postpartum bathroom trip—say, hemorrhoid cream and maxi pads—should stay together in another bag for easy grabbing. You'll know what size zip-top or cosmetic bag to use. I think most categories are evident, but if Dad clutches in emotional situations, go ahead and label the bags for him.

# 39 WEEKS PREGNANT

## Create a "Mom and Baby" Nook Somewhere in Your Home

**This week, you can**

- Prepare a special nook for you and Baby
- Keep this area stocked with supplies
- Consider how to make this nook interesting over the long haul

THIS JUST MIGHT BE the most fun assignment so far. As I mentioned in the introduction, one of the keys of Zen Organizing is creating special places in your home to relax and be at peace. Since you and Baby will be spending a lot of time snuggling, rocking, and nursing over the upcoming months, why not purposely create a peaceful, comforting spot where the two of you can retreat instead of just plopping down wherever you happen to be? And here's the best part: You can have more than one nook. Let's say you love the morning sun and the way it streams into the family room. Why not enjoy that warmth and special time of day with Baby? If he's arriving in the dead of winter, those warm rays from the sun will comfort both of you. As the day fades and night takes over the world, you might enjoy another spot equally well.

What if Baby is coming in the middle of summer and you live in a house with a beautiful back porch that overlooks your yard? You might want to create a nook there so that you and your baby can enjoy the early evening hours outdoors. I have a friend who bought a tiny, nondescript house in an unfashionable part of town. It took about two years but he turned the front and back yards into magical areas. No matter where you look you see beauty and hear the soft trickling from multiple water fountains. It's soothing to the eye, the ear, and the soul to be in those areas. You can create magic as well.

### PICK YOUR SPOT

I want you to pick your spots with care. Let's do the "fresh eyes" exercise. You'll need to leave your home for a bit so if you don't have time this minute or you are feeling sleepy, do the exercise the next time you return home from running an errand, walking the dog, or visiting the doctor's office.

Walk around your home as if you have never been here before. Are there any spots that catch your eye as being particularly inviting? You probably have a candidate in mind but this walk will open your eyes to new possibilities.

## YOUR PERSONAL STAMP

Each of us is unique in some way. Now that you've chosen your spot, how will you make it unique? Here are some considerations to help you decide what you will do in your nook:

Is music important to you? What about an iPod docking station? Or just stash an iPod and some headphones here.

Do you love plants and indoor gardening? See the box below for some tips.

Are you an avid reader? You'll want a good light source and a bookcase or some bookends so that your stash doesn't get sloppy looking.

Do you love rocking chairs or a big, comfy side chair? Do you need to move some furniture to get your favorite chair in your designated nook?

What about items like comfy pillows or beautiful shawls? Do you have what you need to make this nook especially inviting?

Himalayan salt lamps cast a soft magical glow and throw off negative ions. They come in a variety of shapes and sizes. It is recommended that you leave the lamps on twenty-four hours a day. The light bulb in-

### GROW A GREEN THUMB

The idea that only some people have a green thumb is as silly as the concept that only some people can get organized. If you have never had any luck with plants, I'm going to bet I know why. You see, I used to labor under the same false assumption. Like the old me, you are probably prone to bringing home exotic plants that you plop in areas where they can't possibly thrive. Here's the trick with plants: First decide where you would like them to go. Note the light source and the amount of heat or air conditioning that area gets. Then go to a reputable nursery and find the on-site expert. Tell her what your conditions are in detail and she will match you up with the perfect plant.

There is one fly in the ointment: Plants need water! Some need periodic fertilizer. And all will eventually need to be repotted. You'll have to stick with a simple schedule to care for them properly. Plants are alive, and nurturing them and watching them grow is a joy. They absorb pollutants, give off oxygen, and breathe visual life into any environment. A decorator client taught me to mix shades of green and shapes of leaves to create an interesting visual.

Finally, there are varieties of green plants that thrive with very little care. Ask your nursery rep to show you a "cast iron plant." Yes, that's the common name. You find them in malls because, as the name suggests, it's almost impossible to kill them with neglect. If you aren't sure about your ability to care for plants, start with this one. Otherwise, bring home a few silk plants for their decorative value.

side is only fifteen watts so the cost is negligible. I have one in every room. (You'll find a source in the Resources section.)

This might be another great place for a small water fountain. You don't want this to run twenty-four hours a day because the water evaporates and adding water to a fountain isn't high on your to-do list. Turn it on when you sit down with Baby. Again the sound of water may be very comforting to her, as she's just left a water world of her own.

## THE WELL-STOCKED SPOT

No matter where you settle, you're going to want basic supplies at hand. You don't want to get comfy and cozy with the baby asleep in your arms and suddenly realize you don't have that new book you just started (or your e-reader). Here is a list of items you'll want to have on hand. Be sure you replenish this area. (If you have a housekeeper, you might put this task on her to-do list.) Here are some items to get you started:

- Tissues
- Diapers
- Wipes
- Nursing pillow
- Water bottle
- Lip balm
- Burp cloth
- Blanket (a nice-sized one to cover up both you and Baby)
- Quick snacks in case you get settled in with Baby just as your stomach starts rumbling! Granola bars are a good choice.
- Remember the postpartum tote we created last month? You'll want to keep one here stocked with your nursing supplies and medications for at least the first few days after you come home.

## EVERYTHING GROWS

Over time this nook may become a special spot for you and your toddler. Build the possibility of growth into your plans. Here are some ideas:

A small folding/portable bookcase might have been your first choice for this area. It will work well while you're holding a baby. But a sturdy one will work better over the long haul. For example, a toddler might grab one of the legs of the portable bookcase as he crawls by and down it may go!

A bookcase is great because the top can be used for your baby supplies. Keep them in containers to preserve a tidy and welcoming environment. If your baby already has books, start filling the bottom shelf in addition to the bookcase in his bedroom.

If the area has floor space, over time you can set this up as a play area for your growing child. You might want a playpen at first and later set up a small easel for your budding artist.

As your need for baby-related supplies wanes, the bookcase shelves or baskets you used are now free to house toys and more books.

I hope you enjoy setting this nook up as much as you will enjoy sharing the space with your baby. And remember to keep your partner involved in the process. Invite him to sit with your child in this comforting space and read her a story or sit on the floor and play with his son. Moms are flooded with baby-bonding hormones at this time; it's easy to unconsciously ignore Dad. Even if you feel you do everything better for your baby, be sure to involve your partner with Baby's care. After all, without him there would be no reason to create a nook.

# 40 WEEKS PREGNANT

## Take Care of Yourself to Get Ready to Care for Your Baby

This week, you can

- Decide on specific and fun ways to nurture yourself before the baby arrives
- Consider which forms of self-care you wish to permanently incorporate into your life

Y OU'RE ALMOST THERE! If you haven't already had your baby, you're now forty weeks pregnant and have either reached your estimated due date or are very close. Congratulations! Your baby will be here very soon.

Even though it can be frustrating to wait, a "late" baby presents an opportunity. Most likely you're on maternity leave from work or have wound down your duties considerably in anticipation of your baby's birth. Nobody is expecting much of you right now. Take advantage of this slow time of your life and savor it as much as possible. I know, that's easier said than done at times. But think of it this way: No matter how uncomfortable you are right now, your baby will never be as easy to care for again. Right now, your body and your baby are doing all the work of getting her ready to be born.

In a few short weeks you'll probably be tired and overwhelmed and may find yourself looking back on this time with a bit of wistfulness. Don't wish these precious last few days of quiet anticipation away! Instead, look at them as an opportunity to take care of yourself really well so that when the moment of motherhood arrives, you'll be as refreshed and ready as possible.

Now is a great time to:

- Get a massage. Opt for a therapist experienced in pregnancy massage. He or she will know how to comfortably work on your pregnant body. Also, there are certain pressure points that have been shown to stimulate labor— a therapist who specializes in prenatal massage will be aware of these points and stay away from them until your baby is full term.
- Get a pedicure and manicure.
- Read. You may find that your brain is too foggy or full of baby thoughts for *War and Peace*. That's okay. Essay

and short-story anthologies are great for right now since you can read in short bursts. Or, if you're drawn to fashion or home-decorating magazines, that's a great pastime, too.

- Go to the movies.
- Go see a play.
- Go for a slow, gentle walk around the neighborhood or through the woods. Take time to really experience the season—remember, you'll probably be spending a lot of time indoors in the very near future. Will you miss smelling the lilacs or watching the leaves turn color this year because you'll be so busy sniffing your baby's scent and staring at his fingers and toes? Get your fill of nature now.
- Go out with your spouse.
- Spend some time with your baby journal. Whether you're feeling excited, anxious, impatient, or all of the above, getting it out on paper may help you work through feelings that are subconsciously holding you back from going into active labor.
- Get your hair cut and/or colored. Highlights are generally considered safe for pregnant women since the dye doesn't sit on the scalp and so can't be absorbed through the skin. Semi-permanent vegetable-based dyes are also considered safe. Talk to your stylist about a cut that will grow out well and can be worn in a variety of styles that will fit your new life. Trust me, it may be a while before you can dedicate forty-five minutes a day to blow-drying your hair again.

When people are tired, rushed, and working at home, it's easy to forget you haven't brushed your teeth, and flossing becomes nothing more than a good intention. Stop the madness! Plaque has been linked to heart disease and stroke. Brush those pearly whites and floss in the morning when you wake up and at night before you go to bed. After each meal is the ideal and that's a lovely habit to create right now. And while toothpaste actually isn't necessary—it's the brushing that matters when it comes to oral hygiene—the best substance to use is baking soda with peroxide. It alkalizes the system as well, which some doctors consider to be an anti-cancer precaution. It's the perfect time to take care of that beautiful smile!

- Partake in some gentle prenatal yoga. If you don't feel like going out, try a DVD. I recommend Jennifer Wolfe's Prenatal Vinyasa Yoga Short Forms.
- Meditate. By now, sitting in tailor pose may be quite uncomfortable. Try sitting on a pillow so that your hips are slightly higher than your knees. You can also use yoga blocks to prop up your knees on either side so you don't get too intense a stretch.

## IN TOUCH WITH YOURSELF

You've seen her. I know you have. She's been on Oprah, all the morning shows, and most afternoon talk shows, both local and national. She's got long, straggly hair and she hasn't been out of sweats in years. Her shoes are all utilitarian. She doesn't remember the last time she wore makeup or jewelry. And don't ask about what she wears to bed. She carries one large black purse all year long, which weighs a ton, and her shoulders slope under the weight. Speaking of weight, she's packing an extra forty pounds and has the blood pressure to prove it. Who is she? She's a mom. And I don't want you to be like her!

Something happens to certain women after the birth of a baby that is downright scary. These women believe that *all* of their energies are to be poured into their children. Oprah calls them 'schlumpadinka' moms. They've gotten the idea somehow that the more they sacrifice, the better off everyone in their family will be. The little things that once made these women feel feminine or even like a real human being now somehow feel frivolous and even selfish. Go for a jog or buy new underwear? Why, schlumpadinkas have baby bonding and college savings to put first!

I can empathize with these moms. Of course, parenthood equals sacrifice . . . a lot of it. But these women aren't doing their children any favors by sacrificing everything that makes them happy and whole for the pursuit of parenting perfection. It's great to add motherhood to your life. It's not so great to jettison everything that has come before now because . . . you are a *mother*.

On television, the host of the show gifts our schlumpadinka with a head-to-toe makeover. Her husband salivates in the first row of the audience. Her kids can't believe this is their mom. And the makeover artists all take a bow.

It's a fairytale ending, but I've got a better idea. How about remembering to nurture yourself? Of course, we all have our good days and bad. Just remember there are positive things you can do from the start to keep you as close to your personal best as possible. It's the little things really that add up: the regular haircut, a touch of lipstick or gloss on your lips each morning, and wearing something nice to bed instead of that old, torn T-shirt.

So far this week we've focused on ways to care for yourself while waiting for your baby to arrive. But what about when she's here? One day—far in the future, but one day—she's destined to leave home. In order to avoid the empty-nest syndrome, keep your nest filled with your true self. In addition to the restful activities you're enjoying right now while waiting for your baby, here are some small, simple things you can try to incorporate into your life both now and when she's here:

- Put on your favorite lipstick.
- Wear your favorite fragrance.
- Moisturize your face and hands.
- Exercise.
- Babies love shiny objects, so while you tuck your earrings and necklaces away, wear an ankle bracelet!
- Shave your legs and underarms.
- Do yoga and meditate.
- Sleep in something feminine.
- Join a book club.

- Make time for your hobbies.
- Tour art studios. You can continue to do this with your baby in a carrier!
- Get some sensible yet attractive shoes.
- Buy a new music CD.
- Pick up a bouquet of fresh flowers each week at the supermarket.
- Order a DVD of that movie you missed in the theaters but really wanted to see. Better yet, join a program like Netflix and have a monthly movie night with your sweetie.
- Take a class in something you love that's not taxing and comes without homework. For instance: flower arranging, writing poetry, or a cooking demo.
- Change your clothes every day and don't sleep in your sweats.

What would you add to this list? Some of these items may be things you do already do regularly, while others may represent adventures for the future. I'm not suggesting that you embrace *everything* on this list or that you do them all before your due date. Of course there will come a time when running out for a massage, heading to yoga class, or even watching a movie all the way through becomes much more logistically difficult than it is right now. Plan for that eventuality. If massage makes you feel like a whole new woman, figure out a way to work it—and, if needed, the cost of child care—into your budget. Think about your hair. Will you have two inches of dark roots by the time Baby is two months old? Maybe now is the time to get an appointment on the books. Soon enough you might be feeling a little stir-crazy from caring for the baby all day, and your appointment will give you something to look forward to.

Build routines into your week or month that will be easy to keep after Baby comes. For instance, if you love to read, make a certain day of the week your library or bookstore day. Mark it on your calendar so you don't forget. Once your baby is here, you can bring her along. Making it part of your regular routine now will help you keep from letting an important part of your life go by accident.

Your baby is almost here, and she needs you to be the happiest, most whole mother you can be. You are facing down an enormously life-changing event, and nothing will ever be the same again. Take care of yourself . . . now, and in the future. Your baby is counting on it!

# PART TWO
# BABY'S HERE!

# CHAPTER EIGHT

# Weeks 1 to 4 Postpartum

The universe and the light of the stars come through me.

—RUMI

REMEMBER HOW much fun it was when you knew your spouse was "the one" and you started to savor getting to know him? Was he grouchy in the morning? Did he eat vegetables? Did he have an unfailing sense of humor in a crisis? Was there a deep pool of kindness at the center of his being? Now it's time for both of you to get to know your baby. Not the baby you imagined or the one you hope for ("No child of mine is going to . . .") but the real-life, flesh-and-blood human being in your arms. It's a lifetime endeavor that begins this month. Make it a conscious journey. And of course, let Dad run interference with all those well-meaning relatives and friends who know ALL about babies. They don't know this one. No one does just yet.

What would a month be without some organizing projects? This month they are blissfully small in scope and I hope offer you some fun. First you'll need to send out thank-you notes and baby announcements. You'll probably do a mix of cyber thank you's and snail mail versions. It can be fun to match the perfect thank you to the personality of the recipient. By now you know that I can be a bit of a pit bull when it comes to avoiding the old "well run dry" syndrome. Ergo, our third week is all about self-care. It simply can't go by the wayside as new responsibilities and tasks threaten to engulf you. Finally, another area emphasized is sleep. It's crucial to everyone but especially to a new mom. Your body has been through a trauma. You've got to figure out ways to help it heal and sleep is at the top of the list. Grab your resolve and your camera; it's the first month of your new lives as parents! Let's savor every moment.

## HABIT OF THE MONTH

### Start Trying to Go to Bed Thirty Minutes Earlier than You're Used To

Most new moms get by on a lot less sleep than they're used to, and even if your baby starts sleeping through the night early, chances are good you aren't sleeping as soundly as you once did. It's tempting to stay up long after the baby falls asleep for "me time," but adequate sleep is some of the most important time you can invest in yourself. Start moving your bedtime back in five-minute increments until you're falling asleep a full half-hour earlier than you used to. Sleep is such an important part of everyone's life that an entire week is devoted to it this month.

# WEEK 1 POSTPARTUM

## Get into the Groove of Motherhood

**This week, you can**

- Do as much or as little as you want. You're a new mom and you've earned the right!

How you'll feel the first week after having a baby is a big question mark. You may feel fantastic and wonder what all the fuss is about. Or you might be sore, tired, overwhelmed, and teary. Either reaction is normal. Many women seem to ride an emotional and hormone-driven high throughout the early weeks of new motherhood (though, watch it—sometimes that high comes crashing down later!). But even if you're feeling great, you still need to take it easy (which can be easier said than done if you're a get-up-and-go kind of woman). Your organs are returning to their pre-pregnancy size and shape, your body is healing from birth or possibly surgery, and overdoing it can lead to undesirable conditions like infections and prolapsed organs.

So try to stick to a few rules this week: Stay down (whether lying in bed or reclining on the sofa) as much as possible, don't lift anything heavier than your baby, and let other people take care of you so that you and your baby can get off to the best possible start.

### CARING FOR YOURSELF

It's likely that you're taking some kind of pain medication right now and possibly using heat and ice to soothe cramping and soreness. It can be surprisingly difficult to keep track of it all, and the last thing you want to do is accidentally overdose on Tylenol because you lost track. Try these tips:

If you're breastfeeding, you may forget which breast you nursed your baby on last. Feeding twice in a row on one side may make you feel "lopsided" and uncomfortable. To help you remember, leave the flap of your nursing bra down on the side you *finished* on. Then, when Baby's hungry again, you know to feed her on the other side. If that's not comfortable, try putting a safety pin on the side that you last fed your baby on.

Medications work best to manage pain when they're taken 'round the clock. If you wait until you're experiencing cramping or soreness to pop a pill, it won't work as well and you may need to take more of it to control discomfort. If you know you'll be rotating Tylenol every six hours and Motrin every four hours, create a schedule that makes sense and doesn't wake you up every two hours through the night. (For example, maybe your doctor or midwife would OK a larger dose of Motrin right before bed so that you can wait until morning to repeat.)

Once you've set up your medication schedule, you can either keep track of it on a simple hour-by-hour calendar you create in Excel or in a day planner, or set your smart phone's alarm to alert you when it's time to take a medication (with a note about *which* medication to take). After a few days, you should start needing the medications less and less and can slowly wean off of them.

One of the best things you can do to keep uterine cramping at a minimum is to keep your bladder empty. A full bladder presses against your reproductive organs and is not only uncomfortable but can cause you to have heavier postpartum bleeding. But sometimes giving birth actually bruises your urinary tract and you won't feel the urge to go . . . or you may just get so caught up in your baby that you actually forget to pee. It's a good idea to set an

In all the movies that glorify the fantasy of parenthood, Mom and Dad look at their child in the delivery room and are *instantly* in love with their son or daughter. Indeed, your love for this child will be like no other you've ever experienced. But if it isn't instant, don't panic. Whether it's garden-variety baby blues or the more serious postpartum depression, ask for help. There isn't any reason to suffer in silence.

And while we're dealing with reality, let's talk about the changing landscape of your relationship. All couples will need to adjust the "we" you created when you came together in order to accommodate and include Baby. Give yourself the gift of time and allow your relationship to grow. Right now you're also likely feeling sore, tired, and sleep-deprived—but rest assured that although this phase is uncomfortable and a little scary, it will pass. Very often it's the difficult times in our lives that yield the most positive change.

*Darkness deserves gratitude.*
*It is the alleluia point at which we learn*
*to understand that all growth does not*
*take place in the sunlight.*
—Joan Chittister

alarm to remind you to go to the bathroom every couple of hours. Or you can peg bathroom breaks to another frequent task to help you remember: For instance, try going to the bathroom every time you change Baby's diaper or just before you feed her.

Whenever you go to the bathroom remember to switch out nursing pads, ice packs, and sanitary napkins, and ask your spouse or helper to reheat your rice pack for your belly. This will keep you comfortable and clean (helping to reduce the risk of infection) as well as help you monitor bleeding.

## FEEDINGS AND DIAPER CHANGES

In addition to tracking your own medications, you may be trying to keep track of your baby's feedings and diaper changes. You can use Excel to keep tabs on this information, but working on a laptop while juggling a floppy newborn is not always so easy. If your smart phone has a spreadsheet program, now may be the time to try it. Or a notebook by your bedside will work just as well: Remember, you aren't creating a permanent record but a temporary document to help you manage this first week or so.

Your pediatrician or lactation consultant may have asked you to keep track of the baby's feeding times and the number of wet and poopy diapers to be sure she's getting enough to eat. Your doctor or lactation consultant may even have asked you to keep a record of the color and consistency of your baby's poop. Even if it wasn't requested of you, many moms and dads are comforted by keeping a close eye on this information. If you want or need to track feedings and diapers, in Excel or in your baby journal, create a table with three columns, like so:

| Time | Event | Details |
|------|-------|---------|
| 10:11 AM | Ate | At breast for 20 min. |
| 10:45 | Wet diaper | |
| 11:54 | Ate | At breast for 15 min., fell asleep |
| 12:45 | Poopy diaper | Yellow, soft |
| 1:40 | Ate | At breast for 20 min., switched side, nursed an additional 5 min. |

I've kept both the diaper and the feeding information on the same document for two reasons: to make life easier for you and also because in this format, the information makes logical sense. Your baby's care provider or your lactation consultant can look at the data here and see cause and effect right away because everything is listed in chronological order.

This is also a nice way to track your baby's reaction to different kinds of feeding practices. For instance, if you are giving bottles for some feedings and notice that Baby is fussy soon after his bottle, you and his doctor will be able to deduce that he needs a different type of formula or nipple. This document can also accommodate other types of information your doctor may request, like sleeping habits or weight. Keep it simple and accurate.

You probably won't need to track this information for long. Unless your baby has a low birth weight, issue with feedings, or some other health problem, you'll find that tracking every feeding and diaper change becomes annoying and unnecessary pretty quickly. But some parents like to stick the document in their baby's scrapbook to help them remember those first days of his life.

## NO JERKS ALLOWED

Caring for yourself emotionally after giving birth is just as important as caring for yourself physically! You may be disappointed about how your birth experience went. You may find that motherhood is a lot harder than you expected or feel insecure about your parenting skills. And you may feel sad, angry, or down for no specific reason at all. This is all normal and an expected part of the first week postpartum.

In addition to talking over your feelings with a sympathetic friend; your doula, obstetrician, or midwife; or a therapist, be sure to carefully guard your psyche during this time by keeping emotional vampires away! You may be able to tolerate your bossy Aunt Edna just fine when everything is normal, but hearing her opinion on your baby's "outlandish" name or her comments about how you're spoiling her by picking her up too much may be more than you can bear when you're already feeling insecure and shaky.

Now is the time to ask your spouse or a close friend to run interference between you and the difficult people in your life. Limit their access to you. If they do visit, keep it short. Let your husband show off the baby, explaining that you're taking a nap . . . even if you're just in the other room reading a magazine. Ask him to keep visits short—nobody should get to monopolize your baby right now except for you and Dad! You can always use Baby's feeding or nap time as an excuse.

## GETTING TO KNOW YOUR BABY

You'll never have this precious time with your child again. So instead of worrying about whether the dishes are done, trust that whoever is on your "helper" list is doing what needs to be done and get as wrapped up in your baby as you want! It may seem hard to believe, but those delicate fingers and scrunched-up face will fill out all too soon, and even that head of soft newborn hair may soon be a thing of the past (it often falls out). Document all those things you'll want to remember now. Use your baby journal liberally and take more pictures than seems reasonable. You will never look back at this time and think "I wish I hadn't taken so many photos!" or, "I wish I hadn't written down so many details about my baby's first week!"

This is a good time to document your birth story, as well. The details fade fast. Write it yourself, or dictate to a good friend or your doula and ask them to write it up for you. Have your husband do the same thing and then compare notes. It's amazing sometimes how different Mom's and Dad's versions of the big event are, and the different details that stand out as important to one or the other.

### BABY, LOOK AT YOU NOW!

Every week, take one photo of Baby against a plain background or in the same chair.

I've seen some really cute photos done this way—against the backdrop of a chair or other object, it's easier to see how much Baby's growing from month to month. At the end of the year you'll have a digital collage that can easily function as your (digital) holiday greeting card. You can make family and friends scattered across the globe feel connected to your experience. And all it will cost is a few computer keystrokes.

I've given you a lot of information to handle for somebody who's just had a baby. But it's all meant to make your life easier, not more difficult, this week. Feel free to use whatever seems helpful and discard the rest. Or hand this section to your friend or spouse and ask them to create the charts for you. Keep it simple so you can focus your brainpower on your baby!

# WEEK 2 POSTPARTUM

## Send Thank-You Notes and Baby Announcements

**This week, you can**

- Send out your thank-you notes
- Consider safe and sane ways to multitask

I CAN HEAR YOU SAY, "Regina, who cares about thank-you notes at a time like this!" Here's the deal: Thank-you notes are a gracious gesture. They also help you stay connected to the people who love you. You know, those wonderful people who went out of their way to send a gift or participate in this momentous event in your life.

I think the act of writing thank-you notes, over time, also serves another far more subtle need. Children learn from their parents' actions more than they do from their words. From time to time when I was a child my father would ask me to do something and I would say, "But, Dad, you don't do that and neither does Mom!" My father's words ring in my head to this day: "Do as I say in this instance. Don't do what I do." Huh? It was a huge source of confusion for me. Every day you will show your child how to exist in the world. Is there anything more valuable than having manners? So write those notes. Say "please" and "thank you" to everyone you

interact with. You want your child to be smart and successful—and it starts with your example.

### EMBRACE SANE MULTITASKING

As a mom, you'll need to catch snippets of time when Baby is sleeping to perform tasks you might otherwise have simply scheduled in your calendar. Once your baby is on a regular schedule, you'll have more freedom to make plans. Unfortunately, babies don't exit the womb with the knowledge that a regular schedule is good for everyone in the family. While the baby is sleeping or perhaps nestled safely and happily in Dad's arms, you'll have some time to tackle these notes. The first step is to make a plan. The whole of any project is overwhelming, right? You're feeling like you have 25,000 thank-you notes to write and you just can't face it. But once you make a list, you'll realize it isn't in fact

25,000 people who need to hear from you. It's only 17.

Begin by making that list of who is to receive a note from you. Once again, Excel can make it easy, but if you are a yellow legal pad and pen kind of gal, that's great too! Once you have your list, you'll need to decide who will be delighted with an e-mail thank you, who could receive a greeting card via e-mail, and who requires a handwritten note. If you're using Excel you can cut and paste from your master list to create these subcategories; if you're working by hand, find a way to designate your groups. For example, make a check by those who require a written note and put an asterisk by those who get the greeting card.

If "mommy brain" has set in and you're a bit fuzzy about who gets thanked for what, ask your partner to refresh your memory or grab that list someone recorded. Make a notation by some names. When you sit down to write the notes it will go quickly. Here's another tip to help you gain speed.

If Aunt Martha has never met your friend Terry and most likely never will, you can write pretty much the same note to both. Just be sure the gift is mentioned in the body of the note, and be sure it's the correct gift! This is where e-mail and cyber greeting cards are the quickest ways to go. You can write one message and then tweak it for each recipient.

If you aren't familiar with sites online that send out greeting cards, there are some listed in the Resources section (page 325). It's just like shopping at your fa-

## CREATE AN ORGANIZED STASH OF GREETING CARDS

One thing a mom needs is a stash of cards on hand. You can have a separate file tote just for this purpose or you can use a few of your box bottom hanging file folders. Make a space in your file cabinet. On the tab you put on the box bottom make a label that says "Greeting Cards." Inside, place separate file folders (in alphabetical order) for whatever categories you feel you will most frequently need.

Here are some common ones:

Anniversary
Birthday/Adult
Birthday/Child
Blank
Congratulations
Encouragement
Friendship
Get Well
Halloween
Valentine's Day

You can personalize your list to suit your interests, culture, or religious affiliation. You'll find this stash to be a lifesaver. But don't go out and spend several hundred dollars on cards tomorrow! Build your stash over time.

vorite card store except you're looking at a computer screen. If you join a site most will keep track of the e-mail addresses of your recipients. Whenever you return for a new card you'll save time because you won't have to retype the e-mail address. And most sites also log birthdays and anniversaries so you receive an e-mail reminder. Modern technology really helps you be more thoughtful. Some sites require a yearly membership fee, but it's cheaper than paper cards over time. The more you use it the more you save.

Are you afraid this is too impersonal a communication? For some it may well be. Your best friend Ginny who already has three kids may groove on such a communication, but your aunt in Michigan wants to hold something in her hands. If you need thank-you notes, shopping for some might be one of your first outings. Perhaps your best friend or sister could run this errand for you. See if your favorite store is online and browse their selection from your laptop. You can send your sidekick your choices via e-mail or just make the purchase online and have them delivered to you.

Should you elect to have someone shop for you and you send them out with the simple directive "Pick up some thank-you cards for me," be sure you're delegating to someone whose taste is close to yours.

Keep your phone, laptop, and note cards handy so that when the baby falls asleep you can use those minutes to be productive. Of course you don't have to be superwoman and make use of every opportunity to work—it's perfectly OK if you catnap with Baby. Balance is the word. You'll be in quest of it for the next eighteen years. Remember at the start of our journey when I asked you to drink more water, get some exercise, watch what you ate, and get more sleep? I wanted you to cultivate these as habits because once the baby arrives they will all be crucial to your survival.

Birth, especially your first, is a time of upheaval. If these wonderful habits have gone by the wayside, take some time to consciously reinstate them. They will save your life now and over the long haul. Be mindful when you are multitasking whether you are wisely using down time to serve you or whether you are simply driving your body and mind to a state of exhaustion. Being productive during these precious snippets of time doesn't mean using every free second to work either. Next week we're going to consider the things you can do that represent healthy self-care.

# WEEK 3 POSTPARTUM

## Organize Your Self-Care and Delegate

This week, you can

- Pick out some rewards, treats, and indulgences and work them into your day
- Practice the fine art of delegating
- Dismiss all guilt for taking care of yourself
- Remember to consciously nurture your relationship

I BELIEVE THAT taking care of oneself is extremely important. But make no mistake: I'm not encouraging you to become self-involved. People who aren't accustomed to rewards very often make that conclusion. Whenever I give a talk, I hear the most amazing things from audience members. Someone inevitably says that she doesn't deserve a reward for getting organized, doing something that "should have been done a long time ago." Clearly for this personality type, guilt is the norm, and the joy of completion is not to be experienced. Others tell me they don't have the money for indulgences like a manicure or a massage. And yet if I were to comb through their finances or follow them for a day, I would find money being tossed to the wind on items that had no lasting value. When we feel tired, depressed, and sad or overwhelmed we self-comfort ourselves. The key is to take the Twinkie, the

drink, the credit card, or the Xanax tablet out of your hand and replace it with a bowl of fresh strawberries, a cup of green tea, a few yoga postures, or a nice hot shower.

### CALL IN THE TROOPS

As this month goes on, your partner is likely to go back to work full time. If you're a single mom and were lucky enough to have a hands-on, 24-7 helper at first, she's probably had to return to work, too. I trust you have some kind of consistent help at home. Whether it's a professional like a doula, a housekeeper, or a nanny or perhaps just an experienced mom friend or relative, you really need continued support. I'm always amazed when someone espouses the value of doing something all by yourself. I hear it about the publishing world. "Why do you have a publisher,

Regina? If you self-published, you could keep all the money." And I could do all the work. The extra money would no doubt pay for my room at the hospital when I collapsed from mental fatigue and physical exhaustion. The specific endeavor doesn't matter. Whether it's birth, publishing, or anything else, the bottom line is this: The easier you make the journey, the more productive you will be.

Take a few minutes with your baby journal and make a list of the people in your life who have offered to help you. We all know who the good folks are who merely give lip service; they have no intention of putting themselves out. Leave them off your list. Why call and be disappointed?

Who is on your list? Does Marsha have four grown children? Is cousin Jane trying to adopt? Is your mom the best diaper changer on planet earth? I just bet each would understand if you asked her to come twice a week for the next month or so and watch the baby. You need a shower. Greasy hair will make you feel worse. We've all been there. My mother used to say with lipstick and mascara a woman could conquer the world. Maybe lipstick isn't your thing, but a dash of gloss and some scented body lotion can lift your spirits. Assure your relatives and friends that you literally need thirty minutes. You aren't asking them to come over and care for the baby while you go shopping for new clothes!

Here are some things you can do at home while your baby is being watched that will refresh you:

- Take a quick shower. This is a good time to begin mastering the art of the three-minute shower. Meagan's three-minute routine goes like this: Shampoo hair. Use your shampoo-covered hands to lather up your underarms and do a quick wash-down of the rest of your body.

Rinse hair.

Shave underarms. A good razor with a fresh, sharp blade is essential! You're not going for a beach-ready set of armpits here, just comfort, so try shaving diagonally instead of straight up or down for less irritation.

Put conditioner on hair.

Step out of the water stream and use conditioner-covered hands to prep your legs

Shave legs—as much as you have time for. Don't hurry on knees! They get nicked easily. If shaved legs aren't important to you, skip this part when you're in a super hurry.

Use exfoliating wash on face.

Now, step back under the water stream and rinse from head to toe.

All done! With practice, you really can do this entire routine in three minutes or fewer.

- If your helper can spare more time, take a bath, light a candle, and crank up the music. Don't forget the lip gloss and some nice-smelling bath salts!
- Take a nap.
- Read a magazine.

- Start a baby blog. Your relatives will love it!
- Sit in the backyard if weather permits and listen to and observe nature.
- Start reading a new book.
- Write in your baby journal: the one that goes to your child.
- If you enjoy crafts, work on a project that relaxes you. Make a quilt, knit a sweater, crochet a scarf, or make a candle.
- If baking relaxes you make a batch of cookies for your hubby and helpers.
- Rub Fido's belly and toss the ball. He has missed you.
- Do something that puts you in touch with your old life or the outside world. Call a friend, read your favorite news site, or download a new album from your favorite band.

The specific activity doesn't matter. If you asked me to knit a sweater, I would tear out my hair. But many people find it relaxing. And that's the key: Someone is generously giving you the gift of personal time. Use it to refresh yourself. Don't just sit with your helper and watch her take care of your baby! Do something for you. Remember (yes, I am beating this one into the ground), in order to have something to give your baby not to mention your partner, you have to replenish the well inside you.

## WHAT HAPPENED TO "US"?

In the heat of the moment, we jump wholeheartedly into new adventures. At the top of the list of examples would be a new mom with her baby. It's a mix of primal forces, hormones, and what I would call a deep spiritual connection that creates a true "mama bear." She's the warrior woman who would gladly die to protect her child. This great bond has helped the species survive. But mama bear needs to take precautions lest her man be denied the joy of becoming her true partner in this adventure.

The damage isn't planned. It's a series of careless moments. Suddenly you no longer say please and thank you. You're sleep-deprived and it causes you to bark orders. You feel that no one but you cares for the baby correctly. When the baby needs a midnight feeding, you drag yourself out of bed without looking over your shoulder. You get the baby. After awhile you stop bringing the baby back to bed. You feed him in his room. It's a slow, largely unconscious slide from the "we bond" originally created with your partner to the "we bond" of you and the baby. Dad feels left out and begins to become absorbed in his work. His new "we bond" is with that part of his life. If a year goes by, the marriage has been changed. And not for the better.

Here are some easy things you can do to prevent this from happening:

- Always speak in a respectful tone. Use the one you wish to hear in return.
- Acknowledge your partner before you leave the bed to tend to Baby. A quick kiss or the words: "I'll be right

back, Sweetheart" enhance the bond between you.

- Ask Dad to bring the baby to you for a feeding and then share the experience.
- Leave surprise "I love you" notes for your partner.
- Ask Dad to take some of the feedings using milk you expressed earlier that day.
- When you're at the grocery store, remember a treat your partner enjoys and surprise him.
- Communicate with your partner. Never utter the words "If you really loved me, you'd. . . ." And ask him sweetly to never utter them to you. Communicate.

I would also encourage you to make Dad an active participant in Baby's care right from the get-go. Too often moms keep their partners at arm's length when it comes to baby care. Sometimes it's out of good intentions—they see caring for the baby as their job and don't want to burden Dad, who is probably back to work by this point, with more work. Sometimes it's out of a prideful or misguided idea that only moms know what their babies need. This will definitely prove to be true if Dad's never given the chance to figure it out for himself! Once a day if possible, make a point of handing the baby over to Dad and removing yourself from the scene. Take a bath, go for a walk, or simply retire to the bedroom with a book. Without Mom nearby at the ready to either rescue or judge him, Dad will be remarkably good at figuring out what the baby needs and how to soothe and entertain him. But the older the baby gets without having that experience with Dad, the harder it will become for the two of them to get in sync. Don't make things harder than they have to be for you or your partner. Leave them to their own devices often. You may be amazed by how competent and enthusiastic a parent your partner proves to be. In the short and the long run this will make everything easier on you and your child, and he and his father will enjoy a much stronger bond.

While examining her fingers and toes, when she's nestled in your arms, and while she's being bathed, your baby is using her emotional radar. She knows more about your relationship than you imagine. Nurture your partner and the love that originally brought you together and created this child. Check out books like relationship expert Dr. John Gottman's *And Baby Makes Three* and *The Seven Principles for Making Marriage Work*. Anything we give our attention to flowers. Be sure you consciously tend to your relationship during this time of transition.

# WEEK 4 POSTPARTUM

## Plan Your Sleep

**This week, you can**

- Maximize your baby's sleep time
- Reset your body clock in order to get more sleep
- Learn tips and tricks for falling asleep

### MR. SANDMAN, PLEASE PLEASE PLEASE BRING THIS BABY A DREAM!

I am going to begin this week with a harsh bit of truth. While the idea of a baby who magically sleeps through the night from the first day of life is lovely, it's not terribly realistic. Newborns have tiny stomachs and digest each small meal in record time. They're biologically programmed to eat around the clock. Many of them will wake up every two or three hours to eat for the first few months. This is normal and not something you should try to train them out of. They are growing fast and need the nutrition.

You may have read that the "average" baby will sleep through the night by six months of age. First of all, when it comes to babies, the average really doesn't matter. Your specific baby may do things very differently. Second, many of the studies on infant sleep consider any six-hour stretch

of time "sleeping through the night." Let's imagine you put your baby down for the night at 8:00 p.m. That would still only theoretically give you until 2:00 a.m. before he's up again. Doesn't really sound like "sleeping through the night," does it?

You are entering a world in which sleep will be at a premium for at least a few months, possibly longer. You have to figure out a way to get the sleep you need during this time of change. There are no over-the-counter remedies, prescription drugs, healing tapes, or visits to shamans that can replace the benefits of sleep. If you do a little investigating you'll find there are several possible side effects from lack of sleep. Guess what the number-one is? Depression!

The good news is that the typical newborn sleeps sixteen hours a day, so you can technically get in your eight hours *somewhere*. While "sleep when the baby sleeps" is much-dished-out advice that's good in theory, sometimes it is hard to put into practice . . . especially if your baby sleeps in forty-five-minute increments around the clock. Still, for the first couple of months, it can't hurt to try anyway. Lie down when the baby is sleeping, draw the shades, and close your eyes. Even if you don't fall asleep every time, you'll benefit from the rest. Here are some other tips for maximizing your sleep time:

Keep things quiet at night. When your baby wakes up, don't turn on the light or play with her. Change or feed her quietly in the dark, so she won't get confused and think it's daytime. A dimmer switch in her bedroom or a night light near her bassinette will help you be able to see what you're doing without making the room too bright.

Take sleep where you can get it. When your partner gets home from work, maybe you could go lay down for an hour. Or perhaps he will take over the last hour or two of Baby's nighttime care so you can get a jump on bedtime. Yes, there are things we all like to do in the evening— read, watch TV, surf the Internet. But adequate sleep must take priority over any of these activities. Chronic sleep deprivation not only puts you at risk for health problems and depression, it can make you a danger to yourself or your baby. You need your wits about you to drive her to her doctor's appointments, give her a bath, or cook yourself dinner!

If the situation gets desperate, call in the troops. Have friends come over during the day and hold the baby so you can take a

It's not just the number of hours you sleep but the quality. You need to go deep and experience different sleep cycles to be fully refreshed. The only new mom in the position of easily achieving this goal is the one with a full-time night nurse. The realistic goal this week is to create a new sleep cycle that helps you get the quality and quantity of sleep you need while taking into account your new lifestyle. Keep at it, and over time you, Dad, and Baby will all adjust. Without effort, however, a disjointed, disrupted night of fitful sleep will become the norm, with consequences you truly want to avoid.

nice long nap. Sleep is not a luxury. It is a necessity!

Consider co-sleeping. Many moms find that sleeping near or with their babies helps them get the sleep they need. Instead of Mom and Baby waking fully every time Baby is hungry, Mom becomes tuned into Baby's subtler hunger cues and can feed her without having to get out of the bed or turn on the light. Often Baby never fully wakes up and goes back to sleep much more quickly and easily. We've talked a bit about safe bed sharing in previous chapters, but there are books and Web sites in the Resources section that will help you safely and successfully co-sleep if it's something you would like to try.

As your baby grows, you'll want to incorporate flexible routines into your evening so that he begins to associate those routines with sleep. Some quiet playtime after dinner followed by a bath, a feeding, and a snuggle in the rocking chair while you read aloud are all nice bedtime routines that can grow with him. Eventually, he'll start sleeping longer and more predictable stretches.

## THE LAND OF
## WINKIN, BLINKIN, AND NOD

No matter how much of a dedicated sleeper you are by nature, pregnancy and birth and the new demands of motherhood have probably upset your cycle. Sometimes it can be difficult to drop off to sleep even when the opportunity presents itself and you're exhausted.

Here are some tips that can help you fall—and stay—asleep:

Remember how we organized your bedroom with the idea of creating a sanctuary? I had a secret agenda. A room like that will enhance your ability to fall asleep, especially now. Look around and see if you are keeping up what you created. It might be time to reinforce some habits. Take back ownership of the space.

In addition to being organized, your bedroom needs to be dedicated to sleep and play. If you turn it into an office, gym, or full-time nursery, there will be no environmental support to help you relax and fall asleep. Use screens if you can to block your views of gym equipment or the computer.

If your partner prefers to watch TV or listen to music here, give him an early Father's Day gift: headphones.

Check the state of the bathrooms since your return home. Did the reality of the baby cause the order you created to vanish? Take a minute to restore the room.

Avoid stimulants like caffeine, action movies, the news, Aunt Edna, or exercise close to your desired bedtime.

Drink a cup of warm milk to relax late in the evening. If Aunt Edna is itching for something to do, ask her to cook a turkey. Eat the low-in-calorie, high-in-tryptophan white meat. It's what makes everybody sleepy on Thanksgiving. And tell Aunt Edna her turkey-making rivals her diaper-changing skills!

Do some fragrances relax you? Why not introduce them with a scented candle about twenty minutes before you get into bed? It's best to use beeswax or soy candles with pure wicks. Regular candles are petroleum-based products and can put toxins in the environment. The same is true for cheap wicks, which can have lead in them. Try a lavender sachet under your pillow.

Are the sheets clean? Sorry, I had to ask. What about your pj's or nightgown? You may be so sleep-deprived you are too exhausted to do laundry. This is an Aunt Edna assignment if ever I invented one.

Don't toss and turn. You'll associate your bed with not sleeping. After twenty minutes get up and try reading in another

> ### ELIMINATE HAZARDS
>
> Never leave a burning candle untended. If you have toddlers, pets, or live in earthquake country, your candle flame can move from atmospheric to destructive in seconds. In addition, be sure the room is well ventilated. Baby's lungs may find fragrance of any kind irritating so use with caution. And please don't smoke in his presence.

room. Read something gentle and relaxing. Now is not the time to review the history of the plague in Europe!

Do you live in an apartment with noisy neighbors? Try a white noise machine.

Wash your face and do your brush-and-floss routine a few hours before bedtime; that way you won't wake yourself up when the desire to sleep overtakes you.

Stop eating three hours before the time you wish to retire.

Just before you get into bed meditate for a few minutes to calm your nerves. Meditation should ideally follow no less than two hours after eating so your body can first devote its energy to digestion.

Finally, try one of your baby's lullaby CDs. After all they are designed to induce sleep! Put on your headphones and lull yourself to sleep. Or try a guided meditation designed to help you sleep. You'll find my favorite source in the Resources section.

## ROUTINES AND RITUALS

I've previously noted that routines and rituals will serve you when you need to get and/or stay organized. They are equally powerful when you want to induce sleep. Why not try some of the suggestions above and then weave them into a ritual of steps you can repeat each evening? The routine you create may require some tweaking over time. Gradually, however, you'll find yourself getting sleepy the minute you start the first step, even if that happens about three hours before bedtime. If you review your evenings now, you'll see that you may have unconsciously embraced a sleep-repelling routine!

That would be an accurate description of this month. It will never come again. It's overwhelming to bring an infant home. And yet in no time you'll be an old hand offering advice to other mothers. I thought I'd close out this month with a poignant story.

My friend Lynn married Keith right after graduation from college. At the time he was planning to be a career Army pilot. Lynn became pregnant almost immediately and gave birth to their first child in South Korea. Lynn and her daughter came home from the hospital two days after the birth; Dad promptly left for ten days of maneuvers. When Vanessa was seven days old, she cried nonstop for hours. As a new mom, Lynn didn't know what to do to comfort her daughter and get her to stop crying. They lived off base in an apartment building. Lynn had no phone of any kind,

> 🚼 Talk to your doctor if you find it impossible to adjust your sleep cycle. He may prescribe a sleeping aid for short-term use. Be sure he knows if you are breastfeeding (so he can choose a medication that's safe for baby).

no friends, and certainly no family nearby to consult with. Nor did she speak any Korean. She decided to put Vanessa down in her bassinet and do some dishes. In less than a minute the baby's crying stopped. Lynn felt her body flood with relief—until she went to check on Vanessa and found she was listless and turning blue. She quickly tried baby CPR, smacked Vanessa's bottom, and clapped her hands over Vanessa's head. The baby started to breathe normally, but Lynn had no idea how long her infant daughter had been without oxygen.

Clad half in pj's and half in street clothes, she wrapped Vanessa in a blanket and tore out the door. She raced through side streets to get to a major thoroughfare where she could grab a taxi and get to the American base. Minutes later, Lynn was dropped at the base gate. She asked the guard to call the MASH unit and alert them that she had an emergency with the baby. Fortunately Lynn had done volunteer work here during her pregnancy and knew most of the physicians on staff. A base cab delivered her to the MASH unit, where waiting docs grabbed Vanessa and whisked her away. A man Lynn didn't know escorted her into a room, where she waited for two long hours to hear news of her daughter. She feared the worst. She remembers that he tried to take her mind off the situation by engaging her in meaningless chitchat about their hometowns. It didn't work.

Finally a surgeon she knew came in to reassure her that her daughter was just fine. She was breathing; they had examined her and run tests and found that all was well. Lynn was free to take Vanessa home. Lynn burst into tears again and said, "This was all a terrible mistake. You all made a mistake when you let me take her home in the first place! Clearly I can't care for her." Lynn remembers the doctor's kindness. He told her that everyone feels this way at first. In fact he assured her that if she didn't have doubts and concerns, he would think something was amiss. Back on the streets of Korea, Lynn walked home with Vanessa in her arms.

Vanessa thrived and was followed over the years by a brother and a sister. Today she is a mother herself. Remember this story the next time you are overwhelmed and feel certain you just can't be a good mother. Taking care of a baby is a learning curve, but you can do it. And many astonishing moms have been there before you.

# CHAPTER NINE
# Weeks 5 to 8 Postpartum

*Becoming a parent is like falling in love. You can read about it,*
*talk about it, worry about it. . . . But nothing can fully prepare you for it.*
**—MICHAEL ORDONA**

RIGHT ABOUT NOW the feeling of being totally overwhelmed should begin to subside. In its place a feeling of confidence, even mastery, is no doubt growing. You and your baby are getting to know each other and understand how each communicates. Systems, rituals, habits, and routines are saving the day. As you feel yourself falling into them, always leave yourself room to embrace, improve, or overhaul them. As you grow in experience and Baby simply grows, you will find that what works this week may need to be tweaked next week. The first year of a baby's life is a time of rapid-fire change. Be ready to roll with the punches. It's no time to get stuck in the "This is how we do it" mentality. This year will be like no other in your child's life.

This month you will probably be going outside the confines of your apartment, condo, home, or backyard. It's time to venture into the world and I've got you cov-

ered. Won't you be the envy of new moms everywhere as you sally forth with just the right amount of baby gear? I'm always amazed how most women leave home laden down like the proverbial beast of burden. A trip to the grocery store does not require the same abundance of supplies as a three-day hike through the woods, and when your bag is always stuffed, you're not likely to be able to lay hands on those baby wipes just when you need them. I will show you how to pare down your stash so you're only as prepared as you need to be. Yes, it's time to organize the ubiquitous purse and diaper bag.

Of course many of you will be preparing to go back to work. That difficult moment when you need to leave your baby with others is on the horizon. And soon you'll be juggling work and baby needs. Let's make this transition a joy rather than a burden. Many women find they miss work and the company of adults. You want

Baby to experience Mom as a woman fulfilled in many arenas beyond his nursery. We close out the month looking at the world of photos and how to keep them from taking over your home and computer like some virus run amok.

## HABIT OF THE MONTH

### Practice Parental Decision Making

At the heart of getting organized is the ability to make decisions. Without that skill, piles appear everywhere. Guess what? Decision making is also one of the most important things you can learn to do as a parent. This month I want you to become a confident decision maker for all things related to your baby. It's time to abandon second-guessing, overthinking, outside opinions (within reason!), and entertaining guilt. This will be especially critical for moms who are returning to work. You may be called by your sitter and asked to make a decision about the baby. You need to be confident, otherwise your workday will be turned over to fretting about the response you gave.

Use your baby journal if you wish to log five positive decisions you make every day with regard to your child. After 21 days you will have noted 105 decisions. Don't stop to second-guess those decisions. If you look back at something you did and realize that you would make a different choice today, use this as an important lesson: No one parenting decision (within reason) is going to make or break your motherhood career. Instead of dwelling or feeling guilty, simply chalk it up to a lesson learned and move forward. By the time you get to day 21 and see that you've made 105 decisions in that time—and that your baby is still here, happy, and growing—your confidence should be through the roof.

# WEEK 5 POSTPARTUM

## Beat Cabin Fever

**This week, you can**

- Begin to master the art of getting out the door with Baby

YOUR BABY IS about a month old now. Your spouse or partner is likely back to work and your initial flurry of visitors and helpers has probably died down. If you've followed your doctor's or midwife's advice, you've probably been taking it easy since she was born, and chances are good you're starting to feel stir-crazy. So . . . now what?

Now what, of course, is the beginning of the real day-to-day life you'll have with your baby. If you will be returning to work soon, that's likely going to mean a daily shuffle to get the both of you dressed, ready, and out the door by a certain time every day. And even if you plan on being an at-home mom for the foreseeable future, that doesn't mean you'll want to be actually at home all day long, every day. Sooner or later, you and Baby will have to leave the comfort of the very organized nest you've created and head out into the world. This can be both exciting and scary.

This week we'll create some strategies for helping make those initial outings successful and as stress-free as possible.

### GETTING READY TO GO

One of the things you'll need in order to make getting out the door easy is a baby staging area. Little coats and teeny baby shoes don't always logically fit where the grown-up outerwear goes. After all, your newborn won't be putting on her own shoes, nor walking on them, so why put them on the floor? And her pint-sized coat is likely to get lost in the closet among full-sized versions. What you need is a place where you can keep all the items you'll need when leaving the house with your baby. Think about where you will be most likely to put on her shoes and coat, slather on her sunscreen, or fasten the strap on her sun hat. Your bed? The sofa? You will want a place where you can sit down comfortably while you attend to all her needs, but as close as possible to the door you'll be exiting through.

The area may also change in time. When you have a small baby, a changing table might work wonderfully for getting her ready. As she grows and is able to sit up unsupported, you may find that a chair or bench by the front door makes more sense. Don't make any permanent changes. A pretty basket where you can stash her shoes, hats, slings, and a coat is a good solution—it'll look good as a temporary addition to whichever room is baby staging ground du jour. Keep your diaper bag in the same area. We'll be talking about how to stock it next week . . . feel free to peek ahead if you have no idea what to put in it!

Next you'll need to figure out what you'll use to carry your baby while you're out.

### Slings and Carriers

While strollers are typically the first equipment we think of for porting babies around, slings and carriers are great for busy places like zoos and festivals because it's so much easier to navigate crowds with them. The same goes for uneven terrain. And many moms find that Baby is happier and calmer when worn close to her (or Dad's) heart rather than being pushed in a stroller. So which kind should you choose?

**Slings** are wonderful for shorter trips like a trip to the farmer's market or mall. If you anticipate your baby falling asleep while you're out and want to be able to lay her down easily on your return, a sling is a good option. Some very good slings are great for all-day use, but some moms experience shoulder fatigue if they use them on the same side for too long. Either way, slings take practice and knowledge for best results. Read reviews at TheBabyWearer .com before you choose, and after your

purchase, read or watch tutorials and practice getting a comfortable, secure fit. For short trips where your baby will be getting in and out of the sling several times, Meagan loves the Maya Wrap. For longer trips, she loves the Moby Wrap, which can be worn many different ways that distribute her baby's weight across both shoulders.

**Front and Back Pack Carriers** are great for trips where you'll need Baby to be in one place for a long time, like hikes or all-day ventures to the zoo or museum. Since they distribute weight evenly across your back, they're comfortable to use all day. And they are easy to use without help, even the first time. They generally have pockets where you can stash things, and other useful features like built-in sun hoods. Make sure you get a good one—check out reviews on Amazon.com or TheBabyWearer. com. Meagan's favorite is the Ergo Baby.

### Strollers

These baby staples are a fact of life for most moms and are especially convenient for trips where you'll need a place to stash stuff in addition to your little one. And if you'll be jogging with your baby, a stroller is a must. (No jogging allowed with slings or carriers—Baby's neck isn't able to handle the jiggling yet). But what kind do you need for your particular outing?

A jogging stroller is a must if you'll be running, and is also a good choice for uneven terrain, like a rocky path. If you're a cyclist you can buy a jogging stroller that converts to a bicycle trailer.

An umbrella stroller is perfect for short trips or those where you'll need to navigate public transportation because it compacts into a nice bundle. If you haven't gotten an umbrella stroller yet, invest in one now. Find a model that you can fold up with one hand; look for one with a small basket, if possible a carrying strap, and a seat that reclines a bit, and make sure the handles are long enough so you don't have to walk hunched over! Don't be afraid of splurging because it's "just" an umbrella stroller. If you get a nice enough one and use it in conjunction with a carrier or sling, you may find that you don't need a larger stroller.

Larger strollers, prams, and "travel systems" often have deluxe features like cup holders, large wheels to absorb shock, and roomy baskets. They are comfortable to push and make a snug ride for Baby. But they also tend to be heavy, don't fold down as compactly as an umbrella stroller, and are overkill for many outings. If you'll be shopping or walking for hours and need a place to stash a diaper bag, various purchases, and a drink, then grab the big stroller and throw—okay, hoist—it into the trunk or hatchback of your car. Otherwise, leave it at home. Most of the time it can probably live in your garage, where you can use it for long walks around the neighborhood.

## MASTERING BREASTFEEDING IN PUBLIC

One of the best gifts you can give yourself is the ability to breastfeed confidently while out and about. While this is a controversial topic, you should know that breastfeeding in public is legal in all fifty states, and some states even have specific laws meant to protect nursing mothers. Sure, you could always take your baby to the bathroom to eat . . . but wait. Would *you* eat in the bathroom? Of course not! Some museums, malls, and other public places have special nursing rooms for moms to use. These can be lovely, but if you're out with friends or simply not near one, they're inconvenient, too.

There are a variety of nursing covers on the market, and some mothers cover up with blankets. But many moms feel that the blankets and covers just add another layer of complication to the process. It's hard to latch a newborn on even under the best of circumstances, so how are you supposed to do it when you can't see what you're doing? Babies nursing under a blanket often get hot and sweaty, and the cover-ups serve as beacons to announce, "Hey, I'm feeding a baby under here!"

Another approach is to wear a shirt that's loose-fitting enough to be pulled up without showing skin, or a nursing camisole under a cardigan or button-down shirt. With some practice, you can become very adept at lifting the shirt and latching the baby on quickly. Instead of throwing the blanket over the baby's head and your shoulder, try arranging it behind the baby's head and back so that any exposed skin of yours is covered but you can still see your baby's face. Practice this at home until you get comfortable. Make sure you have a burp cloth handy as well as anything else you might need while breastfeeding—you won't want to have to rummage through your diaper bag with one hand while keeping your baby latched on with the other.

Try to find an out-of-the-way place to nurse your first few times. Meagan reports that over the years, she's gotten a lot of breastfeeding mileage out of the lawn furniture section at Target. If you have a friend along, they can help you get Baby arranged and block you from view of passersby until you're settled.

Once you've gotten the hang of it, you can breastfeed so discreetly that nobody around you will know what you're doing . . . unless they've been nursing mothers themselves.

## GETTING OUT THE DOOR

Now you're ready to venture out! For your first outing, choose something simple, not too far from home, and not too long. A stroll around the familiar, insect-free, climate-controlled environment of your local Target, where extra diapers, snacks, bottles of water, and helpful sales staff are all around you, may be a lot more comfortable for a first outing with Baby than a hike through the forest, where worries about heat, cold, bugs, and supplies may make it more complicated. I'm not suggesting you make every trip with your baby to a department store, just that you keep your first outing simple and predictable so you can get a nice rhythm without stressing yourself out. A walk to the coffee shop is another simple choice.

Plan to meet a friend at your destination, if possible. If you haven't practiced breastfeeding on the go yet or dealt with changing a diaper in public, you could probably use the physical and moral support. Whether you'll be meeting anyone or not, give yourself plenty of time to get yourself and your baby ready. Have your shoes and coat on or handy by your baby staging area. If Baby's car seat is the kind that detaches from the base, it might be helpful to bring it inside, especially if the weather is bad or it's cold outside. You can use it as a safe place to stash her while you put on your shoes and coat and also get her completely secure and fastened in before you go outside.

Here's something I'd like to point out: While those bucket-style car seats can be convenient for carrying the baby from the house to the car, I highly recommend that you don't get in the habit of carrying them further than that. They are heavy, bulky, and hard on your shoulders and back, not to mention your thighs, where they tend to bang as you walk. And the poor baby is jerked and swung all about as parents try to manage this awkward piece of hard plastic. Car seats are designed for automobile safety, not Mom and Dad's comfort and spine health! Use a sling, a stroller, or your arms if you'll be carrying your baby farther than across a parking lot.

Get yourself ready first. The less opportunity you give the baby to spit up or poop on himself before you go, the better chance you'll get out the door without incident. Make sure both he and you have eaten— there's nothing like an attack of low blood sugar to make your outing go south. And use the bathroom before you get him ready, too. Before you start getting the baby ready, gather up everything you'll need to take with you and put it by the back door. Hopefully this first trip will be a simple, short venture, and you won't need more than a diaper bag and purse (we'll discuss organizing both next week!). Do this while Baby is somewhere safe and comfortable, like his crib or in his car seat, so you won't have to rush. If you live in a single-family home where your vehicle is close to the door, go ahead and load up the car before you start getting your baby ready. If you are in an apartment building or will be using public transportation, figure out ahead of time a convenient way you can carry Baby and all your stuff. Maybe you can stash a small purse or just your wallet inside the diaper bag so you won't have to carry two bags. Scale down as much as you can. Take the baby to his staging area and get him ready. Now you're ready to go!

While the first outing may be laden with poop, sweat, and tears, it really will get easier the more you do it. Just make things as easy as you can on yourself by sticking to your system. Keep your baby's things where they make sense and prepare as much as you can for the outing before you get him ready. Once you're out, you may be surprised at how smoothly things go. If not, feel free to go home at any time if the situation gets too stressful. Just keep practicing.

# WEEK 6 POSTPARTUM

## Organize Your Purse and Diaper Bag

**This week, you can**

- Streamline your purse
- Organize your diaper bag
- Learn how to downsize your streamlined diaper bag over time

IT HAPPENS EVERYWHERE I go. Clients do it as often as my closest friends. A woman will ask me to pass her purse to her. As I lift it, I drop to the floor. This looks like a purse but it's clearly a medicine ball in disguise. Why do women do this to themselves? I think there are several reasons. Which of these do you relate to?

Most women rarely clean out their purses. The daily detritus of miscellaneous receipts, snacks, beauty aids, flyers, coupons, and notes builds up. It takes about two minutes to clean out your purse if you do it daily. And now you have a file system to absorb the receipts you do need to keep.

Some women like to "save the day." It may only happen once a year, but when someone needs a screwdriver, a safety pin, or any other rarely used item (when you're out and about), you've got it in your bag and will jump in and save the day. I say let everyone take care of her own needs. Find other ways to build your self-esteem.

And then there are the women who have no idea what should be in a purse. Incapable of making a decision, they toss everything that will fit into their bag. And it's no accident that the purse is more the size of a horse's feedbag! I've got a purse primer for you.

### WHAT DO YOU *NEED* IN YOUR PURSE?

Here's a list of the basic items the average woman needs in her purse:

- Hair supplies: usually a small travel-sized brush, comb, or hair pick will suffice. And please note I said *or*, not *and*. If you have long hair, you might toss in a barrette or twisty for the emergency pin-back or ponytail.
- Makeup touch-ups will depend on what you put on before you left the house. In general powder and lipstick

or lip gloss is sufficient. A small emery board is a nice touch.

- A notebook and one pen or pencil. If your life is in a PDA, the notebook should be very small.
- ID: driver's license and one credit card for emergencies should suffice (a debit card if you prefer). DO NOT carry your social security card.
- A wallet for change and cash. Leave the bulk of your change in your car so you can easily feed a parking meter. Empty your change purse out every night. I never carry more than five pennies—the rest go into a piggy bank—or more than one quarter—I squirrel those away for the laundry machines in my building. How much change do you really need?
- A checkbook travels with most of us on a daily basis. Or, leave the checkbook at home and just keep a check or two stashed in your wallet. Don't forget to log them in your check register when you get home.
- If you drive a car you will need your (current) license, registration, and proof of insurance. I keep my car key and clicker on a separate key ring. Use something small, lightweight, and unusual to identify it should you frequently valet park.
- Keys are a source of extra weight for most women. Which ones do you need? I'd guess your house key and front door (if different). What about the key ring? If it's big and heavy it's weight you don't need to lug around. Don't put ID on your keys. Should

you lose your house key, you don't want the wrong person to scamper over and rob you.

- A few photos in a wallet are understandable. "What does your husband look like?" "Do you have other children?" It's nice to have something to show. But if your wallet bulges with photos, you need to weed out and let go. Save those photos for the last week of this month when we discuss how to organize your collection.
- If you're a career woman, be sure you have a few business cards in your wallet.
- A small packet of tissues is indispensible.

## THE BIG CLEAN UP

Now it's time for a fearless inventory of *your* purse. Clear off a surface like your bed (which I know you make every morning) or your dining room table (which is always ready for a meal now that you have an office/work area set up at home) and let's see what you are carting around with you. Take everything out one item at a time. Don't do the big dump! I want you to create categories. Do this quickly and without judgment or commentary. Carly Simon's song said she didn't have time for the pain. You don't have time for the guilt. Baby will be awake soon.

Once everything is spread out before you in neat categories, make an assessment. Ask yourself questions about each item. For example:

## RELIEVE YOUR ACHING BACK

Have you heard that a chiropractic adjustment can make you feel great? It's true! I've been going to chiropractors for over twenty years and they all lament the damage they see in their patients who routinely carry heavy items. The big culprit isn't the weight; it's the way you lift and support the item. Remember these three keys to success: back straight, tummy tucked, and knees bent. As your baby gains weight and you're lugging the diaper bag and various other items, it will become more difficult to keep "the big three" in the forefront of your mind. What mom doesn't suffer from a sore back from time to time? Don't hesitate to seek out a chiropractor because you fear encountering a practitioner who is going to violently "crack you" into place. Try and find a Network Chiropractor in your area. Their touch is so gentle it will be hard to believe the treatment can be effective—until you stand up and feel the relief.

I'm also a big believer in acupuncture. To find a qualified practitioner, your best bet is word of mouth and the experience of others whose opinions you trust. I would suggest you experience someone who is a Doctor of Oriental Medicine and not a Western-trained MD who has merely taken a twenty-week course. If there is a Traditional Chinese Medicine school in your city they may have reduced-rate clinic hours. Advanced students need to practice so it's win/win for everyone.

Stress and motherhood go hand in hand. Stress wears down the body and the mind. It's a major source of illness. You need to have a counterpunch or two in your arsenal in order to stay healthy. Chiropractic adjustments and acupuncture treatments are two powerful tools in your quest for balance. What healing modalities will you use?

- You pick up your compact and think: "Wow! I can't live without this! I don't want a shiny nose." I say that's fair but how heavy is that compact? Could you get a smaller, lighter one?
- How many items are rarely used and hanging around just in case someone needs one of them?
- Do you have enough makeup to be prom-ready in a heartbeat? Leave the bulk at home. If you're going out for a special event and want to be able to touch up your eye shadow, that's the time to take the small size with you. It's not likely you'll have a sudden urge to glam up at the supermarket.
- Paper and pen or pencil is very wise. But are you hauling too much and too many? Scale back.
- If you are an avid reader, I salute you. I trust you will be reading to your baby to foster her love of literature. But do you need to haul a huge hardcover volume with you? Try a small

paperback or invest in one of the electronic readers on the market. You'll have books, newspapers, and magazines all in one device.

- You might need reading or sunglasses and a holder for each. Some eyeglass cases are fashionable but outsized and heavy. See if you can streamline that necessary item.

- Whatever other categories you have, be ruthless in your honest appraisal of the items. Here are some questions to help guide you.

Do you need this item?
How often do you use it?
Could you leave it at home and take a smaller size?
Would you be willing to try going without it for a week or two and see what happens?

Frankly I think the airlines did us a favor when they said we could only take a few ounces of any liquid on board. Why take a full bottle of shampoo when you'll only be gone for a few days? Most hotels will supply grooming items at no charge. And I know your Aunt Edna feels she buys the best, so use hers when you visit. In just the same way, learn to downsize with the items you deem necessary on a daily basis.

## HERE COMES THE GOOD NEWS!

Do these instructions and solutions sound a bit familiar? When I suggested you separate items into categories and store them in separate holders for your hospital bag,

guess what? I was priming the organizing pump for all travel outside your home. Whether it's your weekender or your purse or that huge suitcase you haul out once a year, you want to be able to get to an item easily and quickly. Did you find your hospital bag served you well? Did you feel more powerful and in control when all you had to do was reach for the right zip-top or cosmetic bag rather than rifle through a huge duffle? If you did try this method, you are surely on board for organizing your purse (and diaper bag) in the same way.

If you didn't try this method out for the birth, there's no time like the present to give it a whirl. Visit a beauty supply store for small zippered (usually mesh or cotton) bags meant to store cosmetics. I get mine at The Container Store, which you can visit online if it isn't easy as yet for you to venture outside the home. One word of caution: Don't buy all the same size or color of bag. You'll wind up with a series of mystery packages. Be able to reach in and know what you need by the size and the color of the container. You will save time and energy, especially precious commodities now that you are a mom. (Note: Some containers are plastic and see-through. If you're not going to remember what color you assigned to each category, go for the plastic see-through container. Make life easy for yourself at every opportunity.)

Once you assemble your containers, you might find you need a different size purse. Needless to say, I'm rooting for a smaller one! It might also be true that you want to divide your possessions into two groups. There's the "I need this every day" group and the "I need this some days" group. The former would include items like your ID, cell phone, cash, and keys. The latter might include your electronic reader (Kindle, iPad, etc.) or your makeup. They can pop into a tote or a large purse when you need them. I'd love to see you pare down, but the most important goal is to make everything easily accessible. If this is a big change for you, allow yourself to warm up to the idea that you are no longer carrying *everything* with you. Rome was not built in a day.

## YE OLDE DIAPER BAG

Let's take a realistic look at what the average newborn needs. By now you know I'm going to ask you to categorize your items and then pack them in related containers. With experience you'll develop a system for changing and caring for Baby. And that system will influence how you group items in individual containers.

### Container #1: Ointments and Aids in a Zip-Top Plastic Bag
Nursing pads
Nipple cream

### Container #2: Diapering Essentials in a Mesh Bag or Foldable "Changing Station"
Diapers (Calculate your need based on the average number of changes you make in an hour and how long you plan to be gone. If you don't gauge correctly in the beginning, don't panic. Unless you're

visiting Mars there will be a store in your vicinity with diapers!)
A plastic grocery bag to wrap a poop-filled diaper in before disposal or . . .
A washable bag to put a used cloth diaper in for the trip home
Changing pad. You can purchase a portable "Pronto changing station" with a fold-up pad plus pockets for diapers, wipes, and other changing necessities at www.skiphop.com. Or just use a folded-up receiving blanket in a pinch.
A small container of baby wipes

### Container #3: Baby Supplies/ For Mom's Use, in a Large Pocket of the Diaper Bag
Several burp cloths
A blanket
A small sling you can easily fold up

### Container #4: Baby Clothing in a Quart-Sized Zip-Top container (use to transport soiled clothing home later!)
Hat/bonnet
Extra outfit, including a onesie and socks

### Container #5: Baby Food in a Quart-Sized Zip-Top Container
If your baby takes formula you'll either need a can of powder and some water or the premixed single-use kind.
If you'll be taking breast milk with you, you need a cooler and an ice pack to keep it cold if you'll be gone more than a few hours or if the weather is hot. (According to La Leche League, milk can keep at room temperature for up to six hours . . . it's awesome stuff!)

### Optional

Pacifiers and/or bottles if you use them

Emergency food for Mom: a banana, an apple, or a health food bar. Read the ingredients for the latter if that's your choice. If one of the first three ingredients is sugar, try another brand. If the sodium content is stratospheric, try another brand. And if the ingredients read like a science project (to quote chef Jamie Oliver), try another brand! You may fare better in a health food store than the supermarket. Learning to read labels is a skill every mother needs to master.

### Beach Day Additions

A water bottle for Mom

Sunscreen (reapply often; use the natural kind free of estrogen-making chemicals)

Natural bug repellent

Shade or umbrella for Baby

Create bags with supplies for special outings like the beach, hiking, or overnight trips, and grab as needed. When you get home be sure you replenish, launder, or switch out.

## DON'T LEAVE HOME WITH THEM!

The older your baby gets, the less you will need, and the more experienced you will be. It's a combination meant for success and self-confidence building. You could pare the above down to a diaper, a small container of wipes, a sling, and maybe a

### BAN CONTAINER CLUTTER

Warning! If you put only a few items in a container you will create a new kind of clutter: container clutter. And it will be more difficult to find items because you now have a sea of containers to wade through in your diaper bag instead of a jumble of products. Who is prone to doing something like this? The person who has no confidence in her decision-making ability. And that's why developing that skill is the habit of the month! Try to group items into as few categories—and containers—as possible.

burp cloth by the time your baby is a few months old if you are accustomed to packing light and don't mind being resourceful in a pinch. On the other hand, some moms are reassured by feeling prepared for any possibility and the idea of giving up a well-stocked diaper bag at any phase makes them feel anxious, not free. That's okay. Just be reasonable. Your toddler will not need an economy-sized box of crackers for a few hours' outing. Your infant is not likely to pee and poop her way through sixteen diapers in eight hours. If you are breastfeeding, you won't need bottles. And you are guaranteed not to forget your boobs at home! Have fun with this project because success in this arena gives you freedom to move outside the home. It's a bit daunting at first, but trust me: Within a few months of first going out with your baby you'll be a pro. Every mother becomes one.

# WEEK 7 POSTPARTUM

## Prepare to Go Back to Work

This week, you can

- Make plans to return to work with confidence
- Start to rearrange your closet based on current needs
- Have guidelines to ease back into the work world

At some point or other, most mothers will return to work. For some of you, it won't be until your "baby" is starting school . . . or beyond. For others, it will be much sooner . . . maybe even next week. No matter when it happens, you're likely to feel a flood of emotions, possibly conflicting with one another. You may be simultaneously **excited** to return to work, **sad** about the prospect of leaving your baby in somebody else's care, and **confused** about your new identity as working mother. The proportions in which you experience these emotions will probably have a lot to do with how much you like your job and how positive your experience as a mom has been so far. If you're more excited than sad or more sad than excited, that is also normal.

A smooth transition back to work can help ease your discomfort. Your baby will pick up on your stress and anxiety if the details of your return are messy, and she may reflect them back the only way she knows how—by crying a lot. That certainly won't help make things any easier on you. So let's take some time to get you really ready for your return to work and all the details that might come up.

### PRACTICE MAKES PERFECT

If you knew you would be returning to work at this time—and you paid attention during the first half of this book!—your childcare plans are already set and you may think it's an easy matter of dropping your baby off on your first day back and heading to the office. But going to work is a far different matter when you've got a baby to worry about. Last-minute diaper changes, slower-than-expected feeding sessions, and spit-up sessions have a funny way of derailing the best-laid back-to-work routine. Both you and your baby will likely benefit from a few "dry run" days—preferably a whole week—in which you go through all the motions of a working day, up to and including dropping your baby off at day care or leaving her with a sitter.

If you can't afford an extra week of childcare or your care provider isn't available to take your baby until your actual start date, still go through the morning routine and the daily commute to make sure you've factored in all the possibilities. Do this practice run first thing in the morning, the way you will when it's a real workday. Time how long it takes to get the both of you dressed and ready. Add in fifteen minutes as an emergency-clothing-change cushion, and calculate your new wake-up time. This will vary greatly depending on how long your baby takes to eat. Some babies are no-nonsense eaters, and can complete a feeding in ten minutes

The way you start your morning sets the tone for the rest of the day. When sleep is at a premium, it's easy to get in the habit of waiting until the absolute last minute, then getting up and rushing through your morning routine. But you and your baby will be off to a much better start if you give yourself at least thirty minutes more than you think you'll need. If you don't use it, you'll have a few extra minutes to enjoy breakfast or flip through a magazine. Plan to eat a real breakfast with your spouse rather than running out the door with a piece of toast in your teeth. As your child grows, a morning breakfast routine will continue to be a wonderful part of her family tradition.

or less. Others have a much more leisurely style. As you prepare to spend time away from your baby during the day, you may find that you especially treasure bonding during these morning feedings. Make sure to give yourself enough time to enjoy them—and the rest of the morning with your baby—without feeling rushed.

A trial run is a great way to figure out how your husband or partner will help out in the morning. If he leaves for work earlier than you, perhaps he can get up with the baby and dress her while you take your shower. Then you can feed her right before you leave. Or maybe he'll be the one dropping her off at childcare. Has he considered how much earlier he might have to leave in order to facilitate the drop-off? How can you divvy up the small tasks that will need to be done each morning?

Don't even think about rushing through a three-minute shower while your significant other steams up the bathroom for forty-five minutes. Find an equitable way to share the morning duties. If necessary, write down everything—to the smallest detail—you both need to do every morning for yourselves, everything that will need to be done for the baby, and approximately how long each task takes. Then, together, come up with a logical and fair plan for splitting it all up. During your practice week, you can experiment with certain arrangements until you find one that works the best.

If your care provider will be taking the baby during your trial period, this is also an excellent time to get used to what may seem like a foreign concept: leaving your

Now is the time to take out the literature you received from your caregiver with her policies and procedures and give your mind a refresher. Some of the details that seemed like a vague, far-off concern back when you were shopping for childcare are now very real, and you'll want to make sure you're on the same page. Don't make any assumptions. What will she expect you to provide for your child: diapers, bottles, a cooler for breast milk, a blanket, a change of clothes? When will payment be expected? What if your baby is sick? What if your caregiver is sick? If you need help remembering all the important issues and questions to raise, flip back to the section of the book where we discussed questions to ask potential caregivers (page 63).

baby. You don't have to stay away for an entire eight hours during your practice days, but do go to breakfast or run a few errands without her. Allow yourself to experience the range of emotions you may be feeling now. Tears are normal. Better to do your crying now than on your first day back to work! This trial run will also give your child and her new caregiver a chance to get to know one another in shorter periods of time.

If your spouse or partner will be staying with the baby, a trial run is still valuable! Has Dad handled enough of Baby's care to be really comfortable with a day on his own with her? Does he know where you keep all the supplies? Has he read about

safe handling of breast milk or how to heat up a bottle? Nobody wants to be micromanaged, especially not in the care of his own baby. Taking a few short trial days to adjust to your being back to work will allow Dad to figure things out—or ask you questions—without the pressure of you being gone for a full day.

## YOUR WARDROBE

Chances are good you're not back into your pre-pregnancy wardrobe yet. So what will you wear to work? Look back at the clothing you wore during your second trimester. There's a good chance that the skirts and pants you wore then will fit now, possibly with some modifications. Remember the Bella Band I recommended in chapter 2? They're great for helping keep slightly-too-big maternity pants snug and secure, and can help smooth out any post-pregnancy bumps and bulges, too.

You'll probably want to get a few new tops, just so you can feel like you haven't gone back in time to your second trimester. Look for structured tops, like tailored, button-down shirts—they'll help define your waist and keep you from looking sloppy, even though you'll still be carrying some excess weight and loose skin. If you'll be pumping breast milk during the day, make sure these tops give you easy access, especially if you won't have a private room for pumping in. (Speaking of pumping, do you have enough breast milk stored for your return to work? Check out the Resources, page 325, to help you figure out how much you'll need and safe storage options.)

Next month we tackle reorganizing the closet. At the beginning of this journey, we made room for your pregnancy clothes. Now we're reversing the process. This week we'll get a head start. Let's take this in stages so it isn't too overwhelming.

1. If you work in corporate America, you probably have a wardrobe of suits, dresses, slacks, and separates. Set aside about ninety minutes (have someone watch your baby so this time isn't interrupted) and check to see whether any of the pieces from this wardrobe still fit.
2. If you work outside the home in a less formal setting, you have more leeway. Still, you should go through the process of trying on your pre-baby work outfits to see where you stand. If you wait until your first day back, you're likely to be late and demoralized.
3. Now is a great time to remove from your closet any items from your early pregnancy that you won't need any longer. You'll be faced with making two piles: clothing that gets moved on to the next pregnant woman in your circle or a charity, and the items you would wear again if you plan on having more children. I would store the latter in space bags. They will take up less room this way and be impervious to moths.
4. Include going through your dresser drawers and closet shelves in this phase of the clean-out.

That's it for your closet this week. If

## BE A CHAMELEON

If you have a basic outfit like a classic pantsuit, you can make it look like many different outfits simply by changing the accessories: jewelry, scarves, shoes, and tops/blouses. Draw eyes to these details and they won't notice that the basic canvas is the same. (Besides, everyone at work knows you've just had a baby. They won't expect you to look like a fashion model!)

Do you work from home? When you cross the threshold of your office, be sure you're dressed for the workday. Staying in your pajamas and robe all day can lead to depression, as will not taking a shower for days. Your clients may not see you but you see yourself every time you walk into the bathroom or pass a mirror. Run a brush through your hair; add a dab of lip gloss and maybe a dab of scented oil behind your ears. You'll feel like the queen of the world!

you have items for the cleaner or the tailor, set them by the door to go out on your next foray outside the home. Maybe on one of your practice mornings, you can run some errands. You might also need to pick up, as mentioned above, a few items for this transition phase. Even a simple pair of jeans can be transformed depending on the quality of the top you choose and your jacket and shoes. Build your new choices around a pair of dress jeans (if your company allows) and one or two pairs of classic slacks. You can of course shop at a resale shop or at a good-quality thrift store if you don't want to invest heavily in a transition wardrobe.

## THE FIRST DAYS BACK

If you have a secretary or an assistant, odds are he has called you since the birth to give you a heads-up. If not, call your assistant or someone in your division to see what the lay of the land is since your departure. I'm not suggesting you need to hear the office gossip. It would behoove you, however, to be up to speed on any critical changes in projects and client relationships or due dates.

Hopefully your request to have all mail, memos, and other documents placed in a box has been honored. If you can, eat lunch at your desk the first day back, come in an hour early, or stay an hour after close of business to blast through this box. Don't dump the contents out on your desk! Clear a workspace as we have so many times before and remove each item one at a time.

- Toss or recycle as much as possible.
- For existing projects, sort the papers quickly into a pile for each project. When it comes time to file the material, you can take a closer look. Is there any follow-up indicated? You might want to put that into your general To Do folder or the To Do folder for that project, depending on how you organized these files before you went on maternity leave. Put the pa-

pers you can file away into the sub-categories that make up the project like Budget, Invoices, or Reports.
- You may have acquired new material that needs to be housed in file folders you have to make. Don't forget to add these files to your computer list if you created one before your departure.
- After you complete this work, set aside time to blast through e-mail and voice messages using the same basic guidelines, that is, discard as much as you can, decide what needs your attention, and file by category the material that qualifies as reference.

If you took the time to get organized before you left, it's not going to be difficult to streamline now. Once again you see there was indeed method to my madness. After you get the paperwork cleared out, look around and decide how you wish to personalize your office now. When it comes to your baby's photo, be discreet. Have one or two frames out at most or have some shots rotate on your computer screen. There's always going to be a resident Scrooge who just doesn't want to see that angelic face or hear your stories. It's OK. I doubt there are any universal interests when it comes to offices. Don't take it personally and better yet, don't set yourself up for any negative chatter.

## HOME SWEET HOME

If you are working out of your home, I'm going to bet you have snuck a quick peek

## THE BIRTH ANNOUNCEMENT UPDATE

It might save some time if you send out an e-mail blast to your colleagues, vendors, and clients announcing your return to work. Say a few succinct words about your experience. This may curtail all those conversations about the baby that people feel they need to initiate to be polite the first time you reconnect with them. If you have to give the baby's name, birth weight, and number of hours you were in labor, and say how you feel now that you're back at work twenty-eight times, you're going to be exhausted. And it's a time waster. You need to get caught up. Those who really matter to you will have been in the loop since day one.

at your e-mail, listened to some voice messages, and perhaps even drafted a document during the sleepless nights you've encountered. The guidelines are the same. It's just less likely that you will encounter as much "stuff." You may find that you are like a citizen of two worlds now. Work may provide respite from baby care and allow you to engage your brain in a different way. And your baby will remind you what's really important in life and why you've worked so hard to make your business a success.

As twenty-first-century adults, most of us take out our Blackberries or iPhones at times that older generations would have found impolite. We're plugged in and connected as never before. This is a mixed bag—being always available can lead to feeling always obligated, and constantly multitasking can get in the way of putting your focus where it should be when work is over . . . namely, on your baby. On the other hand, laptops, e-mail, and smart phones make it possible to enjoy flexibility that would once have been impossible. One day soon you may very much appreciate the ability to catch up on some work while home with a sick baby or leave early to go to a pediatrician's appointment and meet your deadline from your home office later. You may even be reaping the benefits of telecommuting or a work-at-home situation, in which communication technology likely plays a large role.

Just try to be the master of the technology rather than letting it master you. Here are some tips for helping to keep your focus where it should be:

**Work while you're at work**. I know, it's hard to keep up with your online entertainment at home now that your arms are always full of a baby, but don't give into the temptation to fritter your work hours away playing Scrabble with your Facebook friends. You'll just end up with more to do later, while you're at home and your baby and partner crave your attention. If you simply must rest your brain from work every so often, set aside the last five minutes of every hour for online "play" and think of it as a reward for working hard the other fifty-five minutes.

**Learn to separate true emergencies from false ones**. Maybe, pre-baby, you were the go-to gal who could be counted on to respond to every message within five minutes, day or night. But that doesn't mean that every request that lands in your inbox is a bona fide emergency that needs your immediate response. Your baby is teaching you to prioritize and recognize which tasks and goals need to be done now, and which can wait. Maybe your coworkers need to learn the same lesson.

**First things first.** For some women, working in the evenings at home is a necessary evil. Just try to manage your time—and your coworkers' expectations—so that you aren't that mom who's constantly got her phone to her ear or one eye on her laptop. Don't take your phone to the park or check your e-mail at the dinner table. Your child needs to learn that, even if your focus is somewhat split, some things are sacred and she can count on times when she'll have your undivided attention.

Whether you work inside or outside the home, whether you devote your working time to motherhood or split your focus, you are entering a time when you may always feel just a bit guilty. It may seem as if everyone needs a piece of you and you fear that no one is getting enough. Welcome to parenthood. All we can ever do is our best, and that has nothing to do with perfection.

Ancient yogis had a wonderful practice you might like to adopt. As you drift off to sleep at night, review your day. Give yourself credit for all the myriad things you did well. This will reinforce your good choices. When it comes to the things you feel you were less than stellar at, decide how you can better handle those situations the *next* time you find yourself dealing with similar demands. Then let go and drift off to sleep. You can't rewind the clock. You can only go forward.

# WEEK 8 POSTPARTUM

## Organize Your Baby's Photos

**This week, you can**

- Decide how best to organize your growing photo collection
- Consider a blog as a way to stay in touch with family and friends
- Make keepsake and digital albums for special family members and friends

LAST MONTH I suggested you take a lot of photos. This month, I caution you to be careful about taking *too* many. What's a parent to do? Recording the first precious days of a child's life is capturing a time that will never come again. However, I'd like to discourage you from attempting to capture every single activity, sneeze, burp, or laugh. Soon you'll have so many photos (or video discs) that you will be drowning in them. And then the desire to "do something with them" will be another item on your already overcrowded to-do list. Your parents probably have boxes of photos they have wanted to organize for years. Your stash simply looks different. You'll have hard drives, CDs, and DVDs eating up space instead of photos in cardboard boxes. Let's get control.

## WHAT IS THE GOAL?

At first, it seems logical to photograph everything your child does. Surely there has never been a more beautiful, smarter, or sweeter child. Take yourself out of today, however, and ask yourself: What is going to happen to all of these photos or videos? Are you going to live in the past and watch endless recordings of birthday parties, graduations, and a series of the first days at school? Or do you envision your child sitting in a darkened room, poring over images of his childhood for years to come? I once heard that a famous basketball star showed videos of himself playing basketball to his dates. His parents so emphasized how special he was that they fostered a nasty case of narcissism. I know that isn't your goal.

## AN OLD FRIEND TO THE RESCUE

What you need is a . . . system! The habits I ask you to cultivate each month are based on repeatable actions. Sometimes an action need not or cannot be repeated every day, but you can still make it a habit. My suggestion is that you set an automatic reminder on your computer for the first of the month (or any other time that is more suitable for your schedule) and on that day you can transfer to a CD, DVD or Blu-ray disc all the photos taken that month. Label the disc and the jewel case. Decide what language you are going to use so there is a consistency to the titles. And above all, date them!

Before you dump all the photos onto that disc, take a few minutes to review them. Delete the ones that are out of focus, show your partner with red vampire eyes, or show you smiling with your eyes shut. We've all seen those in a photo collection and wondered why they were saved. As a matter of fact, do one better: Delete them on your camera before you ever download them onto your computer. And don't print out every single photo just so you can hold it in your hands for closer examination. That can start a whole new wave of clutter.

If you do print out some photos and decide not to use them and you have them stored in your computer, offline, or on a separate drive, don't hesitate to toss them or give them to your toddler to make her own album. In other words, find a way to creatively recycle them rather than saving them. Tossing a photo in the trash or recycle bin doesn't in any way mean you tossed the person into the trash. If I had a dollar for every time a client has said to me: "I can't throw a child in the trash" as we looked at stacks of old holiday cards, I'd be a wealthy woman. People like to share a moment in time with you. They don't expect you to start scrapbooking their family! Literally tossing a child into the trash is frowned upon and will land you in jail. Tossing some photos and cards will help keep your environment under control. Embrace the difference.

## THE NO-COST WAY TO SHARE

You might have relatives or friends who live at a distance and genuinely want to be kept abreast of your baby's life and experiences. You can share photos on a regular basis in a number of ways. Here are some ideas:

- Send your photos electronically to a chain store near your loved ones. Costco and CVS are great examples. Family and friends can go to the store and get either prints or a disc of your photos. Let them decide which ones to keep and how these will be stored/used.
- You can also post albums at a social site like Facebook and invite your friends to view them.
- Upload your baby videos to www.youtube.com or post them on Facebook.
- Open an account at an online site like www.flickr.com, www.snapfish.com,

www.picasaweb.com, or www.kodak gallery.com. You can create online photo albums that your designated guests can view simply by logging in.

Once you get in the groove, sharing and storing photos will be a no-brainer. Most of the parents I know find their photos to be so precious they use more than one method of back-up. With that in mind, you might consider online storage where your files and photos can automatically be saved. You can store a small amount of data for free and then pay for additional space on an as-needed basis. There is a small monthly fee. See the Resources section (page 325) for two such sites.

Macs often come with an online backup program pre-installed. If you have a Mac and an iPhone or iPad, you may want to get a Mobile Me subscription, which will sync the files from all your different devices (including the photos you took with your iPhone last week) so you can back them up. Go to the Apple store or Web site to learn about different features and how you can use them.

What about those boxes of digital recordings and the photos you will soon have lurking about the house? The best way I've seen to get that under control is to buy a media cabinet. You can find a great example at www.exposuresonline.com. Or you can purchase one of those inexpensive bookcases from a store like Ikea. It will nicely hold several storage boxes. Try and use simple storage boxes that are always carried by your favorite vendor. Nothing is more visually crazy-making than a storage cabinet or bookcase that has different kinds of mismatched boxes. Remember: You want the visual to calm you so that when you tackle these photos it's a fun project, not something you dread. As your baby grows and you add to your family, you may want to edit your collection. Remember the old adage: Less is more. Indeed it is! By the way, if you can establish a place to work on your photos, it will be a big help in your quest to streamline this activity. You want to be ready to go and not have to set up or gather supplies when the mood strikes.

## Dear Diary . . .
## Uh, Make That Dear Blog

Just about everyone these days has a blog; why not you? Go to a site like www.word press.com or www.blogspot.com and get started. You'll sign up and use one of the established templates; it doesn't take any real computer savvy. You don't have to be fancy: Just write a few words about your baby's progress, and if you like, post a photo. You can establish a set time to make these entries or take advantage of your baby's naptime. I assure you, relatives and friends in far-flung locations are going to appreciate the feeling of connection to your journey. And all it takes is a few minutes. No need for postage, cardboard, mailing envelopes, or a trip to the post office.

Be cautious, however, at your blog or at any online site like Facebook or YouTube. Follow commonsense guidelines so that you and your family stay safe. For example, don't publish your last name, phone

> ### THIS ZOO IS CLOSED
>
> Set rules for friends and family concerning gifts for Baby. For example, if you live in a tiny apartment, you can't accommodate gigantic stuffed animals. If you prefer books to videos or DVDs, make that clear. Feel free to return or donate all items that are not in accordance with your stated wishes. Better yet, tell Grandma to hold onto that gigantic giraffe so that Baby gets to play with it when she goes to visit Grandma.

numbers, or address. It should be impossible for a stranger to track you down. Don't announce when you are going on vacation! Check the privacy settings at a site like Facebook to be sure you have set your entries to be viewed by official friends and not made available to the world at large. And finally, don't make disparaging remarks about family and friends in a public forum. Aunt Jane may not own a computer but your cousin Wilber does, and he's sure to tell Jane how much you hated the baby shower gift she sent.

## Machines Aren't Perfect!

As wonderful as computers are, we know two truths about them: Photos eat up your storage space and ultimately all computers crash. It's the nature of the beast. A great way to keep your home computer up and running at top speed is to have a separate external hard drive for your photos. Whether you have a Mac or a PC, you can set up your extra hard drive to automatically back up your files.

It's difficult to write about electronic solutions to photo storage and computer backup because it's a world that changes rapidly. Want to know the latest solution? Befriend a teenager! If you don't happen to have one in your immediate family and you can't find a friendly one on your block, there are other ways to investigate. For example:

- If you use a Mac, you can go to the local Apple store and ask questions and/or sign up for free classes.
- Microsoft has online classes you can take as well.
- There are many popular sites that offer articles that will keep you current in this and many other areas. My personal favorite is About.com, run by the *New York Times*.

## Turn Photos into Special Gifts

If you are a person who loves arts and crafts, you may want to make a special thank-you album for some of the good folks who helped you during this time of transition. You can make a lovely hardcover photo book filled with your digital photos using an online template and pick it up within a day or so at your local Walgreens or CVS. Check the Web site of your favorite drugstore or discount store and see what photo services they offer. If you have a Mac, you can create photo albums and other photo gifts easily using iPhoto.

No time to make an entire album? Just use one shot and decorate a frame or make a special card. Whether it's scrapbooking supplies, Creative Memories, or good old-fashioned decoupage, if this kind of project relaxes you, you can turn simple photos into treasures. Before you go crazy making gifts for anyone, however, stop and ask yourself if you have ever seen any item like this in their home. Your friends Jane and Herb may love you and may have given endlessly of their time and talents since the birth. They may not be the kind of couple who has any photos out in their home. Follow their lead.

For those like me who don't have a crafty bone in their body, there are two wonderful gifts for family members this coming holiday season. Purchase an electronic frame or key chain that automatically rotates photos. Every time Grandma walks into her study she'll be surprised by the photo on display. And when Grandpa is at the store, he'll automatically have multiple photos to share with anyone who asks, "Hey, how's that grandson of yours?" You can even purchase digital photo frames that can be updated via a wireless connection from somebody far away. Imagine Grandma coming into her study and seeing a surprise—brand new photos of her grandbaby, sent via the Internet from afar.

## Curb Your (Photo) Enthusiasm

Photo taking has become a multi-million-dollar industry, something akin to a sport, a great way to document your child's life and . . . a source of parental nuttiness. I've been in homes where the parents stalked their poor child like some crazed papa-razzi. I wonder what this does to a child's psyche? "Wow! Every single thing I do is worthy of note!"

Toni McLellan, photojournalist and writer at Toniwrites.com, understands the desire to photograph every moment of life with her three boys. As a storyteller she is drawn to documenting her life. "But sometimes I make the conscious choice to leave my camera behind and just experience the moment with my sons," she says. "It's such a different experience when I stop to look at wildflowers not to get photos, but simply to enjoy them. I'm more present with my family when I'm not constantly recording what we're doing."

Make a conscious decision to participate in your child's life more than designating yourself as her official videographer or portraitist. You're parenting your baby, not reporting on her life. If you know you're taking way too many photos and are really having trouble curbing them, take out your baby journal and see what discoveries you can make as you ponder these questions. I think you may be surprised and ultimately relieved.

- Is there a lack of self-confidence on your part? Perhaps you are making up for the fact that your parents didn't document your life at all or enough or as much as your siblings?
- Has a sibling or close friend been inundating you with photos of their progeny for several years now? Is it unconsciously payback time?
- Does showing off photos of your beautiful baby elevate your self-

esteem? Does it make you feel part of the parent club at work or church?

You aren't a bad person if you found yourself in one of the above scenarios—in fact, it's normal. You're a conscious, self-aware human being trying to be the best parent your child could have. Take a minute and make a decision to find balance.

## Beyond the Photo

When an elderly relative passes away or someone much younger dies suddenly, we all remember snippets of stories they told. Very often we forget the details. Before you completely overwhelm your space with photos and videos of your baby, you might want to take some time to record your family history as a document he will treasure in the future. Make a list of questions and ask your circle to respond on video or in writing. Allow them to use whatever format is most comfortable for them. These historical documents will allow your child to understand his place in the family.

Finally, don't forget to record your feelings, musings, and memories in your baby's keepsake journal. They say a picture is worth a thousand words and the pen is mightier than the sword. Why not combine the power of the word with the visual? Put a photo of your baby in the book and write about what happened that day. Invite Dad to record his thoughts as well. Share the experience of recording your innermost thoughts. This is something your child will treasure all of her life, even when the time comes for her to record the lives of her own children.

# CHAPTER TEN

# Weeks 9 to 12 Postpartum

Let us not pray to be sheltered from dangers
but to be fearless when facing them.

—RABINDRANATH TAGORE

THE QUOTE THIS MONTH is from one of my favorite poets, the great Tagore of India.

I'm sure you've noticed that the road to parenthood is paved with garden-variety challenges. But life very often throws us a curve ball. Whether it's an unexpected job loss, the need to move to a new home, or the flu sweeping in, remember to take a deep breath and be fearless. The longer you live, the longer the list of challenges you never imagined you would have to face will be. Courage, wisdom, and strength lie deep within you. Call upon them. And of course, if you're eating well, drinking water, exercising, and doing a few minutes of meditation each day, you'll be in a better position to ace any challenge that crosses your path. It can't hurt to tattoo this month's quote on your heart.

There is a momentum building now in your life to return to the world with Baby incorporated into it rather than Baby's be-ing the sum total of your daily experience. It's going to be like this for the rest of your life. Oh sure, she'll grow up, go away to college, and get married. But even when she has five of her own children and is president of the United States, your baby will on some level always be your baby. This month we continue with the transition to the new normal of your life.

Clothing is usually a hot-button issue for a woman and remains so all of her life. With your body shrinking down to its own new normal, we want to continue shrinking your closet contents down. If ever there was a time you needed to know exactly where every item you owned was located, it's now!

Along with your changing body is the shifting landscape of your home. Did you ever imagine how much laundry a small person could generate? Before you know it, cereal will be flying all over the kitchen, toys made of tiny pieces will spill onto every floor surface, and you will swear that those stuffed animals in the nursery are having babies of their own at night after the official light's out. The solution? You need to create an equitable division of chores and establish systems to make the maintenance process pretty much a no-brainer. When you feel these time-honored bromides rise up into your throat, take a minute and don't let them escape your mouth: "It's OK. I'll do it." "It's just easier if I do it." "I don't mind. I can take care of that. . . ." Don't create unconscious systems that are guaranteed to bite you in the butt down the road. Unless of course you want to be a martyr.

What would this month be without a hands-on organizing project? Birth generates joy. It also generates an avalanche of paper. Let's make short work of it. Aren't you glad you created that top-notch file system when you were pregnant?

## HABIT OF THE MONTH

### Stand Up Straight, Momma!

There's no time like the present to get in the habit of practicing better posture. After you have a baby, your stomach muscles are often stretched out and weakened. Also, hunching over to nurse the baby, carrying heavy baby seats, and holding a baby on one cocked-out hip are a chiropractor's nightmare. Jennifer Wolfe, yoga instructor, doula, and creator of the Prenatal Vinyasa Yoga DVD series, recommends that moms do several of the following exercises—plank pose into downward dog—each day

to keep muscles engaged and limber as well as help you stand up straight.

Start in a hands-and-knees position with the hands directly under the shoulders and the hands, knees, and feet hip-width apart. Curl the toes under and lift the hips up, pressing the chest toward the thighs and moving into Downward Dog, making an upside-down "V" with the body. Gently press the heels toward the ground and take five long, deep breaths. This pose is really great for fatigue as it brings oxygenated blood to the brain. From Downward Dog bring the body parallel to the ground with the arms straight and hands directly under the shoulders, moving into a Plank (the knees can be on the ground if needed). Make sure the chest and hips are at the same height and pull the navel into the spine, engaging the abdominal muscles. Hold this position for a couple of breaths then gently drop the knees and sit back on the heels and stretch forward into child's pose. You can repeat this several times in a row, several times a day."

Before you do any abdominal strengthening exercises, you'll want to check to make sure you don't have a diastasis, or separation, of the abdominal muscles, very common in postpartum women. Here's how:

1. Lie on your back with your feet flat on the ground and knees up.
2. One hand should be behind the head to support the neck
3. With the other hand place two fingers on the Linea Alba (the midline connective tissue that links to the Rectus Abdominis muscles) at the waistline.
4. Gently lift just the head until you feel the abdominal muscles engage and notice how much space is between the muscles.
5. Repeat this with the fingers one to two inches below the navel as well.
6. The gap your fingers are in should be no more than two fingertips wide; otherwise, you likely have a diastasis.
7. If you suspect you have diastasis recti, check with your health care provider before doing any abdominal exercises. If you strengthen the abdominal muscles too much, the separation may not grow back together completely.

# WEEK 9 POSTPARTUM

## Tune Up Your Wardrobe and Organize the Family's Closets

**This week, you can**

- Restore or maintain the order you created months ago
- Be sure everyone's wardrobe is tuned up
- Establish realistic clothing size goals

LET'S TALK TURKEY for a minute. By this point you should have a closet that was organized when you were pregnant. Hopefully you cleaned it out again last week in preparation for this week's official tune-up. You're also living in a body that is changing daily. You aren't your old self nor are you any longer as big as a house. You've got clothes you fit into right this minute, clothes you're working your way into, and clothes that are waiting for you about nine months down the line. Now, just to complicate matters, there is no such thing as a standard closet. What's a professional organizer to do? Stick to the original plan!

### TRUST THE TRIED AND TRUE

If you start arranging the clothes in your closet by size you're going to make yourself crazy. I'd advise you to stick to the original instructions: Keep types of cloth-

ing together and organize by color. As you grow smaller, keep a bag in your closet for the larger sizes to collect. (The bag should be the size of a drawstring dry cleaner bag, not a brown paper bag from the grocery store.) Each time the bag is full, take a minute to sort the contents. Not having seen them for a few weeks will give you more objectivity. Can this item be passed on to another pregnant mom? Would it be easier to drop it off at the local shelter? Is the possibility of another baby in your future and would you like to add this to your space bag treasures?

Now somewhere out here is a mom who is screaming right now: "But Regina, I don't want to see all those sizes every time I open my closet!" If you live in a big house, apartment, or condo and you have the gift of multiple empty closets, then of course you can divide your wardrobe into separate locations. In large cities like New York, Chicago, and San Francisco, multiple closets are more of a dream and keeping your things organized in one area is a necessity. This inconvenience actually comes with a hidden bonus: Seeing the clothes you want to fit into again can serve as a beacon to you. And watching the larger-sized clothes vanish into the waiting bag is a sign of victory with each deposit you make.

No matter how creative you are about separating out the ranks, keep everything in related groups and organize by color. If you bypass this instruction, your closet will soon look like sale day at the local mall. In other words, good luck finding what you want or need in a New York minute. And that's all you have with a baby in the house! Speaking of Baby, she doesn't need a fashion plate for a mom at this stage. But she (not to mention Dad) would prefer you not become what Oprah lovingly calls a "schlumpadinka mom." Resist the temptation to fall asleep in the sweats you wore today and jump into tomorrow with them still on. It's the small things that can propel us into depression. Yes, everything is going to smell like spit-up for several months, but you can still have an attractive wardrobe of T-shirts and tops that can get popped into the wash along with the baby's onesies and tees. Be mindful of every choice you make.

## DAD'S CLOTHES

If you two share a closet, be sure his clothing doesn't get shoved into a corner. You don't have to organize his clothes for him, but be careful you aren't usurping his space. (By the way, I have from time to time seen it work in reverse: Dad suddenly takes over the closet and Mom's space is marginalized. It's a funny thing how the physical mirrors the world of thought.)

Men come in all sizes and shapes. They also vary widely in what types of clothing are important to them and how much of a particular category they need to have. Read the following tips and decide how your partner's closet will get organized, that is, by you, by him, or as a team sport!

If a man works in corporate America he may have a wardrobe of dress shirts, slacks, and suits. Keep it all according to category and use color within each one. Dad will be able to get out of the house in a flash.

Casual clothes should be organized in the same way: category and color. Be sure casual clothes have their own area of the closet. When Dad is racing for work his weekend flannel shirts will only cause a delay if they are hanging with his dress whites and blues.

He's probably got a selection of jeans, sport slacks, casual tops, and maybe a few sweaters. Keep the latter folded if you can. Hangers may leave marks and allow the garments to stretch. If you don't have the shelf space, try a dresser drawer. And add some form of moth protection just as you did for your own woolens. (Again, I prefer natural solutions like cedar, lavender, or tobacco to traditional mothballs.)

In every man's closet I've ever organized, there's an explosion of two items: baseball caps and T-shirts. He doesn't wear most of them, mind you, but he is certainly attached. You'll be happy to know that stores like Bed Bath & Beyond and The Container Store sell holders for baseball caps. See which style works best with Dad's closet space.

If Dad likes to purchase T-shirts at sporting events, concerts, and other special-occasion venues, now is not the time to talk him into photographing them rather than keeping them. However, you might be able to convince him to put the ones he'll never wear but can't part with into a space bag. Those high stacks will dwindle to an easy-to-store flat package in no time. One day you may decide to turn these treasures into pillows for Dad's den or have his favorites turned into a quilt to keep him warm in the family room. It all depends on how crafty you are and how attached he is.

Items like tie racks and belt racks can work wonders for Dad if there's wall space to install them. Keep everything separated by color and he'll enjoy the same ease in dressing that you do. Yes, even ties and belts can be sorted by color.

Dad's shoes should be up on a shoe rack. Wooden shoe racks work nicely for men's shoes. Find one that's made out of cedar and you'll be protecting Dad's woolens as well.

If Dad has a pair of dress shoes that he wears once or twice a year, pop for a large acrylic shoe drawer and store them on a shelf. They will stay clean and he'll always be able to find them.

Permanent press, wrinkle free, stain-resistant, and flame-resistant fabrics are convenient because they save us from ironing, but there's one important factor to consider: These magical fabrics often are the result of chemicals. And those chemicals are now up close and personal against your skin or your baby's when you are breastfeeding or enjoying an afternoon cuddle. Make the switch. Join the natural movement sweeping the country now: Make 100 percent (organic, if possible) cotton, wool, hemp, and silk your fabrics of choice.

If Dad is lucky to have shoe shelves built into his closet, he can easily separate his dress, casual, and sport shoes. If not, you may want to use two or three racks: one for dress/work shoes, one for casual shoes, and another for sport shoes.

And now a word about Dad's underwear and sock drawers. You can use small containers within the underwear drawer (made for this purpose) to keep things in order. If Dad bristles at the idea of drawer containers just be sure everything is folded nicely.

Nothing is more frustrating to organize than a man's socks. You need a bright sunny day to tell the dark blue socks from the light black ones. It has driven me crazy on more than one occasion. I keep dress socks folded neatly in a drawer.

If Dad has a lot of sports socks, just toss them into their own drawer or use a container that can sit on the floor of the closet near his sport shoes. Men's sport socks not only take up room, they seem to expand in a drawer. Let them breathe a little.

Finally remember that even Dad needs a miscellaneous drawer for his "stuff." If no drawer is free, consider his bedside table. They do make wood containers meant to sit on top of a dresser and hold a man's miscellaneous stuff. It's not for us to judge, ladies; after all, he's mystified by the contents of your purse.

## BABY'S CLOSET: PEEK INTO THE FUTURE

Right now you've got Baby's room set up so everything is handy. But you'll be amazed by how quickly things change. That seven-pound baby may grow faster than you'd ever imagined, and as for the three-month increments clothes are sized in: 0–3 months, 3–6 months, and so on? Well, that's just a guess. You may find that your three-week-old baby is showing two inches of chubby leg out the bottom of her newborn leggings or that his 0–3 month sweater is showing his tummy by the time he's two months old. To make things more confusing, your baby may not outgrow all her clothes at the same pace, so you may find yourself simultaneously making room for 3–6 month tops while turning those 0–3 month leggings into capri pants and then trying to figure out where to fit the sweaters she's about to grow into.

Follow some of the same principles that you're using as you make your way out of maternity clothing. Remember the bag in your closet at the ready to catch your outgrown clothes? Do the same in Baby's closet (or near her dresser if she doesn't have a closet of her own). When the bag is full, sort through it and decide whether to keep, give away, or donate items. You likely have plenty of items in larger sizes waiting for their turn. Store those in totes separated by size, and keep the next size up handy. Every week or so, you can give the tote a quick peek to see if there's anything Baby's ready to wear yet. Don't let this tote sit too long in between inspections. That sweater that seems positively enormous for Baby right now will be just the right size sooner than you'd think. And it's so frustrating when you miss the opportunity for Baby to wear that simply adorable dress because you waited too long!

As clothing comes in, hang it in categories and by color. This way, when you want a party dress, you don't need to wade through your little girl's jeans. As your baby grows and gets to the stage where she'd like to pick out her own outfits, you can put the everyday clothes on a low-hanging bar in her closet and keep the fancy outfits higher up. Now she really can make her own choices without you having to run in to get items off the "big girl bar." You also avoid any potential accidents from a toddler climbing on a step stool. Making items convenient to children as their egos and motor skills grow is part of building self-esteem. In the kitchen, I like to store their bowls and cups in a low cabinet where they can reach them without help.

Finally, as much as possible, remember that Baby's closet needs to belong to Baby. It isn't the place for you or your husband to park off-season clothes, the suitcases you use on vacation, the sports equipment you abandoned after one try, or boxes of memorabilia. Babies grow, rapidly collecting stuff of their own along the way.

## REALITY: WHAT A CONCEPT

Clothing doesn't hang itself up at night and dishes won't jump into hot, soapy water in the sink. Infants never change their own diapers. And Fido will refuse to use the pooper scooper. Life is about maintenance. And now you have a little person who needs more maintenance than you ever dreamed possible! The simple secret is to assign objects to specific homes and honor your decisions. You'll find that's the key. And on those days when the piles appear and you feel overwhelmed, take a deep breath. Beneath all that chaos is order just waiting to be *restored*—not recreated each time but restored. Isn't that comforting?

# WEEK 10 POSTPARTUM

## Create a Household Management Plan

This week, you can

- Come up with a plan for dividing household labor between yourself and your spouse
- Learn to manage paid help

UNLESS YOU'VE HAD lots of help—or you or your spouse are Energizer bunnies—it's a good bet your house is looking a little rough around the edges right now. Yes, having a baby in the house creates a lot of extra mess and you've probably been too busy caring for your baby and getting back on your feet to spend much time scrubbing and polishing over the last couple of months.

Now that you are getting back to normal physically, you may be feeling ready to jump back into your regular routine of cleaning, home maintenance, and more. But as you may have already figured out, it's just not possible to clean as quickly or efficiently with a baby in your arms . . . or even sleeping in the crib (nap time for Mom!). This is why parenthood so often brings housework inequalities to the surface: When it's just you and your spouse, it's not quite so obvious when one person isn't quite pulling his weight. But now

that there's twice as much to do and both partners are stretched much thinner than before, just how much work it takes to run a household is becoming starkly clear.

Though the majority of women, including mothers, now work outside the home, men and women very often fall into traditional gender roles in their off hours. Translation? Mom and Dad might both get home at 6:00 p.m., tired from a long day at the office . . . but most of the time, it's Mom who ends up burning the candle at both ends and managing the housework, too. Not too fair, is it? Even if you'll be staying home with your baby for the foreseeable future, you are going to need help. You won't be able to keep up with everything the way you might have before while also caring for yourself and your baby. If your partner didn't help keep the household running before she was born, you'll need to make a change.

## SHOW RESPECT, BE DIRECT

Okay, so I've got you fired up now, don't I? Settle down, sister! Yes, it's true that women more often wind up with the lion's share of housework. But men aren't always consciously taking the lazy way out. Think about it this way: Imagine you're a man and your wife has a baby. You stay home for a week or so to help her get settled in, and soon after you return to work. You have lots of friends and family stepping in to help out, and things continue to get done up to your (admittedly not too high) standards. After a while the outside help tapers off, and although things look a little rougher for a while, the home stays more or less clean. The dishes are done. The laundry gets folded. There's usually something to eat in the cupboard. Your wife hasn't said a word (though she does seem to have a crazed look about her eyes lately . . . but that must just be a normal part of new motherhood, right?). And you haven't had to do anything to make it happen at all. I guess this taking care of baby stuff isn't so hard after all, you think.

Of course, that's not the real story at all, but if you don't come right out and tell your spouse or partner the truth, he'll never know. Don't assume those heavy sighs and eye rolls get your message across. Nor will passive-aggressively leaving the overflowing trash can in front of the door. Men and women communicate differently: He's not ignoring that hint you're dropping; he just can't see it! Put on your big-girl pants and have a real conversation.

While your spouse needs to be pitching in, he doesn't necessarily want to start cleaning the moment he walks in the door, either. If you're an at-home mom and find it difficult to keep up with the chores while you're home with the baby all day, maybe your partner can play with the baby for an hour or so when he gets home. You can do a half-hour cleaning spree and use the remaining time to put your feet up and read a magazine. After the hour has passed, he should be feeling eased into the house, refreshed, and ready to take on some tasks of his own.

## BE SPECIFIC

So your spouse did the dishes today. It made your evening so much more relaxing and pleasant, and you were sure to thank him. Does that mean he'll do them again tomorrow? Well . . . not necessarily. Maybe he doesn't realize that your life is so much better when he does the dishes, you'd like him to do them *every* day. And everyone has a different standard of cleanliness. Some people don't "see" the same messes others do. This goes for you, too. Maybe while you're gritting your teeth over the sink full of dishes, your spouse is seething about the layer of dust on the computer monitor. The upshot? If doing the dishes is something you really need your spouse to do daily, tell him so!

Of course, all this is assuming that in

your house, you're the one doing most of the cooking and cleaning. I make that assumption because it seems to be the most common scenario. But sometimes, it's the other way around! If your spouse has always been the one holding the house together, he's going to need more help and understanding now.

## KEEP TRACK OF TASKS

One of the biggest challenges to splitting up household labor is to figure out what actually needs to be done—and who's currently doing it. A lot of "unseen" tasks tend to go unnoticed by the person who's not doing them. Your husband may truly have no idea of the amount of work it takes to run a household and may not know that you've been quietly keeping the trash can lid clean all these years.

As a team, keep track of who does what for one week as well as what goes undone because it's currently nobody's "job" or the person who's always done it in the past can no longer manage it. Don't think of this assignment as keeping score. Instead, it's a useful way to determine how often certain tasks need to be done, and who the most logical person is to handle them. For example, maybe you used to always be the person who vacuumed the floors, but it turns out your baby is terrified of the vacuum. Now you'll either need to do the floors when your husband is home and can take the baby out of the house, or the job will fall to him. Or maybe your spouse is an at-home parent, and you were hoping

he'd keep up with the laundry during the week. Have you considered how difficult it can be to carry loads of laundry up and down stairs while your baby is in another part of the house?

Remember to include household management tasks like keeping track of doctor and dentist visits, paying the bills, or getting the oil changed on the car. Once you've mapped everything out, you can sit down together and decide who's going to do what.

Don't feel trapped by gender roles. There's no reason Mom should always handle making appointments and Dad should maintain the car unless you decide it makes the most logical sense to divide the work up that way. Likewise, who says Dad can't cook dinner or that Mom shouldn't take out the trash? Come up with a plan that works for the way you live, and don't feel obligated to divide up tasks by "women's work" and "men's work."

When it comes time to make your household management plan, be specific. If you assure your husband you'll have the bills paid by the fifteenth of the month, he won't have to fret from days one to fourteen wondering if you're going to take care of it. If you know he plans to do the laundry on Tuesdays, you'll know not to expect an influx of clean clothes until then.

## BE FLEXIBLE

Your plan is not written in blood. Maybe your spouse thought he'd be able to make dinner every night but has been asked to

## MONEY MATTERS

If there's one thing that tends to cloud up the "who should do what around the house?" question, it's money. If you don't earn as much as your partner does or plan on taking a big chunk of time out of the paid workforce, you may feel like the house, children, and everything related to them are your "job" and it's unfair to expect your spouse to help out. Sometimes at-home mothers even feel guilty, like they're spending their partner's money, and that they don't have a right to ask for more help.

Keep in mind that your partner's earnings aren't "his" money—the money is there to support your whole family. You are doing an important job by caring for your baby—that's your contribution to the family. Regardless of whose name is on the paycheck, you and your partner have an equal say in what happens to your family's income and should be making financial decisions together. Money is one of the largest stressors in a marriage, so it's important to make sure you're on the same page.

can. This is a partnership, not a competitive sport.

Also entertain the possibility that either or the both of you may need to relax your standards. If you're "neat freaks," you may find that your standards are impossible to maintain now that you've got a baby to care for. And just wait until she's crawling and getting into things!

## KEEP COMMUNICATING

As you put your household management plan into action, there are sure to be snags and bumps along the way. Passive-aggressiveness and attacking won't help regardless of how right you are sure you are. If you aren't happy with how things are going, say so, without making accusations or generalizing (i.e., "You NEVER . . ." or "You ALWAYS . . ."). Tell him what you need him to do, or ask if he has any ideas for how to make the household run more smoothly. You are both likely tired and stressed. Be as forgiving as you can and assume that your partner does want to help.

At some point, you may realize that keeping the house up to your and your husband's standards is simply more than the two of you can manage without stress and fighting. Forget about the "shoulds," for example, "I Should be able to do it all because MY mother did." Your pride is not worth straining your marriage over. If housework is a big stressor in your house and you can make room for it in the budget, consider hiring a cleaning service. Even a three-hour visit every other week

stay late at work for an important project several nights in a row and feels he must be a team player. Maybe you thought it would be a snap to stay on top of caring for the yard but have found it more difficult than you anticipated managing the lawn and a young baby. Check in with one another frequently to see how things are going and help one another out where you will help. This isn't a failing on your part. It's simply being a smart delegator. Not everyone is good at the same things, and just because you're a great mom it doesn't follow that you have to be a crackerjack housecleaner, too.

Of course, hiring help brings with it a host of issues you will have to face. This is especially true if delegating isn't your strong suit. My mother had help at home for the first few months after I was born. She let the woman go because she felt she had to clean up before help arrived. Let's start there! Your job is to direct the person you are paying. It is not your responsibility to make the house tidy before she arrives, make her lunch, or secure her approval for the way you are raising your child.

Here are some additional guidelines to help this new relationship be more successful:

Hiring help is like dating: You wouldn't marry the first guy you ever dated just because he was your first date! You'd want to be sure you were compatible. It's not different for your housekeeper or cleaning service. Ask people you trust whose homes always look tidy how they found their person. Better yet, ask if that person would like to pick up some extra work.

Ask your helper to use the products you prefer for your home. If you have specific ways some items should be cleaned be sure and clearly communicate those instructions. There are many ways to do laundry, dust, or clean the toilet. In your home all tasks must be done the way you desire.

In the beginning, before the two of you have a rhythm and a relationship, direct your helper as to what needs to be done and the order in which you would like her to accomplish it. There's no point in having a perfectly dusted living room when the bathroom and kitchen are in chaos. You're the boss!

Don't leave valuables scattered about your home. As a rule, expensive jewelry and cash should not be left out. One day you may know this person is completely trustworthy but trust is earned, not given as a gift.

In today's political climate be sure your helper is legally in this country. If she will be with you on a regular basis, ask your tax person what you are responsible for in terms of social security and health care.

Is your homeowner's insurance in effect? You don't want someone to sue you in the event of an accident and find you aren't protected.

You may become very close to this person but that isn't a given. Just because someone is cleaning your toilet and changing the sheets on your bed doesn't mean she has to hear all about the issues in your marriage. And guess what? You don't have to hear about her life either!

If this person is going to shop for you she needs to understand what stores you go to and which brands you prefer.

Finally, if your help is with you on a regular basis, work out a schedule of home maintenance with her. It will be comforting to know which tasks are being performed on what days. It will give you something to count on and look forward to.

## A NEW DAY DAWNS

You thought learning about Baby was the only new course you were taking this year. Now you realize you have a new relationship with your partner, new demands on your home environment, and perhaps a new person in the home to assist you. The only way to avoid being overwhelmed is to embrace all this change as one of the great adventures of your life. And on those inevitable days when the world seems to have heaped more on your plate than you can manage, take a step back and ask yourself, *How can I communicate what I need right now?* Be willing to listen as well as speak up. You never know what you might learn.

# WEEK 11 POSTPARTUM

## Organize Your Birth-Related Paperwork

This week, you can

- Organize all the paperwork that your baby's birth generated

IN TODAY'S WORLD there seems to be a paper trail for absolutely everything. If you go to the big chain supermarket and join to take advantage of savings, someone is tracking your purchases. When you surf the Web and sign up for interesting newsletters, you run the risk of being inundated by offers from the site's advertisers. And once you cross the threshold of any medical facility, you can rest assured an avalanche of paperwork is coming home with you, being sent in the mail, and perhaps even being e-mailed to your computer. What's a person to do? I'm so glad you asked.

For those of you who set up a working file system when you were pregnant, this week's assignment will take less than an hour. If you didn't make time for that project when you were pregnant, set aside time this week. There are no shortcuts. Everyone benefits from a well-crafted file system. As you gaze into the future, the paper avalanche is only going to grow. And just wait until little Johnny goes to school! You might as well bite the bullet and devote the

time now. It's easy to update. It's the original creation that consumes the most time. But like baby labor, it's worth the effort.

### GATHER YE SCATTERED PAPERS WHILE YE MAY

I hope you've kept all the paperwork in one place, but with the excitement of bringing Baby home, I understand if it got scattered. You need to collect it all before you can get organized. Clean off a work surface and have someone nearby to tend to the baby so you can focus on the project at hand. When your mind is scattered you will make decisions about the best location for important papers that you probably won't remember down the line. There's a wonderful book called *Be Here Now* by Ram Dass. Whether or not you ever read the book, those are words to live by.

Once you have your stack of papers, I'd like you to separate it into broad categories. Here are some of the likely suspects:

- Doctor's invoices (OB-GYN, anesthesiologist, etc.)
- Doula
- Insurance communications
- Hospital or birthing center
- Prescription receipts

All of these expenses will likely be tax deductible, so you'll want to keep them with your business papers for the current year, rather than creating a separate section just for Pregnancy and Birth. At the end of the year this paperwork will be archived. As noted in the earlier chapter on establishing a file system, that will be for three to seven years depending on your tax status and state of residence.

Every visit to a hospital generates a mountain of paperwork. And much of it can be discarded. It's simply the hospital's policy to send you home with copies. Be sure you pull out anything you want to put in Baby's journal. Discriminate! Your child won't care how much you paid for the delivery but she might be delighted to see the tiny hospital ID bracelet that got put on.

Taking the above groups one at a time, follow these simple steps:

1. Do I need this piece of paper for any reason? If the answer is no, toss/recycle or shred it depending on the sensitivity of the material.
2. If this paper is needed, are you ready to file it away? You don't have to stop and file every few minutes. Make a stack and do it all at once. If you have multiple papers for a particular category, sort as

you go along. It's more efficient to pop ten pieces of paper into a file folder than to have to revisit that folder ten times.

Do you need to make any new files and add them to the system?

3. If you are waiting for additional information or a response of some sort, file this paper in your Pending folder.

Check Pending once a week to see if any office or business entity needs to be "goosed." Do it at the same time each week so it's automatic. You know . . . a habit!

Don't make important follow-up phone calls in a random manner. Literally schedule a time for follow-up phone calls, e-mails, or letter writing. When it comes to phone calls, note the name of the person who is assisting you as well as the date and time. Save the return e-mails and letters if this is an ongoing issue.

4. When a matter is resolved, file as much of the paper trail as you need for taxes or reference (in the event of a legal action for example) in the appropriate folder. Shred or toss/recycle the bulk.

5. Do you have medical reports? Will you need them in the near future? If the response is yes, file them.

If the medical reports are simply interesting but you don't need them for any reason, ask your doctor if he has a copy. If he does, then shred yours and let the doctor clutter his file system. (These reports are your legal property. No medical entity can refuse your request to have copies of them.) If you are the nervous type when it comes to tossing anything medical, you can always scan them into your computer.

6. Keeping track of medical payments is critical, especially if you are paying out of pocket for some of the cost of your pregnancy visits and the delivery. When you need to file a medical invoice with your insurance carrier, be sure you make a copy of it as well as the insurance claim form for the "Pending" file folder. You don't want to have to start from scratch if someone at the insurance company says they never received any communications from you.

Keep these stapled together. Paper clips can get tangled inside file folders and drag unrelated papers along with the originals.

Have a stash of blank insurance claim forms on hand, unless of course you can download them from the company's Web site on an as-needed basis.

7. As your claims are settled, put the final paperwork in the designated file folder for the entity in question. Everyone who was part of your pregnancy and birth experience should have a file folder. You can create a Medical section in your files if you don't already have one. Keep all the files in alphabetical order.

8. Invoices (medical and general) that are due need to be paid. Bill paying should be systemized. To wit:

Some people pay on the first and the fifteenth of the month.

Others schedule their payments on their calendar and pay throughout the month.

Many of my clients turn all of their bills over to an accountant. In lieu of paying individual bills, they have to check a monthly statement.

And still others make all their payments online.

Whether you use one system exclusively or have your own combination, don't fall behind on your bills. You don't want Baby's naptime shattered by phone calls from creditors, do you?

## IT'S RAINING COUPONS!

How it happens is a mystery but rest assured, once Baby is born every company that produces baby products is going to send you coupons. The first decision you have to make is whether or not you plan to use them. Let's face it: Using them is frugal and wise, but some folks are not wired to make use of coupons. They clog up drawers. They rumble around in your purse and car. And then they have the temerity to expire! If you fall into this category, recycle those puppies the minute you take them out of the mailbox. Feel no guilt. The outcome is the same, isn't it? Why entertain a drama? You've got bigger fish to fry.

You may, of course, fall into that other group of shoppers who do indeed use coupons regularly. I'm sure you have a system and the new variety will simply whet your appetite for saving a buck at the store. I never see cause to reinvent the wheel, so please carry on with whatever system you have in place.

And that brings us to the middle ground: those who have never used coupons but would very much like to and have no idea how to keep track of them. Here are some ideas. Hopefully you'll find one that works with your general organizing style.

Pick up a large metal file box with alphabetical dividers. (One usually uses these metal boxes for large index cards or recipes). Put the coupons inside using the first name of the product (corn, hot dogs, bread) or file by type (drinks, vegetables, desserts). Keep this container near your shopping list in the kitchen and check it before you go to the store.

Purchase an inexpensive accordion-style receipt holder. They come in two sizes. The small size would fit in a drawer and the larger size could be tucked into a corner on a shelf in the pantry (as an example). You'll find that some of these holders have the alphabet already printed while others have tabs. You can create your own labels. You might want to divide your coupons by the meal they serve: breakfast, lunch, dinner, snacks, etc. If you ultimately decide you like this solution you can pick up an accordion holder in a more durable plastic. It will take more abuse than the paper ones.

If the above solutions are too detailed for you and you just want one place to stash your coupons, try a project envelope (roughly nine and a half by eleven inches). They can be found at any stationery supply store like Staples. These envelopes are

**COUPON-CLIPPING TIPS**

- If you shop once a week with a list made from a menu, you will save time by not having to trek to the store multiple times a week to shop. You'll also save gas in the process and reduce your carbon footprint by making one less trip in your car.
- Coupons do have expiration dates. Every week keep an eye out for the ones you can now toss. Do check for store policy. As of this writing, for example, Bed Bath & Beyond does accept their store coupons long after the expiration date.
- Remember to cut coupons from newspapers or magazines down to size. They will take up less room—space that can be occupied by more coupons!
- For one month, keep track of the money you have saved by using coupons. Multiply that by twelve and you'll be amazed by the amount you can save over the course of a year. Put that same amount aside in a special family fund. Once a year, plan an outing funded by the coupon angels.

sturdy, durable, reusable envelopes that keep the contents visible. They close with a tie, a snap, or Velcro. You can grab the whole thing on shopping day and flip through it in your car before you enter the store. Wherever you decide to keep this or any coupon holder, make sure it's always in the designated spot. When Dad goes to the market he'll be able to check for coupons without asking you where they are.

If you have a big kitchen with lots of counter space and you fall into the "if I don't see it, I won't use it" category, try putting your coupons in a project box. These can be quite decorative and you certainly won't forget to check it before you head out for the store.

Inside a project box you could have top-loading sheet protectors housing various categories of coupons. Get the heavy-duty ones so they can endure lots of handling.

If you clip coupons in your home office, you could put in a box bottom file folder to catch your prizes. However, this time it should be one with closed sides so that your treasures don't fly all over your file drawer every time it gets closed.

## THE BABY MAVEN

Some of us were born to research. We have a hunger for information. Scouring newspapers, magazines, books, and the Internet is in our blood. But it can also become a vice. Left without (what else?) a *system* to corral the information, a mom like this will have articles about every aspect of life with Baby strewn all over the house. No one you know of course.

Here are some ideas to help keep your research accessible:

- Set aside a section in your file cabinet or use a portable file box. Remember

that the latest information about any subject is always on the Internet. You really don't have to save hard copies of much of anything these days.
- If you have a special newspaper or magazine article, cut it down and staple the pages.
- Divide the material into categories so that all related articles will be in one file folder. You might for example have something like this:

> Books (of interest)
> Breastfeeding
> Food Allergies
> Immunizations
> Toys
> Videos

The tab announcing this category might say: Baby-Related Research. If your individual file folders were small, they might all fit inside one two-inch-wide box bottom file folder. If you need more than one, it's not an issue. Over time as you make purchases like toys, strollers, videos, etc., be sure you add folders in the Warranty section of your files to house any pertinent information that comes with these purchases. You know, like the instruction manual for putting Baby's stroller together. When Cousin Mike did it for you, he clearly made a mistake. If you can't easily put your hands on that manual, it's going to be a long evening punctuated with some colorful language.

Finally, remember to follow the same guidelines for the file system you create in your computer. If information is housed differently in these two worlds, you're going to waste time searching for it. And that waste of time is exactly what a file folder is meant to eliminate from your life. Be consistent.

## THINK OF FILING PAPERS LIKE CHANGING DIAPERS

Some of you are going to resist this work with all of your might. Let me ask you a question: Do you like to change poopy diapers? Would you ever leave one on your child? Would you say to your baby: "I'm so sorry. I can imagine how uncomfortable this must be. However I don't like poopy diapers! You'll just have to endure this, OK?" No responsible adult would consider this an option.

Well, those medical papers are important to you and they need to get filed. Food and drink can get spilled on them if they continue to free float around the house.

Baby will be crawling in the blink of an eye and you know how babies like to put everything in their mouths. And let's not forget Fido and his incredible paper-eating ability. You catch my drift. In addition to the chaotic visual, there's the matter of your financial health. You need to be reimbursed for some of these expenses. You don't want to be stretched too thin because your reserves were depleted. And don't forget that the good folks who are owed money can trash your FICO score with a phone call if your payments are overdue. Paper can be as daunting as poop. But you still have to deal with it. That's the moral of the story.

Don't attempt this work on an empty stomach or after a sleepless night. Set yourself up to win by feeding your brain a nutritious meal and having a trusty glass of water by your side. Ritualize these sessions by scheduling them for the same time each week, and build a reward into the activity.

# WEEK 12 POSTPARTUM

## The Road to Relaxation
## Is Paved with Routines and Rituals

**This week, you can**

- Establish routines that will help you and your baby

CHANCES ARE GOOD you fall into one of two camps. The first type of person seeks to make order out of chaos with to-do lists, a carefully constructed calendar, and a no-fail daily routine. The other type of person believes she thrives on chaos and avoids routines. She worries that they'll make her feel confined and hold back her natural creativity and joie de vivre.

She couldn't be more wrong. A (flexible) routine isn't stifling. In fact, it frees you up. When you create habits and routines that give your day shape, you spend less time digging yourself out of self-created messes and find that you have more time for inspiration and creativity. Here's an example: Say you refuse to set yourself a bedtime. After all, you're much too free spirited for that! Around 10:00 you get sleepy, but you hit a second wind just as you're into the third hour of watching old sitcoms on Nick at Nite. Next thing you know it's 1:00 a.m. and you can't fall asleep. The next day you have to drag yourself out of bed and spend most of the day in a fog, too tired to think. You'd love to go for a hike or check out that new lunch spot downtown, but you just don't have the energy. Instead, you take a nap, then wake up groggy. Your day is shot.

Not much joie de vivre going on here, is there? The fact is that routines are helpful for both type A and type B personalities. Knowing when and where certain things are going to happen will give your life structure and allow you to have more freedom to do the things you really want to do. And now that you have a baby, routines are more essential than ever. You have two people's lives to manage instead of just one, and it's amazing how easy it is to forget to change a diaper or eat if your day has no structure. Your baby will be comforted by knowing when to expect her breakfast, her nap, her bath, and so on. And it will make it easier for you to get things done around the house or plan for outings because you'll be able to plan around your routine and not end up trying to leave a fussy, over-tired baby with a sitter or taking a hungry toddler to the grocery store.

I want to be clear that I am talking about a flexible *routine,* not a set-in-stone *schedule.* Babies don't come with internal clocks. They eat frequently and their early sleep patterns are erratic. And they cry sometimes for no reason at all, requiring comforting just when you'd penciled "load the dishwasher" into your calendar. This is all biologically normal. Just when your baby's behavior starts getting more predictable, she'll throw a wrench into the works. At some point, she'll drop that morning nap. Or she'll stop eating 'round the clock, then go through a growth spurt and be suddenly ravenous at 3:00 a.m. again. With an infant, it's just not possible to plan everything down to the minute.

But what you can do is start creating a basic outline to your day and fit your baby in as much as you are able. Here are some ideas:

Try waking up at the same time whether you need to or not. If your baby always wakes you, see if you can train yourself to get up fifteen minutes or so earlier than she usually does. Take this time to grab a quick shower, pour a cup of tea, or meditate and get ready for your day. When she does awaken, you'll feel wide-awake instead of groggy and overwhelmed—a much better way to start your day with Baby.

Make your bed first thing in the morning and dress yourself and your baby shortly after waking up. Hanging around in a bathrobe for hours is depressing.

If you're an at-home parent, get out for a walk first thing in the morning. One of the biggest challenges of having a baby is that it can seem so hard to get out of the house. The longer you sit around in front of the TV, the harder it'll be to get moving. Put Baby in a front pack and hit the sidewalk!

Don't let breakfast dishes linger in the sink or towels lie wadded up on the bathroom floor. Take a few minutes in the morning, afternoon, and evening to tidy up. It's much easier to stay on top of the housework when you make a habit to do it in small bites throughout the day, and your baby will learn by watching.

It can be hard to get babies on a predictable nap schedule. Some sleep-training books advocate scheduling naps very early using a "cry it out" method. If that's not your style or you don't think your baby is ready for such an approach yet, you can at least make it clear that certain times of the day are for taking it easy. Retreat to a quiet corner with Baby, turn the lights down, and play soft music. Maybe she won't fall asleep today, but if you do this around the same time every day she'll start to get the idea that this is a quiet, restful time. If you choose to sleep train later, it'll be much easier to accomplish now that you've built this groundwork.

Eat breakfast, lunch, and dinner around the same time every day. Sure, Baby is too small to eat food yet, but set up her Moses basket or bouncy seat near you as you eat. She'll learn that dining is a shared experience and an opportunity to be social.

Schedule errands for the same time every day. You'll be able to tell as you get to know your baby what times of the day she is most calm, content, and alert. You'll be making your life a whole lot easier if you choose those times for your trip to the grocery store.

Don't forget to add time for yourself into the routine. Maybe Baby can spend some time in her bouncy seat while you read. Or maybe you'll need to get creative. All babies have different personalities and tolerance levels for being allowed to entertain themselves. If she fusses a lot when put down, maybe you can incorporate her into your activities—for example, try a mom-baby yoga DVD or put her in the sling and put your laptop on the kitchen counter. You can surf the Web while standing and bouncing her.

A bath, pajamas, tooth brushing, and a story are great components of a nighttime bed routine. Of course, most babies don't need a bath every single day and if your baby has dry skin or eczema, your doctor may even recommend that you avoid bathing him too much. In that case, you can still incorporate the bathroom into the routine on non-bath nights. Sit in the bathroom as you wipe down Baby's hands, face, and all those little rolls around her neck with a washcloth and the same soap you would use for her in the tub. Now move on to the next thing in the routine. Baby will learn to associate these wash-up visits to the bathroom with bedtime, even if she doesn't always get a full tub bath.

Plan time for you and your spouse every day. Maybe it's as simple as watching a certain TV show or enjoying a glass of wine together as you both make dinner. When Baby is very small, you may sometimes have to include her in your time together. But as she gets older and her sleeping and eating habits become more predictable, you'll get more and more time alone.

When you start something, finish it. Leaving half-done projects scattered throughout the house is an exhausting visual. Complete even small actions: You open a cabinet to take out a jar of peanut butter. Close the cabinet door! You'd be surprised how many people leave cupboard doors ajar, drawers open, products languishing on the bathroom counter, etc.

Spend a day being mindful of the most common thoughts you entertain. Are you shocked to discover they are negative by nature? Make a concerted effort to think positive, constructive thoughts. If you have an upset in the morning, don't tell everyone you meet what happened. You'll only reinforce the negative. Maybe the day the bathroom flooded was also the day Baby gave you his biggest smile. Tell everyone about that part of the day!

## THE ROAD TO FREEDOM

It is said that the road to hell is paved with good intentions. I'd like to assure you that the road to freedom is paved with good habits and routines. If you are used to flying by the seat of your pants, this habit and routine idea may be very foreign to you. And of course all things that strike us as foreign or strange are also a bit terrifying. What can I say? Open your heart and mind and give it a try. I'm not talking about a few hours or even a day. Try it for twenty-one consecutive days—it takes that long to make a habit stick. Eventually, you may wonder why you resisted. Routines don't inhibit you. Rather, they give you a firm foundation from which your creativity is free to soar.

# ELEVEN

# Weeks 13 to 16 Postpartum

*An ounce of practice is worth more than tons of preaching.*

—GANDHI

Isn't it amazing how many collections of numbers identify us? We have social security cards, bank accounts, investment accounts, credit cards, and more. Baby hasn't taken a step and already he's identified. This month we get him set up in the file system you created months ago.

All filing and no play make Mom a cranky gal. Mom, your body has been through a lot over the past year. I'm going to devote an entire week this month to helping you restore your appearance. Women are givers by nature. It's important to balance the cycle by learning how to receive. One of the best places on earth to receive is a beauty salon. From haircut and color or facial and eyebrow wax to manicure and pedicure, it's time to give yourself some time and attention. By the way, Dad, do you need a haircut? I'm just checking.

Baby will soon be on the move, crawling at lightning speed across your floors. You want to be one step ahead and ready to corral his toys and other paraphernalia.

A quick tune-up of the living room or family room—before it turns into a mini-store or a scene from a horror movie—is in order. You'll find the more you practice the art of completion, the less likely you are to encounter clutter of any kind. If a toy comes out of a particular container for playtime, you close the circle by returning it when you're done.

Baby is only four months old. You can't wait for him to crawl, walk, and utter his first *mama* and *dada*. Right in your neighborhood, however, are other good folks who are eager to know if he's going to attend their school! Yes, it's true. Some schools sign up future students the minute the pregnancy test turns positive. We're going to take a look and make sure you aren't behind the curve. And of course it's never too early to start saving for college. Are you trying to catch your breath? It's OK. Go change another diaper and anchor in today's reality. I'll be here when you get back.

## HABITS OF THE MONTH

There are two related habits this month.

### 1. Be sure to brush and floss at least twice a day

You'll have to forgive me. This may seem obvious. But did you know that a huge percentage of people don't brush their teeth at all? I have a periodontist in the family so I hear all the horror stories. It's easy to forget—and really important to brush and floss at least twice a day. You don't want to set the stage for tooth loss in years to come. I can hear your daughter now as she turns to a friend and says, "Isn't my mom beautiful? It's just too bad she's missing a tooth." The sad reality is that most tooth loss and decay are preventable. In traditional Chinese medicine green tea offers a host of health benefits, including healthy gums. Enjoy a cup in the morning in place of your coffee. It's got caffeine to wake you and properties to heal you.

### 2. Be sure you foster good dental hygiene with Baby

Conventional wisdom had Baby visiting the dentist after she had teeth to be checked. But now the American Academy of Pediatric Dentistry advises bringing Baby in sometime between the appearance of her first tooth and her first birthday. The dentist will check your baby to be sure development is normal and the environment in her mouth is not unintentionally putting out the welcome mat for bacteria that can lead to trouble. Here are some things you can do to be sure her smile will be as beautiful as yours.

- Don't dip her pacifier in anything sweet like sugar or honey to entice her to suck.
- Never let your baby fall asleep with a bottle that has anything but water in it. Make sure Dad is on board with this idea and educate her sitters and siblings.
- Be sure your baby is drinking out of a cup by the ninth to twelfth month.

Line up your pediatric dentist now to see if she has any additional guidelines for you. Children with healthy teeth and gums have no problem chewing solid foods. They learn to speak clearly and, perhaps sweetest of all, they love to smile. Nothing of course trumps your good example.

# WEEK 13 POSTPARTUM

## Organize Your Baby's Documents

**This week, you can**

- Integrate the baby paperwork into your existing file system

ONE MINUTE YOU'RE SAFE and cozy in Mom's womb and the next some nurse is sticking a gigantic syringe up your nose and in your mouth. Before you can say, "Ouch! Hey, lady, that hurts!" you've generated paperwork for Mom to file. What a transition! Welcome to the world, Little One.

Once again you will be grateful you created a file system while you were pregnant. Didn't I promise that the dividends would be endless? Baby is going to have all sorts of important documents coming home with him or arriving in the mail. These documents will be needed for school and doctor's visits and as reminders of personal milestones. What a drag if you have to go looking for things instead of knowing just where to find them when the need arises. I've got two ways to keep track so you have a choice. Isn't it too bad we can't ask Baby what she would like?

### INTEGRATE ALL NEWCOMERS!

Let's assume that your baby isn't going to be an only child. Let's say he's going to be one of several children like in Meagan's household. Why not tweak the existing file system? It's designed to easily absorb all future members. It's a drag to have to stop and reinvent the wheel every time you come home from the hospital.

Baby will probably start life with some combination of the following. Please note that I've divided the items into categories and kept both the categories and the documents within them in alphabetical order.

### Financial
529 account (college savings plan)
Savings account

### Legal documents
Birth certificate
Passport
Social Security card

### Medical documents

Immunization record

Hospital or medical records

### Miscellaneous

Memberships he's given as gifts.

### Sentimental

Foot and hand prints

Hospital/birth center birth certificate
(for posterity, not an official record)

Hospital ID bracelet

### Religious Documents

Religious ceremony certificate
(Baptism, Bris, etc.)

In your file system you already have many if not all of the above categories. The easiest thing to do is to make folders for the various new documents and keep them in areas where you go for similar information regarding yourself or your spouse. Give Baby his own color file folder for quick visual identification. You'll find wonderful choices at any chain office supply store like Office Max or Staples. If you want something fancy you can shop online at a site like www.seejanework.com. I would suggest using a soft pastel. And yes, they do come in pale pink and pale blue!

When you can, group your documents. For example, Hospital and Immunization records would be in separate files in the Medical section; all legal documents can be placed in one file folder in the Business section. I'm going to assume you have a Banking section in your system. We all

---

### HOW SAFE IS YOUR SAFE?

Security is always an issue when you have any valuables at home. You may want to invest in a safety deposit box at your bank (usually a tax-deductible expense) or have a safe in your home. Just be sure that the safe isn't small, compact, and easy to pick up. After all, if you can pick it up so can a thief! Consider one in the wall behind a painting or photo or invest in a heavy one for your master bedroom or office closet. It should weigh several hundred pounds and be deposited by two burly guys named Bubba with a dolly.

Be sure you have secure locks on the doors and windows. If you have a security system, use it. I can't begin to count the clients and friends I have who neither lock their doors nor turn on the alarm when they exit the home. Play it safe. It's a lot more fun than that other game, Sorry!

You might want to put a lock on your office door and another on your file cabinet. Be sure you both know where the keys are and make it a habit to return them to the designated spot. In addition you can come up with a code for your legal documents. (Many of my clients put them in a file called Feng Shui. It's a rare thief who would know what that is and it's even more unlikely you'd find one who wanted to read about it.) Pick out a code name for your legal documents if it makes you feel more secure. But again be sure you both know what the code phrase is.

have credit cards with different banking institutions, savings accounts, and checking accounts. You may also have certificates of deposit, etc. In this section I would put Baby's banking information in a separate file. I'd also create a file folder for his 529 account should he have one. (Schools will, for instance, want to see his birth certificate and his immunization record. But no one is going to ask to see his bank account balance.)

Memberships for all sorts of fun clubs will probably arrive over time. I'd create one file to hold all of them. If the organization sends out a monthly newsletter or generates other paper communication on a regular basis, you might need to make separate folders for each membership entity. But keep them in one section of the file system. I'd say a box bottom file folder would be ideal. You could label it, Memberships/(Baby's name) and then put the organizations' information in individual file folders and of course keep them in alphabetical order. Organizations that send very little material or have a one-time-only communication can have a General file folder.

## SEPARATE THE MINIONS!

Now because this is your first baby, you may not be ready to integrate her files into the system. I understand completely. In that case, make your file folders in the color of your choosing and then keep them together in one section of your file cabinet in one or two box bottom file folders. The tab can simply indicate your baby's name: Erin's Files, for example. If you aren't a file cabinet person, you can purchase a portable file container. I've seen ones made in soft pastel colors designed especially for Baby. Or you can buy a generic one at the above-referenced stores or sites.

## THE BOTTOM LINE

No matter how you decide to keep track of your baby's growing paper trail, remember the bottom line: You need to be able to grab her important information in an instant. I had a client who told me a great story after we completed organization of his home office. One morning, as he was backing out of the driveway, his young son said he had forgotten to tell his father that he needed his birth certificate at school that day. My client said that in the past a huge explosion would have ensued because he'd have had no idea where that certificate was located. Instead he was able to turn off the engine, run up to his office, and grab the birth certificate. His son wasn't even late for school. This kind of ease is at your fingertips. Decide which system works for your personality type. Pick up any supplies you need and devote an hour to integrating your baby's paperwork into your existing system.

# WEEK 14 POSTPARTUM

## Get a Haircut and Speed Your Routines

**This week, you can**

- Consider your new "look" and plan for your beauty routine as a mom
- Improve your time-management skills

WHEN YOU WERE pregnant, you may have noticed that your hair got thicker, more lustrous, and shinier. Its texture may even have changed, becoming straighter or curlier. That's because during pregnancy, hormonal shifts cause you to lose fewer hairs each day than you generally would. Your head holds onto a lot of extra hair throughout your pregnancy and for a few months after your baby is born.

I bet you can tell where this is going, right?

A few months after you give birth, your hormones will shift again. As you return to your normal phases of hair growth and loss, your head will shed all the "extra" hair it saved up during pregnancy within a short frame of time. So no, all that hair on your pillow and coming out in huge handfuls in the shower doesn't mean you're going bald!

What it does mean is that you probably need a new haircut. And while you're at it, it might not hurt to get those highlights taken care of. Or maybe you went on a nine-month hair-color fast while pregnant and *really* need an overhaul now.

There may be other areas where your look could use a bit of maintenance. You couldn't see your feet for months. Even if you got regular pedicures while pregnant, it's probably been a while since you've had a touch-up. How are those toes doing now? While you're at it, check out your hands. Frequent washing after diaper changes may have left your cuticles ragged, your nails weakened, and your skin dry. While a set of fake nails would probably be one of the world's most impractical moves right now, that doesn't mean you have to live with dry, cracked hands or tattered fingernails.

Maybe you were always a low-maintenance gal when it came to beauty treatments. If that's the case, you can probably just schedule a haircut to get yourself back on track. Ask the stylist to give you a cut that can be styled in five minutes or less and that will grow out well so that you don't have to worry about getting back into the salon within a month. (Let's be realistic, here!) And ask her to show you three or four different ways to wear your hair—complete with product and/or accessory recommendations—so that you can make the most of your "in-between cuts" time. If you're new to this stylist, don't feel shy about asking for some advice. If your new cut is a low-maintenance one, it won't take the stylist long to advise you how to wear it.

On the other hand, perhaps before you had a baby you were in the salon regularly getting waxed, washed, colored, massaged, and blown dry. Your schedule is undoubtedly less "free and easy" than it once was and most likely your budget is tighter, too, but if your beauty regimen has always been comforting to you, it may be worth figuring out ways to maintain it.

If making time is an issue, maybe there's a mom friend from work, playgroup, or Mommy and Me classes who's in a similar boat? (Here's how to find her: Approach the woman whose eyebrows look as though they were waxed to perfection . . . about six months ago. Or maybe her hair is beautifully highlighted but she's wearing three inches of dark roots and a desperate look in her eye.) The two of you can schedule your appointments close to one another, meet at the salon with a double stroller or a stroller and a front carrier, and switch off walking the babies around while the other is getting beautified.

If you've got more time than money, try your local beauty school. If you're in an urban area you may be able to find one associated with an upscale salon. Your treatments and services will take a long time since they'll be performed by cautious students under the watchful eye of their instructors, but you can get a fantastic deal on everything from waxing to dyeing to cuts, and you should be happy with the end result (after all, that's what the student is supposed to be learning to do).

## SPEED UP YOUR BEAUTY ROUTINE

Once you're home from the salon and your new style is washed out, it's the moment of truth. In a previous chapter we shared Meagan's three-minute shower routine. But what about a three-minute beauty routine? Well, counting blow-drying time, you may need a little more than that. But you can still pare it way down from your pre-baby routine with a little practice. The trick is mastering a handful of hairstyles you can do quickly—maybe even with one hand—and paring down the number of beauty products you use.

Everyone relies on different cosmetics to achieve their desired look. Maybe you're not a fan of your ruddy complexion, so for you foundation is a must. Or maybe you tend to look pale (especially when you haven't slept more than four hours in a row in months) and blush really helps. Or maybe you have sand-colored eyelashes and really need mascara to make your eyes pop. Prioritize. You don't need to put on a full face of makeup every day to look "put together." You just need to figure out the two or three products that make the biggest difference and make sure they're easy to put your hands on in the bathroom or at your vanity table. Some women don't like using makeup at all but feel naked without a pair of great earrings to accessorize. Whatever your adornment of choice, make it easy to find and use when time is short.

Another great way to reduce the amount of time you spend getting ready and to keep your bathroom organized is to use products that do double duty and take plenty of beauty shortcuts. Some ideas:

Consider a tinted moisturizer rather than a separate foundation and moisturizer. Just make sure it has adequate sun protection. My personal favorite is Jouer's luminizing moisture tint.

Instead of separate compacts for eye shadow and blush, use a palette with several colors you can use anywhere you want. Jouer Cosmetics makes individual cosmetic containers that click together like puzzle pieces. You can custom design a palette that's perfect for you. When your baby is about to wake from her nap, every second counts!

Consider having your eyelashes tinted. You can have this done in many salons and spas, and some beauty schools, too. It'll look like you're wearing mascara all the time, and you won't have to worry about raccoon eyes after an afternoon nap or bother with eye makeup remover at bedtime.

Invest in good makeup brushes. They make the whole job easier, give you better results, and will last longer, too.

Keep a thick moisturizing cream on the sink near the hand soap. After you wash your hands, give yourself a liberal slather every time. This will help keep your hands in good shape in between manicures.

When you do get a manicure, don't bother with colored polish. Go natural or clear. It will last longer since you won't see the chips. Save bright reds and pinks (or purples and blues) for your toes.

Buy a good razor. Those single-blade disposables you buy ten for two bucks just scrape the hair off your legs and underarms. It'll take a lot longer to finish the job and you'll end up with nicks and cuts in the process. Meagan likes the Schick Intuition, which comes with a block of moisturizing shave cream attached so you don't have to squirt out a separate product. (Every second counts!) Experiment with products that help you get the job done quickly and comfortably. Put a small seat in the shower (if there's room) so you can enjoy this task. This is also a great place to give Baby a quick spray-down if you don't have time or inclination to run a full bath.

Treat yourself to products (shampoos, conditioners, soaps, etc.) that moisturize and have a pleasing fragrance. Your bathroom will always smell like a high-end spa.

## THE SECRET SELF-CARE INGREDIENT

No, it's not a gym membership or a series of pole dancing classes. The secret to self-care is having solid time-management skills. With time management you can be sure and schedule the haircut or the pole dancing. Without it, they may never move from wishes and dreams to reality. If you let things occur in a haphazard way you'll always be exhausted, disappointed, and playing catch-up.

Decide what you want to accomplish each week. Make a list. Now schedule those items on your calendar. Whether it's on the computer, a PDA or smart phone, or a paper version on the refrigerator in the kitchen, plot your course. Everything that was dear to you before Baby arrived deserves to have a shot at being integrated into your new life. And this is especially true for all those wonderful, nurturing activities you may have let slide for the past few weeks.

Here are some tips:

Get good at running errands in clusters. Why go to the same area of town multiple times a week when you can hit the cleaners and the shoemaker on the same day you grocery shop? If the beauty salon is there, have your hair cut that afternoon or schedule your manicure. I call this "geographical intelligence."

Make it easy on yourself. If your bathroom is all the way across the house from where you and Baby spend most of your time, why keep your cosmetics there? Can you keep your three "must-have" products and a mirror in a more convenient location? I know a mom who keeps a small cosmetics bag with a compact, mascara, and blush in her glove compartment. She also stashes a hairbrush and some barrettes there. Since her son started crawling, she can't take her eyes off him for a minute. The car is the only place where he is safe and confined (in his car seat) and where she can have a few minutes of peace to fix herself up a little before she starts driving. Plus, there's a mirror and natural light already there!

Schedule and direct your helpers. You will need to know how long things take. If you find you have no clue, time them over the next week. You will realize, for example, that it takes three hours to drive to town and have your hair cut and colored. If you don't know the time required, you may book Aunt Jen to babysit for only two hours. Either she'll be fuming when you get home from the salon or else you'll be in your car with foils in your hair!

Now is the time to establish yourself as a priority in your life. Oprah has enough candidates for her schlumpadinka makeover shows. She doesn't need you. But your partner would like to see the face of the woman he fell in love with, and while I'm at it, you surely want to see the face of that guy you said "yes" to, right? Encourage him to get a haircut. He doesn't have to turn into "metro-sexual man"; he can just fly into the local Super Cuts and get cleaned up. If this is all new to you, don't get frustrated or disappointed if you're not a natural at time management. It takes patience and practice to change. All it requires is a first step.

# WEEK 15 POSTPARTUM

## Prepare the Family Room Before Baby Starts Crawling

This week, you can

- Get your living room, family room, and/or great room ready for Baby's expanding horizon, paraphernalia, and toys
- Learn how to tailor these instructions for an apartment
- As new baby-related items enter, decide how to manage those that can exit or be stored

YOUR LITTLE DARLING will soon be covering new territory. Babies fly like the wind when they master crawling and really take off when those little legs get sturdy. It's fulfilling, touching, and exhausting all at the same time. You don't want to be saying, "Oh! No! Don't touch that!" every five minutes. It's a boring mantra to recite and an even bigger bore to listen to. In fact, after a few repetitions, it runs out of juice. This week we'll do a little preliminary work on those areas of the home that are usually inundated with baby toys and paraphernalia. When Baby is ready to move, both you and your living or family room need to be ready to rock the house.

### YE OLDE LIVING ROOM

In many modern homes the living room has vanished. The more popular home design has a family room that flows organically (i.e., no walls) out of the kitchen space, creating one large area where Mom or Dad can make a meal and supervise the kids. It invites sharing and conversation (provided, of course, that you have rules governing the use of the television and computer). If you have a "great room" encompassing dining, living, and family areas in one open space, you'll need to decide exactly which parts of the room the baby is allowed to grace with her toys. Use furniture placement and area rugs to demarcate the zones.

There are still some homes with a formal living room. Assuming you have a separate family room, the living room's function is to be an area that is always tidy and ready to receive guests. You graciously guide visitors, from family members or coworkers to the UPS guy, into this room and keep the lived-in ambience in your family room private. (And therein tells the tale. Is your living room always tidy and ready to receive guests? The unfortunate answer is usually "yes." I say it's unfortunate because this room is so rarely used that the energy here is generally stagnant. It can feel a bit like you're entering a room in a museum.)

I would suggest you discourage your baby from taking up residence in this area, whether you set up a baby gate or simply keep her toys in another area of the house. You will be grateful over time to have an area always ready to receive guests. However, I'd wake up the energy in this room by actually using it once or twice a week. When you were pregnant, did you create a special nook for yourself and Baby? What about a nook that's just for you—I bet this room has one. Perhaps you have a window seat? Why not curl up here and spend ten minutes watching the world go by when your baby is asleep? No texting, Tweeting, or phoning! Give your brain a break. Maybe this is where you relax in a big easy chair with a guilty pleasure like a romance novel? My father loved classical violin music. Neither my mom nor I shared his passion. Dad would go into the living room, read the paper, and listen to his music. He filled the room with glorious sounds and great happiness. Find a way to put your unique stamp on your living room and enjoy it. Never underestimate the power of living plants to make a room look and feel more alive.

### Are You Ready to Receive Visitors?

Let's look around before we move on to the family room and see if indeed this room is clutter free. What do you see? Have outdated magazines gathered here? Are there one too many knickknacks on the tables and the mantelpiece? Do photos crowd the space? Are any of them current? Take a few minutes one day to toss, recycle, or pack away the excess items in this room. And then be sure you have that baby gate ready to go.

## THE FAMILY ROOM

This room should be where the family can kick back and have fun. Take a minute to sit in this room and take stock. You will be spending more and more time here as your baby grows and you add to your family. It's important for it to be a nurturing place in the home. It's going to see dramatic changes over the course of the next year and beyond. If it's chaotic before Baby's toys and paraphernalia arrive, you will be just like Sisyphus pushing the same rock up the same hill. Or perhaps I should say putting the same DVD into the same jewel case for eternity.

Here are some questions to help guide any work that you feel needs to be done here:

- Is it fun to be here or do you feel overwhelmed in the space?
- If overwhelmed is your response, can you pinpoint exactly what's contributing to that feeling? Very often there's too much furniture in this room. Donate any old, ratty furniture you kept here for sentimental rea-

sons. I know that beanbag chair from college was cool in its day but you need the space for your new room-mate—you know, the teeny tiny one asleep in her bed. She's got stuff comin'!

- Does the room need a little refreshing with new window treatments, a book-case, or a new chair? If you cannot afford to make these purchases at this time, is there a temporary cure?
- Is there too much of something that's clogging the space: reading matter, photos, decorative items, an unwieldy CD or DVD collection, or perhaps a hobby gone awry?

Take stock and make some notes in your baby journal. You might want to surf the Internet and visit sites like www.The ContainerStore.com to see which products fit your pocketbook, lifestyle, and temperament. For the most common clutter culprits in this room, you may want to consider the following product ideas.

- Keep magazines and newspapers in holders designed for this purpose. Very often you can find matching ones. The key of course is to stay on top of your issues. The prettiest container in the world will be useless if it's habitually overflowing. Is it time to cancel some subscriptions? Try reading your favorite magazines and newspapers online. iPad or Kindle anyone?
- Bookcases are just wonderful for holding books as well as CD and DVD collections. Do you need any bookcases in this room? Inexpensive ones are available, but if they are melamine, you may want to let them air out in the garage, backyard, patio, or balcony first due to the off-gassing issue (see page 99). Perhaps Dad or a handy aunt would like to build some out of wood and stain or paint them to go with the room.
- As noted earlier in this book, CDs and DVDs can be divided by genre and stored in binders with special sheets that are designed to hold the collection. You can recycle the jewel cases. Never underestimate the amount of destruction a baby can wreak on an out-in-the-open disk collection.
- If you engage in a hobby in this room, do you have the parts put away in suitable containers? Now is the time to secure the appropriate holders. Baby is going to be into your Creative Memories supplies before you can say "Zen Organizer to the rescue!"
- Computers come with all sorts of cords and wires, even if you are on a wireless system. Wrap the cords and wires in plastic tubing made for this purpose. It will be less inviting for Baby. You'll still need to keep an eagle eye on him but now you'll be keeping him away from one item, not ten.
- Does the room need a trash can? If there is one, is it adequate in size? And does it get emptied regularly? I see a new habit on the horizon, especially if you have older children in need of a chore.

Remember that the best products in the world only keep you clutter-free if you use them. Before you and your husband (and later your child) leave this room you should cultivate the habit of restoring order. Did you take something like today's newspaper, your newest magazine, a CD, or a sheet of stickers out of its container? Everything needs to go back! Did you wrap yourself in the throw on the couch? Refold it so it's ready for your next nap or visit. Did you bring an item like a glass or a dish in here from another room? It leaves with you as you exit. If you make this a habit, your baby will automatically grow into a child who understands that there is a place for everything and everything must be in its place. That little bromide is at the heart of being organized.

## BABY-PROOFING BASICS

Sooner than you can imagine, Baby will be crawling. It's time to consider baby-proofing your living spaces. Some parents go whole hog, covering every corner and padding every surface. Other parents are much more relaxed. Whichever camp you fall into, there are a few basic precautions you should definitely take.

- Make sure small items like coins, marbles, and other choking hazards are put on a high shelf, away from the baby. Better yet, put them in a room that your child rarely plays in. They have a funny way of turning invisible in the pile of the carpet. Guess who will have no problem finding them? You guessed it: Baby.

- Check to see if your houseplants are safe for Baby. Many common plants are poisonous, and yes, Baby will try to eat them.

- Speaking of poisons, if you haven't done so already move toxic household cleaners like bleach or ammonia, medications, alcohol, and other potential toxins to a high cupboard. (This is a great incentive to start using those natural cleaning products we talked about earlier.) That cavernous space above the refrigerator is a wonderful spot, although you'll surely need to keep a step stool handy to access your products. If you don't have any high cupboards or cabinets, be sure you install childproof locks on the cabinet under the sink or any other place you might keep those store-bought or homemade cleaners.

- Shorten drapery and blind cords. You can purchase products to keep dangerous cords out of Baby's reach at stores like Babies "R" Us or at special baby-proofing stores online.

- Put a screen around your fireplace, radiator, and/or electric heater.

- Cover all electrical outlets.

- Keep sharp objects like knives, razor blades, or box cutters out of Baby's reach.

- Invest in good baby gates for the top and bottom of the staircase. The kind that mount with hardware to the wall are easier to use and sturdier. Stairs are fascinating to babies and some will work diligently at tearing down a portable gate.

- Keep a portable gate on hand for other areas you may temporarily want to keep the baby out of.
- Make sure TVs and furniture pieces cannot be pulled over onto Baby. These are often top-heavy and it doesn't take much pulling to bring them crashing down. Consider affixing these items to the wall. Televisions can be closed up into a sturdy armoire.

Use your common sense. If the corner of your coffee table is sharp and right at a toddler's eye level, it probably makes sense to cover it. But as your baby learns about the world, some bumps and bruises are unavoidable. All children are different. Some are climbers. Some are more likely to hunt for marbles under the sofa. As you watch your baby grow, it will become apparent where your baby-proofing may need to be beefed up. Meanwhile, don't go into debt turning your home into the equivalent of a padded room.

## THE CHALLENGE OF AN APARTMENT

Now that you've read this far, if you live in a small apartment, you may be thinking, "O.K., Regina. You can 'great room' *this!*" Believe me, I understand. I grew up in New York City and I've got clients in small apartments and condos all across the United States. There are three keys to san-

> ### CHECK IT OUT!
>
> In the past you may have been lax about checking out the smoke detectors in your home or making sure you had fire extinguishers in strategic places. But now someone tiny and precious needs you to keep him safe. Make a list of household items to be checked once a year (e.g., smoke and carbon monoxide detectors) and once every six months (e.g., AC/heat filters). Set a reminder on your iPhone, PDA, or computer. Be sure your kitchen and bathrooms have fire extinguishers and note the expiration dates. (Please note that there are different types of fire extinguishers for different types of fires. Choose wisely. It isn't one size fits all.)

ity if you have this situation. And one bonus option if you own the apartment.

- More than in any other living condition you must designate a place for everything and return it when you are done. It will take less stuff to make the room appear to be drowning in clutter. If you stay vigilant, you can manage.
- Don't over-buy baby clothing and toys. Tell family and friends they need to follow your wishes because you are space challenged. Grandparents very often are the worst offenders, especially if they live far away. It's well intentioned but still leaves you squeezed for space.

As I suggested in an earlier chapter, you don't have to keep the life-sized panda bear if he's bigger than you, your spouse, and your baby combined. If Grandma and Grandpa don't want to keep it in their home to entertain Baby when she visits, ask them to be sure and send a gift receipt with every item. Return the gift and put the cash in Baby's 529 college fund. When your visitors come over and you are asked, "What happened to the panda?!" simply smile and say, "Oh my gosh! He's busy getting her ready for Harvard."

- You will most likely need outside storage. Most apartment buildings in big cities like New York, Chicago, and San Francisco have storage areas for rent in the building. This is the most convenient solution. If either of you have parents who live outside the city and they have a home and a car, ask if you can use your old room or part of the garage to store things for a few years. The good news is that as Baby grows, her toys generally shrink in size. The bad news is that the small parts multiply and you will need to corral things in containers. But you've got to do that anyway!

- Finally, if you own your condo and have the funds, invite a professional designer or space planner over to give you some ideas about built-in storage designs. This can be pricey but remember: It will increase the value of your condo when it comes time to sell.

When friends and family come by, warn them ahead of time that space is at a premium and the baby has taken over the living room. Even a vigilant mom who has help is going to have a time of it. I doubt you'll be doing any formal entertaining for a few years so take a deep breath and enjoy this time in your life. If anyone balks at the setup, tell her that from now on you can meet in a restaurant or park. Judgment is one thing you don't need to entertain.

## BABY'S STUFF ARRIVES

Here's the unvarnished truth: You've got to stay on top of Baby's stuff; otherwise it will be an avalanche that buries you. I can't reinforce this reality often enough. First we'll talk about Baby's current items. Next we'll get ready to greet the new generation of things she's going to need. I'll also discuss possible systems to keep order as we go along. If you've always had difficulty making decisions, you're going to have ample opportunity to practice over the next eighteen years. Please feel free to adapt these ideas to suit your needs.

Most babies use some combination of the following gear for the first few months of life:

Bouncy seat
Swing
Moses basket
Cradle or bassinet (as soon as she can grab the edges and pull up, it's no longer safe)

Odds are good that you've been using these items in this room. No matter the location, over the next few months your baby will either outgrow them or lose interest. Soon it will be time to start clearing them away to make way for the next wave of age-appropriate items. What's a parent to do? I'm so glad you asked.

- If you borrowed any of these things, it's time to return them to the generous mom who shared them with you. If she no longer needs or want them, you'll have to decide whether to store them or donate them. I have ideas below for both scenarios.

- If you purchased them or received them at your shower, you also have to make a decision. Are you planning to have more children? If the answer is "yes" and "soon," you'll want to store these items. If you have a garage, I'd use large, heavy-duty plastic storage containers for the smaller items. Cardboard containers will disintegrate over time. They may also play host to the creepy crawlies that thrive on paper. The plastic will keep them clean and dry. For additional protection you may want to put wrapped and labeled bags into storage containers.

   Some items of course defy gravity when it comes to storing them. We've all seen baby swings that are four feet high and three feet wide, and then there are the true pieces of furniture like a cradle, a crib, or a bed or a sofa. You have choices.

1. You can save the original packaging, but remember that probably means breaking some items down. You may be loath to do that if you aren't handy at that sort of thing and your sister swears she's not putting together one more item for you.

2. If you have fly space in the garage you can literally hoist these items (covered and well protected of course) into the air or create a loft in the garage. Your local home store will have guidance and the supplies you need for either of these choices. A company specializing in garage makeovers can also assist you.

3. Break your bed down into its parts for easy upright (covered!) storage against a wall in the garage. If there are smaller parts like braces or screws, bag them and store them *with* the items.

4. Protect the outsized items by covering them carefully. Whether it's a cover the manufacturer sells for the product, the special plastic wrap that movers use, or a heavy-duty garbage bag, be sure it's wrapped securely. If you have a garage, store all of Baby's items together in one area. You don't want to embark on a treasure hunt when you need one specific item.

- Label the container as to the contents. Use your label maker or print out a list using your computer. I don't want you out in the garage around midnight one cold winter's night muttering under your breath, "I wonder what the heck is in *that* box?"

- If you have a clear wall, purchase an inexpensive shelving unit from your local home store. Use the shelves exclusively for baby-related items. When you need to access them either for use with your next child or because you realize there isn't going to be another child and it's time to pass these items on to another mom or a charity, you want to be able to get to them easily.

- If you lack a garage, basement, attic, guest room closet, or any other type of storage, it may be time to either rent a space or ask Mom and Dad if you can have some space in their garage. I'm rarely in favor of renting outside storage but there are exceptions. Decide how long it will be before you have your next baby. Multiply the rent by the number of months until you are pregnant. If the amount is greater than the replacement cost of these items, rethink this option!

- Maybe you have a friend or family member who would like to borrow the item. Now that your baby has outgrown clothes and gear and you're done with most of your maternity clothes, you have the option of loaning them out. But you'll need to take shared responsibility for their safe return. Label the items yourself and keep track of what you loaned to whom. Keep track with a document

---

**THE MYSTERY BOX**

All babies and children receive gifts that they simply don't need. One of my clients has a neat trick: She keeps a Mystery Box on a high shelf by the front door. When little people drag their feet about leaving, she tells them when they are ready they can reach into the Mystery Box and take a toy. The catch is that taking the toy means they have to exit immediately. Small stuffed animals, small picture books, party favors, etc. all make great additions to the box. While your baby is still young and nonverbal, you can give visiting moms a parting gift for their baby or perhaps something for an older sibling. Don't go out and purchase items in order to create your Mystery Box. Trust me when I tell you that potential items are going to come flying in your front door!

---

you create in Excel. However, remember that human beings lose, destroy, and stain things, so give items away with an understanding that they might not return or, if they do, they may not be in pristine condition. By the way, the easiest way to mark an item is with a bit of nail polish on a sewn-in tag or underneath a toy where no one will see it. "Crafty" moms may of course have custom-made labels on hand.

- If you know this is your only or last baby, see if anyone in your community of friends would like to have these items. Or simply donate them to your favorite local charity or women's shelter. You'll get a slip for your taxes. Is that win/win or what?

The bottom line is, you can't stash items in their original packaging behind the couch. (And, yes, I have encountered this in some homes as a "solution"!) It's the visual equivalent of living in one of the aisles at Toys "R" Us. Every item that belongs to your baby is going to undergo the same scrutiny. Whether it's the bouncy seat or

---

### MEMENTO OR TREASURED MEMORY?

Every baby will be gifted with special items that will be difficult to part with, especially if you know he is the last of the Mohicans. Chief among these items will be beautiful clothes and cuddly stuffed animals. If you find these are difficult for you to part with, box them up and put them away for a future date. However, I am not suggesting years from today! Mark six months on your calendar, after which it will be time to reassess and make a decision. It would be better to pass these items on to another baby than to hold onto them. They were made to be loved, used, and treasured. They lose some meaning when they are salted away safe from a baby's touch. Treasure the photos you have of Baby wearing or cuddling the item. And then let it go. After all, it represents something you can't hold on to anyway, no matter how hard you try: a time that is past.

---

the onesies he just outgrew, you've got to have things on the move almost constantly. Otherwise you will be overwhelmed with stuff. If ever there was a time to cultivate the art of the decision, it's now. I can't repeat that too often. It's the crux of the matter.

Just as you have a bag waiting in Baby's room to catch those clothes she has outgrown, you will want a staging area for toys and other paraphernalia that can leave the house. Perhaps you make a sweep once a week on Friday afternoons? Maybe you agree on an area and when your husband sees items there, he knows they are on their way out of the house. You can tag them for garage or donation. The way you manage this will be unique to your relationship, any outside help you have, and the size of your home. The concept is universal but the way it gets implemented is an individual matter.

### SQUEAK, RATTLE, AND ROLL!

As Baby gains coordination and muscle strength, the baby gear you acquire will be moving away from things that prop Baby up/do things for her, and moving toward things Baby can really play with (balls, push toys, things that squeak and rattle and have interesting textures). Instead of allowing your entire home to become a toy store, why not designate certain areas for certain toys? Here are some questions to help you decide what goes where:

Where do you want to read to your child? The usual answer is in his room each night before he goes to sleep. Keep his books in his room on a bookcase to facilitate this choice.

In addition to the books you read to him, Baby will have lots of picture books to look at and baby books to touch. Perhaps it's best to keep these in the family room? By dividing your stash you teach Baby to expect a particular book in a designated area.

One way to keep your baby's toy stash manageable is to rotate his collection. Keep some of his toys on a shelf in the closet. In three to six months, when you rotate the toys again, he'll think he's gotten a brand-new stash. Until he's old enough to make an informed decision, be sure that periodically some toys just rotate right out the door!

When your child is old enough to make decisions about which toys will be donated, involve him in the process. Explain that there are children who aren't as fortunate as he is and need toys to play with. A charitable nature is one of the greatest gifts you can give a child. And the first lessons can start sooner than you realized.

When it comes to toys, they all naturally fall into categories. For example, there will be dolls, stuffed animals, balls, rattles, and so on. Purchase containers for the family room (if this is the designated spot for playing) and when a play session is over, let Baby watch as you return things to the container where related items are stashed. The minute he's old enough or coordinated enough to help you, he can put his toys away.

Does this activity remind you of anything? It's no different than putting your clothes away in the same spots after you organize your closet, is it? It's exactly the same as returning your baby's important papers to the same files when you are done with them . . . or your papers for that matter. It's never too early to learn that related items go together and that categories are to be honored to safeguard the system.

By the way, good-quality containers can be decorative and sturdy. They can hold a changing array of toys as Baby grows up and becomes a young adult. One day when he's off at college, you may be using them in the garage to help you sort your gardening tools. You never know what the life history of a good quality item will be.

You may wish to pick up an activity mat. They're a soft, colorful place for Baby to lie and usually feature attached toys, mirrors, crinkly material, and other interesting things to touch and look at. Baby can also play with his toys on this surface rather than on the floor or the carpet. You can keep it clean and you'll also be portable. If you have a cat or a dog, of course, they will want to bless this toy with their energy. 'Tis the nature of the beasts. Baby can be safely at your feet and occupied while you do dishes or chat with your mom about the day's developments. If need be, the mat can be folded or rolled up and stashed behind the couch when not in use.

Another popular baby toy is the Exersaucer. Babies will stay entertained for hours because of all the interesting (and noise-making) parts. You can set it up just about anywhere and move it around the house so that Baby has a safe place to play off the floor and within view, whether you're making dinner or working in the yard. Be forewarned, however: This is one of those space-eating toys and will seem to dominate the space in smaller or cluttered rooms. Perhaps the Exersaucer can live in a closet or in the baby's room and only get pulled out when you need to use it . . . or maybe an activity mat is all you need.

While I'm on the topic of toys that make noise . . . yes, babies often love them. But adults, understandably, usually don't. For centuries, babies grew up to be intelligent, happy people without ever playing with a single battery-operated toy. If you know the beeps, squawks, and endless musical notes emanating from that Exersaucer will drive you batty over the next few months, by all means, remove the batteries now. Baby will never know the difference.

Whenever you designate an area as the zone for a particular toy, Baby will automatically anticipate playing with that item when he enters that room. Remember when I asked you to keep your bedroom free of stimulating items like a TV, a DVD player, or a computer because I wanted you to relax the minute you entered the space? You're creating the same kind of expectation with Baby when you divide his toys. Imagine growing up organized!

# WEEK 16 POSTPARTUM

## Start Investigating Baby's Education

This week, you can

- Begin to plan for Baby's early education placement and her college education
- Investigate your neighborhood in terms of education, transportation, taxes, and child-friendly atmosphere
- Consider education options that aren't tied to your neighborhood, such as private schools, charter schools, and home schooling

REMEMBER WHEN you were pregnant and I suggested you talk to your partner about *everything* concerning your baby? I have a question for you: Did you include education? It can be a surprisingly hot-button issue. You're probably thinking, "Hey, my baby is four months old; what's the rush?" Did you know that some private schools put children on the waiting list while they are still in utero? Did you also know that some schools now cost an arm and a leg? You may be shocked when you hear the tuition. This week, you want to give some thought to the whys and wherefores of your child's education. There's preschool, kindergarten, and then grammar school. Let me ask you some questions to get the ball rolling:

- Do you plan to stay in your residence for the foreseeable future?

- If so, did you pick this area because of the quality of the school district?
- If not, do you have an area you know you want to move to?
- Keep an open mind. There is more to a quality school experience than test scores. Take the time to ask other parents and visit schools to get a real feel for what student life is like. Do students, teachers, administration, and other parents seem engaged, involved, and happy? Is there an active parent-teacher group? Is the curriculum well rounded? Are there offerings in the arts and languages? How strong is the math and science? Is the technology up to date? How's the lunch program? Do you agree with policies on things like discipline, physical education, and recess (in many schools, recess has been cut en-

tirely!)? Okay, that's a big list, and you don't have to care about everything on it. No school is perfect, but some will be a much better match for you, your values, and your belief system than others. Look beyond demographic information and statistics. With caring, effective teachers; a supportive environment; and your encouragement and involvement, your child can excel in a school even if it's not considered "the best."

- Do you want your child to go to public school, private school, or a combination?
- Is the idea of a neighborhood school important to you or are you okay with the idea of driving your children (possibly some distance) to your school of choice? Keep in mind that at some point you may have several children needing to get to different schools.
- Does your religious affiliation run a school for the congregation?
- Have you ever considered home-schooling? Do you know what it entails?
- Do you have friends with school-age children? Are you planning to follow in their footsteps?
- Are you interested in a traditional school or one with a specific approach to learning like Montessori?
- Did you set up your child's 529 savings account for college?
- If you don't have the funds for such an account right now and lack wealthy family members, have you

thought about how your child's college education will be funded? Remember that one of the key ingredients to a scholarship is good grades, which of course brings us back to . . . education. How's that reading at night coming along?
- Are you excited to discover what your child will grow up to be and embrace as far as a career goes? Or do one or both of you have plans for her? You'd be surprised how unconsciously sexist some seemingly hip parents can be when it comes to children and professions. I have friends who wanted their daughter to get married and their son to become a doctor. She was free to basically pursue any path she chose, while the son was not allowed to enter the arts. Do you or your partner view some professions as more suitable for a particular sex?

## FOREWARNED IS FOREARMED

Now that I've officially gotten your eyes to roll back in your head, take a deep breath. You don't have to answer all of these questions this week. But you also can't afford to put this work aside until your child is five and ready for kindergarten! Talk to your partner about this list. Are you in agreement about everything? Try and work out any issues first and then launch into an information-gathering phase. Here is some information you could gather this week:

Whether it's Montessori or your local public school, make some calls one afternoon to find out what the requirements are, when you sign up, and the current cost for an academic year. Also ask about scholarships and other ways to reduce costs.

If you want to stay in your current home but the local schools aren't great, is there a magnet school, charter school, or private school in a neighboring area your child may be able to attend? Keep in mind that with schools of choice, magnets, and selective-enrollment schools, there is no guarantee your child will get in, especially this far in advance. Do you have a Plan B just in case?

If you are interested in homeschooling, call your local Board of Education to find out what the requirements are and what a typical syllabus looks like. Do you think you can/want to handle something like this? Keep in mind that home education is about more than reading, writing, and arithmetic. Where will you be able to seek out extracurricular activities, arts, music, language, and other programs aimed at homeschooling families? Your child will also need peers. Is there an active homeschooling community in your area? Look online. Many are open to families of babies and young children who are considering home education and will welcome you warmly.

If your child is going to preschool and then kindergarten, give those local entities a call and find out the procedures for entry.

## A HOUSE WITH A WHITE PICKET FENCE

Even if you love where you live, the school search may have been the unwelcome reality check that sent you scrambling to check out Realtor.com. Even couples who thought they were choosing a place in a "good" school district are sometimes unpleasantly surprised when they find out that the best schools operate on a lottery system or are great on paper but joyless, high-pressure kiddie colleges in reality.

Whether a move is on the immediate horizon or just a possibility in the future, it's important to think about how your choice of neighborhood and community will impact your child and your family life. There's more to your decision than crime rates and schools. And whether you like small towns, cities, the 'burbs, or life on a farm, there are pros and cons to consider.

For example, right now you are in charge of your baby's comings and goings. Her "social life" consists mostly of you, Dad, and other family members and close friends. But in a few short years, that's going to start to change. Who your neighbors are will matter more than ever before. Are they people you can depend on in a jam? Are there other young families with children in your area? Is your block diverse enough that your child will have interactions with people of a variety of ages, races, and economic levels? Consider your values and how those values will be supported or challenged in the area you're looking at. Think not just about the city as a whole, but about your specific neighborhood.

Mike Lanza, founder of Playborhood. com, a site aimed at getting more kids to play outside, suggests that the most important thing to a child is the block he lives on. Parents might get caught up in the restaurants and theaters downtown or in a specific home's lovely hardwood floors or square footage, but the people who live on your block will have a huge influence on your child as he grows. You can always change the carpets, and you can always hop on the bus or in the car to get to another part of town, but you can't change your neighbors.

Or maybe you are more drawn to country living. That can be a wonderful environment in which to raise a child. Just think about how it will play out not just now but in two or ten years. A lovely farmhouse may lose some of its charm if it's set on a county highway with fifty-mile-per-hour traffic and you can never let your child play in the yard. And sooner or later, that baby is going to grow into a middle-schooler who will want to hang out with his friends in town. Are you prepared to drive . . . a lot?

## EMPOWER YOURSELF AND YOUR CHILD

There you are settling into parenthood and I've thrust you into a future reality that comes all too quickly. Again, I'm not suggesting you make all the decisions for your child's education this week. I am asking you to be aware that on the horizon are life-changing opportunities for her. She can take advantage of the best of the bunch if you have done your homework. Start an online notebook for your cyber research and have one on hand. You can soon phase out of your baby journal and jump into your Zen Organizer mom's journal! How you keep track of your research isn't as important as the fact you need to keep it and update it often. Real estate agents say the most important ingredient is "location, location, location." In this case, your success will be governed by "attitude, attitude, attitude!" If this turns into a big homework assignment, resentment can fill your days. If you make it an exciting adventure, you will enjoy the learning curve as much as you do the planning one. In what will seem about fifteen minutes, you'll be at your baby's college graduation.

# CHAPTER TWELVE

# Weeks 17 to 20 Postpartum

Everybody is unique. Do not compare yourself with anybody else
lest you spoil God's curriculum.

—BAAL SHEM TOV

WHEN WE BEGAN this journey, only your nearest and dearest knew you were pregnant. Now you have a baby—and maybe you're surprised how quickly you became adept at caring for her! Most first-time moms, especially if they didn't get to babysit or have younger siblings, tell me they were somewhat in shock as they left the hospital. They couldn't believe anyone would trust them to take care of a newborn. But nature has a way of acclimating us quickly. What was once a little scary becomes fearless in no time. Keep that in mind the next time you assure yourself that you can never get organized.

If it hasn't started already, right about now a strange thing will begin to happen when you chat with relatives, friends, and especially other moms. A competition of sorts will be created between your baby and theirs. "What do you mean your baby isn't sleeping through the night?" "Is your baby holding her head up, playing with toys, or looking like she wants to crawl?" "No?! Why you must be doing something wrong!" Smile at these dear souls for me, will you? If you are worried, ask your pediatrician what the normal range is for the activity in question. I place emphasis on *range*. Discover your child without holding her to other peoples' standards. The world is full of famous people who contributed much to the world and did things like walk, read, or talk at their own pace. Albert Einstein, for example, was so late in learning how to speak that his parents consulted a doctor. I rest my case.

Your child will soon start the process of graduating to solid food. (Is that your breasts heaving a small sigh of relief?) The purer the food you put into your child's body, the better chance he has to grow strong. He deserves to have a body and mind untainted by unnecessary chemical additives, fat, salt, sugar, and empty calories. You may be surprised to find it's a snap to make your own baby food. You don't have to be Julia Child or Martha Stewart to puree a meal. I've also got a few cookbooks in the Resources section.

If all you do is care for Baby, maintain your home, and go off to work, you are going to become a "mental schlumpadinka!" This month includes some ideas to help you get back into the social swing. Don't worry; you don't have to become a hipster and frequent the local club scene (unless, of course, you did that before the baby and you just won't rest until you are out there again)! Don't be surprised if your priorities change and new things grab your attention. There is having a life and being a hermit. Somewhere between the club scene and trips to the zoo lies social balance.

Speaking of balance, few experiences threaten to knock you off your financial even keel faster than Baby's first holiday season. It's important to be in control of your spending, your decorations, your entertaining, and, oh yes, your sanity! They can all go out the window as you look at your baby's sweet face, listen to holiday music, and see the lights springing up all over town. At this point you have something wonderful on your side: Your child isn't at the stage where she can assure you that everyone else in her circle has the toy-of-the-moment and so should she. (That experience is down the line.) You can have a great celebration and not contribute a single penny to your credit card debt. Now that's truly being a sexy momma!

Lastly, strange things happen in even the most organized home when a baby enters the space. Everything seems to be growing and changing in tandem with your child; it can be a bit overwhelming. This month before I take my leave, we're going to tune up your home. Every few years I do a big clutter purge in my own environment. Someone once asked me how this could be—why would the Zen Organizer have anything to toss? The simple answer is that we all change over time. I don't have to live with a book, knick-knack, or dress forever just because I once loved it. I do feel I have to honor it while it's with me and pass it on in a respectful manner. No matter how perfect your systems are, you are always free to alter them. After all when anything is frozen in place, all growth is stopped and creativity is stifled. The purpose of Zen Organizing is to free you. Always embrace the solution that makes life easier in today's reality.

## HABIT OF THE MONTH

### Use It or Lose It

Weeks of staring into your baby's eyes and singing lullabies can be peaceful, calming . . . and turn your brain to mush. Did you know that neural pathways that don't get used literally atrophy and die off? But using your brain in challenging ways can actually create new pathways: Yes, you can get smarter no matter how old you are. "Mommy brain" might be a perfectly normal phenomenon, but that doesn't mean you can't take steps to stay connected to the world around you and help keep your brain in shape. Here are some ideas:

Keep a brain-challenging game like Sudoku or a crossword puzzle in one of the areas where you settle down to rock or nurse.

Think beyond TV and social media for entertainment. Baby can come along to the art museum or concerts in the park with you.

Make a habit of reading challenging material. You can do this a little at a time, just five or ten minutes a day. Try creating a book club with a group of moms and adjust the pace of the reading to something you all can live with. Create an e-mail list or Google Group so that you can share your thoughts on what you've read between physical meetings.

Keep your paper systems top of mind by giving them five minutes of attention each day. Never thought of paper systems as a way to keep your brain tuned up and firing on all neural pathways? Check the tips in week four for more details. Organizing can be creative and fun if you have the right attitude and embrace the dividends.

# WEEK 17 POSTPARTUM

## Adventures with Baby Food

**This week, you can**

- Consider your baby's first food experiences
- Turn food prep into shared time with Baby

BY THE TIME he's six months old, the average baby has doubled his birth weight. By the end of their first year, babies are typically three times heavier than they were at birth. That's a lot of growing in a short time, and most of the calories he needs to get him there come from milk, whether via breast milk or baby formula.

The American Academy of Pediatrics recommends holding off on starting solids until six months of age, but many parents are thinking about them earlier, especially if your baby is the sort to grab handfuls of food off your plate when you aren't looking! No matter when you start solids, though, it's important to remember that Baby's early experiences with food will shape her eating habits for life. Don't worry about "filling her up" with solids at this point. Breast milk (or formula) will give her the complete nutrition she needs for months to come. Instead, solid foods are her chance to experiment with tastes and textures and figure out how to work her gums and tongue in a whole new way.

If you're starting these foods when your baby is around six months old, you may need to puree or grind them to get them to the right consistency. Older babies may be able to handle foods that are simply mashed or even cut into tiny pieces for her to pick up. The American Academy of Pediatrics' Web site (www.healthychildren. org) is a great resource for figuring out when and how to introduce solids to your specific baby depending on her age and development.

Many babies start out eating rice cereal. This is generally recommended because it's bland with a thin, watery texture, making it easy for Baby to manage. It really took hold as "baby's first food" when, in generations past, mothers were encouraged to start their babies on solids very early . . . sometimes as early as a few weeks. At that early stage, rice cereal was a logical choice because it could be watered down until it was practically the consistency of milk and didn't give babies bellyaches as readily as some other foods.

But nutritionally, commercial rice cereal doesn't have a lot going for it. It's boring. And the ingredients label on the most commonly purchased brand reads like a science experiment. When it comes to your baby's first food, you can think outside the cereal box. Experts are now beginning to recommend nutritionally rich foods: fresh fruits, veggies, and even meats as the building blocks of babies' early diets. Your baby is growing and developing at an amazing rate, and her tummy is too tiny for wasted calories. Plus, you want her to get a taste for flavorful, fresh foods, not just bland, starchy stuff that's reminiscent of the fast-food French fries you'd probably like her to avoid down the road.

Here are some good first choices that are also easy to prepare:

- Avocado. A great consistency for babies and lots of "good for the brain" healthy fat.
- Carrots. Babies have a natural sweet tooth, and carrots cater to it, with plenty of dietary punch.
- Sweet potato. A nutritional powerhouse!

Even if you do decide to go the rice cereal route, you don't have to settle for reconstituted flakes. There are more wholesome options on the market, or you could make your own.

And while we're on the subject, let's talk about jarred baby foods. They can be convenient in some circumstances, but they're also expensive; are often full of sodium, sugar, and other additives; and take up precious space in your pantry. The good news is that it's not hard to make your own baby food.

## MEALTIME AS PLAYTIME

Let's imagine for a minute that it's a few months into the future. Baby is safely ensconced in her bouncer seat. You're busy making her food, chatting with her as you go along, listening to music, and just having a great time. Maybe Fido is curled up in the kitchen contributing to the good vibes. This can be an experience you share every day with your child. Or perhaps you're the mom who likes to prepare a week's worth of meals in advance and freeze the bulk. How long it takes or how often you engage in this activity isn't important. Savoring the time and sharing it with your child are what count. And who knows? Maybe Dad would like to whip up some meals with his son or daughter while you read the paper. Try and keep TV watching to a minimum. Baby, not the boobtube, needs your attention. You'll both be grateful you made it a priority to organize your kitchen. The time you might have wasted searching for the right equipment or tools can instead be devoted to fun with your baby. Next week I'll be helping you integrate fun time with other adults back into your life. Zen Organizing is first and foremost about balance. Moms and dads need the company of other adults just as much as they need to spend quality time with their children.

## BABY FOOD MADE EASY

My good friend Chef Tanya promises you can spend one hour twice a week in the kitchen and whip up a week's worth of meals for Baby. You'll want to have zip-top bags on hand so you can pop your cooked food in the freezer. Or, if you invest in some canning/preserve jars you won't have to freeze anything, and these can be recycled later. No matter which method you choose, always remember to label as to contents and date the bottle or bag. Without a label, your sweet potatoes and carrots may look alike.

Here are Chef Tanya's simple recipes to get you started. All recipes will yield about two cups.

A 2008 study from the International Journal of Pediatric Otorhinolaryngology listed the ten biggest food hazards for children under three. They are: hot dogs, peanuts, (raw) carrots, boned chicken, candy, meat, popcorn, fish with bones, sunflower seeds, and (raw) apples. Be mindful of your choices and how you prepare food for your baby. Call 911 in an emergency. You can't perform the Heimlich on a child under the age of three. Talk to your pediatrician about specific techniques to use in the event of a choking emergency. Forewarned is forearmed.

### Pureed Yams
2 cups (i.e., about 2 whole) organic
   yams or sweet potato
2/3 cup water

Peel yams and cut into cubes. Put in a pot of water and steam yams until tender like potatoes. Pour in blender with two tablespoons of water and blend yams until pureed or desired consistency is reached.

### Pureed Peas
2 cups of organic peas
2 tablespoons of water

Put peas in a glass bowl and microwave for one minute, or steam them in a pot. Pour peas in blender with water and blend until pureed.

### Applesauce
4 medium organic apples
2 tablespoons water

Peel, core, and cut the apples into cubes. Put apples in a glass bowl and steam in the microwave for one minute or steam in a pot until tender.

Pour apples in the blender with the water and blend until pureed or desired consistency is reached.

### Pureed Bananas
4 ripe bananas

Put peeled and halved bananas in blender and blend until pureed or desired consistency is reached.

Preparation tips:

- You may have developed a taste for heavily salted or sugary foods. Consider a simpler, healthier palette for Baby.
- You can make your food more nutrient rich by not shaving off the outer skin. Do wash the skin, however, before you cook it.

- There are special baby food makers and storing trays but you don't really need them. The everyday equipment in your kitchen will serve you. Got an empty ice cube tray? Turn it into your new baby food storage tray. Put in freezer and defrost a "cube" for each meal. Wasn't that easy? Save your money.

# WEEK 18 POSTPARTUM

## Get Back into the Swing of Things

**This week, you can**

- Give your social life a tune-up

A FEW MONTHS AGO we talked about your post-baby social life. Have you experienced the benefits of a community of friends now that your baby is here? Or did an emergency or lonely period prompt you to realize that your network wasn't quite as strong as you'd thought?

If your social life is lacking these days, this is a perfect time to start making new connections. Baby is getting bigger and more interested in the world every day. There will be more opportunities to meet other moms through his activities. His schedule is likely getting more predictable, making it easier for you to plan a coffee or park date during the day. And because he's not quite as needy as he was a few months ago, it's probably starting to seem a lot easier for you to get out by yourself, too.

### NEW "MOM" FRIENDS

Do you have anyone you can call to talk over teething, solids, and crawling? If not, maybe you've been having trouble meeting or connecting with other moms. They're out there, no matter where you live. The trick is finding them.

First, let's re-cover some old ground:

- Have you checked with your local parks department or YMCA about classes geared toward babies?
- Have you looked at the bulletin board of the local baby boutique, toy store, bookstore, coffee shop, library, or yoga studio for activities that interest you?
- Have you checked with your religious institution to see if they offer support groups for parents or playgroups?
- Have you gone online to meetup. com, mothering.com or mommyand me.com to see if there are offerings in your area?
- Have you considered creating your own group and running or advertising it in one of the above locations?

Not everyone is a "group" person. You may find that one Mommy and Me is enough to send you screaming for the exit doors. That's okay. The point isn't that you have to love every activity but that you get yourself out there and meet other people. Perhaps you'll spy another mom who looks like she wants to run screaming out the door, too. That's the one you send a sympathetic glance . . . and connect with after the singing and clapping has wrapped up.

By the way, be sure to keep a small notebook in your purse or diaper bag so that you don't miss out on being able to reconnect with her later. Another option is to plug potential friends' contact information right into your iPhone or Blackberry. Just make sure you have a place to record this information. You don't want to miss out on making a real friendship because you can't find a pen.

It's also just fine if those "baby activities" aren't up your alley. Nobody ever said you had to suffer through endless clapping and singing nursery rhymes to be a good mom. And at this age, your baby really doesn't care. Use activities as a starting point to meet other moms, but feel free to form your own offshoot groups. For example, maybe you could form a book club, meet new friends (and their babies) once a month at the natural history museum, or create a movie club: Rent some romantic comedies, head to one person's house, pop some popcorn, and take in a flick. The sexual innuendo will fly right over the babies' heads at this point.

Just because you became a mom doesn't mean you left your brain at the hospital. You're a grown-up and it's just fine if

you want to act like one! Your baby is your first priority, but that doesn't mean that the focus has to be on him every moment of every day. The best news is, you can learn to carry on grown-up conversations even in a room full of children. It's a skill that mothers have perfected over the millennia. Now it's your turn.

## OLD FRIENDS

Are your old friendships looking a little rough around the edges? Have they fallen by the wayside as you've been adjusting to life as a mom? Understandable. But let's not let any more time go by before you reconnect with your old pals. Here are some ideas:

**Arrange a "girls' night in" at your home.** Dad can do bedtime duty that night, or if you're single or he's not available, you can either invite friends to come after Baby's down for the evening or plan to excuse yourself for a half hour and do it yourself. If you've invited an interesting mix of people and provide wine and snacks, they will keep themselves entertained! The nice thing about a girls' night in is that it's quiet and intimate, inexpensive, doesn't require you to get a babysitter, and brings together several good friends so you can connect with them all at the same time and help them form stronger friendships with each other.

**Schedule some outings that interest you both.** Sit down with your old friend with a local arts and entertainment calendar. Buy the tickets and arrange for child care now. Plans like "oh, we should go see that play when it opens" aren't really plans at all and will almost definitely fall through the cracks unless you lock them in.

**Let Baby tag along.** If you're finding that it's harder than you anticipated to find sitters or schedule evenings out around your spouse's schedule, talk to your friend. Tell her you really want to spend time together but you're having a hard time doing it without the baby. Then brainstorm some ways you two can connect that don't require you to leave him. Some ideas:

- Go for regular walks together. You can have a great conversation even if you're pushing a baby in a stroller. Or put him in a backpack and go for a hike in the woods.
- Put him in a carrier and hit the local art museum together.
- Pick his mellowest time of the day and plan to meet your friend for coffee, lunch, or early dinner. Outdoor seating is a mom's best friend. Babies are distracted and mellowed by the fresh air and activity around them, and the outdoors "absorb" all the little sounds babies make as they take in the world around them.

You may find that some of your pre-baby friendships go through a lull right now. This can happen for many reasons and is sometimes just a part of life: Sometimes friendships reach a natural end or simply hit the "pause" button and get resurrected later. Don't beat yourself up if things cool between you and an old pal. Just do your best and make sure to keep the lines of communication open.

## ALL ROADS LEAD BACK TO THE SAME SPOT

. . . your calendar! At the start of this month I urged you to use your calendar and phone/PDA to keep track of the daily business of your life. You don't want the electricity to be shut off or allow your credit card company to hit you with an exorbitant late fee because you were lost in chaos or baby clothes, right? Your social life deserves to be tracked, planned, and scheduled just like the business aspects of your life. Before Baby, perhaps "fun" was a spontaneous affair. Now you need to look ahead and build it into your schedule. This isn't meant to be viewed as work, by the way; rather, it gives you something to look forward to when things go awry. When you're walking the floor with a colicky baby, it's nice to remember the great concert you will be attending with your partner and best friends in another week. It's mental candy.

# WEEK 19 POSTPARTUM

## Baby's First Holiday Season

This week, you can

- Decide how you want to celebrate the upcoming holidays
- Plan ways to save time, money, and energy

I CAN'T PREDICT how old your baby will be when he experiences his first holiday season. I can predict you will be tempted to go a little crazy. And with good reason! This is probably your first holiday season as a parent. It's a time to treasure. This week I have a few tips and tricks to help you celebrate without breaking the bank, losing your sanity, or greeting the New Year in an exhausted stupor. Let's start with Halloween. Will it be a trick or a treat?

## GHOULS, GHOSTS, AND GOBLINS

Let's face it: Is there anything sweeter than a baby in a costume? Relatives and friends will be waiting for photos of her first adventure. If you are a new mom, you're probably thinking you wish someone else would do this because you haven't regained your strength yet or gotten into a rhythm with your baby. If Baby is eleven months, you're probably getting ready to

stash him in his stroller and join the neighborhood celebration. Remember the quote that opened this month? You need to remember that your celebration can absolutely be unique to you without having to explain yourself to others. Let's look at some ideas that can help you decide what's right for your family.

You don't have to celebrate Halloween. How about that for a hot tip? The great thing to remember is that Baby is so young at this point he has no idea what anyone else is doing. Peer pressure is a thing of the future.

Baby costumes abound online and in stores. Be sure you shop early and are prepared. If you are handy and enjoy sewing, you might like to whip something up. Pick your pattern this week.

If you have been photographing Junior each week as I suggested, you might like to add one of him in costume. Post it online at your blog or on Facebook. The more people you have in these communities, the fewer individual e-mails you'll have to send out.

You'll be inundated with ads for stores offering professional photo packages. Remember it's the extras that will eat into your wallet. Yes, your baby is adorable in his costume. But at this point you don't need to drop a lot of money on multiple poses. Deposit what you save in his 529 savings account.

Will you welcome trick or treaters this year? Best to stock up on the items you'd like to distribute. Candy is certainly traditional, but you can give items like balloons and save neighborhood moms future dental bills.

Decorating your home for this holiday isn't necessary unless you have a toddler in the house who already knows the drill. Why not buy one fake pumpkin or skeleton and add to your stash each year? By the time your child is old enough to request a specific costume your house will be festooned for the holiday. Word of caution: If you live in an apartment, don't buy the biggest fake pumpkin you can find unless you have that storage unit or Grandma's garage. They sell bags of mini-pumpkins at the supermarket that are more size appropriate for a baby. After they start to rot, you can toss them into your trash or compost and be done with it.

When Halloween's over, pop the costume into a space bag with other items if the possibility of another child exists. If you know this is the only or the last child, pass the outfit on and be sure you have photos of Baby as a pirate or pumpkin.

## THANKSGIVING: THE MOTHER OF ALL DINNER PARTIES

What better way is there to describe Thanksgiving? Once you manage this dinner party, every other party is easy. (In my book *One Year to an Organized Life,* I give detailed advice on handling this holiday.) You'll most likely have three choices: travel far for dinner (think plane or train); travel locally (subway, bus, or car); or, of course, stay home and have everyone come to you.

Let's consider the key points so no matter what you choose, things will go smoothly. This is one of the sweetest holidays in the year. We need only be grateful and celebrate. There's no need to shop like a maniac and buy everyone and his brother a gift. Take a deep breath and remember: *You* decide what this holiday looks like, not the other members of your tribe. If you and Dad want to be alone to savor the day with Junior, that is your prerogative and you shouldn't let anyone convince you otherwise.

The first item you need to consider regarding your baby is how much you want him to be handled and have his sleep cycle interrupted. I've seen babies wail at the end of the day because everyone and his brother had to hold him, stimulate him, and play with him. I know Aunt Edna and Cousin Jeff will be annoyed when you enforce the stated rules. But that's OK because you are the one who will be walking the floor at 1:00 a.m.

If Baby is older and eating solid food, be sure you establish rules for who may feed him and what they may feed him. Perhaps you think it's just common sense that a three-month-old baby can't yet gnaw on a turkey leg, but think again: Clueless or pushy adults will be only too happy to "sneak" Baby bits of food she's not ready for yet, and you'll be the one dealing with the upset tummy (and freaky diapers) later. Actually this tip applies to Fido as well! If you come from a family that can't resist feeding animals and children, then they need to spend the night and take care of the consequences. Lovingly make that clear to them. I emphasize the word *lovingly*.

If you are traveling, the weather may be a factor. Be sure you have made forays into the cold winter weather before Thanksgiving. Do you have the additional gear that this time of year demands? In addition to a warm bunting, blanket, or snowsuit to bundle up Baby in the car, plan for the possibility of getting stuck somewhere and waiting out a storm. Any time you're traveling in cold weather you should have emergency gear in your car, but the addition of a baby makes it even more crucial.

For you and Dad, a blanket; a flashlight; extra food like granola bars, jerky, or fruit leather; drinking water; warm gloves; and warm footwear are essential. For Baby, be sure to have extra food and water for Mom or enough formula and water for a few days' wait, plus diapers, warm booties, and a hat, and any medication she takes regularly.

You probably don't have to pack any baby food unless she's taking a lot of solids by this point; for the first year or so of life, breast milk or formula have everything a baby needs and will be easier to pack.

You can also buy emergency car kits that contain road salt, folding shovels, multipurpose tools for chipping ice away from the car, flares, booster cables, and the like. And of course, a first aid kit is always a good thing to have in your car no matter what time of year you'll be traveling.

If you are going by car you have the advantage because you can carry easily all the supplies you need. But don't take advantage and pack the kitchen sink. After all, weight will cut down on your gas mileage, making that unnecessary stuff quite costly.

Be sure you have the car prepped for travel long before the big day. Is your spare tire ready to serve you in an emergency?

Will your dog be traveling with you? He'll need his own ditty bag! Be sure your home lights are on timers and your cat's automatic food and water bowl are in place. Ask your neighbors to keep an eye out and remember to turn on your alarm if you have one. During the gathering itself, Fido and Fifi may need to be left in a separate room with food and water. Overstimulation isn't any better for them than it is for Baby.

Moms and dads who fly with babies and toddlers are true warriors. Here's another checklist to be sure you are ready for the challenges of that adventure:

- Pad or blanket for in-flight diaper changes, plus plastic bags for storing dirty diapers
- Hand sanitizer in case you don't have access to running water and soap
- Pacifiers—even if your baby doesn't take one regularly, the sucking action can help keep ears from popping
- Umbrella stroller—easy to collapse and stash in the overhead container

## Practice Produces Perfect Parties

If you want to be that lucky hostess who enjoys her own gatherings, you've got to be organized. And there's no better holiday to practice these new skills than Thanksgiving. Why? Because your audience is predominately family and they will forgive just about any glitch in the way the day flows.

Here's a list of the elements you might wish to include:

Decorations
Beverages
Music
Food

Break each category down so you know exactly what your choices are. For example, are you going to decorate with traditional holiday fare or do you prefer fresh-cut flowers? Do you come from a family that appreciates the correct wine with each course or do you come from a "Coke goes with everything" tribe? Does your family like conversation or football on TV to fill the air? Would there be a revolt if someone cut together a holiday music selection that played softly in the background? When it comes to food, are you setting up a buffet or bringing each course to the table? Will there be a separate table for the children or is everyone sitting together? How will that choice impact the table settings? Are you using Grandma's fine china or holiday paper plates from the local party store?

The day is yours to plan. Let it be a reflection of your taste, style, and energy level. It may not be perfect but that's OK. Learn from your mistakes. We all make them.

Last but not least is the consideration of a realistic budget. Can you afford the best wine with each course? Perhaps your Uncle Harry would like to bring the wine this year? Maybe those fresh flowers you'd love to have on the table are too expensive and the decorative turkeys you purchased three years ago at the local mall will work after all. Delegate whenever you can. Substitute less-elaborate or -expensive choices if it's appropriate. December is traditionally an expensive month so don't blow your entire holiday budget on Thanksgiving dinner. Save time and money at every turn. After all, the day is really about fellowship, not perfection.

## CHRISTMAS MADNESS

No matter what end-of-the-year holiday you celebrate, it will demand attention to the same social guidelines as Thanksgiving. But layered on may be the desire to decorate with no holds barred and spend money on gifts as if your last name were Madoff. Let's not go there. Take a step back and remember that your baby isn't going to remember this holiday, nor is she going to understand it right now. However, she is guaranteed to feel the tension in you and Dad if you exhaust yourselves, and the joy of the holiday if you are relaxed. I know I sound like a broken record when it comes to these matters but they can't be stressed enough. Emotions can sweep us along unless we're oh so vigilant, especially at this time of year.

Here are my tips for taming the spending monster inside all of us:

You might want to introduce some touches of decoration in your home just to lift your own spirits, especially if this is something you enjoy doing. I remember a mom who told me for the first few years of her child's life she brought home fresh pine boughs so that the apartment smelled good. Slowly she graduated to a tiny tree with small lights and diminutive decorations. She didn't introduce a big tree with presents until the concept of Santa Claus had been embraced.

Lights add a wonderful touch to this time of year, don't they? They will stimulate Baby in a positive way, especially if they blink, but she doesn't need a six-foot tree laden with them! You can put them on those pine boughs or string them across a piece of furniture.

Arrive at the stores with a game plan. Don't follow your heart or your emotions. They are fueled by desire and credit cards. Decide in advance what you are going to get Baby this year. Will it be a holiday outfit? Will more photos be taken at the local photo shop? What about decorations? Will one of those "Baby's First Christmas" ornaments do the trick or do you need more? How many more exactly?

Expect that grandparents and other family will want to spoil your baby rotten for her first Christmas. I know you will, too! Understandable, and hard to do much damage when he's too little to know what's going on. But at some point, you'll have to consider the precedent being set.

If your growing child gets used to every holiday being a blow-out affair with huge piles of gifts or extravagant vacations, what happens when he gets older and you decide you want—or need—to scale back? Pleasing a three-year-old with a big stack of inexpensive toys is easy. Just wait until he's thirteen, far less easily impressed, and all the "cool" gadgets he wants cost a hundred bucks or more. Better to "begin as you mean to go on," that is, with some restraint.

One good way to do this is through establishing rituals that naturally put a cap on the number of gifts given. For example, maybe you'll decide on a four-gift-per-person rule. Then you won't get caught up in frenzied last-minute shopping, throwing things into your cart just to add to the shiny pile under the tree.

If Baby's grandparents have money to burn and want to spend it on your children,

> A funny thing happens when a baby enters your life. All the things you didn't receive as a child (gifts, attention, decorations, etc.) will rise up like hungry specters and want your attention. Be ever mindful as to whether what you are doing is for your child or for the unfulfilled one inside you. Don't be embarrassed. Without exception we all have one. Some are just needier than others.

more power to them! Why not suggest nonmaterial gifts? Here are some ideas:

- A special outing or, later, vacation with Grandma and Grandpa—what could be a better gift than a wonderful memory that will last forever?
- Museum memberships
- Music lessons, art classes
- Contributions to the baby's college fund

The key element, by the way, in any plan is a budget. If you can't afford the items on your gift list, you need to start over. The key is to be creative rather than extravagant. It's the thought that counts, right?

Here's an idea that will help you save money and be thoughtful to many at the same time. Many retailers sell small photo frames that hang on the tree as decorations. Tell family and friends you are opting out of gift giving that costs over $10 for this season. Give everyone one of these frame decorations for their tree with a photo of Baby in his first Santa suit.

What cool ideas can you add to this suggestion that are thoughtful keepsakes but don't cost an arm and a leg?

## CHERISHED OR TARNISHED?

After reading all the choices before you as you face the holiday season, you may feel a bit overwhelmed. Here's an exercise that will help you. Take a few minutes to sit quietly and reflect on your childhood holidays. Did you enjoy the holiday season when you were growing up? What did your parents do that made it special? Or did you have the opposite experience? The vast majority of people unconsciously allow the pressure of consumerism to chart their course. Overspending is the norm. And so is unhappiness. Instead of joy we are depressed. Make notes in your journal or have a discussion with your spouse. Get down to specifics. Align your holiday expectations rather than making assumptions about how you will proceed. If you present a united front you'll be better able to tune out the disgruntled relatives and friends who may not agree with your choices. This is your time to create whatever experience you wish for your child.

# WEEK 20 POSTPARTUM

## Recommit to an Organized Life

**This week, you can**

- Restore order to the areas of your home that have fallen into disarray
- Establish or recommit to routines
- Embrace the reality of life with Baby versus the fantasy

From time to time everyone—even professional organizers!—will turn around and find chaos in the environment. We aren't robots, after all. Maybe everyone in your home has had the flu for several weeks, including you. Or perhaps you work from home and the biggest job of your career coincided with your Aunt Helen and Uncle Christopher's recent visit. The causes are endless. Thank goodness, the fix is simple and unrelated to any particular cause. You just need to restore the system you created.

For example, the family room very easily and frequently falls into disarray. We enjoy this room and stagger out of it exhausted at the end of the evening. It feels easier to confront the mess in the morning. But morning comes and we launch into the day forgetting what we left behind last evening. After a few days the room looks like a tornado blew through. Remorse sets in as we realize we dropped the organizing ball.

Don't be demoralized and wail, "See? I can't get organized!" There is a blueprint for where things go. You created it when you first organized the room and decided what items went in which locations. Order can be restored as you tidy up. For this room the steps are pretty common:

- Return food items to the kitchen.
- Toss the trash.
- Put CDs and DVDs back in their albums or individual cases.
- Put toys back into their containers.
- Fold the throws, fluff the pillows.
- Recycle old newspaper and magazines.
- Put away the elements of your hobby that you worked on, whether it's scrapbooking, stamp collecting, or archiving the family tree.

Now, wasn't that easy? If it isn't, ask yourself these questions:

- Do you have containers for the news-papers and magazines, or are they oozing all over the floor like a melting dish of ice cream?
- Is the trash container in the room big enough for the task?
- Do you have enough containers for your baby's toys?
- Did you decide on a system for track-ing your entertainment library?

Order is within reach but you need to expend a little elbow grease—you know, "no pain, no gain." Every good thing in life comes with a price tag. What's the old say-ing ? "Ain't no free lunches!"

## ORGANIZING FROM SQUARE ONE

From the start I suggested you systemati-cally work to create routines, good habits, and systems in your home. Right about now the reality of their true worth is prob-ably dawning on you. There is a reason surgeons and generals have what they need at their fingertips: It makes them function better, be more powerful, and save lives, time, and energy. Our homes can function with the same precision. If you skimmed over the organizing work, it's easier than you think to go back and start from square one. It won't take you a year because much of the pregnancy and baby-related tasks are now done with. Be aware, however, that getting organized from square one is a task that requires more than a weekend warrior mentality

and forty-eight hours. On the other hand, if you did do the work, you only need to devote about thirty minutes a day to re-store order. After that, if you remember to consciously tidy a room before you leave it—something that should take mere min-utes—you'll be good to go.

Don't set aside a few hours and decide to do the entire house in one morning. You will most likely overwhelm yourself. Give organizing an hour a day. And as you do each room, make note of every thing that is in order. Give yourself credit for how far you have come. This attitude en-ables you to build on your successes rather than browbeat yourself for your perceived failures. From my perspective, you are already a success because you are making a conscious effort.

Be mindful not to wander from one room to the other leaving a trail of half-completed projects in your wake. Stay in one area at a time until completion has been achieved. Let's examine all the major rooms in the home and take a look at what gets away from most of us . . . from time to time!

### The Kitchen
Walk into this room with "fresh eyes." Pre-tend you are a visitor and you've wan-dered in here for a glass of water. How does the room look to you?

Have cupboards and drawers been left open?

Were the dirty dishes left piled in the sink from the last meal?

Has the dishwasher been waiting to be emptied?

In short, does it look like a disaster? Great! Now we know the culprit: lack of completion. If you open a cupboard to take an item out, the completion of that action is to close the cupboard door. If you need a tool from a drawer, after you remove it, close the drawer. (By the way, did you line the drawer and are you using small containers to keep related items corralled? If not, every time you shut the drawer or riffle through the interior for a specific item, you will be destroying any order you created. Invest in these inexpensive but life-changing products. I tell my clients that if they complete these mundane actions in life, they will complete the big ones as well. It's no accident my favorite Zen proverb is "The way a man does one thing is the way he does everything."

## The Mail and Paperwork

Are newspapers and mail eating up valuable counter space? If you haven't set up your office as yet, do so in the next few days.

If you have set up a file system that's waiting to absorb your bills and other important papers, why hasn't the mail migrated there? Do you have a container to catch the mail when you first come in?

Trash or recycle whatever you can before depositing the real mail in your waiting basket. Set a time to take it to your workspace—perhaps after Baby's first nap of the day or at night when the house is quiet?

You'll find the more you ritualize simple tasks, the easier they are to remember. It's as if when you forget, the time of day reminds you. When I hear the *60 Minutes* TV show theme music, I know it's time to water my plants!

## Frequently Used Items

If you organized your kitchen, is there any placement that isn't working for you? Perhaps the coffee filters wound up across the kitchen from the coffee pot. We lose energy and time when we allow simple actions like that to take longer than they need to. Spend some time with the order you created. You haven't failed if you have to tweak the system. You lose only if you are rigid and refuse to admit you could have done it better.

Be aware that this room is often one that is fairly volatile. One minute you're baking cookies like Martha Stewart and then after a few months you don't ever want to touch flour again in this lifetime. Guess what? The baking tools may have to take a back seat and find a new placement in the kitchen. If you've abandoned baking for indoor grilling, a whole new set of tools needs to be front and center. It's not an everyday affair but it would behoove you to recognize the shifts when they occur wherever in the home they happen.

## Your Food

Finally, how are your doing in the food arena? Does your pantry serve you well? Have your categories begun to migrate into each other? What about the refrigerator? Do you still shove food into the far reaches of the shelves where it rots? It takes a minute or two to restore a pantry. You've already decided where things go;

now simply move items to the designated zones. Your invaluable tool if the pantry is a walk-in space is the shelf divider. Toss in a basket or two and you should be good to go.

## Honoring the Systems

If you have outside help who refuses to honor what you created, you need to have a chat. This isn't your new best friend whose feelings you don't want to hurt. This is someone who is in your employ. You spent a lot of time and expended quite a bit of energy to whip this room into shape. Your system must be honored. Ask your helper what they take issue with and decide if you can work things out. The buck literally stops with you. If it is difficult for you to confront others, make this a practice session. Otherwise your spouse, child, employees, and pets will be taking over.

If your partner isn't honoring the systems you created, you'll need to have a talk. You are a team and must be on the same side. Have a non-emotional discussion. Perhaps your partner felt the systems were created without enough input from him? Maybe he has a better way to do some of the things you organized? Keep an open mind and heart. But if you find yourself having huge arguments over where someone put the milk in the fridge, the issue may be a manifestation of a deeper disconnect. You might want to consult a marriage counselor. Talk to someone. It's never about "the stuff."

For more on organizing these areas, see pages 80–90 and 138–142.

### BE THE CHANGE YOU WISH TO SEE IN OTHERS

Never confuse Zen Organizing with rigidity or a means to belittle or control others. If you are on a quest for perfection or wish to demand that of those with whom you live, you are on a path of destruction, defeat, and ruin. We can only do the best we are capable of at any given moment in time. And the surest way to elicit that from others is to ask for it in return by our good example.

*If you want to build a ship, don't herd people together to collect wood and don't assign them tasks and work but rather, teach them to long for the endless immensity of the sea.*

—Antoine de Saint-Exupéry

## The Master Bedroom

On another day let those fresh eyes sweep over the landscape of your bedroom. How is it going in here?

- Are you making the bed?
- Do your clothes get hung up?
- Did the closet stay organized?
- Are there more baby toys here than in FAO Schwartz?
- Has Baby stopped sleeping with you and embraced his room?
- Are there items languishing in your room that can now be moved to the garage or the home of a pregnant friend?

Don't get overwhelmed by the issues. Identify them as the specific challenges they are. Is the solution something you need to purchase? Or is it a change in your behavior? If the home in general provides respite from the world, the bedroom must be a sacred sanctuary within the home. If yours looks like a messy hotel room, you need to do some first aid!

For more on organizing these areas, see pages 44–49 and 119–124.

### Baby's Room

Baby is growing rapidly and the systems used to keep this room tidy are going to change as rapidly. It's tough to stay on top but it's crucial. After the first year, it becomes easier as the day-to-day, month-to-month challenges are not as dramatic. The most common issue I find in a child's room, no matter her age, is the parents' belief that the child is too young to notice. On one hand, of course, an infant isn't going to whisper in your ear, "Hey, what the heck happened in here, Mom?" But she's a sentient being, so count on her feeling the effects of the chaos. Not to mention the tension between you and Dad should you not be supporting each other in the way Baby's care is managed!

For more on organizing Baby's room, see pages 113–118.

### Bathrooms

What do your fresh eyes reveal in each of the bathrooms in your home? The usual suspects when it comes to chaos in this room are:

- Towels are tossed on the floor after a shower.
- Counters don't get wiped off and become sticky with residue from products used in this room.
- The trash can is rarely emptied until it's overflowing.
- No one checks supplies and key items like toilet paper and diapers run low at critical moments.
- There aren't enough hooks, and bathrobes get piled on top of one another.

While it's difficult to feel great in a bathroom that's less than orderly or pristine, the fixes are pretty easy. Hooks, hampers, and bigger trash cans are easy to purchase. This is another room where relationship issues often surface through the environment. You want to work things out now before you have six children, all of whom toss their wet towels on the floor. Don't turn yourself into a maid unless you want to get paid for those skills. In that case, of course, you'd be picking up wet towels in a hotel.

For more on organizing the bathroom, see pages 167–175.

### The Home Office

Whether it's a room, a nook in the kitchen, or a space you clear on the kitchen table, you need an area for paying bills and managing the daily business of life. Critical to your success is a functioning file system. There are no shortcuts. Once you have one, a little chaos may develop when you neglect your filing. It isn't any fun but it must be done. Set a time once a month for filing and just blast through it. If one of you is in charge of the finances, the other might like to do the filing as a way to stay current.

It's also important to monitor the check register. I'm not talking about policing what your partner does, but understanding how your family—which is really a small business on some level—runs. In the event of an emergency, finances and paperwork won't add to your grief.

For more on organizing a home office, see pages 17–23.

## DECIDE ON THE PERKS

Many years ago I worked with a very successful couple. She was a top executive at a large American corporation; he was an entrepreneur with a thriving business. The husband turned to me one day and said, "Regina, you could never be married to me!" I asked him why. He said: "Because I throw towels on the bathroom floor and I never put the toilet seat down." I had to laugh and agreed that, yes, that would drive me right up the wall.

When I asked why he behaved this way, he caught me off guard. It turns out he and his wife had struck an agreement. She catered to him in agreed-upon ways and he pampered her in others. He had no idea what her salary was; she banked it. He bought her a new Jaguar every year. They traveled to exotic locales when they

took a vacation and he paid for everything. You get the idea. In a previous chapter I suggested you divide the labor in the household. If that type of arrangement doesn't work for your partner—and you're the one cleaning up after him—be sure you negotiate something equally valuable in return. Otherwise trouble is on the horizon.

## TWEAK THOSE SYSTEMS

After order is restored, spend some quiet time with your journal. Ask yourself what happens during the course of a day that drives you crazy. After you have one or two items (or a list!), consider each one in turn. Instead of complaining about this setup, how could you change it to make it more functional and supportive? Let's examine two possible scenarios. I grant you these are benign examples, but in my experience it's the little things that set our teeth on edge, not the big-ticket items.

Every morning you stumble into the kitchen to make coffee. You now rise fifteen minutes early just to have a few minutes of alone time before the day starts. You don't like anything on your counter so the coffee machine and grinder are packed away. It takes about six minutes to haul them out, grind the coffee, and get that first cup o' joe. You wish you didn't have to waste this time. If you weren't sleep-deprived and a little cranky it probably wouldn't bother you, but that's not the reality. Don't be rigid about supporting your original organizing ideas. Stay fluid! If the coffee

## STAY ON TRACK WITH THE BUSINESS OF YOUR LIFE

1. **Every day (preferably at the same time) check the To Do folder in your file system.** You can have every important paper in your life filed perfectly; however, if you don't work the system, what good does it do? You don't want to delay an important medical reimbursement, have your electricity turned off, or get dinged with credit card late fees because you are sleep-deprived. Give paperwork just five minutes of attention every morning or evening. Your to-do list for the next day can grow out of the items that need your attention in your To Do folder and your calendar. Check the Pending folder just once a week for any additional tasks.

2. **Keep track of doctor/dentist visits, etc.** Just before you check that To Do folder you'll want to look at your calendar. You may be amazed at the sheer number of expert appointments you'll need to keep during this first year of your baby's life. Most babies will see their pediatrician or family doctor every few months for well-baby visits. In addition to that, if your baby has had any health issues, such as slow weight gain, for example, her doctor may want to see her more frequently. If you are enrolled in any social programs such as state-based insurance you'll likely need to sit down with a caseworker every so often. And dentists now suggest you take Baby in for an exam soon after her first teeth erupt, which may already be happening now!

   The number of health-related appointments and phone numbers you have to keep track of more than double when you have a baby. Other than Baby, your new best friend needs to be your calendar. You don't want to miss an important one because you forgot to write it down.

3. **Keep a contact list.** In addition, you'll need an organized way to keep track of important phone numbers and office procedures until you have them committed to memory. Let's say your pediatrician welcomes phone calls at home after office hours. Do you have his home number handy so you won't have to go searching through the phone book in the middle of the night when your baby wakes up with a fever?

   Have one sheet of emergency or frequently used contact numbers printed out and available. Post this list on the refrigerator so that your family and helpers can contact the right person in an emergency without losing time. Update your list periodically. If you create it in Excel, it will be a snap to update and you are guaranteed never to hear, "but I can't read your handwriting!" Be sure you and your partner have the same contacts programmed into your phones.

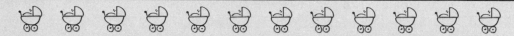

**4. Allow electronic gadgets to serve you.** It's hard to imagine anyone today who doesn't have a cell phone or smart phone. Enter important phone numbers here and check to see if your service provider has automatic back up. If your phone or PDA is ever lost or stolen you won't lose all of your contacts. In fact, most providers keep the list online. Verizon, for example, archives numbers you have deleted. If you have a change of heart a few months down the road, you can cruise online to your account and retrieve the number and your formerly deleted vendor or friend won't be the wiser.

One of the reasons it's great to clean out your bags each evening is that you can look at any business cards you collected that day or check those scraps of paper on which you jotted down important names and numbers. If they relate to Baby and are important for her health and well-being, enter them ASAP into your phone. If you and your partner have iPhones, remember information can be transferred from one iPhone to another by syncing the phones together—consult your manual for instructions. If you like keeping the cards for reference, don't allow them to scatter like snowflakes around your home or office floor. Place them in a card case or a small metal file box. Remember too that in today's economy lots of people are entrepreneurs. Many businesses won't exist in two to five years. You can always relocate the legitimate ones online: www.yellowpages.com or www.whitepages.com will keep you in the loop.

---

grinder and maker stay out and plugged in, you can get going that much faster. In fact, you might invest in one of those machines that will have a fresh cup waiting for you. Clutter on a counter is an eyesore. Equipment that you use every day isn't.

I am always amazed when I organize a space for someone and set up systems to find that my clients are afraid to change any aspect of it. They literally call and ask my permission. If you organized something per my instructions in this book and you find you'd like to do something different, feel free to do your own thing *provided* you are truly staying organized and not simply expressing a desire to buck whatever system an "authority figure" imposes on you. I've had those clients as well! Make your home a creative playground. Getting/staying organized should be signs of your desire to nurture yourself, not inflict punishment or rebel.

## REALITY VS. FANTASY

Despite what you may be thinking, there's no such thing as perfect organization.

Think of your home as alive: always changing, growing, and evolving. As your baby grows and you perhaps add more children to your family, you will need to embrace flexibility and learn to cut yourself a lot of slack in order to keep your sanity . . . and to keep from turning into a control-freak taskmaster. Always remember that your systems are in place to help you, not punish you (or anyone else in your family). If something isn't working, change it. If you need a break, take one. Just remember, tomorrow is another day. While that's true about anything in life, it should really be a mother's daily mantra.

I thought a fitting way to end our journey would be to share some wisdom from a few of my Zen Organizing mothers. Claudette, for example, wrote to me after returning from a short trip out of town with her family. There had been a death in the family and Claudette had little time to prepare. This is just the kind of emergency that can throw a monkey wrench into your newly organized life. Claudette found that rather than being overwhelmed, she simply had to set aside time to put things in their proper places.

"I emptied out my purse, filed some papers and got things squared away pretty fast," said Claudette. "Being organized has not lessened the work but made the work more streamlined and less stressful. There are no questions now as to where things go! If I take a mere 20 minutes a day, I find I can keep my desk and surfaces in order." Claudette has two school-age children, a large home, a small dog, a busy husband, local relatives around the dinner table most nights, and, oh yes, her own thriving career. Do you see elements of your situation in hers?

Sometimes a colicky baby can bring a mother to her knees while a screaming CEO wouldn't ruffle her feathers at all! Like many moms, Denise was most impacted by the way Zen Organizing saved time during those inevitable and unwelcome upsets that can derail a mother's well-planned day. She had been a successful corporate attorney before the birth of her son. Here is what Denise shared:

"Being organized makes everything you do as a mother easier. There is a lot in the day-in, day-out of motherhood that can't be controlled (sick child, temper tantrum, nanny or housekeeper doesn't show up), but by being organized you are better able to handle whatever the day throws at you." Denise added, "You don't have to waste time that could be valuable quality time with your child hunting for a lost this, that, or whatever. Being able to easily move through the house to pick up a fully loaded and ready-to-go diaper bag, your baby, and your keys without event is priceless."

Do you envy her experience? It's yours for the taking!

Finally, there was Jennifer, who got organized just as her baby was about to enter the world. She touched on the bottom line for all mothers when she wrote me this: "If you are organized, you have more time for you—which is the one thing every mommy needs." I hope these are the benefits you see during the course of your journey as a mother.

# EPILOGUE

## As One Door Closes, Another Opens

The future is not some place we are going, but one we are creating.
The paths are not to be found, but made.
And the activity of making them changes both the maker
and their destination.

—JOHN SCHAAR

IT'S HARD TO BELIEVE that a year has flown by since we started our journey. You'll be on your own now, but not without the proper tools. The Magic Formula —eliminate, categorize, organize—and a host of ever-evolving habits, systems, and rituals will carry you across the finish line. Of course once you become a parent there really is no finish line, is there? Your child is your baby even when she's fifty and being sworn in as president of the United States.

The documentary *Babies* shows highlights from the first year in the lives of four babies born in different countries under vastly different circumstances. They hail from Africa, Mongolia, the United States, and Japan. In an interview, the director said that there was one common denominator: No matter what the socioeconomic conditions of his family or country, every baby wanted love. It's love that brought your baby into the world and love that will sustain you on the arduous journey to her adulthood. Remember love when you are sleep-deprived, overwhelmed, or sad. I thought I would close with words that I hope exemplify the relationship you have with your child.

*The greatest gift I can give is to see, hear, understand and to touch another person.*

—Virginia Satir

# ACKNOWLEDGMENTS

Writing *Organized Life with Baby* was a journey that quite literally changed me. As with all journeys of note, I had a host of worthy companions. I wish to thank them publicly because without them it would have been a very different experience.

My literary agent, Marilyn Allen, has guided my career for close to ten years. While I appreciate her skill in this arena, I am equally blessed to call her my friend. She has shared triumphs and heartaches with me over the years. It's an honor to have this honest, compassionate woman represent me. Thank you for always having your eye on "the next book," Marilyn!

*Baby* marks my fourth collaboration with editor Katie McHugh. If the *One Year to . . .* series is worthy of note, it is due to her skillful guidance. As Stephen King said in his book *On Writing: A Memoir of the Craft,* "The editor is always right." Indeed you are, Katie. Thank you for your patience, your guidance and your editorial genius. You elevate every manuscript I send you.

Meagan Francis taught me many things about pregnancy and babies. What really impressed me, however, was her ability to do great work under pressure, never miss a deadline and do it all with tremendous grace. You were the perfect partner, Meagan. Let's do it again!

The incomparable Christine Marra heads the post-production team that gets the final manuscript ready for press. She has shepherded the entire *One Year to . . .* series over the finish line. Your quiet strength and expertise allow me to sleep at night knowing that all is well.

Christine's team is as talented, dedicated and creative as she is. Jane Raese once again designed the interior pages with a sense of style and whimsy. Copy editor Anna Kaltenbach had a big job tweaking the punctuation. I promise some day soon to learn the correct usage of a comma. Donna Riggs created an index that is truly a work of art. Last but not least, kudos to (pregnant) Josephine Mariea for proofreading the final pages as we neared the finish line. I hope you were taking notes!

Jon Resh, what can I say about you? Your book cover designs for the entire series have all been brilliant. A well-written book with a great cover will still languish on the shelf if no one knows about it. My deep thanks to the ladies who head the PR Department at Da Capo, Kate Burke and Lindsey Triebel. They work tirelessly to get the word out. I owe you much.

Each of the moms and dads I have worked with over the past twenty plus years have taught me about the unique organizing needs of parenthood. Without their willingness to lay bare their often chaotic home and work life scenarios, I would have had no idea what to include in this book. Special thanks however must be extended to my attorney client Mandy Dake and her attorney husband Chris Rowley. They each gave generously of their time to answer countless questions I had about all aspects of parenting a new baby. They also demystified the legal aspects of a pregnancy leave.

I extend heartfelt thanks and apologies to Anne M. Jones whose inspiring story didn't make the final cut.

Equally generous with her time was my client Christina Zilber. The ink on my contract wasn't dry when Christina not only consented to a long interview but also sent me home with a stack of baby related books. Christina, you are the Soul of generosity.

Therapist Donna Emmanuel spent countless hours helping me understand what a challenge a new baby can pose to even the best relationship. Her wisdom shines in the pages of this book.

Deep thanks to my family and friends for always being there for me—especially my cousin Dr. Jamie De Stefano, my aunt Dolores Johns Agbay and six extraordinary women I regard as nothing less than sisters: Ann Walsh, Russi Taylor, Susann Jarvis, Cathy Jones, Tanya Russell and Lynn Hernandez. I do indeed get by with a little help from my friends.

Animals have always played an important role in my life. Kudos to the seven birds, who chirped, sang or screamed their support in my home office as I wrote each morning. A special bouquet of gratitude to the late, great terrier mix, Gracie, who sat by my side as I navigated the waters of editorial notes. Thanks for sharing her, Ann.

Writing this book has not only made me acutely aware how challenging it is to prepare for a child, my personal interest in babies has been activated. I can't walk down the street or pass one in a store without saying "hello." It is my sincere hope that this book will enable all new mothers and fathers to more easily navigate the waters of impending and new parenthood. In this way they will have more time to simply love and cherish their baby. We can imprint children with love, acceptance and joy or spend our time searching for stuff. You know which choice has my vote.

# RESOURCES

### BABY CARE

*The Better Way to Care for Your Baby.* Robin Elise Weiss (Fair Winds Press, 2010)

*The Mother of All Baby Books.* Ann Douglas (Wiley Books, 2010)

*The No-Cry Sleep Solution.* Elizabeth Pantley (McGraw Hill, 2005)

*Raising an Emotionally Intelligent Child: The Heart of Parenting.* John Gottman Ph.D., Joan Declaire, and Daniel Goleman (Simon & Schuster, 1998)

### BABY FOOD

Beaba Babycook Baby Food Maker
www.williams-sonoma.com and
www.amazon.com

Vitamix
www.vitamix.com

### BREASTFEEDING

Ameda
www.ameda.com
Breastfeeding education, pumps, and products

Avent
www.avent.com
Parenting and baby products

KellyMom
www.kellymom.com

La Leche League
www.llli.org

Medela
www.medela.us
Breastfeeding products

*The Nursing Mother's Companion.* Kathleen Huggins, Harvard Common Press
www.nursingmotherscompanion.com

### CHILDBIRTH

*Birthing From Within.* Pam England
www.mybestbirth.com

*The Thinking Woman's Guide to a Better Birth.* Henci Goer (Order from Amazon or directly at her Web site: www.hencigoer.com)

### CHILDCARE

Sittercity Babysitting
SitterCity.com

ILoveMyNanny.com

www.Care.com

### COOKING

Chef Tanya Russell, In Good Taste Catering Company, Los Angeles, California
ingoodtastela.com or email
ingoodtastela@aol.com

*The Basic Baby Food Cookbook: Complete Beginner Guide to Making Baby Food at Home.* Julianne E. Hood (AuthorHouse, 2006)

*The Complete Idiot's Guide to Vegan Eating for Kids.* Dana and Andrew Villamagna (Alpha, 2010)

*Cooking for Baby Cookbook*
Available at Williams-Sonoma

*Tofu Cookery (25th Anniversary).* Louise Hagler (Book Publishing Company, 2008)

## CO-SLEEPING

Cosleeping.org

*Sleeping with Your Baby: A Parent's Guide to Cosleeping.* James McKenna, PhD (Platypus Media, 2007)

## DONATIONS

### Clothing and Household Items
Career Gear
www.careergear.org
Provides professional attire for job interviews to disadvantaged men

Dress for Success
www.dressforsuccess.org
Provides professional attire for job interviews to disadvantaged women

Goodwill Industries International
www.goodwill.org
Sells clothing and household goods

One Warm Coat
www.onewarmcoat.org
Collects and distributes coats for free to those in need

Salvation Army
www.salvationarmy.com
Sells clothing and household goods

### Computer Technology
The following sites refurbish and distribute computer technology (laptops, desktops, printers) to economically disadvantaged youth in the United States and around the world.

Computers 4 Kids
www.c4k.org

National Cristina Foundation
www.cristina.org

World Computer Exchange
www.worldcomputerexchange.org

### Miscellaneous Items
Give the Gift of Sight
www.givethegiftofsight.com
Provides free prescription eyewear to individuals in North America and developing countries around the world. Drop off eyeglasses or sunglasses at LensCrafters, Pearle Vision, Sears Optical, Target Optical, BJ's Optical, Sunglass Hut, or Lions Club.

Hungry for Music
www.hungryformusic.org
Distributes used musical instruments to underprivileged children

Luggage
www.suitcasesforkids.org
Provides luggage for foster children who move from home to home

Reader to Reader
www.readertoreader.org
Accepts books for children and teens and distributes to school libraries nationwide

## E-CARDS

Blue Mountain
www.bluemountain.com

Hallmark
www.hallmark.comn

Rubber Chicken Animated e-Cards
www.rubberchickencards.com

## FINANCE

### Children
Money lessons in comics form
www.centsables.com

Saving for College
www.savingforcollege.com

### Credit Card Calculator
Bankrate.com
http://www.bankrate.com/calculators/
managing-debt/minimum-payment-
calculator.aspx

### Credit Reports and Identity Theft
Free Annual Credit Report
www.annualcreditreport.com
or call 1-877-322-8228
Created by the three nationwide consumer
credit reporting agencies (Equifax, Experian,
and Transunion), this centralized service
allows consumers to request free annual
credit reports.

Equifax
www.equifax.com or call 1-877-576-5734

Experian
www.experian.com/fraud
or call 1-888-397-3742

Transunion
www.transunion.com or call 1-800-680-7289

www.consumer.gov/idtheft
For detailed information about identity theft

### Managing Your Money Day-to-Day
Dinkytown
www.dinkytown.com

Expensr
www.expensr.com

Mint
www.mint.com

Quicken
www.quicken.com

wesabe
www.wesabe.com

### Mortgage Calculator
Bankrate.com
www.bankrate.com

Moneychimp
www.moneychimp.com

Mortgage-calc.com
www.Mortgage-calc.com

### Up-to-date Information on Financial Everything
Yahoo finance
http://finance.yahoo.com

Bloomberg
www.bloomberg.com

Cnn Financial News
www.cnnfn.com

Morningstar
www.morningstar.com

Moneychimp
www.moneychimp.com

## FINDING A DOULA

Dona.org

Cappa.net

## GROCERY SHOPPING

www.grocerylists.org

## HEALTH

Coalition for Improving Maternity Services
www.motherfriendly.org

Playborhood.com

Dr. Greene's House Calls
www.drgreene.com

www.healthychild.org

## LEGAL

http://www.dol.gov/whd/fmla/index.htm

## MEMORABILIA, PHOTOGRAPHS, SCRAPBOOKING SUPPLIES

### Supplies and Ideas
*Creating Keepsakes Scrapbook* magazine
www.creatingkeepsakes.com

Creative Memories
www.creativememories.com
Provides scrapbook ideas and supplies

Exposures
www.exposuresonline.com
Offers albums and scrapbooks

Michael's Arts & Crafts
www.michaels.com

Scrapbooking 101
www.scrapbooking101.com
Your guide to the basics of scrapbooking

## Blogs and Online Photo Management and Sharing
www.blogspot.com
www.flickr.com

Kodak Gallery
www.kodakgallery.com

www.picasaweb.com

Shutterfly
www.shutterfly.com

Snapfish
www.snapfish.com

www.wordpress.com

## FENG SHUI

Ariel Joseph Towne
consult@thefengshuiguy.com
www.thefengshuiguy.com

*The Peaceful Nursery: Preparing a Home for Your Baby with Feng Shui.* Alison Forbes and Laura Forbes Carlin (Delta, 2006)

## MIND, BODY, AND SPIRIT

(*Lots of these herbs and treatments can be found at www.motherlove.com*)
After-Ease
Arnica
Crampbark
Lansinoh
Motherwort
Rescue Remedy
Traumeel

Beliefnet
www.beliefnet.com
Inspiration, spirituality, and faith

Daily OM
www.dailyOM.com
Nurturing mind, body, and spirit

Health Journeys
http://www.healthjourneys.com
For help with child care, depression, etc.
Belleruth Naparstek Guided Imagery Center

Jennifer Wolfe's Prenatal Vinyasa Yoga Short
Forms
www.jenniferwolfeyoga.com

Mysteries.Net
www.mysteries.net
Meditation and yoga site

Network Chiropractors, founded by D. Epstein
http://www.donaldepstein.com

Self-Realization Fellowship
www.selfrealizationfellowship.org
Meditation and yoga site

## NATURAL HOUSEHOLD/ CONSTRUCTION PRODUCTS AND TOXICITY INFORMATION

About.comhttp://housekeeping.about.com/
cs/environment/a/alternateclean.htm
managed by the *New York Times*

Baby Safe Finishes
www.babysafefinishes.com

Benjamin Moore
www.benjaminemoore.com

Dispose of old medicine:
www.DisposeMyMeds.org

Meyer's Clean Day
www.mrsmeyers.com

*Naturally Clean: The Seventh Generation
Guide to Safe & Healthy, Non-Toxic Cleaning.*
Jeffrey Hollender, Geoff Davis, and Meika
Hollender (New Society Publishers, 2006)

Natural Resources Defense Council
www.nrdc.org/thisgreenlife/0905.asp

PurePaint
www.purepaint.co.uk

The Real Milk Paint Company
www.realmilkpaint.com

Seventh Generation Products
www.seventhgeneration.com

Sherwin-Williams
Sherwin-williams.com

Tom's of Maine Products
www.tomsofmaine.com

U.S. Environmental Protection Agency
http://www.epa.gov/iaq/voc.htm

## NETWORKING

Craigslist
www.craigslist.org

Facebook
www.facebook.org

Google Groups
www.groups.google.org

La Leche League
www.llli.org

Mommy and Me
www.mommyandme.com

Moms Meetups
moms.meetup.com

momslikeme.com

mothering.com

Mothers of Preschoolers (MOPS)
www.mops.org

Twitter
Twitter.com

Yahoo! Groups
Groups.yahoo.com

YouTube
www.youtube.com

## OFFICE AND FILING SUPPLIES, SOFTWARE, AND DATA BACKUP

Day Runner
www.DayRunner.com

Fitter
www.fitter1.com
Fitter Active Sitting Disc transforms your chair. Check out other ergonomically correct products.

FLAX Art Design
www.flaxart.com

The Geek Squad
www.geeksquad.com
Computer and IT help

Google Docs
docs.google.com

iPhoto
www.apple.comilife/iphoto

Levenger
www.Levenger.com

Mobile Me
www.apple.com/mobileme

Office Depot
www.officedepot.com

OfficeMax
www.officemax.com

Relax the Back
www.Relaxtheback.com
Ergonomically correct office furniture

See Jane Work
www.seejanework.com

Staples
www.staples.com

## ONLINE AUCTION AND SALE SITES

Cash for CDs
www.cashforcds.com

Craig's List
www.craigslist.com

eBay
www.ebay.com

## ONLINE INFORMATION

About.com

American Academy of Pediatrics
www.healthychildren.org

BabyCenter.com

www.chartjungle.com

Childbirth and Postpartum Professional Association
www.cappa.net

International Birth and Wellness Project
www.alace.org

International Childbirth Education Association
www.icea.org

Mothering.com

National Association of Professional Organizers (NAPO)
www.napo.net
856-380-6828

www.whitepages.com

www.yellowpages.com

**Online Assistants**
www.virtualassistant.org

## ORGANIZATIONS

*See also Professional Associations*
American Academy of Pediatrics
www.healthychildren.org

Birthing From Within

Hypnobabies
www.hypnobabies.com

Hypnobirthing
www.hypnobirthing.com

La Leche League
www.llli.org

Lamaze
www.lamaze.com

## PETS AND BABY

*And Baby Makes Four: A Trimester-by-Trimester Guide to a Baby-Friendly Dog.*
Penny Scott-Fox (TFH Publications, 2007).
Available at www.amazon.com.
*Note:* more than one book has this title so it's important to know the author.

*Baby Sounds for Pets,* Kristen Overdurf-Abud
Audio CD available at www.amazon.com

An animal communicator may be able to help your pet's relationship with Baby.
Colette Grace St. Clair
www.animalsconnect.com, call
310.499.4220, or email
colette@animalsconnect.com

The ASPCA has a virtual Pet Behaviorist who will respond to specific questions.
www.aspcabehavior.org

Holistic animal care advice: Dr. Karen Becker
http://www.drkarenbecker.com

The Humane Society has specific information regarding introducing baby at
www.humanesociety.org
Enter this phrase into the search engine:
Introducing Your Pet and New Baby

*Marley & Me.* John Grogan (William Morrow & Co., 2005)

*Oogy: The Dog Only a Family Could Love.*
Larry Levin (Grand Central Publishing, 2010)

## PROFESSIONAL ASSOCIATIONS

Clutterers Anonymous
www.clutterersanonymous.net

Codependents Anonymous
www.codependents.org

Messies Anonymous
www.messies.com

National Association of Professional Organizers (NAPO)

## RECYCLE

1-800-GOT-JUNK?
www.1800gotjunk.com or call
1-800-468-5865
Removes just about anything (furniture, appliances, electronics, yard waste, and renovation debris) and makes every effort to recycle or donate items

Rechargeable Battery Recycling Corporation (RBRC)
www.call2recycle.org or call 1-877-273-2925
Recycles used portable rechargeable batteries and old cell phones

Worldwatch Institute Web site
worldwatch.org/resources/go_green_save_green

## REDUCE AND STOP UNWANTED MAIL

Opt-Out of Preapproved Credit Card and Insurance Offers
www.optoutprescreen.com or call
1-888-567-8688
Official Web site of the Credit Reporting Industry to accept and process consumer requests to opt-in or opt-out of prescreened credit card and insurance offers

Direct Marking Association (DMA)
www.the-dma.org
Reduces your total volume of mail when you register for the Direct Marketing Association's Mail Preference Service (MPS)

## RELATIONSHIPS

*And Baby Makes Three: The Six-Step Plan for Preserving Marital Intimacy and Rekindling Romance After Baby Arrives.* John Gottman PhD and Julie Schwartz Gottman (Three Rivers Press, 2008)

*The Relationship Cure: A Five-Step Guide for Building Better Connections with Family, Friends, and Lovers.* John M. Gottman PhD and Joan Declaire (Crown, 2001)
www.gottman.com

*What Am I Feeling?* John Mordechai Gottman (Parenting Press, 2004)

## SEARCH ENGINES

Bing
www.bing.com

Google
www.google.com

## SHOPPING: COMPANIES/CATALOGS/WEB SITES

Ameda
www.ameda.com
Breastfeeding education, pumps, and products

Avent
www.avent.com
Parenting and baby products

Babies "R" Us
www.babiesrus.com

The Baby Wearer
www.thebabywearer.com
Chat room and forums to discuss and exchange information

Bed Bath & Beyond
www.bedbathandbeyond.com

The Blessed Nest
blessednest.com
Supportive pillows for during pregnancy, childbirth, and caring for Baby

Bridgford (Tanya's favorite rolls)
www.bridgford.com

The Container Store
www.thecontainerstore.com

Costco
www.costco.com

Crate & Barrel
www.crateandbarrel.com

CVS
www.cvs.com

thediaperpin.com

GDiapers.com

Himalayan salt lamp
Solay
http://www.natural-salt-lamps.com

Home Depot
www.homedepot.com

Home Shopping Network
www.hsn.com

IKEA
www.IKEA.com

Joanne's
www.joann.com

The Land of Nod
www.landofnod.com

Medela
www.medela.us
breastfeeding products

Michael's Arts & Crafts
www.michaels.com

www.newbornfree.com

Pier One Imports
www.pier1.com

Pottery Barn
www.potterybarn.com

Pottery Barn Kids
www.potterybarnkids.com

The Roper Collection

www.skiphop.com

www.Solutions.com

Space Bags
Available at Bed Bath & Beyond and
The Container Store

Target
www.target.com

Wal-Mart
www.walmart.com

Walgreens
www.walgreens.com

Williams-Sonoma
www.williams-sonoma.com

## SHOPPING: SPECIFIC PRODUCTS

Bella Band

Catalina 3-in-1

Emergency delivery kit
edeliverykit.com

Ergo

Exersaucer

Jouer Cosmetics
www.jouercosmetics.com

Maya Wrap

Moby Wrap

Pronto changing station

Schick Intuition

Tushies

Vitamix
www.vitamix.com

## THE AUTHORS

Regina Leeds
www.reginaleeds.com

Meagan Francis
www.thehappiestmom.com

# INDEX

# ABOUT THE AUTHORS

**Regina Leeds,** known as the Zen Organizer, has brought order to homes and families for more than twenty years. Named "Best Organizer" by *Los Angeles* magazine, she is the author of eight books, including the *New York Times*–bestselling series *One Year to an Organized Life.* She lives in Toluca Lake, California. Visit her Web sites at www.organizewithregina.com and www.reginaleeds.com.

**Meagan Francis** is a parenting writer and mother of five children. Her other books include *The Happiest Mom: 10 Secrets to Enjoying Motherhood* and *Table for Eight.* Meagan contributes regularly to magazines and websites like *Parenting, Parents, Fit Pregnancy, Good Housekeeping,* Family .com and Babble.com, and at her own blog The Happiest Mom (www.the happiestmom.com). She and her family live in St. Joseph, MI.